CITIZEN BIRD

CITIZEN BIRD

SCENES from BIRD-LIFE in PLAIN ENGLISH for BEGINNERS

A CRITICAL EDITION

MABEL OSGOOD WRIGHT AND ELLIOTT COUES
WITH ILLUSTRATIONS BY LOUIS AGASSIZ FUERTES

Edited and with an Introduction
by Elizabeth Cherry and Meghan Freeman

Rutgers University Press
New Brunswick, Camden, and Newark, New Jersey
London and Oxford

Rutgers University Press is a department of Rutgers, The State University of New Jersey, one of the leading public research universities in the nation. By publishing worldwide, it furthers the University's mission of dedication to excellence in teaching, scholarship, research, and clinical care.

Library of Congress Cataloging-in-Publication Data

Names: Wright, Mabel Osgood, 1859–1934. author. | Coues, Elliott, 1842–1899, author. |
  Fuertes, Louis Agassiz, 1874–1927, illustrator. | Cherry, Elizabeth, 1977– editor. |
  Freeman, Meghan, editor.
Title: Citizen bird : scenes from bird-life in plain English for beginners / [edited by] Elizabeth
  Cherry and Meghan Freeman.
Other titles: Scenes from bird-life in plain English for beginners
Description: A critical edition. | New Brunswick : Rutgers University Press, 2025. | Includes
  bibliographical references and index.
Identifiers: LCCN 2024041321 | ISBN 9781978837065 (paperback) | ISBN 9781978837072
  (hardcover) | ISBN 9781978837089 (epub) | ISBN 9781978837096 (pdf)
Subjects: LCSH: Birds—United States—Juvenile literature. | Birds—United States—
  Conservation—Juvenile literature.
Classification: LCC QL676 .W956 2025 | DDC 598—dc23/eng/20250206
LC record available at https://lccn.loc.gov/2024041321

A British Cataloging-in-Publication record for this book is available from the British Library.

Citizen Bird: Scenes from Bird-Life in Plain English for Beginners was first published in 1897 by The Macmillan Company.

Introduction to this edition and scholarly apparatus copyright © 2025 by Elizabeth Cherry and Meghan Freeman

All rights reserved

No part of this book may be reproduced or utilized in any form or by any means, electronic or mechanical, or by any information storage and retrieval system, without written permission from the publisher. Please contact Rutgers University Press, 106 Somerset Street, New Brunswick, NJ 08901. The only exception to this prohibition is "fair use" as defined by U.S. copyright law.

References to internet websites (URLs) were accurate at the time of writing. Neither the author nor Rutgers University Press is responsible for URLs that may have expired or changed since the manuscript was prepared.

∞ The paper used in this publication meets the requirements of the American National Standard for Information Sciences—Permanence of Paper for Printed Library Materials, ANSI Z39.48-1992.

rutgersuniversitypress.org

Contents

Introduction: *Citizen Bird* in Its Contexts   vii

CITIZEN BIRD
Scenes from Bird-Life in Plain English for Beginners   lxxxiii

---

APPENDIX 1
Supplementary Material on *Citizen Bird*   303

APPENDIX 2
Historical Materials on Nineteenth-Century Birding and Audubon   317

APPENDIX 3
Other Works of Nineteenth-Century Nature Writing and Children's Literature   338

APPENDIX 4
Further Reading   363

Acknowledgments   365

About the Contributors   367

Index   369

Introduction
Citizen Bird in Its Contexts

LIKELY THE FIRST BIRDING GUIDE explicitly intended for children, *Citizen Bird* (1897) was a tremendously influential text in Progressive-Era America, inspiring in a generation of schoolchildren a love of wild birds and the desire to know more about them and to protect them from extinction. More than a century and a quarter later, *Citizen Bird* is today little more than a footnote in U.S. environmental history, most often cited in relation to one of its two authors, the naturalist Mabel Osgood Wright and the ornithologist Elliott Coues, or its illustrator, the bird artist Louis Agassiz Fuertes. This teaching edition of *Citizen Bird* aims to restore the text to its rightful place not just in the history of birding but also in the broader study of nineteenth-century American culture and literature.

Before we begin, we would like to explain what we mean by a teaching edition, as opposed to a scholarly or annotated edition. While this edition of *Citizen Bird* will be familiar to readers of scholarly editions in its inclusion of explanatory footnotes and appendixes, here, the appendixes include almost exclusively primary sources that serve as contextualizing material that are meant to make it easy for scholars in a variety of disciplines to assign and teach the text without the need for outside research. Additionally, the text itself is prefaced by a comprehensive introduction that does not narrowly focus on *Citizen Bird*, but rather seeks to position *Citizen Bird* within a variety of framing contexts: its publication and reception history, its relation to nineteenth-century ornithology and children's literature, and its responses to social and environmental issues in Progressive-Era America. We also provide some suggestions at the end of the introduction about how to pair the supplementary material with readings of specific aspects of the text.

It is our hope that the book will be of interest to scholars and students across various disciplines, including animal studies, environmental studies (especially environmental history), children's literature, American studies, women's studies, Victorian literature, and nineteenth-century material culture studies. While we assume the text as a field guide will be interesting to ornithologists and birders (as much for the ways it deviates from modern understandings and practices as it conforms to them), we believe that *Citizen Bird* can also be a useful text to introduce in a natural sciences classroom, as the ethical questions it grapples with remain central to birding and ornithology today.

Finally, as this introductory chapter will demonstrate, *Citizen Bird* was a landmark work, created by three major figures in early ornithology, nature writing, and bird illustration. Its authors and its publication were highly important to the development of birdwatching and environmental conservation in the late nineteenth century, and yet it does not receive the recognition it should. We hope that all new readers of *Citizen Bird* will enjoy discovering this important text.

BIOGRAPHICAL CONTEXTS

Below, we include individual biographies of *Citizen Bird*'s authors and illustrator for readers who as yet are not familiar with these three pivotal figures of Progressive-Era ornithology, nature writing, conservation, and environmental education.

Mabel Osgood Wright (1859–1934)

Mabel Osgood Wright was born in New York City in 1859, the third daughter of Samuel and Ellen Osgood. A Harvard-educated theologian, Rev. Samuel Osgood led congregations in New Hampshire and Rhode Island before he was appointed minister of the Church of the Messiah, the first Unitarian church in New York, in 1849, a position he held for twenty years. Wright, along with her older sisters Agnes and Bertha, was raised in the family home at 118 Eleventh Street. They spent their summers at their summer estate, Mosswood, later renamed Waldstein, in Fairfield, Connecticut. Wright credited those summers spent in rural Connecticut with inspiring her "Love o' Nature," especially of flowers and wild birds.

First educated at home, Wright later attended the private academy Misses Green (later Misses Graham) School for Girls, where her instructors included the art critic Clarence C. Cook. In the company of her father, Wright visited many of the cultural hubs of post–Civil War New York City, its bookstores, art galleries, and historical societies, and met several prominent artists and intellectuals, including the poet William Cullen Bryant, the sculptor William Wetmore Story, and the educator Elizabeth Peabody. Though Wright was not supported in her desire to pursue higher education, her father did encourage her literary aspirations, and Wright published her first piece of writing in the *New York Evening Post* anonymously at the age of sixteen. After her father's death in

Mabel Osgood Wright. Source: Bird-Lore via Wikimedia Commons.

1880, Wright became engaged to the British antiquarian bookseller James Osborne Wright, whom she married in 1884. The couple spent the first years of their marriage in England before returning to Connecticut to live at Waldstein.

Wright's literary career began in earnest after her husband brought nature articles that she had published in the *New York Evening Post* and the *New York Times* to the attention of George P. Brett Sr., who then was the managing partner of the American office of the British publisher Macmillan & Co. The essays became the core of her first book with Macmillan, *The Friendship of Nature: A New England Chronicle of Birds and Flowers* (1894). Encouraged by the book's favorable reviews, Brett suggested that Wright undertake a handbook on birds aimed at the general public. After an intensive study of ornithology at the Museum of Natural History in New York, Wright penned *Birdcraft* (1895), considered by many to be the first popular U.S. field guide, which quickly became a bestseller and went through nine editions. In 1896, Brett became the president of the Macmillan Company of New York, now an independent publishing venture in its own right, and he continued in this role until 1931, during which time he built the company into a major U.S. publisher with particular strengths in educational and trade publishing. Wright was a particularly prolific author for Macmillan, publishing twenty-three books with the publisher between 1894 and 1931. After *Birdcraft*, Wright expanded into literature aimed at juvenile audiences—*Tommy Anne and the Three Hearts* (1896) was the first in a series of animal-centric fantasy stories, and the following year Wright collaborated with ornithologist Elliott Coues and bird illustrator Louis Agassiz Fuertes to produce *Citizen Bird* (1897), a birding guide for children, with a frame narrative meant to instill "a love of birds and wish to protect them." Wright would continue to publish nature writing on plant and animal life for children and adults, including a sequel to *Citizen Bird* called *Four-Footed Americans and Their Kin* (1898) and *Flowers and Ferns in Their Haunts* (1901). She also wrote a series of popular novels set in New England, initially under the pseudonym "Barbara," the first of which was *The Garden of the Commuter's Wife* (1901).

Wright's popularity as a nature writer provided her with a platform that she used to promote many causes central to the nascent environmental conservation movement in Progressive-Era America, particularly the protection of wild birds killed for sport and fashion. She also played a prominent role in both regional and national organizations devoted to the study and protection of birds. In 1897, Wright was elected as a resident member of the American Ornithologists' Union. She was also a founding member of the Audubon Society of Connecticut (established 1898) and was elected as the chapter's first president. Under Wright's leadership, the group was successful in its petition to make Bird Day a recognized holiday in Connecticut and in instituting nature study curriculums in the public school system. In 1899, Wright stepped into the role of editor for the Audubon Department of the new periodical *Bird-Lore* (published by Macmillan), the precursor of *Audubon Magazine*, whose general editor was ornithologist Frank M. Chapman; her work with the magazine would continue for the rest of her life. Between 1901 and 1907, Wright also penned a series of literature review articles for the *New York Times Book Review*, devoted to recent publications on nature study topics. Starting in 1905, Wright served as a director of the National Association of Audubon Societies, a position she held until 1928. In her home state of Connecticut, Wright is perhaps best remembered today for the founding of Birdcraft Sanctuary in 1914. Built on land across from Wright's family home in Fairfield, Birdcraft was both a sanctuary for nesting birds as well as a museum devoted to public education about the importance of bird life. As the first of its kind in the country, the sanctuary was designated a National Historic Landmark in 1993.

In addition to her careers as a naturalist, a conservationist, and an author, Wright was a gifted hobbyist photographer whose photographs of flora and fauna, rural landscapes, and historic structures were featured in numerous publications, including her own. She was also deeply involved in civic organizations in and around Fairfield. A passionate gardener, Wright helped to found the Fairfield Garden Club in 1915 and served as its first president. She also was an active member of the Colonial Dames of Connecticut, contributing to the Colonial Revival movement popular at the beginning of the twentieth century. After the death of her husband in 1920, Wright increasingly withdrew from public life and published only two more books, including an autobiographical account of her early life called *My New York* in 1926. Mabel Osgood Wright died at her home in Fairfield in 1934 at the age of seventy-five, and she is buried in Fairfield, Connecticut.

Elliott Coues (1842–1899)

Elliott Coues is widely remembered today as an eminent ornithologist, due to his extensive research and publications in the field, and through a national award for ornithology given in his name by the American Ornithologists' Union. However, Coues did not begin his scientific career as an ornithologist. Rather, he trained as a physician and spent a portion of his career working as a U.S. Army surgeon in various outposts in the western United States.

Coues was born in Portsmouth, New Hampshire, in 1842 to a prominent merchant father who took a job with the federal government and moved the family to Washington, DC, when Coues was twelve years old. There, he spent time in the Smithsonian Institution and was mentored by Smithsonian curator Spencer Fullerton Baird, who sponsored Coues's first ornithological expedition off the Labrador Coast of Canada, when he was just seventeen years old. Coues helped to collect eggs and to kill and stuff birds as

Elliott Coues. Source: Smithsonian Institution.

specimens, common practices at the time for the study of birds. In Washington, Coues attended Columbian University (now George Washington University) and then the National Medical College (now the medical school of GWU), while also publishing scientific articles about birds.

During the Civil War Coues served as a medical cadet, first traveling to Arizona in 1863 for a posting. Along the way he kept a journal of his bird observations and even collected some specimens, mailing them back to Baird in Washington. Once he arrived in Arizona he continued to collect specimens, discovered one new bird species and five subspecies, and published two scientific articles on the birds of Fort Whipple. As Coues traveled throughout the United States for his military postings, including to North Carolina, Maryland, and South Dakota, he continued to collect specimens and study birds. During this time he distinguished himself as a naturalist by writing life histories of various bird species. His most famous work of this time, *Key to North American Birds* (1872), was revised and reprinted in six editions, the last two of which, published in 1903 and 1927, respectively, were illustrated by the illustrator of *Citizen Bird*, Louis Agassiz Fuertes.

Tired of life as an itinerant army surgeon, Coues resigned from the military in 1881 and returned to civilian life. He took a position as a professor of anatomy at the National Medical College while continuing to publish books on ornithology. He also served as a founding member of many prominent ornithological organizations. At the time ornithology was not yet an established science, and it required no formal academic training. Through his work in the Nuttall Ornithological Club, Coues and two colleagues, J. A. Allen and William Brewster, founded the American Ornithologists' Union (AOU). They invited about fifty scientists to join them at a convention in New York City in 1883, declaring two major goals: to revise the current list of North American birds and to adopt a uniform system of classification and nomenclature. The AOU successfully established itself as the pre-eminent bird study organization in the United States, and Coues served for seven years as its vice president and three years as its president. He also edited the AOU publication *The Auk*, and he chaired the AOU Committee on Classification and Nomenclature, which published *The AOU Code of Nomenclature and Check-List of North American Birds* in 1886. During this prolific period in Coues's ornithologist career, in June of 1895 Mabel Osgood Wright wrote her publisher at Macmillan and suggested Coues as her coauthor, owing partially to his favorable review of her previous book, *Birdcraft*.

Coues married three times, the first ending in annulment and the second in divorce. He married the suffragist, spiritualist, and occultist Mary Emily Bates in 1887, and this third marriage lasted until his death in 1899. Coues developed an interest in spiritualism and theosophy later in his life, attending seances and serving briefly as president of the Theosophical Society. After disagreements with several other leaders of the Theosophical Society, he was expelled from the organization in 1899.

Coues developed several serious digestive illnesses in the 1890s and in 1899 was diagnosed with cancer. He died at the age of fifty-seven from pneumonia that he developed after a surgery on December 25, 1899. Elliott Coues is buried in Arlington National Cemetery.

Louis Agassiz Fuertes (1874–1927)

Louis Agassiz Fuertes was born in Ithaca, New York, in 1874, the second son of Estevan Fuertes and Mary Stone Perry Fuertes. Of Spanish lineage and from Puerto Rico, his father was an engineer who in 1873 was appointed as the founding dean of the civil engineering department at Cornell University. His parents named him after Louis Agassiz (1807–1873), the Swiss natural historian, professor, and founder of the Museum of Comparative Zoology at Harvard University. Despite this connection, Fuertes's father did not initially support his son's bird illustration work and encouraged him to study engineering at Cornell.

From an early age, Fuertes evinced a notable interest in the study and artistic rendering of birds. Though he did not receive any formal training until later, Fuertes began collecting and drawing specimens of local species in his adolescence, and his amateur efforts drew the attention and support of prominent

Louis Agassiz Fuertes. Source: *The Osprey* vol. 1 (September 1896–September 1897), ed. Walter Adams Johnson. Galesburg, IL: The Osprey Company, 1897.

naturalists and ornithologists, foremost among them Elliott Coues, the uncle of a classmate. In 1895, while Fuertes was still an undergraduate at Cornell, Coues arranged for a showing of Fuertes's portfolio of bird paintings at the annual Congress of the AOU. The exposure Fuertes received from this event led to his earliest contracts for illustration work, the first of which was a series of pen-and-ink illustrations for Florence Merriam Bailey's birding memoir *A-Birding on a Bronco* (1896), quickly followed by Wright and Coues's *Citizen Bird* (1897). The 111 black-and-white drawings that Fuertes created for *Citizen Bird*—many of which were revised or redone under Coues's supervision—launched his career in earnest, convincing Fuertes and, more importantly, his family that he could make a living as a professional bird artist.

After earning his BA from Cornell in 1897 with the thesis "The Coloration of Birds," Fuertes went on to study under the painter and naturalist Abbott H. Thayer, in whose company he went on his first extended field expedition to Florida. This expedition would be quickly followed by others, including the Harriman Alaska Expedition (1899) and a U.S. Biological Survey expedition of the American Southwest (1901), as well as several American Museum of Natural History expeditions to the Bahamas (1902), the Canadian Rockies (1906), the Yucatan (1910), and Colombia (1911 and 1913), many in the company of ornithologist Frank M. Chapman. Fuertes's extensive experience in the field allowed him to sketch birds in their natural habitats as well as amass a large collection of skins for later study.

Fuertes became so in demand as an illustrator that he stopped joining field expeditions after the 1913 Colombia trip so that he could devote his time to his illustrations. Even then, Fuertes received more invitations to publish his work than he could fulfill, producing thousands of illustrations for numerous important works, including Merriam Bailey's *Handbook of Birds of the Western United States* (1902), Keyser's *Birds of the Rockies* (1902), Coues's *Key to North American Birds* (1903), Eaton's *Birds of New York* (1910–1914), and Forbush's *Birds of Massachusetts* (1925–1929).

In 1923, Fuertes returned to his alma mater to work as a lecturer of ornithology. He took a leave of absence in 1926 to join what would be his final expedition with the Chicago Field Museum to what was then called Abyssinia (now Ethiopia). In 1927, just three months after his return, Fuertes died in an accident when a train struck his vehicle, killing him and severely injuring his wife. He was fifty-seven at the time of his death and is buried in Ithaca, New York.

PUBLISHING AND RECEPTION HISTORY CONTEXTS

The Making of *Citizen Bird*

Origins of the Collaboration. Citizen Bird was published on July 14, 1897, but as a project its roots go back to 1895, when the ornithologist Elliott Coues contacted author and naturalist Mabel Osgood Wright to share his positive review of her book *Birdcraft* in the prominent American periodical *The Nation*. Wright had been planning a series of children's nature books with authoritative male specialists as collaborators, and Wright saw a potential coauthor in Coues for *Citizen Bird*. On June 2, 1895, Wright wrote to George P. Brett Sr., her publisher at Macmillan, to share the positive review, admitting, "I am rather pleased by *The Nation's* notice of *Birdcraft*—in spite of the black eye that is given the poor illustrations, for (entre nous) they are awfully lurid. The author of the notice was no less a personage than Dr. Elliott Coues of Washington, who sent me a signed copy of the paper enclosing also his card with 'compliments and kind regards.'"[1] From this early interaction began a partnership, facilitated almost entirely through correspondence, as the three collaborators lived in different places.

Wright wrote Coues back and pitched *Citizen Bird* to him, and his positive response brought the two together as coauthors, with Brett, their publisher, as intermediary. With Coues on board, the two had to find an illustrator. Originally Wright had suggested Robert Ridgway, the Smithsonian Institution's first curator of birds, to provide the images for *Citizen Bird*, and later she had considered wildlife artist Ernest Thompson Seton ("Mr Thompson" in her correspondence below), but it was Coues who brought Louis Agassiz Fuertes into the partnership, having hired him on several previous occasions for illustrations for various ornithologist publications. Coues insisted on Fuertes as the illustrator, and Wright's August 24, 1896, letter to Brett, which explains the original outline of the book, also mentions the bringing on of Fuertes as illustrator. It also foreshadows the workload division issues that would come up during the process:

Dear Mr Brett, I have asked Mr Wright to see you and read such portions of Dr Coues' last letter as bear upon the business part of the new bird book. The literary partnership with a man of Dr Coues' standing is not a thing to be despised, and I am willing to do the greater part of the work. Mr Fuertes he considers a <u>must be,</u> so I hope that you will find that his work equals

Mr Thompson's. "The Child's Book of Birds," or whatever title it may be given, will contain several instructive introductory chapters—"Bones and Feathers" (the difference in structure and covering between birds & other animals), "Citizen Bird" (the bird's value as a farmer, resident & neighbour), etc. The nicely grouped story-biographies of 100 typical N.A. [North American] birds & a field key to them suited to children's comprehension. The book should I think make about 250 to 300 16ᵐᵒ [a unit of page size] pages.[2]

While Wright was recommending Coues and Fuertes to Brett at Macmillan, Coues was coaching Fuertes on exactly how to respond to an invitation from the publisher to participate in the project. On September 24, 1896, Coues wrote to Fuertes telling him to expect an invitation from Macmillan, thanks to Coues, which could make his reputation. In this letter, Coues establishes himself as Fuertes's negotiator and adviser. He also makes sure that Fuertes knows that he has Coues to thank for the commission, telling him that another more established artist was being considered, however: "I have such confidence in you that I have secured the offer for you. If this proposed arrangement can be made, and the result prove satisfactory, you will have been fairly started on the road to fame and fortune." Two days later, Coues wrote Fuertes with the letter from Macmillan, advising him exactly how to respond:

Dear Mr. Fuertes: I return herewith the important Macmillan letter. I should advise you to reply promptly, thanking him for the offer, intimating your willingness and desire to do the work, and inquiring further what style of work he desires before naming your approximate price. You might add that on hearing from him further on this particular, you would be willing to submit the case to my decision, both as to remuneration, and as to grade of excellence in the particular kind of work which may be agreed upon.[3]

My impression is that Mr. Brett desires, not colored plates, but plain black and white pictures in line work, susceptible to reproduction by process, for insertion in text. If the case should be referred to me, I should probably decide upon that sort of work, and I should think you could afford to produce such pictures for about six dollars apiece.

A little money more or less, in such an important case as this, would be of less consequence to your future career than the fine start you would have, if you can come to terms with Mr. Brett. I think he is inclined to look upon you very favorably, from what I have told him, and disposed to be as liberal with you as the business in hand will warrant. I also believe you capable of making pictures which I can accept consistently with my own responsibility, to the publishers.

Coues maintained the role of mentor to Fuertes throughout the partnership, as is demonstrated further below with Coues's coaching Fuertes through the illustrations and giving him advice on prioritizing his illustrations over his senior college thesis.

Working Process. The collaboration makes manifest the relations between men and women authors, and the extent to which Wright had to fight for her vision for the book shows the lower status of women in the male-dominated publishing industry. Additionally, as a nature writer and birdwatcher, as opposed to an ornithologist, Wright also lacked the professional credentials that automatically gave her coauthor Coues professional standing and respect. As the youngest of the three, still in his senior year of college, Fuertes also found himself overworked in an attempt to please his mentor Coues. The correspondence among the three collaborators highlights these tensions.

As noted above, Wright told Brett she was "willing to do the greater part of the work" on *Citizen Bird*, and Wright and Coues came up with a plan to divide the work among themselves, including Fuertes, who they originally tasked with one hundred illustrations. This original plan was outlined in Coues's August 1896 letter that Wright included in her August 24, 1896, correspondence with Brett at Macmillan:

With your letter of the 16th before me, my offer still holds good, and I am willing to take more than half the responsibility for such a non-technical book as you indicate, on Mr Brett's suggestions, if you are willing to do more than half the work.—You write the stories, block out what technical matter you desire, and I will fill in, furnish the "key" and do all the necessary "sandpapering," and what is perhaps the biggest part of the whole, see the book through the press.

I think probably that your ideas of what we want are more fetching than my own, so therefore make out and send me a proper list to a dot. Better communicate at once with Mr Fuertes, or have Mr Brett do so, it is essential to secure his cooperation in illustrating our text, and someone else may already be bidding for his work.

I hope Mr B will engage him for a round hundred figures; if so every one of them could be used twice, in any size desired for Birdcraft and our new book. Probably he would make them for $5 apiece, which would be very cheap for duplicate use.[4]

Here, Coues promises to write a key (which would become chapter 33, "The Procession of Bird Families"), help with editing ("sandpapering"), and see the book through its production process. As in his letter above to Fuertes, Coues implies that the bulk of the success of the book will be due to his professional reputation as an ornithologist. Wright might well have taken umbrage at Coues's suggestion that his reputation was the only one that mattered, as she was already an established author. It is also safe to assume that her experience with Coues was behind her declaration to Brett that all future collaborators would be "editors," not "coauthors," in this 1897 letter: "Dr. Coues is my co-author, but the gentlemen connected with the other volumes, are to be as I understand, editors, as they do not contribute to the volumes except by revision, while Dr. C. writes 20000 words."

Throughout this entire project, the authors and illustrator met in person together only once, at the beginning of their partnership (November 17, 1896), at the Aldine Club, an all-male social club that counted many heads of publishing among its members, including George P. Brett. That meeting occurred fairly early on in their collaboration, with no drafts yet exchanged and very few, if any, illustrations yet furnished. Therefore, one can surmise that the luncheon went off without a hitch, as the myriad causes for complaint that would plague the rest of the book's production had not yet come to pass.

Their original plan seemed solid, if still with a heavier workload for Wright and Fuertes, but what actually happened was even more lopsided. Over the course of the book's writing and production, Wright completed almost all of the manuscript text, served as the primary correspondent for the trio with Brett at Macmillan, and oversaw the details of the book production as indicated by her reviewing illustration proofs before sending them on to Coues. More than simply reviewing the proofs, she also provided editorial guidance with an eye toward how the public would receive these images. In one instance, she notes that "the high lights have not been carefully looked after, as in the case of the sample Thrush." She continues, "this makes great flatness in the case of many birds; the parts appearing a dull gray, where in the original, they are a dazzling white. It is absolutely necessary

INTRODUCTION xix

(please tell Mr. Walton) [the printer] that the high lights should be <u>cut out</u> as in the case of the sample bird."[5]

By the beginning of February, Wright had finished a draft of the book manuscript and had sent it to Coues for his edits and revisions, as Wright communicated to their publisher in one of their many back-and-forths about the manuscript. Having told Brett that she would be returning three proof pages and requiring them to reprint the Downy Woodpecker, Wright then informed him that the manuscript was now in Coues's hands: "Dr C writes me this a.m. that he will have the MS in shape March 1st and promises me opinion of my work in a day or two. He is obviously not accustomed to having women do what they promise, and seems really surprised at having the MS on the day agreed between us."[6] In the end, Coues provided very little toward the manuscript, significantly less than what he had promised, according not only to Wright but also to Coues, as he later admitted. As Wright noted rather wryly in May 1897,

I am glad that [Coues] need not see the final proof. Shall Citizen Bird have an index? I wrote to Dr. Coues asking him to make one as soon as possible & send you his reply. Personally, I do not consider the Table of Contents [which Coues wrote] sufficient as it is not of course arranged alphabetically and someone may wish to turn quickly to some particular bird. If you wish <u>I</u> will make an index from the galley proof adding page numbers later. Also if you think best to have a very brief color-key of say 4 pages I will do it very quickly. Dr Coues has managed to shirk everything but one chapter and a couple of bird biographies.[7]

In the above letter from May 10, Wright suggests that Coues's key is not sufficient, and that a separate index is necessary. She says she can make one herself, which it appears she did from her June 17 letter, wherein she refers to "my index," and in which she acknowledges the rocky path the book has taken to get to printing:

I have now been through the proof of Citizen Bird four times. Galley proof (at Dr Coues request)—galley proof to place cuts (to please myself)—paged proof with cuts inserted,—to add a line here and there to make pages even— finally foundry proof, and I must say it made me wrathy to find a mistake in paging that made my index seem cross-eyed. But I only hope that the book will be successfull [*sic*], and by a long life pay for the trouble [and] expense of its infancy and teething period. When do you expect the book out?[8]

What was Coues doing the entire time that Wright was writing and Fuertes was illustrating? Coues was coaching Fuertes on his illustrations and recommending (on three separate occasions) that he neglect his senior college thesis in favor of completing the illustrations, offering such advice as, "Don't worry about your thesis—it will never be heard of, after your examiners get through with it—while these artistic plates will live for many, many years before the great public."[9] Coues was also, good-naturedly if rather officiously, providing advice on Fuertes's bird illustrations and helping him secure specimens for birds Fuertes needed for illustration models:

> As I think I told you in N.Y., I will accept all the pictures you showed us, with the two exceptions of the nuthatch and the hummingbird, which I should like to have you do over again. Put the nuthatch in the most characteristic attitude, head downward on a perpendicular tree trunk, with a full rounded breast, and bill pointing horizontally out to right or left. Take the frame work away from the hummingbirds, set the ♀ better on the nest, and draw the bills trimmer.
>
> And in general, <u>keep your accessories down</u>. What we want is the <u>bird</u>, with least possible scenery, stage setting, framework or back-ground of any description. You will remember that even in the cases of those very fine pictures of the summer warbler and the yellow rump, the <u>foliage</u> about them somewhat interfered with the effect. Be always careful about this.... I handed Mr. Chapman the list of your desiderata, and he promised to send you the specimens without delay.

Coues's attention to detail here played an important role in Fuertes's development as an illustrator. His suggestion to keep background elements out of the illustrations set Fuertes's illustrations apart from those of other bird illustrators such as Audubon or Fuertes's contemporary (and rival for this book), Ernest Thompson Seton, as Wright herself noted in a letter to Brett:

> Intrinsically, I do not think Mr Thomsons [*sic*] birds are as good as Mr Fuertes, but he has a wonderful gift of placing each bird in its haunt, with the aid of very artistic bits of landscape, so that the whole thing makes a series of complete

pictures. I prefer our method for the birds, taken from the juvenile point of view, but am very sure that the accessories and pictorial skill of Mr. T. will be better for the beast book, where the hut of the prarie [*sic*] dog and the den of the hibernating bear is as necessary as the animals themselves.[10]

It is worth noting that Coues was telling Fuertes to avoid the practice that Wright appreciated about Seton—his incorporation of background foliage as a means of setting the birds in their proper habitat, thus providing important hints about where to look for different species. Fuertes's improvement in incorporating background elements later helped his career as a bird illustrator.

In early March, Coues requested ten extra illustrations from Fuertes and solicited permission from their publisher at Macmillan. He writes to Fuertes, telling him, "I have a letter from Mr. Brett, saying he will be glad to have you do the <u>additional</u> plates I spoke about. They are the following: 101. Sage Thrasher. 102. Rock Wren, 103. Louisiana Tanager. 104. Red-headed Woodpecker. 105. Golden Eagle. 106. American Egret. 107. Dusky Duck. 108. Hooded Merganser. which, with diagram of Sparrow, plate of beaks, and plate of feet, make 111 in all."

This list is notable in that four of the birds (Thrasher, Wren, Tanager, and Eagle) are western birds, and one (Woodpecker) is a southern bird, not northeastern American birds, which disrupted the frame narrative of the story being set in Connecticut but which corresponded to Coues having made a name for himself as the ornithological expert of the western United States (and having lived briefly in North Carolina). It does not appear that Wright was consulted on these additions, as Wright blamed the book's lateness on Coues's request: "Fuertes has given us wonderful work even if we have been delayed. It has just occurred to me that Dr Coues is chiefly to blame for the delay, as he added nearly ten pictures to the list as originally presented to Fuertes, even though he was well aware how pushed the boy was for time. Without these extra drawings, which are in some cases unusable for Birdcraft, we should have had our pictures by April 15—as from the beginning F. has turned out three a week."[11]

It appears that Coues belatedly recognized that he had not done enough to truly deserve the title of coauthor, which he admits in a roundabout fashion in a letter to Wright shortly after the publication of *Citizen Bird*. In that letter, he suggests that it is in their mutual interest to keep the actual distribution of labor a secret between them, as Wright exasperatedly informs Brett:

What can Dr Coues be up to? He writes—"By the way, never give away the secret of the respective shares of authorship of C.B. There is already much guessing about it, always wide of the mark. I shall maintain impenetrability on this point, and it will be wise for you to do the same. Then the glamour of mystery will surround the book like a halo, in addition to its other fine points, and set tongues wagging and pens wiggling, and the publishers will rejoice accordingly." Furthermore, he says he has filed my m.s. away with his other papers "as I know you do not care to keep it!" I thought it best to tell you this, as he is such an odd stick, and also that I wrote him that both you and Mr Chapman know our respective shares in the work.[12]

While couched in a concern for the book's reception, Coues is also obviously trying to hide the fact that he only wrote one chapter and a few of the bird descriptions, while the bulk of the writing, revising, indexing, and production oversight came from Wright. As uncomfortable as it may be to admit, Coues was, in fact, correct that his reputation as an ornithologist was frequently cited in reviews as evidence of the book's quality as a scientific publication, even one aimed at a younger readership. It is equally true that, without Coues's insistence, Fuertes would not have been chosen as the illustrator, and the career of one of America's greatest bird illustrators would not have unfolded as serendipitously as it did.

While Coues certainly did not contribute as much as promised or expected in terms of being a coauthor, he did contribute to the book's success through his tireless promotion of the book in ornithology circles, where he was widely respected. As Wright had noted to Brett when considering Coues as a potential coauthor, "Dr Coues' standing is not a thing to be despised," and certainly he used all of the goodwill at his disposal to make the book a success among his network of professional ornithologists, many of whom might have otherwise dismissed the book out of hand as a work of children's literature. Coues especially championed *Citizen Bird* as the first major work of his protégé Louis Agassiz Fuertes, who he celebrated as the next great American bird illustrator after Audubon. In addition to promoting Fuertes through his work for *Citizen Bird*, Coues presented a number of works by Fuertes at a meeting of the American Ornithologists' Union and to the grandchildren of John James Audubon, whose support for Fuertes further bolstered his career as a bird illustrator. In this sense, Coues was ensuring the success of *Citizen Bird* as a collector's item for those interested in bird illustration, if not in children's literature.

INTRODUCTION xxiii

Even though she did the bulk of the work for *Citizen Bird*, Wright did not rest once the book was in production. As will be discussed at greater length in the section that follows, Wright did what she could to influence the rollout of *Citizen Bird* and to make it a bestseller for Macmillan. Wright was incredibly savvy in her knowledge of children's literature, and knowing that children's books are bought primarily as Christmas presents, she worked with Brett at Macmillan to ensure the book was published well before the Christmas season. Once *Citizen Bird* was published, Wright immediately turned her attention to its reception, encouraging Brett to advertise the book and get reviews in a wide variety of publications:

I have already endeavoured to stir up some New York press notices, but in July and August, many of my friends are away and either have books sent after them for reviewing, which takes time, or else leave the work in the hands of the office cat.

Certainly we have nothing to complain of at the hands of either Chicago or Boston. The New York Herald of last Saturday also had a nice paragraph.

Do you think it would be advisable to advertise in Forest and Stream—and try to have them put the bird books on their list? If so I could write to the editor and see if he would like to publish say three of the handsomest game pictures from the new edition of Birdcraft, at the time the book is issued. The Ruffed Grouse, Wood and Teal Ducks—would be suitable for that paper.[13]

Wright's planning ahead to encourage reviews in popular newspapers and conservation magazines paid off in the book's popularity and positive reception among many different audiences.

The Reception of *Citizen Bird*

Though the process of making *Citizen Bird* did not go as smoothly as its creators had assumed it would, the book's launch in mid-July of 1897 was met with immediate enthusiasm from the U.S. book-buying public, to the immense gratification of all involved. Coues crowed over the triumph in a July 27 letter to Fuertes, asserting that it was "a phenomenal success from the start," which was no mean feat, given that its $1.50 price tag would be equivalent to roughly fifty dollars today. Coues attributed the book's popularity largely to Fuertes's illustrations;

as he told his young collaborator, "the book sells on sight—almost every body that sees it wants a copy."[14] While there is no doubt that Fuertes's illustrations played a pivotal role in selling *Citizen Bird*, the book's attractiveness and utility as a material object must also be credited. Additionally, Macmillan's advertising campaign, as well as the efforts of its authors, especially Wright, to get the book in the hands of as many reviewers as possible, aided in its success.

Wright's letters to George Brett highlight her close attention to the design and quality of the printed book and her investment in its effective marketing. In the months leading up to its publication, Wright kept Macmillan's printer— J. S. Cushing's Norwood Press—on its toes, scrutinizing galley proofs and demanding up-to-date information concerning *Citizen Bird*'s cover, page layout, even the weight of its chosen paper, all with a sharp eye trained on the appeal of the final product and its marketability. The book's front cover signaled that this was a book aimed at U.S. audiences, which promised not just a lesson in birding but also in civics. The first print run of 5,000 copies featured a federal blue cloth cover stamped with a patriotic design of two silver staffs featuring the American flag and a Bald Eagle with outstretched wings; this design framed the book's main title, which was printed in elaborate quasi-Colonial font, with the authors' names directly below. In what was perhaps a concession to Wright's insistence that a field guide must be as portable as possible, the first run of the book was printed in a "duodecimo" or "12mo" size, roughly 5 by 7.5 inches, instead of the larger "octavo" size of 6 by 9 inches. Though generally pleased with the final product, Wright did have one complaint regarding "the Citizen": specifically, "his weight," which was not inconsiderable as the book numbered 430 pages. If later printings of the book were ever to get "into the schools," Wright suggested, "a thinner paper, more like that used by the Century Magazine, could be used."[15]

That George Brett felt optimistic about *Citizen Bird*'s financial prospects can be assumed from the pride of place that he gave it in the numerous ads or "circulars" that Macmillan published in various industry periodicals to promote new titles. In one representative periodical, *The Critic*, an American "weekly review of literature and the arts" aimed at booksellers and serious book-buyers, *Citizen Bird* featured prominently between July and November 1897. The first Macmillan circular in *The Critic* to promote *Citizen Bird* dates from July 3, a little less than two weeks before it landed in bookstores. Situated in the middle of the list of Macmillan's "new books" and separated from the other titles by an ornately twisted decorative frame, this initial advertisement included only the book's title, a truncated version of its subtitle, the names of the authors, and a brief, evocative description that characterized *Citizen Bird* as "a new nature story book," "illustrated with drawings from nature by Louis Agassiz Fuertes." "A delightful story book for young people beginning the study of bird life," it further asserts, "the narrative forms a guide to all the chief varieties of American birds, and gives a great deal of interesting information about their habits, etc."[16] This first promotional salvo deliberately stresses *Citizen Bird*'s bona fides as a work of imaginative literature that will captivate "young people" with a "delightful story" and bird illustrations taken from nature. This framing implicitly distinguishes *Citizen Bird* from other bird literature of a more dryly educational cast intended for older children, such as James Newton Baskett's misleadingly named *The Story of the Birds* (1896), which offered something more akin to a correspondence class in ornithology. As can be seen in a letter she wrote to Brett a few months before the book's publication, Wright was anxious for Macmillan to foreground this difference in their advertising: "May I suggest that Citizen Bird be advertised as 'a bird book for young people, with new and beautiful illustrations from nature' instead of as a reading book? Many people will buy it as a children's story and the reader part can come in later. Even as a volume in 'a new series of Nature Stories for young people' is less forbidding than the word reader."[17] To have advertised *Citizen Bird* as a "reader" would have stressed its educational value at the expense of the pleasure to be derived from its story and images; it also risked the book's guiding mission: to win children over to the cause of bird protection by teaching them how to enjoy birding as an enjoyable and gratifying social activity. Moreover, as Wright cannily observed, people bought books for children as gifts. A children's book promoted as, in essence, a textbook would be less appealing to purchasers looking for suitable presents during the Christmas season, when booksellers enjoyed the briskest sales.

Reviews of *Citizen Bird*

Wright's opinion was clearly shared by her publisher, as subsequent advertisements further underscored that *Citizen Bird* was "for the young folks," a point that it reinforced through blurbs from its earliest reviews. In a circular published at the end of July 1897, *Citizen Bird* was given top billing on Macmillan's list of new books, and underneath all of the relevant information, including its size and purchase price, the publisher included an excerpt from a glowing review in the *New York Times*, which stressed that it was "a delightful book for young people" that would satisfy even "teachers of natural science." This review also allowed the publisher to trade on the name recognition of its authors—"Lovers of Mrs. Wright's larger and more technical work 'Birdcraft' [would] not need to be told of the interesting style of the new work" and the addition of "Dr. Coues" on the title page was itself a testament to the book's "accuracy and scientific value."[18]

As the reviews continued to come in from across the United States, Macmillan made sure to excerpt them in later circulars, such as in *The Critic*. The *New York Herald* asserted that whether "young or old" "none of us know as much as we ought about birds," a deficit that could be easily overcome "by spending an hour or two in perusing 'Citizen Bird.'"[19] The *Chicago Tribune*, on the other hand, doubled down on *Citizen Bird*'s value for its intended audience, claiming that "there is no other book in existence so well fitted for arousing and directing the interest that all children of any sensibility feel towards the birds."[20] The cumulative effect of these positive notices is evident in the book's sales. The first printing of 5,000 copies sold out within two months, and by the end of September 1897, Macmillan was advertising its second printing, this one in the slightly larger "octavo" size of 6 by 9 inches. The new edition of Wright's *Birdcraft*—illustrated with larger sizes of the same images Fuertes had produced for *Citizen Bird*—had also launched by this time, which allowed Macmillan to promote Wright's field guides for children and adults to the public simultaneously, suggesting that the average U.S. household could benefit from possessing them both.

Throughout 1897 and well into 1898, reviews of *Citizen Bird* continued to accumulate, echoing with common themes that help to account for the book's extremely positive reception by the press. Numerous critics noted the book's timeliness, its publication coinciding with a growing national awareness of the impending environmental catastrophe if the current rate at which wild birds were being eradicated was not drastically reduced. "This volume," noted the *Boston Advertiser* (quoted in Macmillan's *Book Reviews*), "has been issued just at the right moment, when from many sources the leaders among people of intelligence are trying to arouse the public conscience to the fact that a great wrong has been done to the birds of our country."[21] Several reviews also noted how the book's appeal to the general public served as an important supplement to fledgling legislative efforts to protect bird populations, such as "the recent Massachusetts law protecting insectivorous birds from the ravages of milliners."[22] The New York

Outlook seconded this opinion, arguing that works like *Citizen Bird* were vitally important as "many specimens of birds peculiar to this country are fast becoming extinct, due to the misdirected energies of egg and bird collectors, and the aimless cruelty of men who call themselves sportsmen, and of the thoughtless or wicked small boy."[23]

Though they varied widely in their beliefs as to which groups were principally to blame for the extinction event facing numerous bird species in the United States, the reviewers largely shared with Wright the conviction that the success of the bird protection movement depended on the enlistment of the nation's children to the cause. *Citizen Bird* was thus celebrated as a powerful recruitment tool, owing to its winning "union of science and sentiment," providing its child readers with an elementary grounding in the basic principles of ornithology while inspiring them to care about the natural world and about birds as neighbors and fellow citizens. In this way, noted the *New York Times*, "information is given that does not 'dust the mind by its dryness,' nor lead it astray by inaccuracy."[24] In the reviewers' general approbation of how the frame story exhibited for children an active, interrogatory approach to learning about birds, one can see the changing attitudes toward early childhood education as well as the influence of the burgeoning environmental and wildlife preservation movement. Unlike other works of juvenile bird literature, one critic observed, *Citizen Bird* did not make the mistake of treating its intended audience "like an audience at a lecture, who are to be seen and not heard."[25] Instead, the example of the story's fictional children, who Frank M. Chapman in *The Auk* praised as "eager questioners and often keen observers," promoted a more participatory model of education, while the nature study program developed by their fictional ornithologist uncle encouraged adult readers to recognize the value of supplementing classroom lessons with experiential learning in the field.[26] Numerous reviews underscored the heuristic value of the early chapters, which outlined a "step by step" process wherein the children first learn to recognize the diversity of birds in their local environment, and then to study them more closely by keeping personalized "bird tables" in which they record the defining characteristics of every "unfamiliar bird" they encounter.[27]

At the same time, most reviewers recognized that *Citizen Bird*'s ostensible function as a birding guide (i.e., to teach children how to correctly identify birds) was in service to a larger preservationist agenda, one that was, in some ways, in conflict with ornithology as then practiced. As one critic observed, in "teaching children about our domestic birds, by encouraging them to observe the living creature rather than the inanimate 'specimen,'" *Citizen Bird* was promoting a new model of bird study, one that was open to nonspecialists and, more importantly, could be undertaken "without a gun."[28] The palpable enthusiasm of the book's reviewers—even in academic periodicals like *Science*—for its goal of cultivating a rising generation of "bird-lovers," "filled with a healthy sentiment against the wanton destruction of birds and their eggs," evidences the degree to which the bird protection movement had already infiltrated the public discourse by the century's end.[29] Moreover, the various narrative and poetic strategies that Wright employed to make *Citizen Bird*'s subject not just intellectually stimulating but also emotionally affecting and morally edifying were so well-received because they were already part of an established protectionist playbook. By anthropomorphizing the birds—whether by opening the story with an imaginary conversation between birds on a telegraph wire or by organizing the birds into quasi-medieval "guilds" based on their shared "occupation" ("Seed Sower," "Weed Warrior," etc.)—*Citizen Bird* put them within the bounds of human sympathy and aligned them with Progressive-Era ideals, including the right to protection, positing birds as "citizen[s] both in name and in reality."[30]

Interestingly, *Citizen Bird*'s framing of the wild bird as both a natural and "naturalized" citizen was cited as one of its major failings by British reviewers. Wright was baffled and angered by the book's treatment in the "London notices," protesting that the "the English papers have always been nice to me until this season."[31] Three of the negative reviews she mentions critiqued the book largely on ideological grounds, arguing that national differences in temperament, taste, and education made the book unlikely to find favor with British children. In the journal *The Academy*, the unsigned reviewer likened *Citizen Bird* to a piece of protectionist propaganda; its "peculiarly waterish sentiment" might appeal to "American children," it asserted, "but in England especially we should probably shrug shoulders... and utter the time-worn complacencies that boys do very little damage to our feathered populations, and that birds'-nesting is an excellent means of inculcating a spirit of hardiness and adventure."[32] Though milder in his review in *Nature*, the British ornithologist W. Warde Fowler also dismissed the book as too sentimental and didactic to recommend to the intrepid "English boy," "who would probably learn better from a sound and scholarly handbook."[33] *The Zoologist* made a similar argument, suggesting that *Citizen Bird* is "too elementary in style" and insufficiently scientific, complacently concluding that "a young naturalist will grapple with and surmount many difficulties when his heart is in the subject."[34]

The British reviews all judged *Citizen Bird* based on the preferences and needs of the prototypical English schoolboy, which limited the potential readership to older, upper-class boys, the kind likely to attend an elite "public school" (similar to a private school in the United States). They also took umbrage with the assumption that bird protection as a common good should trump the privileges of these schoolboy readers to rob nests and shoot birds for pleasure and for study. Seen in this light, their shared contemptuousness of *Citizen Bird*'s "sentimentality" might be read as more than the usual tactic by which literature written for women and children was often devalued, the implication being that its emotionality comes at the expense of intellectual and moral rigor. These critiques also betrayed an anxiety about the potential for affecting works of environmental literature to disrupt existing socioeconomic ecosystems, both by encouraging an understanding of civic responsibility that extends to nonhuman agents and by inspiring legislation that might prohibit industry's unfettered access to birds and other "natural resources."

Though Fuertes's illustrations did not receive the same criticisms from hostile critics as Wright's frame story, there is no doubt that the images reinforced the text's protectionist message. As Chapman noted in *The Auk*, Fuertes's depictions of different species as they might look in their natural habitats encouraged the viewer to view them as one might "portraits of the leading characters in a fascinating story."[35] Indeed, Wright had been insistent about this feature of the illustrations from the beginning. However, over the course of their collaboration, Fuertes's willingness to accept Wright and Coues's numerous requests for revision led to his rapid improvement in this aspect of bird illustration, and by the time the book was published, even the fastidious Wright could find no complaint, willingly acknowledging to Brett that "Fuertes has given us wonderful work."[36] The reviewers heartily seconded her praise for Fuertes's ability to render the *living* bird as if one were seeing it through a pair of binoculars in the field. In the words of the *New York Times* review, "Mr. Fuertes has caught the characteristic attitude, the poise of the body, the intelligence of the eye, and the gently modeled surfaces with great skill and insight; he has made his birds live upon the page instead of presenting them with hopelessly stuffed and distorted bodies, after the manner of the average illustrator of bird books."[37] Though Fuertes also used "skins" for his bird studies (and was, especially in later life, an avid hunter-collector of rare birds), his illustrations for *Citizen Bird* supported Wright's oft-stated maxim that "a bird in the bush is worth two in the hand," with the majority depicting a particular bird perched on the type of tree branch or bit of brush or marshland where it would typically nest or find its food. In this way, Fuertes's illustrations exceeded the ornithological goal of rendering birds with scientific accuracy for identification purposes; they also served the aims of birdwatching as a recreational activity, helping prospective birders learn where they should be looking in the natural world that surrounded them when searching for particular birds.

Bird Day and Educational Material

For all of the buzz and sales generated by its coverage in the Anglo-American periodical press, had *Citizen Bird* been made available only to child readers whose parents could afford such literary luxuries, it never would have reached a broader audience beyond the upper-class elite. As evidenced by her suggestion to Brett about printing future editions on thinner—and thus cheaper—paper (which never came to pass), Wright foresaw this limitation and was already considering alternate strategies for the book's broader dissemination. To reach a wider audience, *Citizen Bird* required advocates beyond its publisher, advertisers, booksellers, and critics, and it found them in two main arenas: the larger bird-protection movement, which was then formalizing itself as the Audubon Society, and the U.S. public school system. The years surrounding *Citizen Bird*'s publication saw the rebirth of the Audubon Society as an interconnected network of state chapters, including the Connecticut chapter, which was founded in January 1898 with Wright at the helm as its first president. In this role, Wright was well positioned to promote outreach to children as one of its major objectives, and the Audubon Society of Connecticut quickly adopted a multipronged approach to bringing young people into the fold. One strategy used by many state chapters including Connecticut was to allow all those under eighteen years of age to join as "junior members," without the fees required of adult members.[38] The Audubon Society of Connecticut also pioneered the creation of circulating lending libraries of bird books, pre-scripted lectures, and magic lantern slides that town libraries could borrow to engage their local populations in bird study (see appendix 2). Several of those lending libraries were designated specifically for children, and *Citizen Bird*, of course, featured prominently in these circulating collections.

Yet, grassroots efforts by state Audubon chapters could accomplish only so much on their own. These organizations required governmental support to institutionalize bird study for children, and their most successful inroad into public school curriculums was a new holiday just then being adopted by states throughout the country: Bird Day. The brainchild of school superintendent C. A. Babcock, Bird Day was first observed in Oil City, Pennsylvania, on May 4, 1894, and over the next decades it was enthusiastically promoted by public school educators committed to bringing nature study into the classroom and students into the natural world. The Audubon Society of Connecticut made the adoption of Bird Day in the state one of its first orders of business, with Wright leading a contingent of members on a trip to the capital city of Hartford to petition the legislature to "amend an act related to Arbor Day" so that the governor would "annually in the spring, designate by official proclamation an Arbor and Bird Day to be observed in the schools and in any other way as shall by indicated in such official proclamation."[39] Their efforts were met with immediate success, and in 1899, Governor George E. Lounsbury issued the first such proclamation, declaring May 5 as Connecticut's Arbor and

Mabel Osgood Wright's bird study group, 1897. Source: Fairfield Museum and History Center Archives.

Bird Day. Lounsbury's proclamation especially "recommend[ed] to all teachers of the state that on that day they so give instruction and direct the exercises of the schools, that the children may take increased interest in Forestry, feel in their hearts a response to all that is kind and gentle in Nature, have a higher appreciation of the innocent and beautiful birds that sing in our forests and nest about our homes, and so give glad obedience to all protecting laws."[40]

With Bird Day now a recognized holiday in Connecticut, Wright and others quickly set about creating educational materials for distribution in the public schools, which included a variety of bird-centric readings and activities that ran the gamut from recitations of poems about birds to games involving the recognition of local bird species to birdhouse-building projects. In an 1899 editorial in *Bird-Lore* magazine, titled "A Bird Class for Children," Wright provided a model for how children between the ages of six and twelve might be introduced into bird study, a model that she had patterned in *Citizen Bird* and that she had herself tested through an informal bird-study group she organized for local children on the grounds of her Fairfield, Connecticut, estate. To teach the rudiments of how to observe birds in the wild, Wright suggested that educators borrow stuffed birds from already existing collections and place them in outdoor spaces where live birds of that species would most likely to be spotted (the Song Sparrow in a bush, Chipping Sparrows on the ground). "Let the children look at them near by and then at a distance," she advised, "so that a sense of proportion and color value will be developed unconsciously." "After this," Wright concludes, "the written description of the habits of birds, which you must read or tell the children, will have a different meaning. This method may be varied by looking up live specimens of the birds thus closely observed."[41]

Though Wright does not explicitly promote her own book as the best source for these "written description[s]" of birds for a juvenile audience, numerous educational publications printed at the time make clear that *Citizen Bird* had already achieved the status of urtext when it came to bird study for children. In a column titled "Nature Study for Grammar Grades" in an 1898 edition of the *Journal of Education*, prominent Massachusetts educator Arthur Clarke Boyden proclaimed *Citizen Bird* "the guide" for teachers interested in "developing the spirit of the naturalist in children" by instructing them in "the grouping of birds according to their habits, and in the studying of their relations to human interests."[42] Boyden followed this declaration by providing his readers with a model curriculum for juvenile bird study, which alluded to the book's organization of bird life into particular "citizen" groups and which highlighted individual chapters in *Citizen Bird* as preparatory material for specific lessons. A year later, pioneering ethnographer and natural science educator Lucy Landon Wilson also singled out *Citizen Bird* as required reading for all teachers "preparing for the proper celebration of Bird Day," and, in her own ideas for Bird Day lessons, she borrows heavily from the mnemonic words and phrases that Wright developed to help birdwatchers identify and memorize the songs and calls of different birds.[43] Boyden and Wilson's promotion of *Citizen Bird* to an educator audience suggests it had a broader dissemination and greater impact within the U.S. school system than what might have been expected of a non-textbook. Equally germane to lessons in civics and the natural sciences, *Citizen Bird* resonated with many of the core beliefs that fueled Progressive-Era educational reform: it conceptualized a child-centric model of bird study; it promoted an experiential learning approach that was, by virtue of relying almost exclusively on the observational faculties, applicable to schoolchildren of all classes; and it fostered in children a sense of social responsibility by enlisting them as protectors of local birdlife and of the natural world more generally.

Citizen Bird's Print Run

By the turn of the twentieth century, the field of bird literature for children had become considerably more crowded, with contributions from, among others, Florence Merriam Bailey, Olive Thorne Miller, and Neltje Blanchan. Wright herself reviewed many of these books in a recurring column devoted to new nature writing in the *New York Times*. Yet, *Citizen Bird* remained in circulation throughout this period, with reprints in 1898, 1900, 1904, and 1907, at which point it went out of print until Macmillan reissued it for a final time in 1923.

Its continued popularity can be attributed to its complex embodiment of Progressive-Era aspirations and anxieties about the future America it was rapidly building and the gifts and burdens it would be leaving for the next generation. While *Citizen Bird* did not challenge any of the major shibboleths of the period, remaining optimistic about America's industrial and economic development, its framing of bird study as a form of meliorative environmental stewardship that even children could practice was incredibly compelling to an audience just awakening to the idea of anthropogenic impact.

Birds, *Citizen Bird* cautioned, were the bellwether of greater environmental devastation to come if the country did not avert its current course. Moreover, the book educated the next generation of children how to manage and protect its natural resources instead of exploiting and destroying them. *Citizen Bird*'s reception thus reveals how receptive the U.S. public was to the wisdom of what Wright called "The Heart of Nature."

ORNITHOLOGY AND CHILDREN'S LITERATURE CONTEXTS

Citizen Bird *in the Context of Ornithology, Birding Culture, and Environmental Conservation.* With its publication in 1897, *Citizen Bird* came out at the height of newfound interest in birdwatching and environmental conservation, its popularity aided by the development of ornithology as a science. Birdwatchers were now able to take portable field guides out on their walks for aid in identifying birds, complete with illustrations of birds for reference. *Citizen Bird* encapsulates the skills of its three creators in each of these areas: Mabel Osgood Wright's expertise in writing one of the first popular field guides (*Birdcraft*, 1895), Elliott Coues's background in ornithological manuals and checklists, and Louis Agassiz Fuertes's bird illustrations.

Drawing by Louis Agassiz Fuertes on envelope. Source: Cornell Archives. Photo by Meghan Freeman.

Birding Culture and the Rise of Ornithology

Birding developed as a hobby in the United States in the late nineteenth century as the culmination of several historical trends related to ornithology, natural history writing, and bird illustration. The establishment of ornithology as a new science during this period helped make birdwatching an acceptable leisure pursuit, as hobbyists were engaging in a productive, admirably scientific form of leisure. In the absence of established universities and degrees in ornithology, the lines between amateurs and professionals were blurred, until Elliott Coues (among others) helped to establish the first ornithological society in the United States in 1883.

In early 1883, Elliott Coues, J. A. Allen, and William Brewster, all members of the Nuttall Ornithological Club in Cambridge, Massachusetts, began discussions about organizing a countrywide professional ornithological society. The three sent formal invitations to a variety of men, primarily scientists, but also well-connected and moneyed individuals who could aid the society with their social networks and funds. In September 1883, the American Ornithologists' Union (AOU) held its three-day organizational meeting at the American Museum of Natural History in New York, with twenty-three ornithologists in attendance. In addition to all the typical election-holding (wherein Coues was elected chair), constitution-writing, and bylaws-producing, the group focused on three main issues relevant to the creation of *Citizen Bird*: membership, committees, and publications.

Part of the purpose of the creation of the AOU was to professionalize ornithology, but very few members of the AOU worked as ornithologists. Therefore, the AOU created a tiered membership of "active" and "associate" members. "Active" members referred to those who worked in science and ornithology, or those with great expertise in the area, while "associate" members included those whose work supported ornithology, such as taxidermists, specimen collectors, and parties interested in bird life in a hobbyist capacity. The initial committees created by the AOU included committees devoted to professionalizing ornithology by formalizing species lists and naming conventions for birds. The Committee on the Classification and Nomenclature of North American Birds played a significant role in this area, as did committees devoted to obtaining government support for ornithology. Later that year, the AOU launched a new periodical, *The Auk*, with four associate editors (Coues among them).

This work was intended to professionalize and popularize ornithology in the late nineteenth century, but what did ornithology look like in practice at this time? These days, much of the fieldwork of ornithologists consists of wildlife observation and species counts, but in the late 1800s, much of the work of both ornithologists and bird illustrators included killing birds for study. (To be sure, contemporary ornithologists continue to use study skins, as they are called, but contemporary ornithologists are much more conservation-oriented than were their predecessors.) In fact, Elliott Coues is widely cited for his advice to ornithologists to kill and collect as many birds as possible: "How many examples of the same bird do you want?—*All you can get*.... Bird skins are *capital*,"[44] and "begin by shooting every bird you can, coupling this sad destruction, however, with the closest observations upon habits."[45]

The importance of taxidermy for bird study is represented in *Citizen Bird* with Uncle Roy's (Dr. Roy Hunter) "wonder room," described in detail in chapter 2 ("The Doctor's Wonder Room") and referenced throughout the book, when the children are introduced to birds via taxidermy when the weather is too poor to go out birdwatching.[46] Ornithology as a scientific profession is represented in *Citizen Bird* when Uncle Roy repeatedly refers to ornithologists as "the Wise Men." In chapter 4 ("The Building of a Bird"), Uncle Roy explains the different body parts of birds to the children, making frequent allusions to "the Wise Men" and their development of terminology and names for bird study.

The term "Wise *Men*" also indicates the gender makeup of ornithology at the time. The AOU did not allow women into its membership at first. In 1885, two years after its founding, the AOU allowed its first woman member, Florence Merriam Bailey (then Florence Merriam, whose early field guide is described in more detail below). Mabel Osgood Wright also became an associate member in 1895. By 1900, eighty women held AOU membership at the "associate" (amateur) level, representing about 11 percent of its membership. In 1901, the AOU created a new category of "elective" members, at the level between "associate" (amateur) and "active" (professional) membership, and inducted six women as elective members, including Bailey and Wright. Despite its gender imbalance at the professional level, the development of ornithology as a profession contributed to the rising interest in birding as a hobby for men and women. Bird observation and identification were seen as useful contributions to the new profession of ornithology, and thus birding as a hobby was seen as an acceptable leisure pastime, as its emulation of the work of science fit squarely into the Protestant work ethic. In addition to the cultural acceptance of birdwatching, another key development that aided the rise of birding at the end of the nineteenth century was the publication of the first true field guides for birders, complete with realistic bird illustrations.

Field Guides and Bird Illustrations

The end of the nineteenth century brought a key development in birding with the publication of the first true field guides for birders, with Florence Merriam Bailey's *Birds through an Opera-Glass* (1889) and Mabel Osgood Wright's *Birdcraft: A Field Book of Two Hundred Song, Game, and Water Birds* (1895). Before these publications, birders did not have portable field guides. Those interested in bird study needed to refer to scientific ornithological manuals, nature writing, and bird illustrations.

Ornithological manuals included information about bird anatomy, as well as maps and ranges of birds, and therefore could be useful in bird identification. However, such manuals were also quite large and therefore not portable for use in the field. Elliott Coues's *Key to North American Birds* (1872, 361 pages) and Spencer Baird, T. M. Brewer, and Robert Ridgway's *History of North American Birds* (1874, 684 pages) were the most popular manuals of the time. Most importantly, these manuals were aimed at identifying stuffed bird skins for study, not live birds in the field. Coues's *Key* includes directions titled "How to Use the Key," which begins, "We have in hand a bird which we know nothing about, and desire to *identify*, that is, to discover its name and position in the system; and to learn whatever else the present volume may afford."[47] The specification of having the bird "in hand" indicates a dead specimen, and the rest of the key continues in that manner, with "How to Measure a Specimen" instructing ornithologists to use "a tape line showing inches and fourths" for large birds, and "a foot rule, gradated for inches and eights, or better, decimals to hundredths" for small birds, and all of the ways to handle, measure, and identify dead specimens.[48] Later editions specified the types of guns ornithologists should use to kill and collect birds and how to prepare and stuff birds for study skins.

Nature writing and bird illustration also contributed to the growing interest in birdwatching and ornithology. In the second half of the nineteenth century, many authors wrote narratives about birds, extolling the virtues of birds' beauty and of communing with birds in nature. Mabel Osgood Wright contributed to such nature study writing in her 1894 book *The Friendship of Nature: A New England Chronicle of Birds and Flowers.* As Wright described it, "The character study of the bird is beyond the mazes of classification, beyond the counting of bones, out of the reach of the scalpel and the literature of the microscope."[49] Her poetic depictions of wild birds exemplify a goal of nature writing: to encourage people to appreciate birds in the wild, rather than in a cage, and to spend more time in nature. Likewise, bird illustration piqued people's interest in the beauty of birds, as it had been established as an artistic tradition, if not yet fully used for bird identification. The most famous bird illustrator of the time was John James Audubon, whose comprehensive volume *The Birds of America* had been published in 1840.

In crafting his illustrations for *Citizen Bird*, Louis Agassiz Fuertes used his observations of live birds as well as dead bird specimens and skins that Coues helped source for him through his vast ornithology networks. Even though Coues encouraged shooting birds for ornithological study, he could recognize the difference between the drawings Fuertes made from live and dead birds, as he claimed in a letter to Fuertes's mother:

> As soon as he has finished with this contract, and graduated from college, I hope he will be able to take a long rest, go off in the woods, and get fresh inspiration from contact with nature. Do you know, I can see a difference between the pictures he makes of birds he knows alive, and those he has only dead specimens of to work from? I should like to have him turned loose for the summer, with his field glass, pencils, & sketch book. There is nothing like it, for the ends we have in view.[50]

Whereas Coues had been more of a traditionalist in the sense of wanting Fuertes's illustrations to be only of birds, without foliage, here he shows himself to be somewhat forward-thinking in his assertion that drawing from nature will create better bird illustrations. His communication of this preference to Fuertes (via his mother) likely influenced the young artist's artistic habits moving forward.

Finally, one last development, not of a publication variety but of a technological one, contributed to the development of birdwatching: binoculars. Though devices for seeing farther away had existed for centuries, modern prism binoculars that allowed people to view with both eyes at six to ten times magnification were invented in the mid-nineteenth century. Nineteenth-century birdwatchers also used opera glasses, which cover both eyes and allow for three to five times magnification. This development in optics helped move bird study from being able to closely observe only dead birds to being able to observe live birds in the field.

These developments culminated in the first popular field guides: Florence Merriam Bailey's *Birds through an Opera-Glass* (1889) and Mabel Osgood Wright's *Birdcraft: A Field Book of Two Hundred Song, Game, and Water Birds* (1895). These books combined scientific information about birds, visual clues for identifying birds in the field, portability, and accessibility, all framed by a subtle message in support of environmental conservation and wildlife protection.

Florence Merriam Bailey's *Birds through an Opera-Glass* (1889) began in 1887 as a series of articles in *Audubon Magazine* called "Hints to Audubon Workers: Fifty Birds and How to Know Them." The subsequently published book was small and portable and included seventy species and a field key, which was a first for identifying live birds in the field rather than dead birds in a lab. Before the chapters describing each bird, Merriam Bailey provided tips on the main details to assess for identifying birds: "locality, size, color, details of marking, song, food, flight, eggs, nest, and habits."[51] She also promoted birdwatching as opposed to bird collecting, for scientific as well as sentimental reasons: "Photography is coming to hold an important place in nature work, as its notes cannot be questioned, and the student who goes afield armed with opera-glass and camera will not only add more to our knowledge than he who goes armed with a gun, but will gain for himself a fund of enthusiasm and a lasting store of pleasant memories. For more than all the statistics is the sanity and serenity of spirit that comes when we step aside from the turmoil of the world to hold quiet converse with Nature."[52]

The other major field guide of this era was Mabel Osgood Wright's *Birdcraft: A Field Book of Two Hundred Song, Game, and Water Birds*. Wright's guide was more popular than Merriam Bailey's in part because it contained more birds—two hundred, as opposed to seventy—and it was more scientific in its approach to describing and identifying birds. Her introductory chapters describe a variety of elements related to birds' life cycle: in spring, their breeding plumage and song, in summer, their nesting, and their fall migration and winter survival. The next chapter, "How to Name the Birds," provides tips similar to those of Merriam Bailey for bird identification. Beginning with a plate of the different parts of a bird's body, Wright goes on to instruct readers on the features to note in bird identification: size, color, habitat, behavior, and food, using the book's "Synopsis of Families" and "Key to the Birds" to locate the exact species. Further, Wright distinguishes her field guide for the "novice who wishes to recognize the birds by sight"[53] and opposes it to ornithological manuals such as those from Robert Ridgway, Elliott Coues, or Frank Chapman (Coues's she described as "modern and charming."[54] Like Merriam Bailey, Wright cautioned against killing birds—unless done by an expert scientist:

> A mere dogged persistency will not do for the study of the *living bird*, and it is to the *living bird* in his love-songs, his house-building, his haunts, and his migrations, that I would lead you. The gun that silences the bird voice, and the looting of nests, should be left to the practiced hand of science; you have no excuse for taking life, whether actual or embryonic, as your very ignorance will cause useless slaughter, and the egg-collecting fever of the average boy savours more of the green of possession than of ornithological ardour.[55]

Just as humans can engage in virtuous or unsavory behaviors, such as looting nests or killing birds, so too can birds, according to Wright. In *Birdcraft*, as in *Citizen Bird*, Wright anthropomorphizes birds to depict their instinctual behaviors as good or bad. In her description of Cowbirds' nest parasitism (the practice of laying their eggs in other birds' nests, like some species of Cuckoo), Wright begins: "The Cowbird is the pariah of bird-dom, the exception that proves the rule of marital fidelity and good housekeeping."[56] In *Birdcraft*, Wright goes on to decry Cowbirds as "socialists" who "send their young to free kindergartens and mission schools that they may be fed and clothed at the expense of others."[57] In *Citizen Bird*, her language is geared more toward the civics lessons she seeks to imbue in her young readers, calling Cowbird parents "lazy and shiftless" for their nest parasitism, and chastising the young for leaving the nest "without so much as saying 'thank you' to its foster parents."[58]

Birdcraft was a popular field guide; it was reprinted nine times and remained in print for thirty years. It went out of print with the advent of the more technical field guides as exist today, starting with Roger Tory Peterson's 1934 *A Field Guide to the Birds*. Peterson's innovative contribution to bird identification was "field marks" or, as they put it, the "trademarks of nature." Field marks denote the unique physical features that can be used to identify a bird. Additionally, these new field guides do not use any narrative descriptions of bird species and describe their range, habitat, behaviors, calls, and habits in more technical and less sentimental terms. Now, in Peterson, Cowbirds are described this way: "Often seen being fed by smaller birds whose nests have been parasitized.... Parasitizes a wide variety of smaller bird nests. Never builds its own nest."[59]

The move from a sentimental, conservation-minded approach to a more technical one represents the developments in wildlife and environmental conservation during this time. Whereas Merriam Bailey and Wright were attempting to encourage people to become conservationists by getting them interested in birds, Peterson's field guide represents the development of birding as a hobby and the successes of the conservation movement. Below, we describe the context for *Citizen Bird* in terms of environmental conservation in the nineteenth century.

Environmental and Wildlife Conservation

The industrialism of the mid-nineteenth century brought with it a newfound interest in nature, especially from urban elites who would escape their urban environments to go renew themselves in nature, developing new interests in fishing and hunting, as well as in hiking and birdwatching. These urban elites also began participating in the burgeoning environmental conservation organizations that sprung up during this time. Many of today's large and established conservation organizations were founded in the nineteenth century, like the Sierra Club and the Audubon Society. Those interested in birds and wildlife could find conservation organizations to suit their interests, as opposed to organizations devoted to the protection of companion animals, such as the ASPCA, or the nature study movement.

These newfound nature interests and participation in conservation movements were highly gendered, though. Aside from those in the Transcendentalist movement, men's interest in nature skewed heavily toward the conquest of nature, with nature posing a challenge to be overcome. The frontier of the western United States became a favored spot for wilderness exploration and for hunting, especially big game hunting. Theodore Roosevelt, a childhood friend of Mabel Osgood Wright (whom she called "Teddy Spectacles"), famously enjoyed big game hunting out West and saw hunting as a laudatory, masculine way of enjoying nature. Elliott Coues also participated in this movement and made his name as an ornithologist in part by documenting the birds of the West when he was stationed there in the army, killing them by the hundreds to ship back to Washington, DC, for study. While men were outside conquering the outdoor environment, women were charged with maintaining a sanitary home environment and engaging in domestic activities; the extent to which they enjoyed nature outdoors was in tending to gardens around their homes. This theme was the feature of one of Wright's planned books in her Heart of Nature series, of which *Citizen Bird* was to have been the first book. After introducing children to birds, mammals, plants, insects, geology, and astronomy, Wright had planned a final book in the series called "The House People," on "The making of home sanitation, out doors and in."[60]

Perhaps the most gendered element of this newly forming environmental conservation movement related to who was to blame for environmental problems. While men killed scores of birds for ornithology, bird study, and collecting more generally, women were the ones largely blamed for the plight of wild birds owing to the fashion trend of wearing bird plumes, or even whole dead birds, on hats. Both men and women used feathers in hats at the time—fedoras trimmed with feathers were particularly fashionable for men in the late nineteenth century—but women took the brunt of the blame for killing birds for fashion purposes.[61]

Ornithologists, outdoorsmen, and burgeoning conservationists all came together to support the campaign against women using birds in hats. *Forest and Stream* editor George Bird Grinnell had been working with the American Ornithologists' Union on their bird protection committee, and in 1886 he founded the Audubon Society with the goal of strengthening the work of the AOU committee. Grinnell publicized the new Audubon Society and tried to get non-ornithologists involved through his publication, calling for people to start Audubon chapters and targeting women's fashion as the central cause of bird destruction. Ornithologist Frank Chapman visited several Audubon Society events and gave a speech titled "Woman as Bird Enemy" on the topic of feathers in hats.

Though initially quite popular, the Audubon Society founded by Grinnell was short-lived. It had too much overlap with the AOU, was short-staffed, and could not keep up with the work demand, especially from its *Audubon Magazine*, which ceased publication in December 1888. The society was shut down shortly thereafter. However, the focus on blaming women's fashion for bird destruction continued, and this time, the charge was led by women. In the 1890s, women began reviving the Audubon Society, state by state and city by city. Women were behind the founding of these state and local chapters—Mabel Osgood Wright herself founded the Connecticut Audubon Society in 1898—and women made up

80 percent of the membership. These new iterations of the Audubon Society again centered their campaigns on using feathers in women's hats, so much so that the Great Egret, whose long plumes were popular and prized features in hat decorations, became the symbol for the Audubon Society and remains so to this day.

Ever of its time, *Citizen Bird* engages in this anti-feather campaigning throughout the text, but especially in two stories (in chapters 15 and 28, respectively), of the Scarlet Tanager and of the Snowy Egret (which is called the "Bonnet Martyr" in the book). In their description of the Snowy Egret, the authors associate using feathers in hats with "savagery": "In an evil moment some woman, imitating the savages, used a bunch of these feathers to make a tuft upon her headgear. From that day the spotless bird was doomed to martyrdom. Egrets, as the plumes are called like the birds themselves, became a fashionable trimming for bonnets and have continued so to this day, in spite of law and argument; for many women seem to be savages still, notwithstanding their fine clothes and other signs of civilization."[62] This accusation of "savagery" invokes both race and class: upper-class white women who wear these feathered hats are now associated with lower-class and "uncivilized" Indigenous people of color. In a time when the leisure class was being asked to engage in charitable works as part of the civilizing process, these upper-class white women were accused of the opposite behavior. *Citizen Bird* thus contains lessons for adults as well as for children. After hearing the story of the "Bonnet Martyr," the youngest girl child character, Dodo, proclaims, "I never, never will wear any kind of bird's feathers again, and when I go back to school I am going to make a guild for people who will promise not to either."[63]

Written and published in the context of this newfound interest in wildlife and environmental conservation, as well as the rise of ornithology and birdwatching, *Citizen Bird* brings all of these lessons together into what was likely the first field guide for children. *Citizen Bird* adapts the typical field guide entry that describes a bird and helps the observer identify it, to make it more child friendly. Its narrative frame provided the key element to engage child-readers' imaginations.

CITIZEN BIRD IN THE CONTEXT OF LATE NINETEENTH-CENTURY CHILDREN'S LITERATURE

While *Citizen Bird* was from its conception a collaborative effort, the roles of its two major authors were also clearly demarcated from the very beginning. In the

August 1896 letter to Wright, in which he agreed to participate in the project, Coues made clear that he deferred to his future coauthor in all of the imaginative aspects of this work of children's literature. "You write the stories, block out what technical matter you desire, and I will fill in," Coues suggested, then admitted, "I think probably that your ideas of what we want are more fetching than my own."[64] Coues's faith in Wright's abilities as a children's author rested on firm, if recent, evidence. Besides her two previous publications geared toward adult audiences—*The Friendship of Nature* (1894) and *Birdcraft* (1895)—Wright had just completed her first work of children's literature for Macmillan: *Tommy-Anne and the Three-Hearts* (1896). A work of fiction, *Tommy-Anne* was organized around the fantastical conceit of a pair of magic spectacles, which allowed its titular heroine to see and directly communicate with the myriad inhabitants of the natural world—from blades of grass to its wild creatures—thus learning from the source all the mysteries of the "heart of Nature." In spite of this whimsical framework, Wright took pains to make sure that all the lessons concerning plant and animal life learned by its child protagonist were within the realm of established fact, thus distinguishing *Tommy-Anne* from the work of so-called nature fakers, whose stories about the miraculous behavior of animals often strained credulity, especially of informed audiences.[65]

Samuel Osgood's "Books for Children" and *Citizen Bird*

If the example of *Tommy-Anne* was more than sufficient to justify Coues's confidence in Wright's talents as a storyteller, he still could not have known certain aspects of her upbringing that had helped to shape her—almost from the cradle—into an author particularly well-suited to the bustling market of Anglo-American children's books that flourished in the last decades of the nineteenth century. Mabel Osgood Wright was born in 1859, more than a decade after the second of her two older sisters, and her early childhood coincided with the Civil War and the first years of the Reconstruction period. It also coincided with the beginnings of what scholars still, if with reservation, refer to as the "Golden Age" of children's literature, a period roughly spanning the mid-nineteenth century through the early twentieth century, in which children's literature as a genre both solidified and diversified, becoming an increasingly dominant force in the publishing world and contributing to increasingly lively debates regarding the nature and function of childhood and the importance of early education.

Wright's Unitarian minister father, Samuel Osgood, held strong opinions on both topics, contributing to popular periodicals on subjects relating to the war effort and the rebuilding and reunification of the United States in its aftermath as well as on the nation's "home life," including its domestic values and the proper rearing of children.

Both of those interests converged in his article published in an 1865 issue of the American periodical *Atlantic Monthly*, titled "Books for Our Children." Osgood's viewpoint in this piece aligned him with those progressive educators active in the post–Civil War period who helped to shift children's literature away from the largely religious and didactic model dominant in the late eighteenth and early nineteenth centuries, as exemplified by the English author Maria Edgeworth and the prolific U.S. author Jacob Abbott, creator of the immensely popular *Rollo Series*. The error of these earlier authors, Samuel Osgood asserted, is that they sought to "cross the first instincts of children" by trying to "mak[e] of them little moralists, metaphysicians, and philosophers, when great Nature determines that their first education shall be in the sense and muscles, the affections and fancy, rather than in critical judgment, logical understanding, and analytic reason."[66]

In this belief, Samuel Osgood exemplified the new perception of the child— as an innocent, whose natural instincts should be developed through free play and gentle instruction—that had emerged out of Romanticism, supplanting the earlier understanding of children as sinful human creatures in need of the restraining influence of moral education to ensure their spiritual salvation. Often produced by religious tract societies, much of the children's literature of the early nineteenth century sought to "civilize" the child reader by inculcating dominant mores and beliefs, often through stories that threatened outsized punishments for minor infractions against parental and societal injunctions By contrast, the emerging school of juvenile literature that Osgood champions in his article prioritized the "cultivation" of the sensory and emotional faculties through the engagement of the child's inherent curiosity in natural phenomena and their attachment to the simple goings-on of everyday domestic life. Though still often religiously inflected, the work of these new "masters of the nursery" represented the natural world as the manifestation of a benevolent God and children's natural impulses as the God-given means by which they can be taught to understand and appreciate "the whole world of truth and goodness and beauty."[67]

While Osgood's arguments were predicated on an understanding of childhood as a developmental stage through which all children must pass, he also shared with other American educational theorists of the period a belief that children's literature had to speak to the unique cultural conditions facing the nation's children at the beginning of the Reconstruction period. The Civil War had damaged the concept of a cohesive American identity; thus, American children were badly in need of books "true to all our just American ideas," most fundamentally the belief that "*here* the opportunities for education, labor, enterprise, freedom, influence, and prosperity are to be thrown open to all."[68] At the same time, Osgood cautioned, these same books must also "rebuke the ready American failings," such as "the haste to be rich, the passion for ostentation," as well as "the failing to which our children are tempted—the morbid excitement, precocious sensibility, and airs and ambitions to which they are prone."[69] To forestall the development of these weaknesses of character—all of which were bound to be exacerbated in the period of rapid industrialization the United States was entering into— Osgood prescribed a national natural education; children must be trained to be "observers of Nature," to see the country's "flowers, plants, trees, minerals, animals, lakes, rivers, seas, [and] mountains" as their shared "property" as U.S. citizens.[70] And "good books and magazines," he argued, would play a critical role in helping to foster in children this sense of civic stewardship toward the nation's natural resources.[71]

Importantly, Osgood's article was not an endorsement of extant works of American children's literature so much as it was a prescription for texts yet to be written. In 1865, Osgood shared with many of his contemporaries the belief that the country had yet to craft for itself a national literature on par with the literary traditions of Europe: "As fruitful as America has been and is in children's books," he argues, none as yet belong "to the first rank of juvenile classics."[72] To produce American masterworks of children's literature, Osgood intimates, requires first that children of the present be educated according to the paradigm set forth in his article, the same model he practiced with his beloved youngest daughter, "May," his nickname for Mabel. Blessing the "Good Providence" that allowed him to purchase his country house, Mosswood, around the same time as Mabel's birth, Osgood holds up his daughter as the model child for the natural education for which he is advocating, an education that he argues is also a *re-education* for the adults in her immediate vicinity: "She noticed first only bright colors and moving objects and striking sounds; but with what zest she noticed them, and jogged our dull eyes and ears. Then she observed the finer traits of the place, and learned to call each flower and tree, and even each weed, by name, and to join the birds and chickens in their glee. She gathered bright weeds as freely as garden flowers, and, with a larger wisdom than she knew, came shouting and laughing with a lapful of treasures."[73] The developmental narrative that Osgood charted here for his daughter reinforces the Romantic ideal of childhood as a period of innocent, healthful attachment to the natural world, which, if fostered, facilitates emotional, then intellectual, then moral and spiritual maturation. Moreover, in this period of awakening, the child offers to adult observers the chance to relearn by proxy all those natural lessons they have forgotten owing to the corrupting influence of civilization: joy in one's perceptual faculties, interest in one's natural environment, and love of the humble "treasures" that nature provides. This "larger wisdom" that Osgood attributes to childhood is what he argues educators and authors of children's literature must seek to inspire, and in the example of his daughter, he implies, "a little child shall lead them." Osgood ends his article with an optimistic prediction: "Give us a thirty years' fair training of our children in schools and reading, galleries and music-halls, gardens and fields, and our America, the youngest among great nations, will yield to none the palm of strength or beauty."[74]

Wright's Childhood Library and *Citizen Bird*

Two years past Samuel Osgood's thirty-year deadline, his "darling May" published *Citizen Bird*, a work of children's literature that, had he lived to see it, one imagines would have met with his approval. Sharing her father's core belief that the "bright child" is always superior to the adult as an "observer, interpreter, and lover of Nature," Wright crafted the framing fiction surrounding this birding guide for children so as to loosely parallel the conditions of her own childhood at Mosswood. Indeed, the "Orchard Farm" of *Citizen Bird* is a clear stand-in for her family's country home, and the story's orienting conceit—that two children hailing from New York City are sent to spend the summer in "rural" Connecticut—is patterned on the seasonal migrations of her family between their two homes, a common practice among those in the city with the financial means to escape the summer's heat, noise, and pollution, not to mention periodic outbreaks of cholera, smallpox, and other viruses especially lethal to young children.

Yet, as much as *Citizen Bird* realized Samuel Osgood's vision for a story that speaks to the specific nature and needs of the post–Civil War child reader, it also displays Wright's canny understanding of how the market in children's books had evolved in the three decades since her father's article. At least part of this understanding can be attributed to her own precociousness as a reader. In her memoir *My New York* (1926), Wright devoted almost a full chapter to her childhood bookshelf, tracing her own process of *Bildung* through the books she read at specific developmental stages.[75] In doing so, she provides a valuable record of the variety of texts available to children in the United States in the second half of the nineteenth century. Among the works that Wright mentioned receiving as a very young child (all of which were written prior to 1865), two—Maria Edgeworth's *Harry & Lucy* stories (1815–1825) and Jacob Abbott's *Rollo Series* (1835–1842)—are exemplary of the didactic tradition, with impeccably behaved child protagonists who modeled for their early readers deference to adult authority and tractability to all forms of instruction. Other children's stories, though, like *Leila; or, The Island* (1839) by Scottish author Ann Fraser Tytler and *Esperanza: or, The Home of the Wanderers* (1855) by British author Anne Bowman, offered more thrilling fare for young readers by placing their child heroines and heroes in perilous exotic locales, reinforcing the values and norms of Western (Christian) society through confrontations with "Nature" (and natives) "red in tooth and claw." And, in the form of *Memoirs of a London Doll* (1846) by Richard Henry Home, Wright possessed an early work of fantasy literature for children, a subgenre often frowned on by those who viewed overly imaginative literature as encouraging idleness and daydreaming at the expense of industry and lesson-learning.

As Wright grew older, her bookshelf also grew to include a number of works intended for more advanced juvenile readers, which, in their more explicit targeting of differentiated readerships, illustrate the diversification of children's literature as a genre in the latter half of the nineteenth century. This development can be linked to several factors, including a larger total audience of young readers owing to population growth and rising literacy rates; the growing demand for children's books by public school educators and as a supplement to subjects not covered by public education; and innovations in the publishing industry that allowed for texts—especially those with illustrations—to be printed quickly and at a price point within the reach of more consumers. At the same time, these books also were responding to the increasing stratification of nineteenth-century society. The rigid gender norms that structured the period's ideal of family life and dictated that the place of women, or, at least, of middle- and upper-class women, was in the home drove the development of subgenres aimed specifically at "girl" and "boy" readerships, with "domestic fictions" like Louisa May Alcott's

Little Women (1868), a particularly cherished favorite of Wright's, marketed to the former and adventure stories such as Robert Louis Stevenson's *Treasure Island* (1883) to the latter. These same texts also inscribed other societal divisions in their stories, reinforcing extant class- and race-based hierarchies through their tendency to represent the experiences and perspectives of white, upper-middle-class children as normative.

Wright's childhood bookshelf predictably included several juvenile novels for female readers, including *The English Orphans: A Home in the New World* (1855) by Mary Jane Holmes and *Lilian's Golden Hours* (1857) by Eliza Meteyard. Both adapted the sentimental tropes of adult domestic fiction to preadolescent female audiences, crafting heartrending stories of girls, often orphaned or otherwise socially displaced, whose inherent virtues eventually win them a new home and family. Proving, however, that readers often refuse the efforts of publishers (and society at large) to corral them into specific consumer groups based on gender, class, or ethnicity, Wright also counted among her favorite children's books a number aimed at juvenile male readers, including adventure stories, such as *In the Wilds of Africa: A Tale for Boys* (1871) by W.H.G. Kingston, and boys' memoirs, such as *Tommy Try and What He Did in Science* (1869) by C.O.G. Napier. Rounding out this eclectic mélange of various subgenres of children's literature, Wright also listed two works that adapted Western "classics" for children, which served to familiarize them with literature too advanced for them as readers: *Tales from Shakespeare* (1807) by Charles and Mary Lamb and *The Girlhood of Shakespeare's Heroines* (1850) by Mary Cowden Clarke.

Citizen Bird as Didactic Children's Literature

Itself a microcosm of the bustling market in nineteenth-century children's literature, Wright's childhood library helps to account for her own success as a children's author and to explain the alluring genre-bending nature of *Citizen Bird*. Wright's letters to her publisher at Macmillan evidence her awareness of the different demographics to which *Citizen Bird* could appeal by framing a birding guide for juvenile audiences with an engaging story, which borrowed from a multiplicity of subgenres, including animal fables, didactic literature, domestic fiction, and adventure stories. The most fantastical parts of *Citizen Bird* are its opening and closing chapters, which presume to tell of the doings at Orchard Farm from the perspective of the wild birds on the estate. As with Rudyard

1 INTRODUCTION

Kipling's wildly popular *The Jungle Book* (1894), the anthropomorphizing of the book's animal subjects serves a dual function, allowing for the "translation" of the otherwise incomprehensible sociality of the animal world into human language but also offering a productively estranging perspective on the human world by looking down on it through a literal bird's-eye view. The latter function allows for Wright to introduce certain key ideas that will be central to the larger pedagogical project of *Citizen Bird*—namely, that modern industrial society has blunted the natural faculties (sensory, aesthetic, and moral) of most human beings, creating what British aesthete Walter Pater called in 1873 a certain "roughness of the eye that makes any two persons, things, situations, seem alike."[76] The bird-observers in chapter 1 are mostly different species of swallows, of which the narrator observes, "had [you] glanced at these birds carelessly, you might have thought they were all of one kind," the implication being that most human beings, who have yet to be enlightened as to variety to be found among "the citizens of the air," make just such a mistake.[77]

By contrast, the birds show themselves to be advanced students of human society, capable of drawing nuanced distinctions between the "house people" who have arrived to spend the spring and summer months on Orchard Farm. Gossiping together on a telegraph wire, they express satisfaction in the actions of the adult characters, particularly those of the master of the house, Dr. Roy Hunter, an amateur ornithologist. The Chimney Swift relays a conversation wherein the doctor dictates that one chimney remains unused "until after [the birds] have nested," and all the birds note with approbation that the family chooses to keep dogs rather than cats, outdoor cats being a perpetual threat to wild bird populations. Yet, importantly, the birds' first impressions of the child protagonists are not nearly so sanguine. While they are relatively unbothered by the "big girl" (the doctor's teenage daughter Olive) and "the little girl" (his young niece Theodora, called Dodo), they note with horror the addition of "a BOY!" (Dodo's older brother Nathaniel, called Nat). Their anxiety is not without cause, because, as the Phoebe reports, "the BOY has a pocket full of pebbles and a *shooter*," which he clearly intends to use on the birds themselves. As seen from the birds' point of view, Nat's intentions are hardly to be dismissed as harmless hijinks; rather, they are indicative of a kind of savage ignorance that can be traced to his urban upbringing, which has alienated him from the natural world to the point that he cannot see anything of value about the birds beyond the pleasure to be gained from hunting them. Wright drives this point home when

INTRODUCTION li

Nat's plans are thwarted by Olive, and in frustration he exclaims, "Do let me shoot some, Cousin Olive. I don't see why Uncle Roy likes them. What good are birds anyway?"[78] Nat's question is dismissed by Olive as the result of his life up until this point—"You say that because you have always lived in the city"—and her prescription for a cure to this very modern ailment is directed not just to him but to the child readers of *Citizen Bird*: "But *here* you will see all the beautiful wild birds" and after "this summer, when you have made friends with these wild birds, and they have let you see their homes and learn their secrets, you will make up your mind that there are no *common birds*, for every one of them has something very uncommon about it."[79]

Olive's promise to Nat and Dodo sets in motion what will become, in effect, a re-education program for children in the workings of the natural world, in which Nat and Dodo will soon be joined by a third child protagonist, Stephen Hawley (Rap), the child of a local washerwoman who they find birdwatching on the grounds of Orchard. Unlike Nat and Dodo, the disabled Rap, whose nickname has been rather cruelly given him for the sound of his "crutch hitting the stones," is country-bred and thus already more in tune with the natural surroundings.[80] When discovered by the other children, Rap is reading a discarded segment of an ornithology book he rescued from the bag of a traveling rag picker. Identified as about twelve years old, Rap comes to fill the role of surrogate brother to the other children, younger than the adolescent Olive but older than Nat and Dodo, whose ages based on their school readers identify them as ten and eight years old, respectively. Together, and with Dr. Hunter as their parental guide, the quartet come to form a natural family, bound by circumstance and affection, which could exist only in natural spaces like Orchard Farm, where social divisions based on class and gender are held at bay.

While far less exotic than the imaginary East Indian island of Johann David Wyss's popular *Swiss Family Robinson* (1812), *Citizen Bird*'s Orchard Farm operates similarly as a kind of natural classroom, providing the children with learning opportunities disguised as experiences. Every lesson is understandably focused on bird life, but the implications extend far beyond the realm of the ornithological, leading the child protagonists to mull over ethical complexities, aesthetic profundities, and civic responsibilities. The children are also challenged to reconsider the solipsistic human-centric worldview they have inherited, whether by thinking through the long-term effects of every child feeling entitled to take "just one" egg from a bird's nest (chapter 5) or of adults to deny their bird neighbors the right to a few berries from their fruit trees (chapter 13). In an elegant testimony to the effect of these lessons, chapter 16 finds the children begging Uncle Roy to help them purchase a pair of Cardinals who have been caged as pets by the wife of the local miller. That Nat, who at the novel's beginning valued only his family's pet Canary, is now repelled by the idea of keeping wild animals in cages serves as a yardstick by which to gauge his moral development. Moreover, it is intimated that the growing sympathy of Nat and Dodo with the animal world has a salutary effect on their dealings with the human world as well, most obviously in their relations with Rap. At *Citizen Bird*'s commencement, these two pampered city children hold certain class prejudices that cause them to treat Rap as a social inferior. Their snobbery dissipates as their continued contact with Rap reveals his superiority as a budding naturalist, whose observational faculties and kindness toward animals far outstrip their own. Moreover, it is clearly Rap who the doctor treats as an ornithologist-in-training, which provides *Citizen Bird* the opportunity to reinforce the very American Horatio Alger myth: that hard work and natural talent will always prove out in a democratic society, allowing even a washerwoman's son the opportunity to rise in society through his labor and good character.

Of all the lessons the children learn during their summer at Orchard Farm, it is arguably the lessons of chapter 5, which shares the title of the book, that convey the bulk of *Citizen Bird*'s ideology. Herein, Uncle Roy explains to the children his reasons for granting citizen status to wild birds (a status that is denied domestic birds like chickens and ducks and "immigrant" birds like the English Sparrow). Sending Olive into the house to consult "the big dictionary," most likely based on the *Webster's Academic Dictionary*, Uncle Roy organizes his civics lesson around a secondary definition of "citizen": "Citizen—a member of a nation, especially of a republic; one who owes allegiance to a government and is entitled to protection from it."[81] On this definition rests not just *Citizen Bird*'s argument for bird protection but also its larger justification for looking to birds for lessons on how to be a model American citizen. Wild birds, as Uncle Roy describes them, are "natural"—as opposed to "naturalized"—citizens. They are by "habits and character...citizen[s] of our Republic, keeping the laws and doing the work of the land."[82] Birds are also instinctually patriotic, engaging continually in a "Battle of the Bugs" that, if left unfought, would destroy the farmer's crops and thus the country's food supply.[83] Their nesting behavior, which Uncle Roy represents in deeply heteronormative as well as anthropocentric terms, is held up as an ideal

INTRODUCTION   liii

of American domestic life: "Parent birds love each other and their little ones," "they build their homes with as much care and skill as House People," and "they work hard, very hard indeed, to collect food to feed their children."[84] Finally, even their migration habits are rendered as proof of their status as loyal citizens; no matter how far they roam, they come home to nest and produce the next generation of American birds.

In the "bird stories" that follow the "Citizen Bird" chapter of *Citizen Bird*, the "bird-as-citizen" argument moves from foreground to background, but it remains the foundational concept that informs how each bird's value is weighed and measured. As discussed elsewhere, the different means by which various birds "hold the plant-destroyers in check" and aid in seed dispersal and plant pollination are used to group the birds into specific quasi-medieval "guilds." This organizational model also has an ideological underpinning, however; if bird society, like American society, is inherently democratic, it is nevertheless highly stratified. This stratification, it is argued, is both natural and necessary, so that different species do not compete with each other for spaces and resources. In this way, *Citizen Bird* is complicit in naturalizing divisions in human society, intimating that it is instinctual for a creature to keep to its own kind and to protect its territory from the encroachment of outsiders. What is more, the association of bird citizens with their labor facilitates the exclusion of certain species from citizenship status owing to their "shiftless" behavior, such as the Cowbird, which is deemed "lazy and shiftless" for its habit of laying its egg in other birds' nests. Nature, *Citizen Bird* implies, is not a welfare state, and unless a bird earns its keep by building its own nest, raising its young, and aiding in pest management and agricultural production, it is not just "disagreeable" but also "a bad neighbor, a worse parent, a homeless vagabond, and an outlaw in Birdland."[85]

Full of anecdotes, descriptive flourishes, and, as we see above, coded social commentary, the individual bird stories that make up the "field guide" part of *Citizen Bird* offered quite a bit of entertainment for child readers interested in learning about birds. However, by their very nature, field guides typically are not intended to be read as one would a story. Birders consult them for identification purposes, using the index to find information pertaining to specific birds about which they desire to know more. Wright created just such an "Index of English Names," and Coues supplied a supplementary list of scientific names in Latin for those children who aspire to "Wise Man" (ornithologist) status. As a work of children's literature, though, and, what is more, a work that Wright intended to be the first in a series of nature books for children, it was vital that even the field guide portion of *Citizen Bird* have enough of a story that children would want to read the book straight through. To generate this degree of interest, Wright would have to overcome a problem that also plagued writers of literary utopias, another subgenre that flourished at the end of the nineteenth century. Fictional utopias are conceptualizations of perfect worlds, threatened only by the actions of a humanity easily led astray by its own inherent tendency toward dissatisfaction with the status quo, even when that status quo supports an ideally balanced, regulated, and just society. For all of their virtues, utopias typically do not offer a great deal of dramatic incident and neither does *Citizen Bird*'s Orchard Farm, wherein bird life can proceed without fear or disruption of its natural cycle.

Wright's solution to this narrative conundrum was to create a simulation of narrative progress by the movement of her characters through physical space. Much like Wright's beloved childhood home, Mosswood, Orchard Farm was mapped out in *Citizen Bird* as a plot of natural land encompassing multiple ecosystems, possessing fields, forests, and even a riverside that the children could visit to observe different birds. The vagaries of weather also provide a sense of movement, as the children continually travel between the "outside" of the natural world and the "inside" of the Doctor's "Wonder Room," a museal space filled with stuffed birds that they would be unlikely to glimpse in nature, either owing to the time at which these species are active (like nocturnal birds of prey) or to their geographical location (like the Louisiana Tanager), or because they are already extinct or verging on extinction (like the Passenger Pigeon). *Citizen Bird* also generates something akin to narrative incident in the form of two "summer excursions" the children take to the Connecticut seashore, where they study shorebirds and meet two other human guides to "Birdland," Jim, the son of a local dairy farmer, and Olaf, a lighthouse keeper who lives in a cabin on the coast.

Ultimately, the engine driving *Citizen Bird*'s narrative is the process of *Bildung*, the emotional, intellectual, and moral development of the story's child protagonists as they move from a state of relative ignorance regarding their feathered neighbors to one of perpetual and passionate experience, in which the love of birds provides a never-ending source of interest and investment in the natural world. In short order, Nat transforms from a bored, would-be bird assassin to an environmental advocate; Dodo evolves from a childish crybaby into an emotionally mature little-woman-in-training; and Rap is set on the path of ornithological greatness. The future consequences of their individual journeys are clear—each, as adults, will have a role to play in the protection of bird life, whether as a captain of industry, society matron, or scientist, and together, they will work to repair the damage done by the previous generation, those "civilized" Americans who "never think of natural law at all, and having a coarse streak in their natures desire to kill wild things merely for the sake of killing."[86] Even before reaching adulthood, though, it is suggested that these children can all contribute to the cause of bird protection, mostly by acting as guides to the benighted adults in their own families and neighborhoods. Nat and Dodo are given just such an opportunity at *Citizen Bird*'s conclusion—when their parents arrive to retrieve them from Orchard Farm at the beginning of autumn, the children immediately petition for a longer stay, begging to attend the country school with Rap and to continue their lessons at the knee of their uncle. Ever the shrewd promoter of her own work, Wright uses this culminating moment—in which the birds overhear Uncle Roy suggesting a winter trip to a northern logging camp to see "the foxes and little fur beasts"—as an opportunity to advertise the subsequent book in the series, which would be published in 1898 as *Four-Footed Americans and Their Kin*, with Frank M. Chapman as an editor and Ernest Thompson Seton as the illustrator.[87]

In spite of Dodo's expressed wish for "another bookful about water and fish, and crabs and sky," "a butterfly book," and "Olive's flower book" and Rap's desire for a children's book with "something about the stars—and the rocks too,"[88] *Four-Footed Americans* was the only other book by Wright to feature the characters from *Citizen Bird*, spelling the end to the Heart of Nature series as she initially imagined it. Subsequent years witnessed the publication of further works of children's literature by Wright, including *Wabeno the Magician* (1899, a sequel to *Tommy-Anne and the Three Hearts*), *The Dream Fox Story Book* (1900), and *Dogtown* (1902), and one further nature guide, though aimed at an adult audience, titled *Flowers and Ferns in Their Haunts* (1901). Though all sold well enough to be reissued in the author's lifetime, none came close to reaching the broader cultural impact of *Citizen Bird*, which, beyond its own afterlife in the Audubon movement and Bird Day celebrations, also inspired a rising generation of children's authors to put their imaginative faculties in the service of environmental education and activism. On the surface a deceptively simple tale of two city children spending the summer learning about local bird life, *Citizen Bird* shares with all great works of children's literature a healthy respect for its intended audience, manifesting

lvi INTRODUCTION

in the beliefs that amusement and instruction are not mutually exclusive and that children deserve a literature of their own to help them to understand the world that they occupy and to aspire to a better one beyond it.

ENVIRONMENTAL AND SOCIAL CONTEXTS

The late nineteenth century encompasses the Gilded Age (1877–1896) and the beginning of the Progressive Era (1890s–1920s), and *Citizen Bird* engages many of the major societal, economic, environmental, and cultural happenings of these periods. This section demonstrates how *Citizen Bird* was of its time in how it discusses the environmental issues related to industrialization and urbanization, as well as how it uses a "nature as nation" framework to discuss nationalism, immigration, and race.

Industrialization and Urbanization

Connecticut provided a perfect setting for the fictional Orchard Farm. At the time of *Citizen Bird*'s publication, Connecticut was also seen as the "countryside," where well-to-do urbanites were encouraged to visit and get back in touch with nature. These urbanites' return to nature created the foundation of the nascent environmental movement of the time. Although it was the countryside, the locale also provided an opportunity to discuss several areas of concern to ornithologists and wildlife conservationists, such as telegraph lines and lighthouses, and the dangers they pose to birds.

In an early chapter of *Citizen Bird*, when the authors are still introducing young readers to different ways of understanding and categorizing birds, Wright and Coues discuss bird migration as a way of differentiating resident and migratory birds—or, as they put it in their civics framework, "citizens" or "visitors." They present industrialization and "the inventions of man" as harmful to birds, which sets up their argument for bird protection:

"Suppose, Uncle Roy, when they are travelling, a storm comes up and it grows so foggy they can't see how to follow the rivers—don't they sometimes lose themselves?"

"Yes, very often they become confused and fly this way and that, but always toward the nearest place where they see a light, as if it meant escape for them.

But this instinct is frequently their death, for they fly against the towers of great lighthouses, or the windows of tall buildings, or even electric wires, and thus break their necks or wings."

"That is why I have so often found dead birds along the turnpike under the telegraph wires," said Rap.

"Yes, Rap, the inventions of man are very wonderful, but some of them have been sad things for Bird People, and this is another reason why we should protect them whenever we can. These journeys that the birds make when they leave their nesting haunts for the winter season, and return again in spring, are called *migrations*. The word 'migrate' means to move from one country to another with the intention of remaining there for some time. The birds who only make little trips about the country, never staying long in one place, we call visitors."

The first sentence of *Citizen Bird* depicts a group of Swallows on a telegraph wire on the highway by Orchard Farm, the setting for the story. The use of telegraph wires as perches, and the dangers of telegraph wires to birds, is referenced on several other occasions throughout the text. In 1876, Coues had written a notice in the journal *American Naturalist* decrying the plight of birds being killed by running into telegraph wires: "Few persons, probably, even among ornithologists, realize what an enormous number of birds are killed by flying against these wires, which now form a murderous network over the greater part of the country."[89] He went on to describe the one hundred dead birds he counted in one hour while riding along the road by a telegraph wire. However, Coues concludes, in a very tongue-in-cheek manner, there seems to be little people can do about this problem, outside of abolishing telegraph wires: "Usually, a remedy has been or may be provided for any unnecessary or undesirable destruction of birds; but there seems to be none in this instance. Since we cannot conveniently abolish the telegraph, we must be content with fewer birds. The only moral I can discern is that larks must not fly against telegraph wires."[90] The above discussion between Rap and Uncle Roy also mentions lighthouses as another danger to migrating birds, which are referenced on a few other occasions in the text of *Citizen Bird*. In chapters 28 through 31, the children and Dr. Hunter go to the seashore and sail over to the fictional Great Gull Island, where they learn about shorebirds and water birds, and where they visit a lighthouse. Ornithologists also studied the phenomenon of birds flying into lighthouses, finding damning evidence of their danger to birds, though once again having no suggestions for a solution. In the *Bulletin of the Nuttall Ornithological Club*, J. A. Allen, the first president of the American Ornithologists' Union, listed the results of a survey of lighthouse keepers on the number of birds killed at twenty-four different lighthouses across the country. His conclusion offers no solutions: "The foregoing shows that the destruction of birds by light-houses on the coast of the United States must amount to many thousands annually. Adding to these the number killed by flying against vessels, of which the case of the 'Glaucus' already cited affords an example, and the vast number undoubtedly destroyed by being blown out to sea and drowned, the elements, aided by man, appear to exercise a powerful check upon the increase of bird life." If ornithologists did not have solutions to the destruction of bird life, environmentalists did. Before getting into the environmental and wildlife protection movements of this time period and the new laws protecting birds, it is important to denote the differences between the terms conservation and preservation, as they held different meanings at the late nineteenth and early twentieth centuries. During this time, "conservation implied a utilitarian view of natural resources: that is, they should be developed and used for the current generation. Preservation implied saving resources for their own sake or their intrinsic value. The needs of future generations played a major role in the decision to preserve resources."[91] One can see the tension between the two approaches in the early successes of the environmental movement:

- 1891: Congress passes the Forest Reserve Act (which repealed the Timber Culture Act of 1873), which empowered the president to withdraw land from the public domain and create "forest reserves," now known as national forests. This was the foundation for the National Forest System.
- 1897: Massachusetts state legislature passes a law prohibiting wild bird feather trading.
- 1900: Congress passes the Lacey Act, the first federal law protecting wildlife. This law prohibited market hunters from selling poached game (wild animals or birds) across state lines.
- 1901: Audubon Model Law is passed, which protected water birds from plume hunting.
- 1903: First National Wildlife Refuge is established in the United States in Pelican Island, Florida (led by state-level Audubon chapters). This was the beginning of the National Wildlife Refuge System.

INTRODUCTION   lix

- 1910: New York State legislature passes the Audubon Plumage Law, which prohibits the sale or possession of feathers from protected bird species.
- 1918: Migratory Bird Treaty Act is passed, which protects all migratory birds at the federal level.

Mabel Osgood Wright celebrated these conservation successes in the preface and appendix of the 1923 edition of *Citizen Bird* (which can be found in appendix 1 of this volume). In the appendix, she outlines the Migratory Bird Treaty Act and other international laws protecting birds. The preface thanks Dr. Hunter and the Wise Men for their work: "He and the Wise Men thought and worked year in and year out until we [birds] have come truly to be Citizens and protected, so far as law may do it." Wright goes on to encourage the child readers "to see that these laws are kept in spirit and in letter," as more and more children were spending time in nature than when the book was first written.

Immigration, Race, and Nation-Building

Citizen Bird lies squarely at the center of then-current events in birding, conservation, and ornithology. Its anthropomorphism of birds and its discussion of bird behavior, however, also place it squarely at the center of Progressive-Era discussions of nation-building, especially as they related to immigration, race, and ethnicity.

"Citizen" Bird. Just as the book teaches children how to be good environmental citizens, it also describes birds in terms of their environmental benefits. *Citizen Bird* anthropomorphizes birds and describes their behaviors in terms of birds acting as good—or as bad—citizens.

Birds are good citizens because they provide ecological and economic benefits—for people. Therefore, birds "pay their taxes" and "do their civic duty," and as such, people should learn about, appreciate, and protect them. One primary way birds provide these ecological and economic benefits is by eating insects that cause damage to farms and gardens. This example comes from the first bird depicted in the book, the Bluebird:

> As a Citizen the Bluebird is in every way a model. He works with the Ground Gleaners in searching the grass and low bushes for grasshoppers and crickets; he searches the trees for caterpillars in company with the Tree Trappers; and

in eating blueberries, cranberries, wild grapes, and other fruits he works with the Seed Sowers also. So who would not welcome this bird, who pays his rent and taxes in so cheerful a manner, and thanks you with a song into the bargain? A very few straws are all that he asks for his housekeeping, and every time he promises a meal for his household, scores of creeping, crawling, hopping garden enemies are gobbled up.

This argument, of course, has implications for who does or does not belong under the category of citizen. *Citizen Bird*'s anthropomorphism of birds and its discussion of bird behavior also place the book squarely at the center of Progressive-Era discussions of nation-building, especially as they related to immigration. The book's discussion of nonnative birds that were introduced to the North American continent, such as English Sparrows, demonstrate how birds stand in for immigrants in broader cultural discussions. These phenomena produce a "nature as nation" narrative that is part of *Citizen Bird*'s civics lessons for young children.

Throughout the text of *Citizen Bird*, English Sparrows (also known as House Sparrows) are depicted as "bad citizens." Of the 108 birds depicted in the book, the English Sparrow did not count among them. Instead, the English Sparrow was presented throughout the text as a "bad citizen" to be counterposed with the "good citizens" that provide ecological and economic benefits for people, not to mention food (in the case of game birds). The English Sparrow provides no such benefits and therefore is not presented as a species of bird to be protected. At the beginning of the first chapter of the book, the boy cousin Nat laments to his older cousin Olive, who lives at Orchard Farm, that she took away his slingshot and would not let him kill the birds at the farm. When he questions her as to the value of birds at all, she responds, "You say that because you have always lived in the city and the only birds you have watched are the English Sparrows, who are really as disagreeable as birds can possibly be." Further in the book, in the discussion of the Northern Shrike, a predatory bird known as the "butcher bird," Dr. Hunter explains to the children that part of the Shrike's utility is in killing English Sparrows, who are "bad citizens": "In fact, the Shrike is especially useful in helping us to drive out the greedy, quarrelsome English Sparrow. This disreputable tramp not only does no work for his taxes—he hates honest work, like all vagrants—but destroys the buds of trees and plants, devours our grain crops, and drives away the industrious native birds who are good Citizens; so the Wise Men, who have tried the Sparrow's case, say that he is a very bad bird, who ought to suffer the extreme penalty of the law." The Protestant work ethic and narrative of citizens paying taxes also run throughout the book, as the "good birds" who are "good citizens" work hard and pay their taxes, and therefore provide economic and ecological benefits to people. People should care about birds, because birds are good citizens, is the argument—and the title of the book.

The Sparrow Wars. Citizen Bird was published shortly after the decades-long ornithological debate over English Sparrows known as the "Sparrow Wars," in which Elliott Coues played a central role. A European bird, the English Sparrow was introduced to the North American continent, purposefully, on a number of occasions, beginning in 1850. The first pairs brought by the Brooklyn Institute did not thrive, and thus the organization brought more in 1852 and 1853. In the 1860s, thousands were released in New York, Boston, Washington, DC, and Philadelphia. Two introductions in the early 1870s in San Francisco and Salt Lake City aided their proliferation in the western United States.

The original purpose of their introduction was to control insects that ate farmers' crops. Unfortunately for the farmers, English Sparrows mostly eat grains and seeds, and with up to four broods of up to eight eggs per nesting season, they reproduce quickly and abundantly. Within a couple of decades since their initial importing, the English Sparrow had expanded its range across the entire North American continent, and people began debating its right to exist. In the first edition of his *Key to North American Birds*, Coues did not wade into the debate, but shortly after it went to press, Coues became the most vocal critic of *Passer domesticus* in the Sparrow Wars. His primary opponent was Thomas M. Brewer, a Boston ornithologist who defended the English Sparrows because of their sometimes eating pest caterpillars, but primarily for sentimental reasons, as their ubiquity meant children everywhere could enjoy them, and the birds represented the "Old World." Coues's ornithological critiques centered on the birds' primarily eating crops and their competing with native North American birds for food and nesting locations.

However, the Sparrow Wars were about more than just the Sparrows. Historians point out that, without formal education or employment as an ornithologist, Coues could have been using the Sparrow Wars as an opportunity to situate himself as an ornithological expert, as he wrote in a letter to J. A. Allen that agitating against the Sparrows was a "shrewd action" that could help the Nuttall Ornithological Club become an "American Ornithologists Union."[92]

But more than internal bickering among ornithologists jockeying for position in this newly established field, the critiques of English Sparrows grew beyond ornithological journals and into agricultural and sportsmen's journals and magazines, as well as into scientific journals and daily newspapers.[93] The economic argument that Sparrows were ruining farmers' crops fell apart, as there was no evidence that the birds were destroying fields. Instead, the critique of English Sparrows centered on their "foreignness" as birds. In ornithological debates, the Sparrows were referred to as "immigrants" and "foreign vulgarians,"[94] and the anti-immigrant rhetoric used against human immigrants was used against these Sparrows, arguing that they were doing harm to the native birds of the country. With this anti-immigrant, nativist language, the English Sparrows were painted as immoral. Coues likely influenced the depiction of the English Sparrow in *Citizen Bird*, when the birds are called "disreputable tramp[s]" who "hate honest work, like all vagrants." The implications of this rhetoric for its human characters and readers is discussed in more detail below.

Race and Ethnicity in Citizen Bird. *Citizen Bird*'s anthropomorphizing of birds served many ends. By humanizing wild birds as a species, the authors sought to engender sympathy in their child readers, who would be much more likely to devote themselves to the cause of bird protection if they saw birds in the same way the children of Orchard Farm were learning to: as loving parents with homes and children of their own. Not only would this mindset halt destructive actions against birds by children, like shooting birds or stealing eggs, it would also make them aware of the effects of industrialization and urbanization on bird populations, thus encouraging them to intervene in the adult world's thoughtless eradication of birds and the destruction of their natural habitats. At the same time, as in the case of English Sparrows, Cowbirds, and Crows, attaching to specific bird species negative human characteristics allowed the authors to make exceptions to the general protectionist rule. Cowbirds are described as "lazy and shiftless" because they make no nest of their own; they are "tramp parents" who lay their eggs in other birds' nests, at the expense of the fledglings of those responsible parent birds who now have to feed the baby Cowbird to the detriment of their own children.[95] As for the larger Crows, they are singled out as the only wild bird Uncle Roy will not allow on the grounds of Orchard Farm, as they are "crafty" as well as "dismal and noisy neighbor[s]," "who make themselves hateful by destroying grain and the nests and young of song birds."[96] And English Sparrows, while deemed unremarkable in their native country, are made out to be the feathered scourges of the United States, foreign interlopers who destroy natural resources and repopulate themselves at an alarming rate, "quarreling with and driving out the good citizens," "taking their homes and making themselves nuisances."[97]

If the explanations for the outsider status of these three birds sound familiar, it is because they are similar to those used, both then and now, to justify the control and exclusion of minority human populations within a nation-state. And once that correlation is acknowledged, it cannot be overlooked how these "bad" citizens of American bird land were being humanized using descriptors that align them with humans of different races, ethnicities, and countries. We see this most profoundly in the insistence on the color of the Cowbird and the Crow—the former is described as "a glossy black, excepting the head and neck, which is a shiny dark brown like burnt coffee," and the latter also "glossy black, from the tip of its beak to the end of its toes."[98] To a late nineteenth-century audience in the United States, such descriptors would have had parallels to how variations in skin color were foregrounded in descriptions of Black Americans. In the case of the English Sparrow, it is its "foreignness" that is harped on, an essential, though not visible, foreignness that is represented as hostile to the culture, values, and resources of native bird citizens. This threat of the adulteration of "pure" American culture by foreign agents is also a familiar tactic used in anti-immigrant discourse, aimed to engender fear in those native-born that they will be outnumbered and replaced.

For as much as urbanization and industrialization were hot-button issues in early Progressive-Era America, of equal concern to many people were the twin "problems" of migration and immigration. The last decades of the nineteenth century, starting with the end of Reconstruction, which followed the withdrawal of federal troops from the southern states in 1877, witnessed the beginning of a massive demographic shift. This would become known as the Great Migration (1910–1970). Fleeing the repressive Jim Crow laws that largely stripped them of the rights granted them in the aftermath of Civil War, Black citizens moved in large numbers to the North and West, with the Black population doubling in these regions between 1870 and 1890, with at least 50 percent of this growth attributable to migration.[99] The same period also oversaw a great boom in the immigration of foreigners to the United States. Between 1877 and 1900, there was a net increase of 8 million immigrants to the country, the majority still coming from northern and western Europe but with increasing numbers coming from southern and eastern Europe.[100] While both Black Americans and immigrants to the country played vital roles in development of the United States—particularly in the settling of the western frontier and the urbanization of the northern and midwestern states—they were often viewed with suspicion by the predominantly white and Protestant communities in which they settled, and both openly hostile and more subtle reactions against their presence flourished in the national discourse.

While *Citizen Bird*, thankfully, does not direct toward any of the human characters the vitriol it seems to reserve for English Sparrows, its representation of racial and ethnic "others" does require some careful handling, especially as these characters are confined to the margins of the narrative. As discussed elsewhere, the fictional family at Orchard Farm, like the authors, belong to established upper-middle-class U.S. society. One might even go so far as to say that Dr. Roy and Olive are intended as stand-ins for Coues and Wright, respectively, and that Nat and Dodo are the prototypical American children of the same class whose parents can buy them a copy of *Citizen Bird*. And while Rap, owing to his parentage and his disability, is outside of this charmed circle, he can be easily assimilated into it, most obviously because of his natural aptitude for ornithological study but, also, one might argue, because his Christian name, Stephen Hawley, identifies him as of Yankee blood, albeit of a lower class. Yet, two other characters are named in *Citizen Bird*'s list of characters, which precedes the story, who contribute materially to the children's summer adventures in bird land but who remain segregated from the intimate story-world that is built over the course of the narrative. These two characters are (in the language of the character list) "Mammy Bun, an old colored nurse" and "Olaf, a fisherman."[101] In Mammy Bun and Olaf we have *Citizen Bird*'s only efforts to represent racial and ethnic diversity in the United States, and the treatment of both characters is enlightening insofar as it reveals some of the limitations in the "progressive" values of Progressive-Era America. In comparison to the other characters, Mammy Bun and Olaf hew much more closely to recognizable stereotypes, and, what is more, they shed light on what we might call an inverse tactic to the anthropomorphizing of bird life that is central to the book's birds-as-citizen argument. If the birds of *Citizen Bird* are made candidates for citizenship through attributing to them human behaviors, those characters marked as racially and ethnically other are "naturalized" in ways that suggest they are less human—and thus less worthy of citizen status—than the main characters.

First, in the case of Olaf, who is later further identified as "Olaf Neilsen, a Finlander," his naturalization is more understated, which we can attribute to the fact that he is, for all of his ethnic alterity, white.[102] However, Olaf is truly a marginal character in that he is a complete outsider to the world of Orchard Farm. The only times he is present in the story is on the two occasions the children are taken to study shorebirds on the Connecticut coastline, where he acts as a sort of "native guide" for the denizens of Orchard Farm as they travel through coastal habitats studying, among other birds, Ospreys, Egrets, Plovers, Sandpipers, and Ducks. A bachelor fisherman, Olaf is geographically and culturally associated with the shore; he "ke[eps] boats, fishe[s], and tend[s] two buoy lights at the river entrance for a living."[103] Though he is represented as deeply knowledgeable of the bird life surrounding him, Olaf is laconic and unimaginative, and his connections to the shoreline are rendered in ways not dissimilar to how Native Americans were frequently depicted in literature of the period: as instinctual almost to the point of being animalistic. He is likened repeatedly to the shorebirds, especially the Osprey, who is made his bird-double by virtue of being described as a "feathered fisherman."[104]

When Olaf does speak, his speech is not rendered in such a way that would lead the reader to assume an accent or a less-than-perfect grasp of Standard American English.[105] That said, when called on to describe the shorebirds about which he is the de facto expert, Olaf deferentially bows to the authority of Dr. Roy specifically, and ornithology in general, taking no ownership of the facts he is relaying. Regarding the Osprey, he says, "It's the Fisherman Bird.... Some call it the Fish Hawk and others the Osprey. They say it lives all over North America, but it goes far south in the winter, and when it comes back in the spring we know the fish are running again; for it lives on the fish it catches, and won't come until they are plenty."[106] In Olaf's version of a "bird story," he draws a clear line between the "they" of professional ornithologists and the "we" of amateur naturalists like him. The former possess the right to name the birds and know where they go when they leave the local environment. The latter, though, have something more akin to an intuitive understanding—in the case of the Osprey, based on a common livelihood, but more generally owing to the fact that both belong more to the natural world than the man-made one. At a later point in the story, Olaf attempts to take over for Dr. Roy in lecturing about other shorebirds, only to be reprimanded by Dodo, who exclaims, "Do stop a minute, please, Olaf, and don't tell quite so fast.... Uncle Roy never does. You have said the names of ever so many birds that we don't know, and when he does that he always stops and explains. Snipes and Spotted Sandpipers—please begin with those." But Olaf cannot, at least not like Dodo's uncle, because while "he knew all the game and water birds—in fact, they were intimate friends of his;... it was not so easy for him to describe them."[107]

While there is nothing about this scene that explicitly links Olaf's inability to "explain" the birds to the children's satisfaction to his immigrant status, it is worth noting that as the only immigrant in the story, Olaf's character becomes representative of an entire group of U.S. citizens, who are "naturalized" in more ways than one. Olaf is naturalized in the sense that he was born in Finland but now is a citizen of the United States, but he is also "naturalized" in the sense that he has a closer relationship to "nature" than the native-born Americans to whom he acts as a boat pilot and nature guide. The birds are his "intimate friends" in a way that they can never be to residents of Orchard Farm, and it is implied that this is because, hailing from a coastal Scandinavian country, he is from a culture not so developed as the one in which he now resides. Moreover, he is a nonnative speaker of English who, at the same time, is more poetically fluent in the language of birds than are the other characters. As he tells the children, when he encounters what he calls "another mite of a Sandpiper...the very littlest of all," he doesn't just recognize its call; he understands it: "I've often had them run along in front of me on the beach, piping as sad as if they were telling me how little and helpless they were, and begging me to ask folks not to shoot them."[108] Thus, Olaf translates for the children the birds' vocalizations, which he is only able to do because he, in essence, speaks their language, being closer to them in his lifestyle and his way of being in the coastal ecosystem to which he belongs.

Yet, there is another character whose orientation vis-à-vis the natural world is even more complexly tied to her alterity than Olaf's, and that is the character of the Hunter family housekeeper, Mammy Bun. Introduced at the beginning of the story in "Overture by the Birds," Mammy Bun is first described by the Catbird in terms that leave no doubt as to her differences from the other inhabitants of Orchard Farm: "She is a very big person, wide like a woodchuck, and has a dark face like the House People down in the warm country where I spend the winter."[109] Issuing from a nonhuman character, this delineation is able to call attention to something that would be so self-evident as to not warrant commentary by the human members of Hunter household: namely, that Mammy Bun is a person of color and, moreover, that her blackness marks her as racially and geographically other, associating her, in spite of her current location, with the South. For Progressive-Era readers of *Citizen Bird*, we might argue that this description only reinforced what is already clear from her name: namely, that Mammy Bun is not just a character, but a racial stereotype in U.S. culture, a version of what we now know as the mammy figure. Originating in the antebellum period as an idealized depiction of a loyal Black female domestic, a surrogate mother figure for the children of slaveowners, the mammy figure featured both in pro-slavery as well as abolitionist literature, one of the most famous instantiations being the character of Aunt Chloe in Harriet Beecher Stowe's antislavery novel *Uncle Tom's Cabin* (1852). In the Reconstruction period, though, the mammy figure became increasingly associated with the myth of the Old South, a revisionist historical narrative that depicted the institution of slavery in benevolent and paternalistic terms. Epitomized in Joel Chandler Harris's Uncle Remus stories, the first collection of which was published in book form in 1881 as *Uncle Remus: His Songs and Sayings*, this nostalgic reimagining of plantation life largely elided the brutal realities of slavery while at the same time promoting racist tropes about formerly enslaved Black Americans.

Mabel Osgood Wright was the daughter of a Unitarian minister, who she proudly recalled had married at least one Black couple in the family home, which allowed her as a child to witness the proceedings.[110] In her memoir *My New York*, she also recorded her family's reverence for Abraham Lincoln and her own childish sorrow upon his death at the thought that "the poor black children" might "be sold away from their mothers again."[111] Yet, as was also the case for so many of her contemporaries, Wright's staunch opposition to slavery as an institution did not prevent her trafficking in racial stereotypes in her writings, and *Citizen Bird* was very much of its time in its treatment of Mammy Bun and the way in which it situated her in relation to the natural world and the bird stories with which she is associated. Before touching on the bird story she narrates, it is first necessary to tease out how Mammy Bun's character—like other iterations before her—promoted the racist idea that Black people are less civilized and therefore closer to nature. A variation of the noble savage trope, the mammy figure was usually depicted as naturally maternal, like a mother hen, and Mammy Bun is no different in this regard. Throughout *Citizen Bird*, her abiding preoccupation is that the family at Orchard Farm is well-fed and well cared for. Moreover, her presence in the story almost always indicates the end of the day's bird lessons (lessons that she never joins) because she arrives with nourishment in the form of "hot flannel cakes," strawberry ice cream, and her signature "buns, as light and brown as good yeast and careful baking could make them."[112] The reader learns that Mammy Bun's name is, in fact, a nickname given her by "Miss Olive," who names her on account of those baked goods, and her real name never appears in the text. Mammy Bun is also the only resident of Orchard Farm who never leaves its borders; like a bird in a nest, she remains at Orchard Farm when the rest of the family travels to the seaside, the suggestion being that her primary bond is to the house and the land, in a way that feels uncomfortably similar to the life of a plantation slave.

In chapter II, it is revealed that Mammy Bun was formerly enslaved; what is more, her enslaver was Olive's maternal grandfather, who owned a plantation down in Louisiana. Mammy Bun conveys this bit of her history herself through her one bird story, which is about the Mockingbird. The logistic reason for Mammy Bun telling this tale is that she, like the Mockingbird, is identified as a "Citizen of the southern United States, often straying northward to New England."[113] However, the other reason for the authors' choice in this regard is that the bird story of the Mockingbird is a very different kind of bird story from the majority of the others. In point of fact, it is much closer in style and substance to one of Harris's southern "beast fables," which puts Mammy Bun in the role of (former) slave-raconteur. Mammy Bun has spoken only a few times prior to this scene in *Citizen Bird,* but a reader will have noted that her comments have been rendered in an "eye dialect," a caricature of African American Vernacular English (AAVE), full of contractions, nonstandard spellings, and colloquialisms. It must be stated that this use of eye dialect is not the result of the authors' study of the actual speech of Black Americans but rather a literary creation that is indebted to previous white authors like Stowe and Harris. If not intentionally racist, its effect is still the perpetuation of racial stereotypes that differentiate Black storytellers from their white counterparts as less educated and more comic, not unlike the performances of white minstrels of the period who created Black characters for the pleasure of their white audiences. To put it more bluntly, by virtue of how they represent Mammy Bun in this chapter, the authors of *Citizen Bird* must be acknowledged to be performing a form of literary blackface, and given that

INTRODUCTION lxix

the book was published at the beginning of Jim Crow in the South, there is no way around the fact that the representation of Mammy Bun participated in the oppression of Black Americans through the co-opting of their culture for comic effect.

Like the tales of Harris's Uncle Remus, Mammy Bun's Mockingbird story is also set in the past, during her time as a slave on the plantation, though the protagonist of the story is not Mammy Bun herself, but another slave by the name of Sambo, a name often used pejoratively in the Jim Crow era to indicate a person of African American descent. (The name would become even more common in the world of children's literature in 1899 when the Scottish author Helen Bannerman published her book *Little Black Sambo*.) In Mammy Bun's story, Sambo falls afoul of plantation rules and the rules of the natural world when he steals the eggs from the nests of Mockingbirds—which have been deemed a protected group by the "Massa Branscome" of the plantation, who "jes' loved ter hear 'em sing, an' den he 'lowed dat dey was powerful fond o' cottin worms, what was mighty bad some years."[114] These Mockingbirds, Mammy Bun elaborates earlier in the story, are represented as in league with the plantation owner, serving unofficially in the role of overseers; in March at the start of cotton season, the Mockingbird "comes inter de bushes and orange scrub round de field a-makin' a fuss and tellin' folks to git along to work, or dere won't be no cottin, and he keep it straight up all de day long till cottin's out of bloom."[115] That the Mockingbird is made to serve this function in this instance highlights a different relationship between humans and the natural world than what has been seen before, and it is not too much to assume that this dynamic depends on the race of the humans involved. The unavoidable implication is that these citizens of "Birdland" see themselves not just as citizens who benefit the nation's agricultural output by eating cotton worms and spreading seeds but also by keeping the slaves at their labor for the overall good of the plantation.

The darkly "comic" turn of this story hinges on the revelation that Mockingbirds do not take kindly to the robbing of their nests, and they seek justice in the form of complaining to the plantation's owner. Even though Sambo has stolen the eggs with the goal of selling them to "white trash dat ud tote 'em down the ribber an' sell 'em agin in N'Orleans, to be fotched off in ships" in order to buy himself a banjo, this action is seen as a theft of something belonging both to "Nature" and to Master Branscome, and therefore, it cannot go unpunished. In fear of that punishment, Sambo confesses to the master and his daughter

Miss Jessamine, telling them that "I sol' 'em down de ribber," to which Branscome replies, "I'se a great mind to sell you down de ribber, too."[116] At this moment in the story, Mammy Bun pauses to tell the children that, contrary to what he just said, Olive's grandfather "nebber sol' nuffin'—gib us all our freedom"—which is hardly plausible, but nevertheless serves to cover up how slavery is based in the economic trade in human beings and how many slaves historically were punished and sold for no offense whatsoever. The story ends thus "happily," with Sambo returning the eggs to the nest and asking "pardin" of "dat he-bird" (the she-bird apparently does not need to be consulted), and Mammy Bun ends her story with a song about the "Mockers" the enslaved people sang on the plantation, which is also full of lines that suggest the enslaved people are closer to nature than the white characters: "Did I tole you dat I know'd whar dere's a possum? / Did I tole you dat I know'd / whar dere's a coon? Oh, mah lady, come out soon! / Oh, mah honey, come out soon! / While de Mocker, while de Mocker / Am a-singin' to de moon!"[117] That Mammy Bun herself used the racist term "coon" earlier in her story to describe her fellow slaves (among other more offensive terms) codedly reinforces the association between persons of color and the lower orders of the animal kingdom, and with the song itself, her story concludes in a way familiar and palatable to a nineteenth-century white audience, which delighted in minstrel songs that plagiarized heavily from the actual songs and stories of Black southern culture.[118]

Though Mammy Bun does not herself narrate this second story, importantly, she is identified as the source of a fanciful story told later in the text about the Cardinal. This "legend" Uncle Roy describes as "one of Mammy Bun's strange stories that came from the Indians to the negroes, always growing larger and stranger."[119] Though Cardinals are sacred in numerous Native American mythologies, the legend that Uncle Roy here relays is entirely a fictionalization, which serves an ornithological end, explaining why the Cardinal is "classed with Sparrows" as opposed to the colorful birds of more tropical climates. In both cases, these bird stories use the culture of nonwhite Americans for entertainment value, utilizing common racial tropes that suggest these human citizens are, like the birds, less evolved, if more beautiful and natural, and in need to paternalistic protection owing to their inability to thrive in a modern industrial world. We must not ignore this uncomfortable association, as it influenced and continues to influence Western environmentalist movements, which often fail to treat minority communities as equal partners in their efforts, partners with invaluable knowledge of the land that comes from their experiences and their history. Moreover, these scenes in *Citizen Bird* require our close attention because they do point out some of the limitations of the book's theorization of the Heart of Nature, that quasi-deity to which all plants and animals belong and from which humans have become estranged through their obsession with progress. While *Citizen Bird*'s prescription that all humans may be healed through the kind of reacquaintance with the Heart of Nature that comes through watching and caring about birds, the natural world as the authors depict it is hardly ideal when it comes to creating a truly inclusive, democratic society in which all citizens may make a life for themselves as they see fit. Like Progressive-Era America, the Heart of Nature is depicted as inherently stratified and, what is more, this stratification is deemed necessary for the ecosystem to function and flourish. As Uncle Roy tells the children, "To prevent confusion Heart of Nature has divided the habits and appetites of Birdland, so that instead of a great many families all building in one kind of tree, or eating the same sort of insects or seeds, each has its own manners and customs. Thus they divide among themselves the realms of the air, the water, the trees, and the ground."[120] Nature, as it turns out, is also benevolently paternalistic, confining different bird citizens to different places and tasks based on "habits and appetites." That this declaration immediately precedes Mammy Bun bringing to the "Massa Doctor" and children a plate of refreshments, having "jess guessed" that they would be hungry, is a sadly eloquent testimony to the ways that even this very progressive Progressive-Era text could not yet imagine a way for its characters of different races and ethnicities to take a seat at the table in the common goal of environmental protection.

CONTEMPORARY CULTURAL AND PEDAGOGICAL CONTEXTS

A hybrid text from its inception, *Citizen Bird* was always intended for multiple audiences, and it reached them—children, schoolteachers, reviewers, environmental advocates—on both sides of the Atlantic. Our intention with this teaching edition, reissued more than 125 years after the first edition was published, is to facilitate an encounter with *Citizen Bird* for modern audiences, who we hope will find the book as interesting, useful, and timely as we have.

Yet, while we believe that *Citizen Bird* will find favor with the children of today as it did with the children of the late nineteenth century, children are not the primary audience for this reissue. Instead, our aim has been to create a teaching edition for a variety of adult audiences, including scholars and teachers as well as professional and amateur ornithologists and naturalists who are interested in this small, but important, piece of ornithological history. We do not expect that all of these readers will be equally interested in all aspects of the book, which is why we have created a number of appendices that put *Citizen Bird* in a number of different historical, environmental, literary, and artistic contexts.

In the discussion that follows, we would like to offer modern readers a few justifications for this scholarly edition, first, by explaining why we think *Citizen Bird* is worth revisiting at this moment in history, when the politics and practices of birdwatching are again being discussed in relation to contemporary social and environmental issues and, second, by offering a few different pedagogical approaches to teaching *Citizen Bird* in twenty-first-century educational spaces, from college classrooms to nature center programs aimed at budding child naturalists. For those readers who are simply interested in *Citizen Bird* as a children's story and birding guide, you may or may not find these supplementary materials, including the annotations and appendices, necessary to your enjoyment of the text, but they are at your disposal nonetheless.

Modern Ornithological and Cultural Contexts

Contemporary birders reading *Citizen Bird* can enjoy reading these early descriptors of birds, especially the former names of birds now commonly known by different names (as noted in the footnotes). Contemporary birders can also enjoy seeing the parallels between environmentally minded birdwatching as promoted in *Citizen Bird* and the efforts of current environmental and wildlife conservation organizations. The nineteenth-century child (and adult) readers of *Citizen Bird* learned to appreciate the common birds in their own backyards, as do contemporary birders through citizen science efforts such as the Great Backyard Bird Count. *Citizen Bird*'s authors sprinkle in calls for legislation to protect birds, and the preface to the 1923 edition highlights the passing of the Migratory Bird Treaty Act (see appendix 1). Environmental and wildlife conservation organizations still work to pass, enforce, and maintain such legislation.

As *Citizen Bird* was promoting birdwatching at the very beginning of its evolution as an environmental hobby, the authors infused conservation lessons for those interested in birds, such as not collecting eggs or birds' nests, not disturbing birds during sensitive periods like breeding or nesting, and not killing birds for fashion or fun, all of which still ring true today. Although "listing" did not yet exist—the habit of seeking birds out primarily to add to one's life list or list of species one has seen in one's lifetime—the entire thematic of the book promotes the opposite practice, that of appreciating individual birds, even the common ones, learning as much as one can about them, and reveling in the wonder of each new species through new eyes, much like the children at the center of the book. While much of this introduction has highlighted the ways in which *Citizen Bird* was of its time culturally and historically, in these ways, *Citizen Bird* was ahead of its time in its conservation message and lessons.

Citizen Bird was also ahead of its time when it came to children's environmental education. Teaching children about their backyard birds is now a common practice, as teaching children to learn about and appreciate the birds they see every day is seen as the foundation for learning more. As Uncle Roy says to the children: "In learning anything, whether of bird, insect, or flower, begin at home, and let this be the centre from which you work your way onward and outward. Then you will be sure of what you learn; and ever afterward, though you may follow strange birds all over the known world, you will come home again, to find that there are none more charming and lovable than those few whose acquaintance you will make this summer."[121] One difference, though, is that children now are simply taught how to identify House Sparrows and European Starlings, without the heavy-handed lessons about them being "bad citizens." At a later stage, children might learn about invasive species, but when they first learn about birds, they simply learn the birds as birds.

Where *Citizen Bird* was of its time, and lagged behind contemporary understandings, was in its now obviously retrograde treatment of Black Americans both as citizens and as naturalists, as discussed in more detail above. Many contemporary birders and naturalists recognize the need to make birding and the outdoors inclusive spaces, whereas *Citizen Bird*—and the growing naturalist organizations of its time—implicitly assumed and explicitly emphasized that outdoor hobbies were only for white people, as was scientific knowledge of the natural world.

The growing contemporary cultural awareness and celebration of Black birders encompasses both current and historical naturalists. Harriet Tubman is now also recognized as an expert naturalist, using her knowledge of geography, astronomy, and botany to make her way through the Underground Railroad. Her understanding of ornithology also played a role, as her secret call to announce her arrival in a new area was the call of a Barred Owl. Current efforts include Black Birders Week, a nationwide week of events highlighting Black naturalists and birders, as well as books and television series on birding by Black birders and ornithologists such as J. Drew Lanham and Christian Cooper. And, the National Audubon Society and its various state and local chapters are grappling with the legacy of John James Audubon, and the recent revelations that he actively owned, bought, and sold enslaved people, leading to many groups dropping his name from their organizations. The American Ornithological Society (the new iteration of the AOU) announced in 2023 it was changing all common English names of birds named after people, to avoid associating birds with people linked to slavery and racism. With increasing awareness of the structural and systemic issues affecting people's experiences of the natural world, the cultural landscape has greatly changed since the publication of *Citizen Bird*.

Modern Teaching Context

We previously noted how *Citizen Bird* was used in Progressive-Era efforts to provide the rudiments of an environmental education and to engender a love of birds in the nation's schoolchildren. The book's success depended on a robust network of adult bird protectionists who promoted the book and adapted its lessons, foremost among them members of the Audubon Society and the politicians and educators involved in Bird Day. But how might the descendants of those groups use *Citizen Bird* today? In the following pages, we respectfully offer this preliminary list of pedagogical strategies, many of which we have developed through our own teaching of *Citizen Bird*.

When we started this project, our first objective was to gauge the "teachability" of *Citizen Bird* to contemporary college students in our different areas of specialization: sociology and literary studies, respectively. One of us taught a section of the book in an environmental sociology course and the other introduced it into a historical survey of children's literature. We handed out an extensive survey to both classes, and the student responses guided how we approached the construction of this scholarly edition. Foremost among their responses, our students

INTRODUCTION lxxv

expressed a desire for easily accessible contextualizing historical information, which would help them make sense of why *Citizen Bird* was such a success when first published and how it was engaging in Progressive-Era social and environmental issues. They also felt strongly that its few "problematic" features—specifically, its depiction of nonwhite U.S. citizens and immigrants—should be foregrounded rather than elided, as those features created robust discussions of the politics of race and ethnicity and, more generally, of what constitutes a "good citizen," be it human or animal, in nineteenth-century America and today. The unanimous consensus of those we polled was that we print the text unexpurgated, which meant that we included the Mammy Bun chapter (chapter 11) in its entirety—we have done so, but with an important caveat: we include in appendix 1 a translation of Mammy Bun's speech in largely Standard American English with the hurtful racial epithets replaced, both for readers who do not want to read this chapter in its original "eye dialect" and for teachers who should not read such epithets out loud in contemporary classrooms and other educational contexts.

As for the different types of classes in which *Citizen Bird* might be a productive text to teach, we see it of most value to those teaching environmental science, environmental sociology, environmental and nineteenth-century history, nature writing, children's literature, and children's education. The various appendixes have been created with these different teachers and students in mind:

- For those who would like more contextualizing information about *Citizen Bird*, we have collected in appendix 1 supplementary material pertaining to the book's publication and reception. We are including advertisements and reviews of the 1897 edition as well as the new preface and appendix that Wright composed for the 1923 edition. This appendix also contains the editors' version of Mammy Bun's speech in chapter 11, which removes the deliberately nonstandard spelling and racial epithets. In order to link *Citizen Bird* to Mabel Osgood Wright's lifelong campaign to interest children in bird protection, we also include an article by Wright on the subject of bird education published in *Bird-Lore*, the official journal of the Audubon Society.
- For those teaching environmental sociology and ornithological history, we have included material on nineteenth-century birding and the rise of the Audubon movement and founding of Bird Day (appendix 2). There are excerpts from field guides intended for adult audiences, including a selection from Wright's

Birdcraft (1895), an op-ed by Elliott Coues on the Sparrow Wars (a topic also raised in *Citizen Bird*), and another article by Coues on the destructive effects of telegraph wires and lighthouses on bird populations. Also included are other printed materials that were intended to raise public awareness on the plight faced by birds owing to destructive human behavior, including sport hunting, egg collection, and the killing of songbirds for the decoration of women's hats.

- For those teaching eco-literature, nature writing, and/or children's literature, we have included, in appendix 3, an excerpt from Wright's book of nature writing, *The Friendship of Nature* (1894), and an excerpt from her first published children's book *Tommy-Anne and the Three Hearts* (1896). For comparison's sake, we have also included excerpts from two birding/ ornithology books for children published just before and after *Citizen Bird*: James Newton Baskett's *The Story of the Birds* and Florence Merriam Bailey's *Birds of Village and Field: A Bird Book for Beginners* (1899). To draw attention to the prevalence of racial stereotypes such as we see with the Mammy Bun character in children's literature of the period, we have also excerpted from Joel Chandler Harris's *Uncle Remus: His Songs and Sayings* (1881).

CONCLUSIONS

The nineteenth-century lessons imbued in *Citizen Bird* continue to resonate today. With its instructions on how to locate and identify birds, *Citizen Bird* still serves nicely as a field guide, and its message on environmental protection still shines. Mabel Osgood Wright explicitly wrote *Citizen Bird* to get people excited to learn about and protect the natural world. This naturalist movement is experiencing a renaissance right now. During the pandemic, birdwatching grew in popularity as a safe hobby people could engage in from the comfort and safety of their homes, or on walks outdoors. People also more generally turned to nature as an escape and a solace during this time, and as a result, people have sought to learn more about the natural world. As the pandemic itself was initially caused by people encroaching on the natural world, and specifically on wild animal habitats, this book serves as a very relevant reminder of the need to appreciate and protect nature. In a time when people are rediscovering and reconnecting with nature, this book that brought together new knowledge on ornithology, birdwatching, and natural history writing and illustration, created by three towering historical figures in these areas, should rightfully claim its place as a foundational text.

INTRODUCTION lxxvii

NOTES

1. Mabel Osgood Wright to George P. Brett, June 2, 1895, Macmillan Company records, Manuscripts and Archives Division, The New York Public Library, Astor, Lenox, and Tilden Foundations (hereafter Macmillan Company records).

2. Mabel Osgood Wright to George P. Brett, August 24, 1896, Macmillan Company records.

3. Elliott Coues to Louis Agassiz Fuertes, September 26, 1896, Louis Agassiz Fuertes Papers, #2662, Division of Rare and Manuscript Collections, Cornell University Library (hereafter Louis Agassiz Fuertes Papers).

4. Elliott Coues to Mabel Osgood Wright, August 1896, enclosed in a letter from Mabel Osgood Wright to George P. Brett, Macmillan Company records.

5. Mabel Osgood Wright to George P. Brett, January 19, 1897, Macmillan Company records.

6. Mabel Osgood Wright to George P. Brett, February 4, 1897, Macmillan Company records.

7. Mabel Osgood Wright to George P. Brett, May 10, 1897, Macmillan Company records.

8. Mabel Osgood Wright to George P. Brett, June 17, 1897, Macmillan Company records.

9. Elliott Coues to Louis Agassiz Fuertes, April 21, 1897, Louis Agassiz Fuertes Papers.

10. Mabel Osgood Wright to George P. Brett, January 19, 1897, Macmillan Company records.

11. Mabel Osgood Wright to George P. Brett, May 21, 1897, Macmillan Company records.

12. Mabel Osgood Wright to George P. Brett, August 8, 1897, Macmillan Company records.

13. Mabel Osgood Wright to George P. Brett, July 29, 1897, Macmillan Company records.

14. Elliott Coues to Louis Agassiz Fuertes, July 27, 1897, Louis Agassiz Fuertes Papers.

15. Mabel Osgood Wright to George P. Brett, August 8, 1897, Macmillan Company records.

16. "The Macmillan Co's New Books," *The Critic: A Weekly Review of Literature and the Arts* 28, no. 802 (July 3, 1897): ii. Published in New York by The Critic Company.

17. Mabel Osgood Wright to George P. Brett, April 14, 1897, Macmillan Company records.

18. *The Critic*, July 31, 1897, xii.

19. *The Critic*, August 14, 1897, xvi.

20. *The Critic*, August 14, 1897, xvi.

21. "Citizen Bird," *Book Reviews: A Monthly Journal Devoted to New and Current Publications* 5, no. 3 (September 1897): 59.

22. *Book Reviews*, 64.

23. *Book Reviews*, 61.

24. *Book Reviews*, 61.

25. *Book Reviews*, 59.

26. Frank M. Chapman, "Citizen Bird (Review)," *The Auk* 14 (October 1897): 414.

27. *Book Reviews*, 27.

28. *Book Reviews*, 62.

29. Clinton Hart Merriam, "Review of Citizen Bird," *The Auk* 6 (1897): 706–707.

30. *Book Reviews*, 60.

31. Mabel Osgood Wright to George P. Brett, October 14, 1897, Macmillan Company records.

32. "About Birds," *The Academy: A Weekly Review of Literature, Science, and Art* 52 (July–December 1897): 258.

33. W. Warde Fowler, "Citizen Bird (Review)," *Nature* 56, no. 1457 (1897): 516.

lxxviii   INTRODUCTION

34. *The Zoologist: A Monthly Journal of Nature History*, fourth series, vol. 1, edited by W. L. Distant (London: West, Newman, and Co., 1897), 483.

35. Chapman, "Citizen Bird (Review)," 414.

36. Mabel Osgood Wright to George P. Brett, May 21, 1897, Macmillan Company records.

37. *Book Reviews*, 61.

38. Note here that for "sustaining members" in Connecticut, a $1.00 fee was asked, and for "junior members" a "10 cent fee." That said, all fees could be waived for anyone who could not pay, except for sustaining members, as long as they "subscribed to the principles of the Society." "Second Report of the Audubon Society of the State of Connecticut," 1899 (Bridgeport, CT: Marigold Printing Company, 1900).

39. "Second Report of the Audubon Society of the State of Connecticut," 8.

40. "Report of the Board of Education of the State of Connecticut," 1901 (Hartford, CT: Hartford Press, 1900), 216.

41. Mabel Osgood Wright, "A Bird Class for Children," *Bird-Lore* 1, no. 3 (1899): 100–101.

42. A. C. Boyden, "Nature Study for Grammar Grades," *Journal of Education* 47, no. 14 (1898): 212–213.

43. L.L.W. Wilson, *United States History in Elementary Schools: Teachers' Manual* (New York: Macmillan, 1899).

44. Elliott Coues, *Field Ornithology Comprising a Manual of Instruction: Procuring, Preparing and Preserving Birds* (Salem, MA: Naturalists' Agency, 1874), 17, cited in Mark V. Barrow Jr., *A Passion for Birds: American Ornithology after Audubon* (Princeton, NJ: Princeton University Press, 1998). Emphases in the original.

45. Coues, *Field Ornithology*, 29, cited in Dorceta E. Taylor, *The Rise of the American Conservation Movement: Power, Privilege, and Environmental Protection* (Durham, NC: Duke University Press, 2016).

46. Wright's original name for Uncle Roy / Dr. Roy Hunter was "Dr. Frank Byrd," as indicated in the preface and outline of *Citizen Bird* that she sent to Mr. Brett at Macmillan in January 1897. This move changed the Uncle's association with birds to one that associated him with hunters.

47. Elliott Coues, *Key to North American Birds*, 4th ed. (Boston: Estes and Lauriat, 1890), 227. Emphasis in the original.

48. Coues, *Key to North American Birds*, 55.

49. Mabel Osgood Wright, *The Friendship of Nature: A New England Chronicle of Birds and Flowers* (New York: Macmillan, 1894), 87.

50. Elliott Coues to Mrs. Fuertes, March 29, 1897, Louis Agassiz Fuertes Papers.

51. Florence A. Merriam, *Birds through an Opera-Glass* (New York: Houghton Mifflin, Chautauqua Press, 1889), 3.

52. Merriam, *Birds through an Opera-Glass*, v.

53. Mabel Osgood Wright, *Birdcraft: A Field Book of Two Hundred Song, Game, and Water Birds* (London: Macmillan & Co., 1895), 37.

54. Wright, *Birdcraft*, 38.

55. Wright, *Birdcraft*, xv–xvii. Emphasis in the original.

56. Wright, *Birdcraft*, 167.

57. Wright, *Birdcraft*, 168.

INTRODUCTION lxxix

58. Mabel Osgood Wright and Elliott Coues, *Citizen Bird: Scenes from Bird-Life in Plain English for Beginners* (New York: Macmillan, 1897), 263–264.

59. Roger Tory Peterson, *Peterson Field Guide to Birds of Eastern and Central North America* (New York: Houghton Mifflin, 2010), 322.

60. Mabel Osgood Wright to George P. Brett, undated letter, Macmillan Company records.

61. Taylor, *The Rise of the American Conservation Movement*, 193.

62. Wright and Coues, *Citizen Bird*, 370.

63. Wright and Coues, *Citizen Bird*, 371.

64. Elliott Coues to Mabel Osgood Wright, August 24, 1896, Macmillan Company records.

65. "Wright took particular care to ensure her readers that she did not go beyond the bounds of verifiable facts … a particularly sensitive issue at the time, given her vocal criticism of such 'nature fakers' as William J. Long." Daniel J. Philippon, *Conserving Words: How American Nature Writers Shaped the Environmental Movement* (Athens: University of Georgia Press, 2004), 87.

66. Samuel Taylor Osgood, "Books for Our Children," *Atlantic Monthly* 16 (December 1865): 725.

67. Osgood, "Books for Our Children," 729.

68. Osgood, "Books for Our Children," 730. Emphasis added.

69. Osgood, "Books for Our Children," 730.

70. Osgood, "Books for Our Children," 730.

71. Osgood, "Books for Our Children," 731.

72. Osgood, "Books for Our Children," 724.

73. Osgood, "Books for Our Children," 731.

74. Osgood, "Books for Our Children," 732.

75. Mabel Osgood Wright, *My New York* (New York: Macmillan, 1926), 78–81.

76. Walter Pater, *Studies in the History of the Renaissance* (London: Macmillan, 1873), 211.

77. Wright and Coues, *Citizen Bird*, 1.

78. Wright and Coues, *Citizen Bird*, 6.

79. Wright and Coues, *Citizen Bird*, 6–7. Emphasis in the original.

80. Wright and Coues, *Citizen Bird*, 21.

81. Wright and Coues, *Citizen Bird*, 51–52. The definition in *Webster's Academic Dictionary* (1895) reads, "2. One, native or naturalized, owing allegiance to a government, and entitled to protection from it" (109).

82. Wright and Coues, *Citizen Bird*, 52.

83. Wright and Coues, *Citizen Bird*, 56.

84. Wright and Coues, *Citizen Bird*, 52.

85. Wright and Coues, *Citizen Bird*, 265.

86. Wright and Coues, *Citizen Bird*, 346–347.

87. Wright and Coues, *Citizen Bird*, 418.

88. Wright and Coues, *Citizen Bird*, 281.

89. Elliott Coues, "The Destruction of Birds by Telegraph Wire," *The American Naturalist* 10, no. 12 (1876): 734.

90. Coues, "The Destruction of Birds, by Telegraph Wire," 736.

91. Taylor, *The Rise of the American Conservation Movement*, 27.

92. Daniel Lewis, *The Feathery Tribe: Robert Ridgway and the Modern Study of Birds* (New Haven, CT: Yale University Press, 2012), 85.

93. Michael J. Brodhead, "Elliott Coues and the Sparrow War," *New England Quarterly* 44, no. 3 (1971): 424.

94. Gary Alan Fine and Lazaros Christoforides, "Dirty Birds, Filthy Immigrants, and the English Sparrow War: Metaphorical Linkage in Constructing Social Problems," *Symbolic Interaction* 14, no. 4 (1991): 381.

95. Wright and Coues, *Citizen Bird*, 264–265.

96. Wright and Coues, *Citizen Bird*, 277–278.

97. Wright and Coues, *Citizen Bird*, 204.

98. Wright and Coues, *Citizen Bird*, 265, 278.

99. "The African-American Experience in the Gilded Age," accessed February 11, 2024, http://www.sscnet.ucla.edu/history/waughj/classes/gildedage/private/african _americans/history/african_american_experience.html.

100. I am not counting here non-European immigrants, like those from China, as *Citizen Bird* is limited imaginatively and geographically to the East Coast.

101. Wright and Coues, *Citizen Bird*, x.

102. Wright and Coues, *Citizen Bird*, 266.

103. Wright and Coues, *Citizen Bird*, 266.

104. Wright and Coues, *Citizen Bird*, 281.

105. One possible reason for that authorial choice might be the relatively privileged status afforded to immigrants from Protestant countries like England and Scandinavia as opposed to Catholic countries like Ireland and Italy.

106. Wright and Coues, *Citizen Bird*, 282.

107. Wright and Coues, *Citizen Bird*, 382.

108. Wright and Coues, *Citizen Bird*, 384.

109. Wright and Coues, *Citizen Bird*, 5.

110. Wright's father, Samuel Osgood, DD (1812–1880), is not to be confused with the Rev. Samuel Osgood (1784–1862), who was an important figure in the abolitionist movement and a conductor of the Underground Railroad.

111. Wright, *My New York*, 58.

112. Wright and Coues, *Citizen Bird*, 86, 247, 58.

113. Wright and Coues, *Citizen Bird*, 137.

114. Wright and Coues, *Citizen Bird*, 134. See also the translation of Mammy Bun's speech in appendix 1.

115. Wright and Coues, *Citizen Bird*, 133.

116. Wright and Coues, *Citizen Bird*, 135.

117. Wright and Coues, *Citizen Bird*, 136.

118. For more on how American literature and popular culture both co-opted and derided Black culture and traditions, see Eric Lott, *Love and Theft: Blackface Minstrelsy and the American Working Class* (New York: Oxford University Press, 1993); Brian Roberts, *Blackface Nation: Race, Reform, and Identity in American Popular Music, 1812–1925* (Chicago: University of Chicago Press, 2017); W. Fitzhugh Brundage, ed., *Beyond Blackface: African Americans and the Creation of American Popular Culture, 1890–1930* (Chapel Hill: University of North

INTRODUCTION lxxxi

Carolina Press, 2011); and John Strausbaugh, *Black Like You: Blackface, Whiteface, Insult and Imitation in American Popular Culture* (New York: Penguin Random House, 2007).

119. Wright and Coues, *Citizen Bird*, 236.

120. Wright and Coues, *Citizen Bird*, 57.

121. Wright and Coues, *Citizen Bird*, 88–89.

Long-eared Owl.

CITIZEN BIRD

Scenes from Bird-Life in Plain English for Beginners

BY

MABEL OSGOOD WRIGHT

AND

ELLIOTT COUES

with One Hundred and Eleven Illustrations

BY

LOUIS AGASSIZ FUERTES

1897

To

ALL BOYS AND GIRLS

WHO LOVE BIRDS

AND WISH TO PROTECT THEM

This Book is Dedicated

BY THE AUTHORS[1]

---

[1] With this dedication, Wright and Coues mark out the specific audience for this text, an audience that *Citizen Bird* was intended to create: not just children generally but, specifically, boys and girls who have committed themselves to the cause of bird protection.

SCENE:

THE ORCHARD FARM.

TIME:

FROM SPRING TO AUTUMN.

CHARACTERS:

DR. ROY HUNTER, a naturalist.

OLIVE, the Doctor's daughter.

NAT and DODO, the Doctor's nephew and niece.

RAP, a country boy.

MAMMY BUN, an old colored nurse.

OLAF, a fisherman.

Table of Contents

CHAPTER 1	OVERTURE BY THE BIRDS	1
CHAPTER 2	THE DOCTOR'S WONDER ROOM	7
CHAPTER 3	A SPARROW SETTLES THE QUESTION	12
CHAPTER 4	THE BUILDING OF A BIRD	19
CHAPTER 5	CITIZEN BIRD	33
CHAPTER 6	THE BIRD AS A TRAVELLER	43
CHAPTER 7	THE BIRD'S NEST	50
CHAPTER 8	BEGINNING OF THE BIRD STORIES	59
CHAPTER 9	A SILVER-TONGUED FAMILY Bluebird—Robin—Wood Thrush—Wilson's Thrush—Hermit Thrush—Olive-backed Thrush.	64
CHAPTER 10	PEEPERS AND CREEPERS Golden-crowned Kinglet—White-breasted Nuthatch—Chickadee—Brown Creeper.	80

xc TABLE OF CONTENTS

CHAPTER 11 MOCKERS AND SCOLDERS   88
Sage Thrasher—Mockingbird—Catbird—Brown Thrasher—
Rock Wren—House Wren—Long-billed Marsh Wren.

CHAPTER 12 WOODLAND WARBLERS   105
Black-and-white Warbler—Yellow Warbler—
Yellow-rumped Warbler—Ovenbird—Maryland
Yellow-throat—Yellow-breasted Chat—American Redstart.

CHAPTER 13 AROUND THE OLD BARN   120
Red-eyed Vireo—Great Northern Shrike—
Cedar Waxwing.

CHAPTER 14 THE SWALLOWS   128
Purple Martin—Barn Swallow—Tree Swallow—
Bank Swallow.

CHAPTER 15 A BRILLIANT PAIR   133
Scarlet Tanager—Louisiana Tanager.

CHAPTER 16 A TRIBE OF WEED WARRIORS   138
Pine Grosbeak—American Crossbill—American
Goldfinch—Snowflake—Vesper Sparrow—White-
throated Sparrow—Chipping Sparrow—Slate-colored
Junco—Song Sparrow—Towhee—Cardinal—
Rose-breasted Grosbeak—Indigo Bird.

CHAPTER 17 A MIDSUMMER EXCURSION   170
Bobolink—Orchard Oriole—Baltimore Oriole—
Cowbird—Red-winged Blackbird—Purple
Grackle—Meadowlark.

CHAPTER 18 CROWS AND THEIR COUSINS   188
American Crow—Blue Jay.

CHAPTER 19 A FEATHERED FISHERMAN   192
The Osprey.

TABLE OF CONTENTS xci

CHAPTER 20	SOME SKY SWEEPERS	195
	Kingbird—Phoebe—Wood Pewee.	
CHAPTER 21	HUMMERS AND CHIMNEY SWEEPS	200
	Ruby-throated Hummingbird—Chimney Swift.	
CHAPTER 22	TWO WINGED MYSTERIES	207
	Nighthawk—Whip-poor-will.	
CHAPTER 23	A LAUGHING FAMILY	211
	Downy Woodpecker—Red-headed Woodpecker—Flicker—Yellow-bellied Sapsucker.	
CHAPTER 24	TWO ODD FELLOWS	219
	Kingfisher—Yellow-billed Cuckoo.	
CHAPTER 25	CANNIBALS IN COURT	223
	Bald Eagle—Golden Eagle—Screech Owl—Long-eared Owl—Snowy Owl—Great Horned Owl—Marsh Hawk—Sharp-shinned Hawk—Red-shouldered Hawk—Sparrow Hawk.	
CHAPTER 26	A COOING PAIR	236
	Passenger Pigeon—Mourning Dove.	
CHAPTER 27	THREE FAMOUS GAME BIRDS	240
	Bob White—Ruffed Grouse—Woodcock.	
CHAPTER 28	ON THE SHORE	246
	A Long-necked Family: Black-crowned Night Heron—American Bittern—A Bonnet Martyr and a Blue Giant—Snowy Egret—Great Blue Heron.	
CHAPTER 29	UP THE RIVER	258
	Turnstone—Golden Plover—Wilson's Snipe—Spotted Sandpiper—Least Sandpiper—Virginia Rail.	

xcii TABLE OF CONTENTS

CHAPTER 30	DUCKS AND DRAKES	267
	Wood Duck—Black Duck—Mallard—Pintail— Green-winged Teal—Blue-winged Teal— Redhead—Old Squaw—Hooded Merganser.	
CHAPTER 31	GULLS AND TERNS AT HOME	280
	Canada Goose—American Herring Gull— Common Tern—Loon—Pied-billed Grebe.	
CHAPTER 32	CHORUS BY THE BIRDS	287
CHAPTER 33	PROCESSION OF BIRD FAMILIES	289
INDEX OF ENGLISH NAMES		299

CITIZEN BIRD

CHAPTER 1

Overture by the Birds

"We would have you to wit, that on eggs though we sit,
And are spiked on the spit, and are baked in a pan;
Birds are older by far than your ancestors are,
And made love and made war, ere the making of man!"

ANDREW LANG[1]

A PARTY OF SWALLOWS perched on the telegraph wires beside the highway where it passed Orchard Farm. They were resting after a breakfast of insects, which they had caught on the wing, after the custom of their family. As it was only the first of May they had plenty of time before nest-building, and so were having a little neighborly chat.[2]

If you had glanced at these birds carelessly, you might have thought they were all of one kind; but they were not. The smallest was the Bank Swallow, a sober-hued little fellow, with a short, sharp-pointed tail, his back feathers looking like a dusty brown cloak, fastened in front by a neck-band between his light throat and breast.

Next to him perched the Barn Swallow, a bit larger, with a tail like an open pair of glistening scissors and his face and throat a beautiful ruddy buff. There were so many glints of color on his steel-blue back and wings, as he spread them

---

[1] The epigraph is taken from an 1887 poem by the Scottish scholar and folklorist Andrew Lang titled "The Barbarous Bird-Gods: A Savage Parabasis." Inspired by Aristophanes's play *The Birds*, the speakers of Lang's poem are a chorus of mythological bird deities, who recite their many gifts to humanity in a variety of creation myths and lament the cruel treatment of living birds in the modern world, particularly the extinction of certain species: "Thus on Earth's little ball to the Birds you owe all, yet your / gratitude's small for the favours they've done, / And their feathers you pill, and you eat them at will, yes, you / plunder and kill the bright birds one by one; / There's a price on their head, and the Dodo is dead, and the Moa / has fled from the sight of the sun!"

[2] This opening chapter features an imagined conversation among a variety of local species of birds, who are discussing the arrival of the Hunter family to Orchard Farm. As will be evident throughout the chapter and the rest of the book, the birds are anthropomorphized, meaning being given human characteristics. Moreover, from their lofty perspective on the telegraph wire, they are looking down at the human world below, viewing it with the kind of distanced objectivity that human beings typically reserve for themselves vis-à-vis the animal world. This anthropomorphism will serve as a foil for discussing the civics lessons *Citizen Bird* will teach its young readers, as discussed in the introduction to this book.

in the sun, that it seemed as if in some of his nights he must have collided with a great soap-bubble, which left its shifting hues upon him as it burst.

This Barn Swallow was very much worried about something, and talked so fast to his friend the Tree Swallow, that his words sounded like twitters and giggles; but you would know they were words, if you could only understand them.[3]

The Tree Swallow wore a greenish-black cloak and a spotless white vest. He was trying to be polite and listen to the Barn Swallow as well as to the Purple Martin (the biggest Swallow of all), who was a little further along on the wire; but as they both spoke at once, he found it a difficult matter.

"We shall all be turned out, I know," complained the Barn Swallow, "and after we have as good as owned Orchard Farm these three years, it is too bad. Those meddlesome House People have put two new pieces of glass in the hayloft window, and how shall I ever get in to build my nest?"

"They may leave the window open," said the Bank Swallow soothingly, for he had a cheerful disposition; "I have noticed that hayloft windows are usually left open in warm weather."

"Yes, they may leave it open, and then shut it some day after I have gone in," snapped Barney, darting off the perch to catch a fly, and grasping the wire so violently on his return, that the other birds fluttered and almost lost their footing. "What is all this trouble about?" asked the Martin in his soft rich voice. "I live ten miles further up country, and only pass here twice a year, so that I do not know the latest news. Why must you leave the farm? It seems to be a charming place for Bird People. I see a little box under the barn eaves that would make me a fine house."

"It *is* a delightful place for us," replied the Barn Swallow; "but now the House People who own the farm are coming back to live here themselves, and everything is turned topsy-turvy. They should have asked us if we were willing for them to come. Bird People are of a *much* older race than House People anyway; it says so in

---

[3] The anthropomorphizing of the birds serves a number of functions, the first being its didactic purpose for this book's intended audience of children. Whereas birdwatching field guides can go right to teaching their adult readers about bird calls and songs for identification purposes, this text begins by explaining to children that birds have a language of their own, just like people do. Then, the next goal is that children learn the birds' language so that they can understand the valuable wisdom that the birds are trying to communicate to them, such as lessons about the natural world and why it must be protected from human predation. Throughout this chapter runs a subtle critique of the anthropocentrism of the adult world; by representing these birds as capable of understanding human speech, *Citizen Bird* suggests to its child readers that birds know more about humans than humans do about birds, implying a lack of sympathy and interest on the part of the adult world.

OVERTURE BY THE BIRDS 3

their books, for I heard Rap, the lame boy down by the mill, reading about it one day when he was sitting by the river."[4]

All the other birds laughed merrily at this, and the Martin said, "Don't be greedy, Brother Barney; those people are quite welcome to their barns and houses, if they will only let us build in their trees. Bird People own the whole sky and some of our race dive in the sea and swim in the rivers where no House People can follow us."

"You may say what you please," chattered poor unhappy Barney, "everything is awry. The Wrens always built behind the window-blinds, and now these blinds are flung wide open. The Song Sparrow nested in the long grass under the lilac bushes, but now it is all cut short; and they have trimmed away the nice mossy branches in the orchard where hundreds of the brothers built. Besides this, the Bluebird made his nest in a hole in the top of the old gate post, and what have those people done but put up a new post with *no hole in it*!"

"Dear! dear! Think of it, *think* of it!" sang the Bluebird softly, taking his place on the wire with the others.

"What if these people should bring children with them," continued Barney, who had not finished airing his grievances—"little BOYS and CATS! Children who might climb up to our nests and steal our eggs, boys with *guns* perhaps, and striped cats which no one can see, with feet that make no sound, and *such* claws and teeth— it makes me shiver to think of it." And all the birds shook so that the wire quivered and the Bank Swallow fell off, or would have fallen, if he had not spread his wings and saved himself.[5]

The Martin had nothing to say to this, but the little Bank Swallow, though somewhat shaken up, whispered, "There *may* be children who do not rob nests, and other boys like Rap, who would never shoot us. Cats are always sad things for birds, but

---

[4] The reference to Bird People being of a much older "race" than House People refers to the biological class of birds, Aves, being much older than the species *Homo sapiens sapiens* of the biological class Mammalia. This scientific reference the birds make comes from the bird field guide that Rap is reading, and it complements the authors' support for the Darwinian theory of evolution. (In chapter 3, "A Sparrow Settles the Question," readers will learn that Rap's book is Thomas Nuttall's *Manual of Birds*, a famous ornithological manual from 1832.)

[5] This paragraph exemplifies the didactic nature of *Citizen Bird*; the authors are explicitly teaching children how to act in an ethical manner toward birds. Children—boys specifically—should not steal eggs or shoot birds with guns, for example. The lessons of "good versus bad" children is repeated throughout the book as naturalist lessons for children alongside the civics lessons they receive on "good versus bad" birds. That being said, while this passage leaves open the possibility that children can be taught good behavior toward birds, it leaves open no such redemptive future for cats. From the beginning of the bird protection movement through the present day, the impact of domestic cats on wild bird populations has been a hot-button issue. In the early years of Birdcraft, the songbird sanctuary that Wright would later help found, cats found on the premises were trapped and forcibly removed.

these House People may not keep any!" And then he moved down a wire or two, frightened at having given his opinion.

At that moment a Chimney Swift joined the group. This Swift, who nests in chimneys, is the sooty-colored bird that flies and feeds on the wing like a Swallow, and when he is in the air looks like a big spruce cone with wings. He was followed by a Catbird, who had been in a honeysuckle, by one of the farmhouse windows, and peeped inside out of curiosity. Both were excited and evidently bubbling over with news, which half the birds of the orchard were following them to hear. "I know all about it," cried the Swift, settling himself for a long talk.

"I've *seen* the House People!" screamed the Catbird.

"They wish well to the Bird People, and we shall be happier than before!" squeaked the Swift, breathless and eager. "Listen!"—and the birds all huddled together. "This morning when I flew down the chimney, wondering if I should dare build my nest there again, I heard a noise on the outside, so I dropped as far as I could and listened.

"A voice said, 'Mammy Bun, we will leave this chimney for the birds; do not make a fire here until after they have nested!' I was so surprised that I nearly fell into the grate."[6]

"And I," interrupted the Catbird, "was looking in the window and saw the man who spoke, and Mammy Bun too. She is a very big person, wide like a woodchuck, and has a dark face like the House People down in the warm country where I spend the winter."[7]

"There are children at the farm, *I've* seen them too," cried the Phoebe, who usually lived under the eaves of the cow-shed; "three of them—one big girl, one little girl, and a BOY!"

"I told you so!" lisped the Barn Swallow; and a chorus of *ohs* and *ahs* arose that sounded like a strange message buzzing along the wires.

"The BOY has a pocket full of pebbles and a *shooter*," gasped the Phoebe, pausing as if nothing more shocking could be said.

---

[6] This paragraph demonstrates another didactic naturalist lesson for children on birds, explaining that birds' lives revolve around different seasons. Nesting season is in spring, with young being reared throughout the summer, until it is time for fall migration, after which time it would be appropriate to make a fire, so as to not disturb the nesting birds.

[7] In the Catbird's description, the Hunter family housekeeper "Mammy Bun" is immediately racialized; she is distinguished from the other human characters by virtue of her skin color and is identified with the antebellum South. Moreover, her name, her physical characteristics, and her speech all serve to associate her with a racist stereotype prevalent in nineteenth-century U.S. literature and culture: the Mammy figure. For more on the cultural significance of *Citizen Bird*'s representation of Mammy Bun and the role that such demeaning representations played in the rise of the Jim Crow South in the 1890s, please see the introduction.

OVERTURE BY THE BIRDS   5

"Yes, but the big girl coaxed the shooter away from him," said the Chimney Swift, who was quite provoked because his story had been interrupted; "she said, 'Cousin Nat, father won't let you shoot birds here or do anything to frighten them away, for he loves them and has spent half his life watching them and learning their ways, and they have grown so fearless hereabouts that they are like friends.'

"But Nat said, 'Do let me shoot some, Cousin Olive. I don't see why Uncle Roy likes them. What good are birds anyway? They only sit in the street and say "chuck, chuck, chuck" all day long.'

"'You say that because you have always lived in the city and the only birds you have watched are the English Sparrows, who are really as disagreeable as birds can possibly be,' said the big girl; 'but here you will see all the beautiful wild birds.'[8]

"Then the little girl said, 'Why, brother, you always loved our Canary!'

"'Yes, but he is different; he is nice and yellow, and he knows something and sings too like everything; he isn't like these common tree birds.'"[9]

"Common tree birds indeed!" shrieked the Catbird.

"That is what the boy called us," said the Chimney Swift, who then went on with his story about what he had heard the children say.

"'Why you silly dear!' cried the big girl, laughing a sweet little laugh like the Bobolink's song, 'that only proves how little you know about wild birds. Plenty of them are more brightly colored than your Canary, and some of those that wear the plainest feathers sing more beautifully than all the Canaries and cage birds in the world. This summer, when you have made friends with these wild birds, and they have let you see their homes and learn their secrets, you will make up your mind that there are no *common birds*; for every one of them has something very uncommon about it.'[10]

---

[8] This is the first reference to English Sparrows, deriding them through the anti-sparrow lens Coues developed during the Sparrow Wars, as explained in the introduction. English Sparrows will serve as an example of "bad birds" throughout the book, demonstrating their "poor citizenship" as birds.

[9] Nat's preference for his caged Canary over "these common tree birds" offers the authors another opportunity to advocate for the value of nature study for children, particularly for activities that bring children into nature spaces.

[10] The line "there are no *common birds*" outlines a goal of this book and of birdwatching as a naturalist hobby. Children reading this book, and anyone taking up birdwatching as a hobby, will start by learning the most common birds, as they are the most abundant species of birds in an area. When Nat derides the Catbirds and Chimney Swifts as common as compared to their colorful singing pet Canary, Olive encourages Nat to see the beauty in the wild birds that surround them. Children, and birdwatchers, will learn to appreciate even the most common species of birds, as they learn more about their songs, behaviors, and needs. For more information on how birdwatchers appreciate common birds, see Cherry, *For the Birds: Protecting Wildlife through the Naturalist Gaze* (2019).

"Then our brother B. Oriole began to sing in the sugar maple over the shed. The sun was shining on his gay coat; the little girl pointed to him and whispered, 'Hush, Nat! you see Olive is right; please empty the stones out of your pocket.'"

The Chimney Swift had hardly finished his story when there was another excitement.

"News, more news!" called the Bank Swallow joyfully. He had been taking a skim over the meadows and orchard. "These House People do *not* keep cats!"

"They may not have any now, but that doesn't prove they never will," said a Robin crossly. He had just flown against a window, not understanding about the glass, and had a headache in consequence.

"They *never will keep cats*," insisted the little Swallow boldly.

"How do *you* know?" asked the birds in one breath.

"Because they keep *dogs*!" said Bankey, twittering with glee; "two nice dogs. One big and buff and bushy, with a much finer tail than the proudest fox you ever saw; and the other small and white with some dark spots, and as quick as a squirrel. This one has a short tail that sticks up like a Wren's and a nose like a weasel; one ear stands up and the other hangs down; and he has a *terrible* wink in one eye. Even a poor little Bank Swallow knows that where one of *these* dogs lives the Bird People need not fear either cats or rats!"

"I love dogs," said the black-and-white Downy Woodpecker, running up a telegraph pole in search of grubs; "dogs have bones to eat and I like to pick bones, especially in winter."[11]

"Me too," chimed in the Nuthatch, who walks chiefly head down and wears a fashionable white vest and black necktie with a gray coat; "and sometimes they leave bits of fat about. Yes, dogs are very friendly things indeed."

Then a joyful murmur ran all along the wires, and Farmer Griggs, who was driving past, said to himself, "Powerful lot of 'lectricity on to-day; should think them Swallers would get shock't and kil't."[12] But it was only the birds whispering together; agreeing to return to their old haunts at Orchard Farm and give the House Children a chance to learn that there are no such things as "common" birds.

---

[11] The birds' stated affection for dogs was shared by Mabel Osgood Wright, who besides being a dog owner herself also included a talking dog, Waddles, in her first children's book, *Tommy-Anne and the Three Hearts* (1896).

[12] Here is the first reference in *Citizen Bird* to the impact of new technologies on the natural world. Later references, such as when the children find the corpse of a bird shocked to death below the telegraph wires, underscore the point that bird populations are threatened not just by individual human actions but also by industrial development and urbanization.

CHAPTER 2

The Doctor's Wonder Room

NATHANIEL AND THEODORA, who were called Nat and Dodo for short, were standing in the hallway outside Dr. Hunter's door, engaged in a very lively argument.

"I say birds are animals," blustered Nat, pounding his fists together after a fashion of his own.

"And I'm as sure as anything that they *can't* be," persisted Dodo, "because they have feathers, and nothing else has."

"That doesn't prove anything. Everything that lives and grows is either an animal or a vegetable. Do you think that birds grow like potatoes and are dug out of the ground, or come off trees like apples?" And Nat gave himself an air of great wisdom, such as brothers are apt to wear when they are in the fifth reader, and their sisters are only in the third.[1]

"But isn't there anything besides animals and vegetables that they might be? Perhaps they are minerals," said Dodo, brightening up as she thought of the word.

"Oh! oh! what a stupid you are, Dodo! Minerals! Why those are rocks and such things, that can't move and don't live." Nat laughed rather rudely, and, putting his hands in his pockets, began to whistle.

"I think you might tell me *what* kind of an animal a bird is, and why it has feathers and can fly, instead of laughing," said Dodo in a shaky voice; for her feelings were very tender and she remembered too late what minerals are.

---

[1] That Nat is here identified as in "the fifth reader" and Dodo in "the third" refer to the age-based textbooks assigned in U.S. public schools at the time. Nat is thus roughly ten years old and Theodora is eight.

"Yes, tell her, Nat," said Olive, who came through the hall just then. "Are you holding your knowledge tight in your pockets, or whistling to keep from telling it?"

Nat scowled a minute and then said frankly, for every one was frank with Olive, "I really don't know what sort of an animal a bird is, though I'm sure it *is* an animal. Don't you think Uncle Roy will tell us?"

"I'm sure he will be glad to, if he is not very busy, and he is seldom too busy to talk of birds. He is writing a book now of all the things he knows about them. Knock on the door, Dodo."

"I'm afraid to," said Dodo, clasping her hands behind her. "Mammy says that room is *full* of birds, and that we must never go in there. Suppose when the door opens they should get out and fly away?"

"Mammy was right in telling you not to go in without asking, because there are a great many books and papers there that father values, and you might upset them. But the birds that are there are not alive. They are dead birds that father has collected from all parts of America—stuffed birds, such as you have seen in the glass cases in the Museum."

"But, Cousin Olive," said Nat in astonishment, "if Uncle Roy has shot enough birds to fill a big room, why won't he let me pop at a few with my shooter?"

"You must ask him why yourself, Nat. Knock again, Dodo. Father, may we come in? The children are here, with pockets full of questions"; and Olive opened the door of the study, which Dodo named "the wonder room" that very day.

It was a very long room on the southwest side of the house. The sun streamed in through three wide windows, and at one end there was a deep fireplace with brass andirons upon which some logs smouldered, for though it was a mild May day the great room felt cool. Around the room were deep cases with glass doors, from which peeped all kinds and sizes of birds, while between the tops of the cases and the ceiling the spaces were filled by colored bird pictures. The Doctor's desk stood in front of one window, heaped with papers and books; down the middle of the room were low book-cases standing back to back, and where these ended, before the hearth, was a high-backed settle, almost as long as a bed.[2]

The children stood still for a minute, speechless with surprise and delight. Then Dodo made a rush for the Doctor's chair, and hugging him round the neck, cried, "Dear Uncle Roy, will you please let us stay in here a little while, so that

---

[2] This section introduces Dr. Hunter's study as the office of an ornithologist, as his study is full of stuffed bird specimens in addition to scientific books.

we can learn what sort of animals birds are, and all about them? And will you tell Nat why you let yourself shoot birds when you won't let him?"[3] Here Dodo stopped, both for lack of breath and because she knew that her sentences were mixing themselves dreadfully.

"So you have been here two whole days without finding me out," said the Doctor, seating Dodo comfortably on his knee. "Aren't you afraid of the old ogre who keeps so many birds prisoners in his den, and bewitches them so that they sit quite still and never even try to fly? You want to know about birds, do you, Miss Dodo, and Nat feels grieved because I won't let him pop at our feathered neighbors that live in the orchard? Oh, yes, my boy, I know all about it, you see; Cousin Olive has been telling tales. Come round here where I can see you. I can answer your question more easily than I can Dodo's. Don't look ashamed, for it is perfectly natural that you should like to pop at birds until you learn to understand the reasons why you should not. It was because you two youngsters have seen so little of Nature and the things that creep and crawl and fly, that I begged you from your parents for a time.[4]

"House People are apt to grow selfish and cruel, thinking they are the only people upon the earth, unless they can sometimes visit the homes of the Beast and Bird Brotherhood, and see that these can also love and suffer and work like themselves.

"Now, my boy, before we begin to learn about the birds I will partly answer your question, and you will be able to answer it yourself before summer is over. Animal life should never be taken except for some good purpose. Birds are killed by scientists that their structure and uses may be studied—just as doctors must examine human bodies. But if you kill a bird, of what use is its dead body to you?"

"I would like to see if I could hit it, and then—I—guess," hesitating, "I could find out its name better if I had it in my hand."

---

[3] These next several paragraphs address the question of who "should" and "should not" be allowed to shoot birds. As explained in the introduction, the development of ornithology was built on dead birds as specimens. Ornithologists such as Coues and wildlife illustrators such as Fuertes routinely shot, killed, and stuffed birds for study. As people began to recognize that bird populations were endangered by humans' actions, the narrative that developed was to blame women for using feathers in fashion and children for shooting birds and collecting eggs for fun. Ornithologists, despite killing far more birds than they needed for study, were rarely blamed for declining bird populations. Therefore, according to this logic and narrative, ornithologists can shoot birds, as it is for "some good purpose," as explained on the following pages.

[4] That Uncle Roy has requested this visit of Nat and Dodo specifically to counteract the negative effects of an urban upbringing speaks to the authors' belief that living at a remove from nature fosters anthropocentrism, or humans seeing themselves as the center of the world. The solution to anthropocentrism, the authors propose, is to learn more about the natural world.

"Ah, Nat, my lad, I thought so; *first* to see if you can hit it, and *perhaps* because you want to know the bird's name. Did you ever think of trying to cut off one of your fingers with your jack-knife, to see if you could do it, or how it is made?"

"Why, no, uncle, it would hurt, and I couldn't put it on again, and it wouldn't do me any good anyway, for I could find out about it by asking a doctor, without hurting myself."

"Yes, that is right; and for the present you can learn enough about birds without shooting them yourself, and if you learn your lesson well you will never shoot a song-bird."

"May we see the book you are writing, Uncle Roy, and learn all about the birds out of it?"

"It is written in words too long and difficult for you to understand. Here is a page on the desk—see if you can read it."

Nat stood by the Doctor's chair, but the longer he looked at the page the more puzzled he became, and at last he said, "I think, if you please, I'd rather have a book with only the birds' plain American names." Then he spelled out slowly, "C-y-a-n-o-c-i-t-t-a c-r-i-s-t-a-t-a. Why, that's Latin, but it only means Blue Jay."

"Couldn't you write a *little* book for us, uncle—just a common little book, all in plain words?" pleaded Dodo. "There's plenty of paper here, and of course the know-how is all in your head; because Olive says you know about every bird that lives in our America—and then you need not put them quite all in our book."[5]

"Bless your innocent heart! How many different kinds of birds do you think there are in 'our America,' my little Yankee?" "More than a hundred, I guess," said Dodo after a long pause.

"Nearly a thousand, my lady!"[6]

"A thousand! I think we couldn't remember so many. Does Olive know about 'nearly a thousand'?"

---

[5] This section clarifies the differences between birdwatching books written for adults and those for children. Traditional bird identification books geared toward adults include scientific names (*Cyanocitta cristata*), in addition to the common name (Blue Jay), as Nat notes when looking at Dr. Hunter's ornithological work in progress. Dodo's request that Dr. Hunter write a "common little book, all in plain words" fictionalizes *Citizen Bird*'s origin story, with Uncle Roy and Olive as stand-ins for its real authors Coues and Wright.

[6] Dr. Hunter cites nearly a thousand bird species in the United States at the time of *Citizen Bird*'s writing in the late nineteenth century. According to the Cornell Lab of Ornithology, 2,059 species are listed now, in the early twenty-first century. While some changes will be due to the "splitting and lumping" of bird species—that is, splitting species into subspecies or lumping subspecies into one species—the expanded species list of today should mostly be attributable to the expansion of ornithological knowledge and the discovery of entirely new species.

"No, nor about a quarter of them, Dodo. There are a great many birds that are rare or curious, but are not very interesting to people like you and me," said Olive.

"Suppose you make us a little book about some of the very nicest American birds," put in Nat, who had been looking at the row of stuffed birds in one of the cases, and began to feel a real interest in knowing their names and something about them. "Oh, Uncle Roy! Here's a Robin. See! Dodo, see! I knew it in a minute; it's like meeting a fellow you know"; and Nat pranced about while the Doctor laughed as if he was well pleased.

"Now, children," said he, "I have an hour's more work this morning, and then we will talk over this bird matter. Here is a little blank book, and a pencil for each of you. Go down in the orchard, and when you find a bird, write in the book how it looks to you. So—size, color of head, throat, breast, back, tail, and wings—that will be enough for once; but try to remember, also, how it sings.[7] You had better help them a bit to begin with, daughter," he continued, turning to Olive, who went as gladly as if she were only ten years old like Nat, instead of being seventeen, and nearly as tall as her father, with skirts that covered her boot tops.

---

[7] Dr. Hunter's instructions to the children of what parts of the bird to note include most of the basic elements that birdwatching field guides use to identify birds.

CHAPTER 3

A Sparrow Settles the Question

THE APPLE TREES were not yet in bloom in the orchard, but the cherries were tricked out in dazzling white, and the peaches were blushing as prettily as possible. On either side of the walk that led down through the garden, hyacinths, great mats of single white violets and bunches of yellow daffies were in flower, and as far as the children could see the fresh green orchard grass was gilded with dandelions.[1]

"Isn't it lovely?" cried Dodo, "I want to pick everything." She began to fill her hands with dandelions. "Only I wish that mother was here"—and a little quaver shook the merry voice.

"She will come by and by, dear," said Olive. "You know your father had to go away on business, and you wouldn't like him to go all alone."

"Why do people have business?"

"To earn money, to be sure, to buy your pretty frocks and shoes, and give you plenty to eat."

"But House People are the only ones who must work for what they have—everything else takes what it wants."

"There is where you are very much mistaken, Miss Dodo. Everything works for its living in some way. Take, for example, the birds that you are going to

---

[1] Wright's talents as a nature writer as well as her extensive knowledge of plant life are in full display in this description of Orchard Farm, which is modeled closely on Wright's country home Mosswood, located in Fairfield, Connecticut. In 1901, Wright would publish *Flowers and Ferns in Their Haunts*, a popular guide aimed at adult audiences. For more on Wright as a nature writer, see Philippon (2004), *Conserving Words: How American Nature Writers Shaped the Environmental Movement* (2004).

study. They have to build their own houses, and feed their children, and travel about every year on their own particular business."[2]

"Travel—do birds travel?" cried both children in the same breath. "Oh, where do they go, and what for?"

"Father will tell you about that. Now you must do what he said—each find a bird, and see if you can describe it. Suppose we sit on this great root. It belongs to the oldest tree in the orchard, and Grandmother Hunter used to play house up in the top of it when she was a little girl. Father told me he had a perch up there when he was a boy, so that he could watch the birds. Perhaps, if you are careful and really want to keep quiet and see the birds, he will have one fixed for you."

"How jolly!" said Nat. "Sh-h! I see a bird now—such a queer little thing—it's running round like a mouse. Oh! oh! it goes just as well upside down as any other way." And Nat pulled out his pencil and book and waited for the bird to come in sight again, which it was kind enough to do very soon.

"Size"—wrote Nat, struggling with his pencil, which would squeak, because he had foolishly put it in his mouth. "How big would you call it?"

"Little," said Dodo promptly.

"Kind of little, but not so very. I've seen smaller in the Museum," said Nat.[3] "What would you call it, Olive?"

"I should call it rather a small bird, if I were not speaking exactly. But if you wish to be more particular you must try to guess its length in inches. When I was about your age father measured my right-hand middle finger and told me it was three inches long. Then he made two marks across it with violet ink, which takes a long time to wash off, so that my finger made a three-inch measure. I soon grew accustomed to look at a bird and then at my finger, from nail to knuckle, and then try to tell how many times longer the bird was from the point of his beak down over his back to the tip of his tail. Of course I made a great many mistakes and could seldom tell exactly, but it was a great help."

"How long is my finger?" asked Nat eagerly, spreading out a rather large hand for a boy of ten.

---

[2] This particular type of anthropomorphism is on display throughout the text, as birds are anthropomorphized in terms of their work ethic and utility to people. A bird who is a good citizen "works for its living" and takes care of its children, and its migration is attributed to traveling "for business" (as opposed to for finding new sources of food).

[3] Likely the American Museum of Natural History in New York, where Wright spent two years studying bird specimens in preparation for writing *Birdcraft* under the tutelage of ornithologist J. A. Allen.

"About four inches."

"Then that bird is quite a little longer than that—five or six inches anyway." And he wrote, "Length, five or six inches."

"Ah, he has gone," wailed Dodo. "Oh, no, he hasn't. He has come round the tree again—he says *squank, squank, squank,* as if his voice was rusty. Is that his song, Cousin Olive?"

"No, he is only talking now."

"Talking? It seems to me that birds can do ever so many more things than I thought they possibly could."

"Black head," said Nat, as he continued writing; "sort of gray on top and white in front; his tail is black and white and rusty looking underneath, and—there, he has flown away! Do you think that will do, and will uncle know his name? Oh, I forgot, he says *squank,* goes head down, and picks things out of the tree bark." "Yes, that will do for a beginning, but father will tell you some simple names for the different parts of every bird, so that your descriptions need not confuse you. If every one gave his own names, no two people would quite understand each other."

"Oh! I see a bird," whispered Dodo, pointing to the grass at a little distance. "See! it's quite as big as a Pigeon and speckled all over black and brown and has a red mark on the back of its neck. Please write it down for me, Olive; it takes me so long to write, and I haven't seen it in front yet. There, it's turning round—oh! it has a black mark in front of its neck like a cravat and it's speckled underneath. It has flown a little further off and is walking up a tree, and it's very white on its back where its tail begins. Oh! do hear it laugh, Nat." And the Flicker, the big Woodpecker with golden lining to its wings, for it was he, gave out peal after peal of his jolly call-note.

"Can't we go in now to ask Uncle Roy the names of these birds, and see if he won't begin our book this afternoon?"

"It isn't an hour yet since we came out. Come down through the orchard; I hear some Bluebirds singing and perhaps you can see them. They are very tame, and often make their nests in the knot holes in these old trees."

"See, Olive," said Dodo, "what is that down in the grass by the fence? It is something moving. Do you think it can be any sort of a wild animal?"

"No, it's a boy," said Nat. "I see his head. Perhaps he has come to catch some birds. Let's drive him away." "Gently, gently, Nat," said Olive; "it is a boy, but you are not sure that he is doing any harm, and besides it was only yesterday that you were vexed with me because I wouldn't let you pop at the birds yourself. We will ask him what he is doing."[4]

They went through the orchard, and found a boy, about twelve years old, lying in the grass. He had dark hair and eyes, and a sun-burned face, but was very thin, and a rude crutch was lying beside him.

"Well, little boy," said Olive pleasantly, "what is your name, and what are you doing here?"

The child looked frightened at first and hid his face on his arm, but finally looked up, and said timidly, "My name is Rap, and I was watching the birds. Please, I didn't know anybody lived here, only cows, and I've been coming in most times for two years."

Then they saw that he had a tattered piece of a book in one hand, which he slipped inside his jacket as carefully as if it were a great treasure.

"Watching them to like them or to catch them?" asked Nat suspiciously, then feeling ashamed the next moment when Rap answered:

"To like them. I'd never kill a bird! I've sometimes found dead ones that have hit against the telegraph wires; and it makes you feel lumpy in your throat to see how every little feather lies so soft and lovely, though they never will fly any more."

By this time the three were seated in front of the strange boy, looking at him with great interest.

"What is the book you were reading when we came up?" asked Olive. Rap pulled it out and laid it on her lap, saying, "I don't know its name—the beginning part that tells is gone—but it's all about birds. Here's a picture of a Bluebird, only it isn't quite right, somehow. Oh, I do wish I had all of the book."

Olive turned over the leaves that looked familiar to her and saw that it began at page 443. "Why, it is part of the first volume of Nuttall's 'Manual of Birds.'[5] My father has the whole of this book," she said. "Where did you find this bit?"

"The rag pedler that comes by every fall lets me look in his bags, 'cause sometimes there are paper books in them, and he gave me this for nothing, 'cause it was only a piece."

---

[4] Olive's comparison of Nat's hostile reaction to a strange boy on the property of Orchard Farm to his desire to shoot songbirds makes explicit the book's message of the meliorative effects of nature study. As the children come to treat the natural world more kindly, so will they behave with other human beings.

[5] Nuttall's "Manual of Birds" likely refers to the 1832 publication *A Manual of the Ornithology of the United States and of Canada; The Land Birds* (Cambridge, MA: Hilliard and Brown), written by Thomas Nuttall, an English botanist and zoologist. The Nuttall Ornithological Club, founded in 1873, was named after Thomas Nuttall. As described in the introduction, this is the club from which Coues and several other members eventually founded the American Ornithologists' Union.

"Why don't you ask your father to buy you a whole book, instead of grubbing in rag-bags?" said Nat thoughtlessly.

Rap looked from one to the other, as if in his interest he had forgotten himself for a time, and then he said quietly, "I haven't any father."

"I haven't any mother," said Olive quickly, putting her hand gently on the thin brown one. "We must be friends, Rap."

Her sympathy soothed him immediately, and his gentle nature instantly tried to comfort her by saying, "But you said your father owned the whole of my book. How glad you must be!"

Then they all laughed, and Nat and Dodo began telling about their uncle's room and all the books and birds in it, and about the book he had promised to write for them, until Rap looked so bewildered that Olive was obliged to explain things a little more clearly to him. "Come home with us," cried Nat and Dodo, each seizing him by a hand, "and perhaps uncle will tell you all the names we must learn—head, throat, wings, and what all the other parts are rightly called—and then we can go around together and watch birds."

But as Rap turned over and scrambled up with the aid of his crutch, they saw that he had only one leg, for the trouser of the left leg was tied together just below the knee.

Acting as if they did not notice this, they led the way to the house, going close to the fence that divided the orchard from the road, because there was a little path worn there.

"What is the whole of your name?" asked Dodo, who could not keep from asking questions.

"Stephen Hawley," he answered. "My mother is Ann Hawley, who lives by the mill, and does all the beautiful fine white washing for everybody hereabouts. Don't you know her? I suppose it's because you have just come. I believe my mother could wash a cobweb if she tried, and not tear it," and a glow of pride lit up his face.

"But you said a little while ago that your name was Rap."

"Everybody calls me Rap, because when I go along the road my crutch hits the stones, and says 'rap—rap—rap.'"[6]

---

[6] An onomatopoeia for the sound of his crutch, the nickname reduces Stephen Hawley, the only working-class child in the group, to his disability, not unlike Dickens's Tiny Tim. Yet, also like Tiny Tim, Rap's disability as well as his comparative poverty are presented as reasons for his moral superiority to the other children—he models for them the doctrine of self-help, laboring on behalf of his mother, a local washerwoman, while also exhibiting from

A SPARROW SETTLES THE QUESTION 17

"Here's a dead bird," said Nat, picking something from under the fence.

"It's a White-throated Sparrow," said Rap, "and it's flown against the telegraph wire in the dark and been killed."

"We will take it to uncle and ask him to tell us all about it."

"Yes, yes," said Dodo, "we will all go"—and Rap hopped off after the other children so quickly that Olive had hard work to keep up with him.

This time Nat and Dodo did not hesitate outside the study door, but gave a pound or two and burst into the room.

"Uncle Roy, Uncle Roy, we have seen two birds and written down about them, but we didn't quite know what to call the front part where the neck ends and the stomach begins, or the beginning of the tail, and Olive says there are right names for all these parts. And we found Rap in the orchard and he only has half a book, and here's a White-throated Sparrow, and we want to know how it's made and why birds can fly and why—"

Here the Doctor laughingly stopped them and turned to Olive for a clearer account of what had taken place in the orchard, while Rap stood gazing about the room as if he thought that heaven had suddenly opened to him.

"Now, children," said the Doctor, as soon as the youngsters had stopped chattering, "I will first *tell* you some stories about the birds; then if you like them I will make them into a little book that other girls and boys may read." And as the children began to dance about, he continued: "But before I tell you the names and habits of some of our home birds, you must learn a few things that are true of all birds—what they are; where they belong among animals; how they are made; how they do good and why we should protect them; and the wonderful journeys some of them take. To-morrow I will begin by answering Dodo's questions whether a bird is an animal, and why it has feathers."

"I think a bird is something like a boat," said Rap eagerly. "When it flies its wings are like sails in the air, and when it swims its feet row under the water, and the tail balances behind like a rudder and the head sticks out in front like the bowsprit."

"You are right, my boy," said the Doctor, looking at him attentively; "and would you also like to know how this beautiful boat is made? If a ship-builder

---

the outset the curious, patient, and sympathetic attitude toward nature that the other upper-class, city-dwelling children can develop only through a summer spent at Orchard Farm.

could plan a vessel that would go through wind and water as birds do, he would be the wisest man in the world. But you see, Rap, a man did *not* plan any bird.

"I will go down and ask your mother to let you come and hear the stories with the other children—how would you like that, Rap?"

"Will you? Will you really let me come? Oh, I am so glad! I know mother'll let me any day but Monday and Thursday, because I have to watch clothes on those days."

"Wash clothes?" said Dodo in surprise.

"No, watch them," replied Rap, laughing. "Those two days the miller lets mother spread her things to whiten in his big meadow, and I have to watch and see that they are not stolen or don't blow away."

"Isn't it very stupid to sit there so long?"

"Oh, no, it's lovely; for there are lots of birds and things about."

"To-morrow will be Wednesday," said the Doctor. "Come up to Orchard Farm by nine o'clock, Rap, and we will begin our lessons with this little White-throated Sparrow Nat has found."

"And uncle!" cried Dodo, "you must make inch measures on our middle fingers with violet ink, the way you did to Olive's when she was little."

CHAPTER 4

The Building of a Bird

It rained on Wednesday—a warm spring rain, swelling the rivers and ponds, and watering the newly planted garden; but discouraging the birds in their nest-building, and disappointing Nat and Dodo, who wished to have their lesson in the orchard.

"Come in here, children," said the Doctor. "The wonder room, as Dodo calls it, is a good place for a talk about feathers and bones, and the rest of the things birds are built of. I have sent for Rap, too, so that the trio may be complete."

"Feathers and bones for building birds?" said Nat. "What a queer idea for a bird story."

"Not a bird story exactly," answered the Doctor. "But some things are true of all birds, and you must know them if you wish to understand the *reason why* of any bird in particular."

In a few minutes the three children were seated on the wide settle, with a cheery log fire, to make them forget the outside dampness. Quick, the fidgety little fox-terrier, sat by the hearth, watching a possible mouse hole; and Mr. Wolf, the tawny St. Bernard, chose the rug as a comfortable place for finishing his morning toilet.

Olive presently joined the group. The Doctor took the dead White-throated Sparrow from the table, and began to walk about the room, stopping now in front of the fire and then by the window.

"Here is a Sparrow, different from every other kind of Sparrow, different indeed from any other sort of bird in the world—else it would not be the particular sort of a Sparrow called the White-throated. But there are a good many things that it has in common with all other birds. Can you tell me some of them?"

"I know!" said Dodo; "it has a good many feathers on it, and I guess all kinds of birds wear feathers, except some when they are very little in the nest."

"Quite right, little girl," said the Doctor. "Every bird has feathers, and no other animal has feathers. So we say, 'A bird is known by its feathers.' But what do you suppose its feathers are for?"

"To make it look nice and pretty," said Dodo promptly.

"To make it lighter, so's it can fly," added Nat.

"To keep it warm, too, I guess," was Rap's answer.

"Well, you are all three partly, but not quite, right. Certainly the beauty of a bird depends most on its feathers, being not even skin-deep, as you may well believe, if you ever noticed a chicken Mammy Bun had plucked. But, Nat, how can feathers make a bird lighter, when every one of them weighs something, and a bird has to carry them all? They make a bird a little heavier than it would be without them. Yet it is quite true that no bird could fly if you clipped its wings. So some of its feathers enable it to fly—the large ones, that grow on the wings. Then, too, the large ones that make the tail help the bird to fly, by acting like a rudder to steer with. Perhaps the small ones too, all over the body, are of some help in flight, because they make a bird smooth, so that it can cut through the air more easily—you know they all lie one way, pointing backward from their roots to their tips. Then when Rap said feathers keep a bird warm, he guessed right. Birds wear plumage as you do clothes, and for the same purpose—to look nice and keep warm."

"But what is 'plumage,' Uncle Roy?" asked Dodo; "I thought you were talking about feathers."

"So I was, missy. Feathers are the plumage, when you take them all together. But see here," added the Doctor, as he spread the Sparrow's wings out, and held them where the children could look closely; "are the wings all plumage, or is there something else?"

"Of course there's something else to wings," said Dodo; "meat and bones, because I've eaten chickens' wings."

"Why didn't you say, Dodo, because there has to be something for the feathers to stick into?" said Nat decidedly.

"You both have very good reasons," said the Doctor. "The plumage of the wings grows out from the skin, just as feathers grow from any other part of the body, only the large ones are fastened to the bones, so that they stay tight in their proper places. If they were loose, they would fly up when the bird beats the air with its wings, and get out of order. See how smoothly they lie one over another! When the bird closes its wings, they come together snugly along its sides. But when the wing is spread, they slide apart—yet not too far to form a broad, flat surface, quite stiff, but light and elastic. By beating the air with the wings birds fly along. It is something like rowing a boat. This surface pushes against the air as the flat blade of an oar pushes against the water. That is why these large stiff feathers are called the rowers. When the Wise Men talk Latin among themselves, they say *remiges*, for 'remiges' means rowers."[1]

"But, Doctor," said Rap, who was looking sharply at the Sparrow's wing, "all the feathers are not like that. Here are a lot of little ones, in rows on top of the wing in front, and more like them underneath, covering over the roots of the rowing feathers. Have they any name?"

"Oh, yes! Everything you can see about a bird has its own name. Those small feathers are called *coverts*, because they cover over the roots of the rowers. Those on top are the upper coverts; those underneath are the under coverts, or lining of the wings. Now notice those two pretty bands of color across the Sparrow's wing. You see one band is formed by the tips of the longest coverts, and the other band by the tips of the next longest coverts. Those two rows of feathers are the greater and middle coverts, and all the smallest feathers, next to the front edge of the wing, are called lesser coverts. Now look at the tail, Rap, and tell me what you can find."

"Why, there is a bunch of long stiff feathers like rowers, that slide over each other when you spread the tail, and a lot of short feathers that hide the roots of the long ones. Are they rowers and coverts too?"

"A bird does not row with his tail—he steers with it, as if it were a rudder; and the long feathers are therefore called rudder-feathers—or *rectrices*, which is Latin for rudders. But the short ones are called coverts, like those of the wings—upper tail-coverts, and under tail-coverts."

"How funny!" said Dodo, "for a bird to have to row himself and steer himself all at once. I know I should get mixed up if I tried it with a boat. How do feathers grow, Uncle Roy?"

"Just like your hair, little girl," said the Doctor, patting her on the head, "or your nails. Didn't you ever notice the dots all over the skin of a chicken? Each dot is a little hole in the skin where a feather sprouts. It grows in a sheath that pushes

[1] The name "Wise Men" is a child-friendly term used in this book to describe ornithologists, while also possibly a coded criticism by Wright of ornithology as a field for university-educated men "talk[ing] Latin amongst themselves." As discussed in the introduction, *Citizen Bird* was published around the same time ornithology began to specialize and professionalize, and the American Ornithologists' Union did not allow women members until well into the twentieth century, so "Wise Men" is a more accurate descriptor than one would think at first glance.

out of the hole, like a plant coming up out of the ground from its root. For a while this sheath is full of blood to nourish the growing feather; that is why new feathers look dark and feel soft—pin-feathers they are called. The blood dries up when the feather has unfolded to its full size, leaving it light and dry, with a horny part at the root that sticks in the hole where it grew, and a spray-like part that makes up most of the feather. The horny part becomes hollow or contains only a little dry pith; when it is large enough, as in the case of a rowing feather from a Goose's wing, it makes a quill pen to write with. But the very tiniest feather on this Sparrow is built up in the same way.

"See! here is one," continued the Doctor, as he twitched out a feather from the Sparrow's back. "You see the quill part runs in the middle from one end to the other; this is called the *shaft*. On each side of it all along, except just at the root, the spray-like parts grow. They are called the *webs* or *vanes*. Now look through this magnifying glass at the web."

The children looked in turn, and each, exclaimed in wonder at the sight.

"Yes, it is very wonderful. The web, that looks so smooth to the naked eye, is made up of a great many small shafts, called *barbs*, that grow out of the main shaft in rows. Every one of these small side-shafts has its own rows of still smaller shafts; and these again have little fringes along their edges, quite curly or like tiny hooks, that catch hold of the next row and hold fast. So the whole feather keeps its shape, though it seems so frail and delicate."

"Are all feathers like this one?" asked Rap.

"All are equally wonderful, and equally beautiful in construction; but there is a good deal of difference in the way the webs hold together. Almost all feathers that come to the surface are smooth and firm, and there is not much difference except in size, or shape, or color. For example, the largest wing-feather or tail-feather of this Sparrow is quite like the one I pulled out of its back in texture, only the back-feather is smaller and not so stiff. But near the roots of these feathers you notice a fluffy part, where the webs do not hold together firmly. Some feathers are as fluffy as that in their whole length. Such are called down-feathers, because they are so downy. Birds that run about as soon as they are hatched are always clothed in down, like little chickens, before their other feathers sprout; and some birds, like Ducks, wear a warm underclothing of down their whole lives. Then again some feathers do not have any webs at all—only a slender shaft, as fine as a hair."

"Do feathers keep on growing all the time, like my hair?" asked Dodo.

THE BUILDING OF A BIRD   23

"No, my dear. They stop growing as soon as they are of the right size; and you will find your hair will do the same, when it is long enough—though that won't be for a good many years yet, little girl. When the blood that has fed the growing feather is all dried up, the feather ceases to grow. Then after a while longer, when it has become ragged and worn, it gets loose in the skin and drops out—as I am sorry to say some of my hair is doing already. That is what we call *moulting*."

"I know about that," interrupted Nat. "It's when hens shed their feathers. But I didn't know that it was moulting when people grow bald."

"It is very much the same thing," said the Doctor, "only we don't call it moulting when people lose their hair. But there is this difference. Birds wear out their feathers much faster than we do our hair, and need a new suit at least once a year, sometimes oftener. All young birds get their first new clothes when the down is worn out. Old birds generally moult as soon as they have reared their broods, which in this country is late in summer or early in the fall. Many also moult again the following spring, when they put on their wedding dress; and one of the curious things about this change of plumage is, that the new feathers often come out quite unlike those that were cast off. So a bird may differ much in appearance at different seasons and ages—in fact, most birds do. The male also differs in many cases from the female, being more handsomely dressed than his mate."

"I don't think that's fair," said Dodo. "I shouldn't like Nat to have nicer clothes than I wear."

"But it is best for Bird People," replied the Doctor, "that the mother bird, who has to keep house and tend to the little ones, should not be too conspicuous. She is best protected from enemies when her colors are plain, and especially when they match the foliage in which she sits on her nest. If her mate has only himself to look out for, it does not so much matter how bright his plumage may be. The colors of some birds are so exactly like their surroundings, that you might look long before you could find the sober, quiet female, whose mate is flashing his gay plumage and singing his finest song, perhaps for the very purpose of attracting your attention away from his home. 'Protective coloration,' is what the Wise Men call it."

"What makes all the different colors of birds, Doctor?" asked Rap.

"That is a hard question to answer. It is natural for birds to have particular colors, just as some people have black eyes and hair, while others have blue eyes and yellow hair. But I can tell you one thing about that. Look at this Sparrow. All the colors it shows are *in* the feathers, whose various markings are due to certain substances called 'pigments,' which filter into the feathers, and there set in various patterns. The feathers are painted inside by Nature, and the colors show through. You see none of these colors are shiny like polished metal. But I could show you some birds whose plumage glitters with all the hues of the rainbow. That glittering is called 'iridescence.' It does not depend upon any pigment in the substance of the feathers, but upon the way the light strikes them. It is the same with the beautiful tints we see on a soap-bubble. The film of water itself is colorless, but it becomes iridescent. You might divide all the colors of birds into two classes—those that depend upon pigments in the feathers, and those that depend upon the play of light on the feathers."

"That's pretty hard to remember," said Nat; "but I know how a soap-bubble looks, though I never saw any birds look that way. Please show us one."

"I will show you two," answered the Doctor, who then went to his glass case, and took out a Wild Pigeon and a Hummingbird. "Look at the shining tints on the neck of this Pigeon, and see how the throat of this Hummingbird glitters when I turn it to the light."[2]

"That's the prettiest color I ever saw," said Nat, "and I can remember about it now. But," he added, thinking of the way he had seen hens mope when they were moulting, "does it hurt birds to lose their feathers, uncle?"

"It is probably not as comfortable as being nicely dressed, and sometimes they seem quite miserable, especially if they shed old feathers faster than new ones can grow to replace the lost ones. Some birds, like Ducks, lose their wing-feathers all at once, and cannot fly for quite a while. But Heart of Nature is kind to his children, as a rule.[3] Most birds shed their rowing feathers one at a time in each wing, so that they never lose their power of flight. Now this will do for wings, tails, and feathers. Come! what is the next thing you notice about this Sparrow? Is it entirely covered with feathers?"

"Of course it isn't," said Dodo; "it hasn't any feathers on its beak or on its feet, else how could it eat and hop about?"

---

[2] The "Wild Pigeon" mentioned here likely refers to the Passenger Pigeon, though it also could refer to any undomesticated pigeon more generally. In chapter 26, "A Cooing Pair," Dr. Hunter presents a Passenger Pigeon skin to the children as an example, which could be the same one mentioned here.

[3] The "Heart of Nature" is the poetic conceit used by Wright in *Citizen Bird* but also in other works like *Tommy-Anne and the Three Hearts* to describe the workings of the natural world in a way that combines both a belief in a higher power with contemporary scientific theories, such as the theory of evolution. Here, rather than describing molting in great scientific detail, it is said that the "Heart of Nature" will take care of birds so that they do not lose all their feathers at once. This term is used on several occasions throughout the book to gloss over other scientific elements, such as bird cognition, the natural balance / symbiosis, the division of birds into different species, and so on.

THE BUILDING OF A BIRD 25

"That is right. These parts of a Sparrow are bare; they never have any feathers; and the skin on them is hard and horny, as different from soft thin skin as finger-nails. Now look at the beak, and think how many things a Sparrow has to do with it. He has no hands or paws, and so he must pick up everything he eats with his beak. He has no teeth, and so he must bite his food with his beak. He feeds on seeds like a Canary bird; so his beak comes to a sharp point, because seeds are small things to pick up; and it is very strong and horny, because seeds are hard to crack, to get at the kernel. Notice, too, children, that his beak is in two halves, an upper half and a lower half; when these halves are held apart his mouth is open, so that you can see the tongue inside; and when the two halves are closed together the mouth is shut. These halves are called the *upper mandible* and the *lower mandible*."

"Why, it's just like people's mouths," said Nat, "only people have lips and teeth."

"Certainly it is like our mouths. Birds are built like ourselves in a great many things, and live as we do in a great many ways. Bird People and House People are animals, and all animals must eat to live. A bird's beak is its mouth, and the under mandible moves up and down, like our chins when we eat or talk. Birds can talk as well as sing with their beaks. This Sparrow can say 'Peabody,' and some kinds of Parrots can repeat whole sentences so as to be understood. That is another thing in which birds' beaks are like our mouths. Now look again—can you see anything else about the Sparrow's beak?"

"I see a pair of little holes at the root of the upper mandible," said Rap.

"Well, those are the nostrils!" said the Doctor. "Birds must breathe, like ourselves, and when the beak is shut they breathe through the nostrils."

"So do I," said Dodo; and then she pursed up her pretty red lips tightly, breathing quite hard through her nose. "I do think," she said, when she had finished this performance, "birds have faces, with all the things in them that we have—there are the eyes, too, on each side, like people's eyes, only they look sideways and not in front. But I don't see their ears. Have birds any ears, Uncle Roy?"

"I can show you this Sparrow's ears. See here," said the Doctor, who had run the point of his penknife under a little package of feathers on one side of the back of the Sparrow's head, and lifted them up; "what does that look like?"

"It's a hole in the skin that runs into the head," said Nat. "Can birds hear through that?"

"Of course they can. Ears of all animals are made to hear with. This Sparrow can hear quite as well as you can, Nat. Now think, children, how many things we have found about this Sparrow's head that are quite like our own,—ears, eyes, nose, mouth, and tongue,—only there are no lips or teeth, because the horny beak, with its hard edges and sharp point, answers both for lips and teeth. I want you to learn from this how many things are really alike in Bird People and House People, though they look so different at first sight. When we come to the bird stories, you will find that birds differ very much among themselves in all these things. I will show you all sorts of beaks, of different sizes and shapes. Here are pictures of several kinds of beaks—see how much they differ in shape! But they are all beaks, and all beaks are mouths. They all answer the same purposes in birds' lives, and the purposes are the same as those of our mouths. But now, what do you notice about this Sparrow's feet?"

"They are not a bit like my feet," said Dodo; "they are so long and slim and hard, and the toes stick out so all around. I think mine are nicer."

"But they would not be so useful as this Sparrow's if you had to live in a bush and hop about on the twigs," said the Doctor. "The bird's feet are fixed as nicely for that, as yours are for walking on the ground. I can show you, too, little girl, that a Sparrow's feet are a great deal more like yours than you think. Come, Rap! Tell me what you see about this bird's feet."

"Why, they are the ends of its legs, and there is a long slim part beyond the feathers, hard and horny like the beak, and at the end of this are four toes, three in front and one behind, and they've all sharp claws on their ends."

"Very well said, my boy! Now I will show you that such feet as the Sparrow has are as much like Dodo's as a Sparrow's beak is like her mouth. Begin with the claws—"

"I know!" exclaimed Dodo, "toe-nails! Only I think they need cutting!"

"Of course they are toe-nails," said the Doctor. "Don't nails grow on the ends of toes? All kinds of claws, on the ends of birds' and other animals' toes, are the same as nails. Some are long, sharp, and curved, like a cat's or a Sparrow's, and some are flat and blunt, like ours. I could show you some birds with claws that look just like our finger-nails. Toes, too, are pretty much the same; only this Sparrow, like most other birds, has but four, with three of them in a line in front, and the other one pointing backward. That is what makes its foot as good as a hand to hold on with when it perches on slender twigs. Almost all birds have their toes fixed that way. Some, that do not perch, have no hind toe;

and birds that swim have broad webs stretched between their front toes, like Ducks. All the different kinds of feet birds have are fitted for the ways they move about on the ground, or water, or among the branches of trees and bushes, just as all their shapes of beaks are fitted for the kind of food they eat and the way they pick it up. Here are two pictures that will show you several different kinds of feet. Now you must answer the next question, Nat; what do toes grow on?"

"Feet!" said Nat promptly, then adding: "But this Sparrow hasn't any feet except its toes; they grow on its legs, because the rest of the horny part stands up—I've noticed that in Canaries."

"But all this horny part is the foot, not the leg," answered the Doctor, "though it does stand up, as you say. How could toes grow from legs without any feet between? They never do! There has to be a foot in every animal between the

1. Insect-eating bill of Robin; 2. Seed-crushing bill of a Sparrow; 3. Snapping bill of Whippoorwill; 4. Needle bill of Hummingbird; 5. Chiselling bill of Woodpecker; 6. Climbing bill of Paroquet; 7. Tearing bill of Falcon; 8. Grooved drinking bill of Dove; 9. Gleaning bill of Ruffed Grouse; 10. Wedge bill of Plover; 11. Straight probing bill of Snipe.

toes and the legs. Now what do you call the end of your foot which is opposite the end on which the toes grow?"

"It's the heel in people, but I should think the hind toe of a bird was its heel," said Nat doubtfully, and beginning to think he did not understand.

"You might think so," said the Doctor; "but you would be wrong. All this horny part that a bird stands up on is its foot. And the top of it, nearest to the feathers, is the heel. Don't you see, when I bend the foot *so*," continued the Doctor, as he bent the Sparrow's foot forward, "that the top of the horny part makes a joint that stands out backward, in the same position your heel always has? All this slender horny part of the foot, above the roots of the toes, corresponds to the instep of your foot, and of course the heel comes next. You must remember the name of it—the Wise Men call it the *tarsus*."

28 CITIZEN BIRD

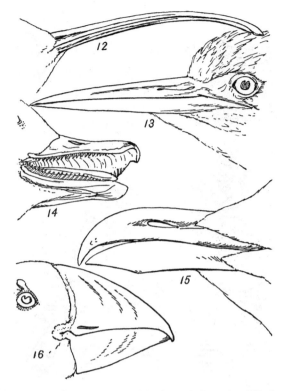

12. Curved probing bill of Curlew; 13. Spearing bill of Green Heron; 14. Strainer bill of Duck; 15. Hooked bill of Gull; 16. Ornamental bill of male Puffin in breeding season.

"Then hasn't a bird got any legs, Uncle Roy, only just feet?" asked Dodo.

"Oh! yes; legs too, with a knee-joint and a hip-joint, like ours. But all these parts are up closer to the body, and hidden by the feathers, so that you cannot see them."

As the Doctor said this there was a great commotion. Quick, who had been watching the mouse hole all the while, gave a sharp bark and pounced on something. There was a feeble squeak, and it was all over with a mouse which had ventured too far from its hole.

"Poor little mousey!" said the Doctor, as he took the limp body from the terrier's mouth. "It is quite dead. I am sorry, but it might have nibbled some of my birds.[4] Besides, this is exactly what I wanted to teach you something about. Who can tell me the difference between a mouse and a Sparrow?"

"I can!" said Dodo; "it's all difference; a mouse hasn't any feathers, or any wings, and it has four feet, and a long tail and whiskers and teeth—"

"That will do, little girl, for differences; do you see anything alike between a Sparrow and a mouse, Rap?"

"I think the fur is something like feathers, Doctor," answered Rap; "and you told us how a beak was like a mouth without any teeth or lips; then a mouse has four feet and legs; but a bird has only two feet, and two wings instead of four legs and feet like a mouse."

"That is just what I want you all to think about," said the Doctor. "Now listen. If a Sparrow has a pair of feet that correspond to a mouse's hind feet, what do

---

[4] Though a brief aside, the justification for a pet dog's killing of a mouse—that it might have nibbled some of the bird specimens—marks the boundary between a love of wild birds specifically and a love of animals more generally. *Citizen Bird* promotes the elimination of "vermin" and "pests"—be they bugs, mice, cats, or English Sparrows—as necessary to the proper functioning of relations between humans and the natural world.

you think a Sparrow's wings correspond to in a mouse?"

"I should think they would be something like a mouse's fore feet," answered Rap, after thinking a moment.

"That is exactly right. Birds and beasts are alike in many respects. They have heads, necks, and bodies; they have tails; and they have limbs. Beasts have two pairs of limbs. We call them fore legs and hind legs. People have two pairs also. We call them arms and legs. So you see our arms correspond to the fore legs of beasts, though we never use them for moving about, except when we go on our hands and knees, or climb trees, or swim in the water. And as for birds—why, their fore limbs are turned into wings, to fly with, so that they walk or hop on their hind limbs only, just as we do. Animals that go on all fours are called *quadrupeds*. Animals that go on their two hind limbs only, like Bird People and House People, are called *bipeds*. A Sparrow's wings are just as much like a mouse's fore legs, as a Sparrow's feathers are like a mouse's fur."

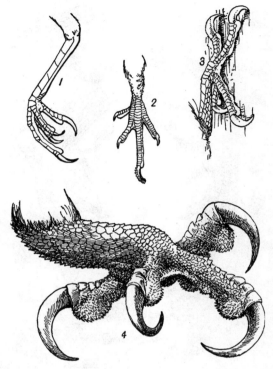

1. Ordinary foot of perching birds; 2. Foot of Nighthawk, with a comb on claw of middle toe; 3. Climbing foot of Woodpecker, with two hind toes; 4. Grasping foot of Osprey, for holding prey.

"How funny!" said Dodo. "But how are a bird's wings like fore legs, when they haven't got any paws or toes—or fingers—or claws—only just long feathers?"

"They have fingers, and some birds' wings have claws; only you cannot see them, because they are all wrapped up in the skin and covered over with the feathers. Some day—not to-day, because you have had a long lesson already—I will show you a bird's wing with only its bones. Then you will see that it has finger-bones at the end, then hand-bones next, then bones that run from the wrist to the elbow, and then one bone that runs from the elbow to the shoulder—almost the same bones that people have in their fingers, hands, wrists, and arms. So you see wings are the same to a bird that fore legs are to a mouse or arms are to us.

"I could go through all the inside parts of birds, and show you something like the same parts in people,—stomach and bowels, to take care of the food they eat and

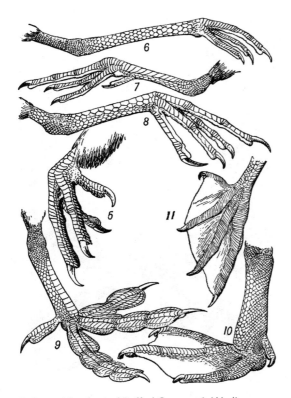

5. Scratching foot of Ruffed Grouse; 6. Wading foot of Golden Plover, with only three toes; 7. Wading foot of Snipe, with short hind toe; 8. Wading foot of Green Heron, with long hind toe; 9. Swimming foot of Coot, with lobed toes; 10. Swimming foot of Canada Goose, with three toes webbed; 11. Swimming foot of Cormorant, with all four toes webbed.

turn it into blood to nourish them; lungs to breathe with, and keep the blood pure; heart to beat and thus pump the warm blood into all parts of the body; brain and nerves, which are what birds think and feel with, just as we do with ours; and all their bones, which together make what we call the *skeleton*, or framework of the body, to keep the flesh in shape and support the other organs."

"Dear me!" sighed Dodo; "there must be ever so many more things inside of birds that we can't see, than there are outside."

"Of course there are!" said the Doctor. "It won't be very hard for you to remember the outside parts, and learn the names of them all. I have told you most of them that you need to remember, to understand the stories I am going to tell you about birds. See here! What do you think of this?"

So saying, the Doctor unrolled a large sheet of drawing-paper that hung on the wall. "Here is a picture of the White-throated Sparrow, drawn so big you can see it almost across the room, with all the outside parts of which you must learn the names. You see the names are all on the picture, too; I am going to make it smaller, and put it in the book I will write for you, so you can look at it whenever you wish.

"It is almost dinner-time now, and you must be very hungry. But now I must tell you one thing more. You know there are so many, many different kinds of birds and other animals that nobody could remember them unless they were classified. To classify is to put things that are most alike closest together, then next nearest them things that are next most alike, and to keep furthest apart those things that are least alike. Now it is true that all beasts, birds, snakes, lizards, frogs, and fishes have some things alike, though each has some other things different from all the

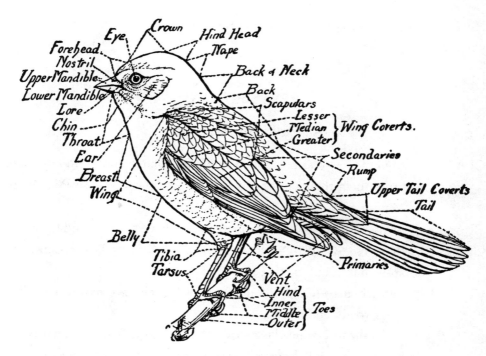

Diagram of the parts of a bird.

rest. If they were not all alike in some things, we could not call them all animals. One of the things in which all the animals I have named are alike is, that they all have skeletons. One of the things in which all their skeletons are alike is, that they have backbones. Backbones are the chains of bones that run along the back from the head to the tail. Backbones are called by the Wise Men *vertebrae*; animals that have backbones are named *Vertebrates*; and animals that lack backbones are named *Invertebrates*."[5]

"Tell us the names of some Invertebrates, please, Doctor," said Rap.

"Well, all sorts of insects are Invertebrates, and so are lobsters and crabs, oysters and clams, worms, starfishes, jelly-fishes, corals, and even sponges. Then there are some too small to see without a microscope. But never mind about Invertebrates now. I only want you to remember that all beasts, birds, reptiles, and fishes are Vertebrates, and that there are five principal classes of them. If I should tell you as much about them as I have about the Building of a Bird, you would see that they are all built on what we call the Vertebrate plan of structure.

[5] The term "Wise Men" appears in this instance to refer to scientists or zoologists more generally, though it is primarily used to refer to ornithologists.

Here is a chart of the Classes of Vertebrates—you can study it this afternoon, till you learn it by heart."

VERTEBRATES

Animals with Backbones

CLASS I.   Mammals.—Warm-blooded animals which have fur or hair, bring forth their young alive, and nurse them. House People are Mammals.

CLASS II.   Birds.—Warm-blooded animals which have feathers and lay eggs.

CLASS III.   Reptiles.—Cold-blooded animals which have scaly skins, like lizards, snakes, and turtles.

CLASS IV.   Batrachians.—Cold-blooded animals which have naked skins, like frogs, toads, and newts.

All the foregoing classes, except a few of the Batrachians, breathe air in lungs, and almost all, except snakes, have legs; none now living can fly, except bats and birds; but bats are Mammals.

CLASS V.   Fishes.—Cold-blooded animals which have either scaly or naked skins, but no fur or feathers; which live in the water, breathe it with their gills, and swim in it with fins.

CHAPTER 5

Citizen Bird

THE APPLE TREES were in full bloom the day that the Doctor again found time to be with the children. It was exactly the kind of a day that birds like. The ground was soft enough to let the earthworms come up to breathe, so that Robins could catch them easily, and the air was full of all kinds of insects newly out from their long winter sleep in their soft cocoon beds, much to the delight of the Swallows and Flycatchers.

It was also a beautiful day for House People to watch their bird neighbors; for it was mild but not too bright, and every one knows how it hurts the eyes to look at flying birds with the sun shining in them.

Olive, Dodo, and Nat went out first and found Rap waiting. The Doctor followed, carrying something in his hand in a black leather case. When they arrived at the old tree in the orchard, he told them to look up. There was the perch arranged as it had been when he was a boy. Not a perch for birds, but for House People—narrow board seats fitted in between the largest branches and a bar fastened across some of the highest ones, so that it was quite safe to climb up and look out of the top of the tree. The branches had been trimmed away here and there, so that a good view could be had of what was happening elsewhere in the orchard. A scream of surprise and delight came from the group, in which Olive joined. Quickly as the children scrambled into the tree, the Doctor was up there first, laughing and saying that it was thirty years since he had climbed that apple tree; for after he went away to college the old seats had decayed and fallen down.

"Give me your hand and I'll help you up," called Nat to Rap, who had dropped his crutch and was looking up at the others.

"No, you needn't," said Rap. "I can climb all right. Sometimes it isn't so handy for me, but other times it's easier, for in tight places one leg doesn't take up as much room as two"; and he swung and pushed until he was up as high as the rest.

"Here's a nest with eggs in it," whispered Dodo, who had crept out on a limb, where a rather large round nest, made of grass and little sticks plastered together with mud, was saddled on the branch—in fact, a Robin's nest.

"Four lovely smooth eggs, not quite blue and not quite green! Please, can I have them? I saw them first."

"Think a minute, Dodo," said the Doctor. "A bird will come from each of those eggs. Suppose you take the eggs away from the poor Robins, you will be killing four young birds, besides hurting the feelings of their parents and making them leave the orchard, very likely. You must not take any eggs in the nesting season—not even one. I will tell you what happened once in a field where there were some birds' nests in the bushes.

"The man who owned the field was fond of birds and wished to protect them, but he was so good-natured that when his little boy came to him and said, 'I wish so much to have some birds' eggs—all the boys collect them—*please* let me take a few, father—only on our own land,' he did not wish to say 'No.' Sometimes, to be good-natured is as bad as to be cruel. This man said, 'You may take one egg from each nest, but only *one*, remember.' So the boy went out and took a few eggs, but then he carried them to school, showed them to the other boys, and told them where they came from. Then each boy said to himself, 'It will be all right if I take only one egg from each nest.' But when four or five boys had each taken one, all the nests were quite empty. So the poor birds left that man's field, where the bugs and worms grew and throve, till they ate up his hay and all the rest of his crops.

"When the nesting season is over eggs that have not hatched are often left in the various nests, that you can take without doing any harm. Of course I know it is not easy to keep your hands off such pretty things as birds' eggs; but if by doing so you can be patriotic and useful, it is an act of self-denial that you will be glad to do for the good of the country."[1]

"What is in that black case, uncle?" asked Dodo. "Is it a pistol to shoot birds? I think it looks too fat for that."

---

[1] Here, the children in the story receive a civics lesson in addition to their lessons in bird identification and protection, as resisting the urge to take birds' eggs from nests is framed as a "patriotic and useful" act of self-denial that serves the greater good of the country.

"Not the kind of a pistol that you mean, Dodo, but the only kind that you youngsters need to bring down birds so that you can see them. It is a double-barrelled gun, but you must use your eyes for bullets, instead of leaden balls.[2] See!"—and he took a fine pair of field-glasses from the case, moved the screw a little, and held them before Dodo's eyes—"what do you see down there in the grass?"

"Why, it's a Robin, but how big it looks! Every feather shows by itself, and it has white rings round its eyes like spectacles. I never saw them before, I'm sure."

Then, as the Doctor handed the glasses to Nat, Dodo looked in her lap, expecting to find the bird there instead of a hundred feet away.

"This is jolly!" cried Nat, taking a peep and passing the glasses to Rap, who put them to his eyes, gave a little "ah," and looked through them until the Doctor said, "That will do now. Olive shall keep the glasses, and whenever you children want them she will give them to you; but you must be careful never to scratch them or rub your fingers over the lenses at either end. With this magnifying instrument you will be able to see the shape of beaks and wings, and many color markings you would never notice otherwise. But what did I promise to tell you of to-day, children?"

"Citizen Bird, you said," replied Nat, "though I don't think I quite know what you mean."[3]

"What does *citizen* mean?" asked the Doctor, smiling.

"I think it is a person who lives in a city, but birds aren't people and they don't live much in the city."

"You are right in one sense, my boy, but the word *citizen* has also a far wider meaning. Do you know what it is, Olive?" But Olive was not sure, and the Doctor asked her to go to his study and look for the word in the big dictionary.

In a few minutes she returned with a slip of paper from which her father read: "Citizen—a member of a nation, especially of a republic; one who owes allegiance to a government and is entitled to protection from it."

"Now, if you listen carefully I think I can prove to you that every bird you can find is such a citizen of this country, and show you why we should protect him.[4]

[2] The comparison of binoculars to guns recalls Florence Merriam Bailey's *Birds through an Opera-Glass* (New York: Houghton Mifflin, Chautauqua Press, 1899), one of the first birdwatching field guides, in which she encourages people to watch birds through binoculars or opera glasses as opposed to shooting birds for study. Wright also exhorted people to watch birds rather than shoot them in her 1895 birdwatching field guide, *Birdcraft*. For more information on these books' contributions to conservation, see the introduction.

[3] Here is the most complete explication of the bird-as-citizen conceit so central to the authors' argument about the rights of wild birds to legal protection from human predation.

[4] This section explains citizenship for humans and for birds, who can also be "good citizens" of the country by performing environmental duties that, ultimately, help humans, as described in detail in the introduction.

"I told you the other day how the body of a bird was planned and built to fill a place no other animal could take. Thus by his habits and character every bird fills a place as a citizen of our Republic, keeping the laws and doing work for the land that House People, with all their wisdom, cannot do. Every such fellow-animal of ours, besides having eyes to see with, and a brain which, if it does not tell him as many things as our brains tell us, yet teaches him all that he need know to follow the laws that Heart of Nature has set for him, has the same feelings and affections as ourselves. Parent birds love each other and their little ones, and often lose their lives in trying to protect them. They build their homes with as much care and skill as House People use in making theirs. Then they work hard, very hard indeed, to collect food to feed their children, for bird children are, oh, so hungry! They grow very quickly, and must eat constantly from morning until night.

"With them it is breakfast, luncheon, dinner, five-o'clock tea, and supper, with a great many other meals between times that would not be wholesome for House Children. So you can see for yourselves that we may well call the bird a fellow-being."

"Yes," said Rap, his eyes beaming as if he had something to tell, "some birds work as hard as mother does. I watched a pair of Robins all one day last spring, when I was sick. They had a nest in a bush by our kitchen window, where I could see it well, and all day long either the mother or the father came about every two minutes with something for the little ones to eat. I timed them by the clock until I was nearly dizzy, and they seemed to do the same thing every day until the young ones flew away. Then they went over to the grape vines, made a new nest, and raised four more the same way"—and then Rap stopped suddenly, as if he feared that he had been talking too much.

"That is all true," said the Doctor, looking very happy at finding that one of his listeners not only saw for himself but remembered and thought about what he had seen. "If you have used your eyes so well, my lad, when we come to the bird stories I shall expect you to tell some of them yourself." And the Doctor held out his hand to the child with a look that sent him to bed to dream happy dreams for many a night.

The children gazed at Rap in surprise. It was a new idea that a poor little fellow like him should know more than they, who had both parents and nice clothes, and had been to school in a big city. That he should be able to tell stories about birds seemed wonderful. But they were not selfish, and instead of being jealous felt a great respect for Rap.[5]

---

[5] Here, the authors highlight how birdwatching as a hobby is not only for those who can afford binoculars. With his unclouded and innocent natural sensibility, Rap as a "model child" is intended to demonstrate that formal

"Now," said the Doctor, "we will see what a good neighbor to House People a bird is, and how in working for himself he helps them also."

"How can birds possibly work to help people?" asked Dodo and Nat together; but Rap smiled to himself as if he knew something about the matter, and said, "They eat the bugs and worms and things that kill the gardens and fields."

"You are right again," said the Doctor heartily. "What is one thing that man and every other animal must have to keep him alive?"

"*Food*!" shouted Nat, and then grew very red, as the others laughed, because since he had been at Orchard Farm his appetite had grown so that though he ate twice as much as Olive and Dodo he seemed always hungry.

"Yes, food. Bread, meat, vegetables, and fruits, but bread first of all. What is bread made of?"

"Wheat, I think," said Nat.

"Rye, too—mother's rye-bread is drea'fly good," said Rap.[6]

"Don't forget Mammy Bun's corn-bread," added Olive.

"All your answers are right, for many different kinds of bread are used in various parts of the country; but whether it is made from wheat-flour, or rye-flour, or corn-meal, it all grows from the ground, does it not?

"Now the next sort of food—meat, the flesh of animals—oxen, sheep, pigs, and poultry—what do they feed on?"

"Oxen eat grass and hay and meal," said Dodo, in great haste lest some one else should speak first.

"Sheep eat grass and hay too. I've seen them over in the pasture on the hill," said Nat.

"Pigs will eat any old sort of thing," said Rap. "Sour milk and snakes and swill and rats."

"Ugh!" shivered Dodo. "Are all those nasty things in sausages?"

"No, Dodo," laughed the Doctor; "when pigs are shut up they eat a great many dirty things, but naturally they prefer clean food like other cattle—corn, acorns, apples, and so forth. Besides, those 'nasty things,' as you call them, turn into pork before they are put in sausages, for pigs know how to make pork.[7] So you see that

---

education and expensive equipment are not necessary to be a keen observer of the natural world. For more on childhood as a state of nature, see Judith Plotz, *Romanticism and the Vocation of Childhood* (New York: Palgrave, 2001).

[6] That Nat associates bread with wheat and Rap with rye indicates the difference in their social classes, rye or "black" bread being considered poorer fare.

[7] The proverbial phrase "pigs know how to make pork" highlights the latent anthropocentrism of the text, even if the book is attempting to decenter people and center birds in people's consciousness. It assumes that animals exist

all the food of the animals whose flesh we eat comes out of the ground; and that is what the Bible means where it says, 'All flesh is grass.' But what other things are there that grow up out of the earth, tall and strong, each one holding a beautiful green screen to keep the sun from drawing all the moisture from the ground and making it too dry; shading the rivers that their waters may not waste away; some making cool bowers for House People to sit under, others bearing delicious fruits for them to eat, and all in good time yielding their bodies to make fires and give out heat to warm us?"

"Trees! Yes, trees of course," cried the children eagerly; "all kinds of trees, for trees grow apples and pears and plums and cherries and chestnuts and firewood too."

"Now what is there that preys upon all this vegetable life—upon every plant, from the grass to the tree, destroying them all equally?"

"Bugs and worms and all kinds of crawlers and flyers and hoppers," said Rap.

"Yes, every plant has an insect enemy which feeds upon its life juices. So a set of animals has been developed by Heart of Nature to hold the plant destroyers in check, and these animals are the birds.

"Man may do all he can to protect his gardens, his orchards, his fields and forests, but if the birds did not help him the insects that work by night and day—tapping at the root, boring inside the bark, piercing the very heart of the plant, chewing off the under side of leaves, nipping off the buds—would make the earth bare and brown instead of green and blooming. Yet House People, both young and old, forget this. They shoot and frighten away the birds, either because some few of their feathered friends take grapes or other fruits and berries by way of pay, or merely from thoughtlessness, to see how many they can hit."

"Do *all* birds eat bugs and such things?" asked Nat. "Olive said she used to put out grain and crumbs in winter for some kinds."

"Some birds eat animal food and some seed food, while others eat both; but almost all birds feed their babies upon insects. The nesting season is chiefly in spring, when all plants begin or renew their growth. Spring is also the season when the eggs of many insects hatch out and when others come from the cocoons in which they have slept all winter.

---

for human uses, just as the citizen birds "pay their taxes" by acting in ways that have environmental and ecological benefits for people. By the same token, animals whose actions are seen to pose a threat to humans—such as insects eating a farmer's crops—are rendered in no uncertain terms as hostile combatants who must be exterminated.

"Then the farmer begins his annual war upon them, and day after day he fights the Battle of the Bugs. But if he stops to think, and remembers that Heart of Nature has a use for everything, he will win this battle against the creeping, crawling, squirming regiments more easily. For above him in the trees of his forest, in the hedgerows and bushes of his pasture and garden, on the rafters of his barn, even in the chimney of his house, live the birds, willing and eager to help him. And all the wages they ask is permission to work for a living and protection from those of his fellowmen who covet the Oriole and Cardinal for their gay feathers and the Robin and Meadowlark for pot-pie."

"Singing-bird pie is wicked. I would like to pound them all," said Dodo, striking her fists together, as Nat did sometimes, not making it clear whether it was pie or people she wanted to pound. "But uncle, it is right to eat some birds—Ducks and Chickens and Geese and Turkeys."[8]

"Yes, Dodo, they belong to another class of birds—a lower order that seem made for food—not singing nor helping the farmers; but even these should not be shot needlessly or in their nesting season. But the higher order—the perching Song Birds—should never be shot, except the common Sparrow of Europe that we call the English Sparrow. His habits are wholly bad; he meddles with the nests of useful birds and is a nuisance to his human as well as bird neighbors.[9]

"To prevent confusion Heart of Nature has divided the habits and appetites of Birdland, so that instead of a great many families all building in one kind of tree, or eating the same sort of insects or seeds, each has its own manners and customs. Thus they divide among themselves the realms of the air, the water, the trees, and the ground. Some birds, as the Swallows and Flycatchers, skim through the air to catch winged insects. Others, like the Woodpeckers and Warblers, take the scaly insects from the bark of trees. Others that walk on the ground, like the Robin, the Thrush, Meadowlark, Crow, and Red-winged Blackbird, eat ground things, such as the fat cutworms which mow with sharp jaws the young plants of corn, cabbage, and onions."

---

[8] The discussion of which birds are "right to eat" and which birds are not highlights the symbolic boundaries between farmed animals, including farmed birds, and wild songbirds. Symbolic boundaries refer to culturally created categories people use to define themselves and others, including animals, often into "us versus them" groups. For more information on symbolic boundaries between animals, see Arluke and Sanders, *Regarding Animals* (1996), and Cherry, *For the Birds* (2019).

[9] This section includes the first of several anti-English Sparrow references throughout the text (beyond a brief mention on p. 6). As explained in the introduction, Coues was one of the leading anti-Sparrow figures in the Sparrow Wars. For more on the Sparrow Wars, see Fine and Christoforides, "Dirty Birds, Filthy Immigrants, and the English Sparrow War" (1991).

"Please, Doctor Hunter," asked Rap, "I thought Crows and Blackbirds were wicked birds that ate up grain and corn, for the miller always puts up scarecrows to keep them away."

But before the Doctor could answer the children caught sight of Mammy Bun coming down from the house carrying a tray. Upon this was a pitcher, some glasses, and a plate full of cakes, which, when she came under the tree, they saw were delicious-looking buns, as light and brown as good yeast and careful baking could make them.

"Ah, mammy, mammy," cried Olive, Dodo, and Nat together, "how did you know that we should be hungry now, and we are simply famishing?"

"Well, honeys, I jess guessed it, I reck'n.[10] I know'd massa was a-learnin' you'uns suffin', and it allers 'peared to me that learnin' was mighty empty work. I know'd Massa Doctor was never a one to keep his patients holler, and least his own folks!" Mammy gave a big comfortable laugh as the Doctor took the tray from her hands and the children thanked her heartily, while little Rap smiled hopefully on seeing that there were six buns on the plate—that meant one for each and two for the Doctor, he thought.

"No one can make such buns as mammy," said Olive, old as she was breaking hers in half, to find the lump of sugar soaked with lemon juice that she knew was inside. "She used to make them for me when I was a little girl; that is why I named her Mammy Bun, and we've called her that ever since."

"I thought it was a funny name," said Rap.

"One for each of us, and one for the dish," said Olive, passing the plate around.

"One for the dish? What do you mean?" said Dodo.

"Mammy says it is always nice to have more food on a dish, than people are likely to eat, so that they shall see there is enough and the dish shan't feel lonely. You see, that last bun belongs to the dish."

"This time the dish will have to feel lonely," said the Doctor, who had noticed that Rap was looking at his bun, and not eating it; "for I think that Rap would like to take that one home to his mother by and by."

---

[10] In her name, speech, and appearance, Mammy Bun bears all the hallmarks of the racial stereotype of the "mammy figure," a caricatured depiction of a Black female servant as a surrogate mother for the children of the family that enslaved or employed her. Originating in the antebellum period, the mammy figure remained a pervasive trope in U.S. literature and culture through the twentieth century, especially in the Jim Crow South. For more on the history of the mammy figure, see the introduction and Kimberly Wallace-Sanders, *Mammy: A Century of Race, Gender, and Southern Memory* (Ann Arbor: University of Michigan Press, 2008).

From that day Rap always believed that the Doctor could look into his head and see what he was thinking of.

"As we have been talking about the insect-killing that Citizen Bird does in order to pay his rent and taxes, as a good citizen should, I will tell you of the six guilds in Birdland, into which these citizens are divided in order to do their work thoroughly."

"What is a guild?" asked Rap.

"A guild is a band of people who follow the same trade or occupation, and birds are banded together according to the ways in which they work, though some may belong to several guilds. We will name each of the six guilds:[11]

1. GROUND GLEANERS. The birds who feed largely upon the insects which live in, on, or near the ground.
2. TREE TRAPPERS. The birds who feed on insects which lurk about the trunks and branches of trees and shrubs.
3. SKY SWEEPERS. The birds who, while on the wing, catch flying insects.
4. WISE WATCHERS. The large, silent birds, who sit in wait for their prey of field-mice and other little gnawing mammals, as well as insects.
5. SEED SOWERS. The birds who eat wild fruits and berries, and after digesting the pulp and juice, sow the seeds with their bodily wastage.
6. WEED WARRIORS. The birds who crack seeds in their stout beaks, eat the kernels, and so destroy millions of harmful weed-seeds.

"You must write the names and definitions of these six guilds down in your books, because when you hear about each bird I will tell you to which guild he belongs, and if you know where and upon what a bird feeds it will be easier for you to find him. All the Land Birds belong to one or more of these guilds; but perhaps we shall find before we are through that some of the Water Birds have a guild of Sea Sweepers."

---

[11] In contemporary birdwatching field guides, birds are typically grouped by their order or family. The order Gruiformes, for example, includes all cranes and crane-like birds such as Gallinules and Rails. The family Corvidae includes all of the Corvids such as Blue Jays, Common Ravens, and Fish Crows, even if they have different diets. In *Birdcraft* (1895), Wright used six broad categories for birds: Perching Song-Birds; Perching Songless Birds; Birds of Prey; Pigeons, Quails, Grouse; Shore and Marsh Birds; and Swimming Birds. In *Citizen Bird*, the authors group the birds into six broad categories, here called "guilds" in order to indicate the birds' particular craft or trade in performing environmental services for humans, such as eating insects, sowing seeds, or eating weed seeds. It should be noted that these categories do not include all birds, as they note below that "all the Land Birds belong to one or more of these guilds; but perhaps we shall find before we are through that some of the Water Birds have a guild of Sea Sweepers."

For a few minutes the children scribbled away in silence.

"My book will be very mussy," said Dodo, "for I can't write well when I sit all humped up on a branch."

"Of course you cannot," said the Doctor; "but by and by you can copy it out neatly in a clean book, and it will give you something to do on rainy days, for there are some things that we always remember better if we have once written them down." Presently Rap said, "It must be because you never have let any birds be killed here that there are more kinds than I ever see anywhere else—some of every guild, I think. I've often wondered how it was."

"There are four Robins' nests in this one tree," said Olive, "and the old birds have been flying to and fro while we talked, and never dreamed of being afraid."

"Yes, children, Orchard Farm always has protected its Bird Citizens, and it always will, in my time."

"And in mine, too," said Olive. "You see if each person would care for the birds on his own land, the Battle of the Bugs would soon become less terrible."

Then the children laughed to think how funny a real battle would be, with an army of little bugs drawn up on one side of a field and big House People with guns and cannons on the other.

"But even against cannon," said Olive, "the bugs would have the best of it, because they can fly or hop, and the worms can crawl into the ground."

Then the Doctor finished this lesson by saying, quite seriously: "Every time you children deny yourselves the pleasure of taking an egg from a nest, or think to spread a little food for hungry birds, when cold and snow almost force them to starve, you are adding to the food-supply of your country. To be sure, it may be only a few grains of wheat here and an ear of corn there, but it all means bread-food of some sort, and the bread of a nation is its life. So we must learn to love and protect this feathered neighbor of ours, who works for his own living as well as ours, pays his rent and taxes, and gives, besides, free concerts to the public, daily. He certainly deserves the name of Citizen Bird. His patriotism, which is simply his love of the country where he was born, leads him to return to it whenever he thinks of settling down in life and making a nest-home, no matter how far he may have wandered away at any other time; and this patriotism makes him one of the greatest travellers on the face of the earth."[12]

---

[12] This segment perfectly encapsulates the double civics lesson that is the heart of *Citizen Bird*. Children learn they can act as good environmental citizens by protecting birds, and they also learn how birds themselves act as good citizens by patriotically providing ecological benefits ("pays his rent and taxes").

CHAPTER 6

The Bird as a Traveller

Rap went up to Orchard Farm one morning very early to take Nat for a walk through the fields, down to the river, to see some birds that had arrived in the night.

It was only five o'clock, but Dr. Hunter was walking to and fro in the garden, listening to the burst of bird-music as eagerly as if it were for the first time in his life. That is one of the best parts of our friendship with Bird People; they never weary us by talking too much, and every spring after winter's silence their music is as new as ever.

"Please, Uncle Roy, can I go with Rap?" pleaded Nat. "I will wear my rubber boots."

"You may go if you eat something first. I wonder if Rap would invite me also?" said the Doctor, leading the way to the big kitchen pantry.

"I know he would!" cried Nat joyfully. "He wished and wished you would go with us, but we didn't think you'd care to, because you have been to the river woods so many times before. But why must I eat something, uncle? I'm in such a hurry to go."

"Because, my boy, the life in us is like a fire that must be supplied with fuel to keep it burning, only instead of wood or coal we need food. Very early in the morning this life flame of ours, that is called vitality, is very low, like a fire that has burned down, and if we go out in the damp air and breathe the mists that rise from the ground our vitality has not strength to resist them. But if we put fresh fuel on our inward fire by eating something before we go out, then that bad little mischief-maker, which we call malaria, has harder work to creep into us."

"How funny! May I call Rap to tell him? Rap! Rap! come in and have milk and something to eat, to make your inside fire burn up chills and fever!"

Rap thought at first that Nat must be crazy, but very soon understood what the Doctor meant, and was overjoyed at the prospect of having him join the expedition.

"Dodo will cry when she wakes up and knows where we have gone," said Nat, who had been much more kind and thoughtful of his sister since coming to the Farm. But kindness is very catching, and at the Farm everybody was kind, from the House People to the big gray horses in the barn, which let the chickens pick up oats from between their powerful hoofs, without ever frightening them by moving.

"It is too long a walk for little sister, but you must remember everything that you see and hear, and tell her about it. Don't forget the field-glass," said the Doctor, following the boys along the road where telegraph wires made bird-perches between the high poles.

"You said a lot of birds came last night," said Nat to Rap; "but how do you know that they came last night and where did they come from?"

"I know they came last night because they were not here yesterday," answered Rap; "but I don't know where they came from, except that it must be from where it is warmer than it is here, because they went away just before it grew cold last fall. See, Doctor, there are some of them now on those fence rails and more up on the telegraph wires. The miller calls them 'Bee Martins,' and says that they eat up all the honey-bees. Have they any other name—because I have never seen them catch bees?"

Nat looked at them first with the field-glass, then without it as they drew quite near the fence, and saw a fine bird, twice as long as his middle finger. Its back and wings looked dark gray; it was white underneath, with a touch of gray on the breast, and had a black tail, with white at the end of it. As Nat looked the bird raised a little tuft of feathers on top of its head, as if angry, flew into the air, giving a shrill cry, seized an insect, and returned to its perch.

"That is the Kingbird," said the Doctor; "one of the most useful of the insect-catchers. Instead of living on honey-bees, as many people think, he eats very few of these, but kills instead thousands of the bad robber-fly, which is the honey-bee's worst enemy. This bird is really king of the air and of all fly-catching birds. See how graceful his flight is, and how easily he moves!"

"Why did he go away last fall?" asked Nat. "Does he feel the cold weather very much?"

THE BIRD AS A TRAVELLER 45

"He does not stay in the United States until the weather is cold enough to dull him; but he has to move away for another reason. The same reason that forces so many birds to leave us—he must follow his food. This food consists of insects—different kinds of flies, ants, and grasshoppers, which disappear or die as the air grows cold.[13]

"Rap, have you ever noticed the difference between the sounds in a spring night and a night in autumn? In spring the air is humming with the calls of all sorts of insects, but in autumn it is silent, and even the crickets have stopped chirping.

"So about the last of September our Kingbirds, who live everywhere in the United States, gather in flocks, start to find a place where insects are still stirring about, and fly southward, following the sea-coast and the great rivers for paths. Those from the eastern part of the country stop in Central America or fly on to South America, and those from the western part often stop in Mexico."

"But how can they fly so far?" said Nat; "it's hundreds of miles; and how do they find the way?"

"The flight of a bird is a wonderful thing, my boy. He spreads those frail wings of his, and launches into the air, up, up, above trees and steeples, then on and on, being able to fly several hundred miles without resting. Some birds, when the wind aids them, cover more than a hundred miles in a single hour.

"As to the way, the eye of the bird is like a telescope. It magnifies and sees from very far off. Flying through the upper air the bird watches the line of coast and river, and the instinct that is placed in him says, 'Follow these.' So he follows them, remembering that by doing so he has found a place of safety in other seasons. All through the spring and all through the autumn birds take these mysterious flights—for so they always seem to House People, as flock after flock gathers and disappears. You can watch them sometimes passing by day so high in the sky that they seem like dust-motes—then perhaps you will only hear a faint call-note and see nothing. At night the sound of many voices falls from the clouds. Sometimes it will be the tinkling bell of Bobolinks, sometimes the feeble peep of Snipes, and sometimes the hoarse honk of Wild Geese."

"Why, Uncle Roy! Can you tell a bird's name without seeing it, only by one little cry?"

---

[13] In this segment, the authors incorporate environmental education about birds' migrations and how they are tied to seasonality in terms of food availability, and not because birds get too cold.

"Yes, my lad. When you have lived with birds as long as I have, you will know their different voices as you do those of your own family. When some one calls you in the garden, can't you tell whether it is Dodo or Olive?"

"Yes, but their voices are so *very* different."

"So are the voices of birds, when you know them well."

"But the young birds who have been hatched up here—how do they know about going the first time?" asked Rap.

"The young ones are led in their journeys with signals and cries by their parents; they in turn lead their own young, and so the knowledge is kept up endlessly."

"I can see why they go south," said Rap, after thinking a few moments, "but why do they come back again? Why don't they stay and build their nests down there?"

"That is a difficult question to answer," said the Doctor, "and one that we House People try to explain in different ways. I think that the love of the place where they were born is strong enough in birds to bring them back every season to build their nests. So you see that Citizen Bird is a patriot; for, though he may be in the midst of plenty in a tropical forest, when the time comes he travels hundreds of miles to his native land to make the young, that will fly from his nest, citizens like himself."[14]

"But the birds that can eat seeds and other things do not travel so far, do they?" asked Rap.

"No, the birds who rove about the United States throughout the year are either Weed Warriors, or Seed Sowers, or those Tree Trappers who creep about tree-trunks picking the eggs and grubs of insects from the bark. Or else those great Cannibal Birds, the Wise Watchers, who eat the flesh of their smaller brothers, as well as of rats, mice, and all such vermin—the Hawks and Owls; or else they are Gulls, Terns, Fishing Ducks, and a great many other kinds of sea birds who feed on fish and pick up the scraps floating on the surface of sea, lake, and river."

---

[14] As the authors explained a few pages earlier, birds migrate in order to follow their food sources, which includes migration south for the winter and migration north for the spring nesting season and summer. Here, the authors add "patriotism" to the reasons why birds migrate and return to the same area to build their nests, likely as a way of both fulfilling the thematic explanandum of the book (birds as "citizens") but also addressing a question for which scientists did not yet have the answers. There is no one clear explanation of why birds return to the same area for nesting season. The Cornell Lab of Ornithology reports that 20%–60% of migratory songbirds return to the same area two years in a row, and other explanations include the suitability of a nesting site (free from predators, ample food sources, etc.). See ornithological research on the phenomenon of "natal philopatry," the term for the phenomenon wherein animals return to their place of birth to reproduce.

THE BIRD AS A TRAVELLER 47

"Do the Barn Swallows that are making nests in the hayloft go as far south as Kingbirds?" asked Nat.

"Yes, indeed! The Swallows' swift flight carries them far and wide, for not only do they make homes all through North America, but they are so sure of wing and confident of outstripping any cannibal birds who might try to chase them, that when they leave us they fly by day and often stop for a little visit in the West Indies on their way to South America."

"Suppose, Uncle Roy, when they are travelling, a storm comes up and it grows so foggy they can't see how to follow the rivers—don't they sometimes lose themselves?"

"Yes, very often they become confused and fly this way and that, but always toward the nearest place where they see a light, as if it meant escape for them. But this instinct is frequently their death, for they fly against the towers of great lighthouses, or the windows of tall buildings, or even electric wires, and thus break their necks or wings."[15]

"That is why I have so often found dead birds along the turnpike under the telegraph wires," said Rap.

"Yes, Rap, the inventions of man are very wonderful, but some of them have been sad things for Bird People, and this is another reason why we should protect them whenever we can. These journeys that the birds make when they leave their nesting haunts for the winter season, and return again in spring, are called *migrations*.[16] The word 'migrate' means to move from one country to another with the intention of remaining there for some time. The birds who only make little trips about the country, never staying long in one place, we call visitors.

"Birds may be divided according to their journeys into three groups, which will help you to place them:

1. CITIZENS. Those Bird People whose families stay in or near the same place the year round, roving about somewhat according to the food-supply and weather.

---

[15] Building on the point made in Chapter 1, "Overture by the Birds," Doctor Hunter here stresses the negative impacts of anthropogenic activity—the erection of lighthouses, skyscrapers, and telegraph wires—on the natural activities of the animal world.

[16] This is the first use of the term "migration." Previously, the authors referred to birds as "traveling for business." In *Birdcraft*, Wright used the ornithological terms "migratory" or "resident" birds; the use of "citizen" or "visitor" is an artifact of this children's version of a field guide.

2. Summer Citizens. The families that, though they are with us but six or eight months of the year, make their homes here, and pay their rent and taxes by working for the common good. As they are almost all insect-eaters, they are even more useful than the stay-at-home Citizens, who are chiefly seed-eaters or cannibals.

3. Winter Visitors. The birds who come down from the North in severe weather, but do not stay in one place for any particular time, arriving one day and disappearing the next. They glean for their scanty board and return to the cold countries, of which they are Citizens, before nesting-time.

"Please tell me the names of some of the birds that live here all the time," said Nat. "Have I seen any yet?"

"I think the Bluebird, the Robin, and the Song Sparrow are Citizens," said Rap, "because last winter I used to see one or two almost every day, unless the snow and ice were very thick."

"Yes," said the Doctor, "the Bluebird is a Citizen in the Middle and Southern States, and the Robin also. But in the more northerly parts they are Summer Citizens, returning early and staying late. But the Song Sparrow is a Citizen almost everywhere, and is known about every bushy garden from the east coast to the west, and from the cotton plantation to the land of snow."

"Please tell me the names of some winter visitors," said Rap. "Isn't the Great White Owl one of these?"

"Yes, the Snowy Owl is one of them; so is the Snowflake, who comes to us on the wings of the storm; the tiny Winter Wren, the Great Northern Shrike, and many others, who arrive when snow-tide is upon us in the temperate part of the country, after our song birds have flown to the warmer south. You shall hear of all these, and learn where each one lives, in the bird stories I am going to write for you. But now let us go down by the river and see what some of these newly arrived birds are doing after their long journey.

"Hark! I hear the notes of a Thrasher in those bushes, and the Red-winged Blackbirds are calling all through the marsh meadow. When I was a boy the alder bushes were always full of nests."

"They have nests there now," said Rap eagerly; "a great many nests, and they are very pretty. Ah! There is the big brown bird that you call a Thrasher, with his striped breast and long tail that spreads like a fan. I see him—he is building in that barberry bush!"

THE BIRD AS A TRAVELLER   49

"Then the nest comes pretty soon after the up-journey," said Nat.

"Yes," answered the Doctor, as he watched the antics of the Thrasher; "right after the journey the mate, and next the nest. Do not forget the mate, Nat, for it is Mrs. Bird who usually makes the nest and *always* lays the eggs, besides working in the guilds with her husband, whose greatest distinction is in being the family musician."

"When do the Summer Citizens begin to come back to their nesting places?" asked Nat. "And when do they go away again?"

"The great bird procession begins the first of March with Bluebirds, Robins, Redwings, and Meadowlarks, but it is the first of June before the latest comers, the little Marsh Wrens, are settled. Then in autumn, from September until the first snows of December fall, the procession flutters back south again, one by one or in great flocks, dropping away like falling leaves in the forest, and the birds that we see later are likely to be Citizens.

"The early Robin may have a second brood and the Hummingbird eggs in her nest, before the Marsh Wrens have even been seen.

"In the Southern States the birds arrive and build sooner than in the Northern. A cold spring may delay the on-coming migration, or a warm autumn retard the return movement. But as you study birds you will soon see that each one has his own place in the procession, and usually keeps it. Year by year this vast procession goes on in the air, back and forth, night and day, like the ceaseless ebb and flow of the tides at sea. Bird-waves flow on forever, in their appointed times, and none of Nature's aspects are more regular or more unfailing. It almost seems, boys, as if birds made the seasons—as if winter in the Middle and Northern States might be called the 'songless season.'"

CHAPTER 7

The Bird's Nest

"I WONDER WHY SOME BIRDS build their nests so very early, when it is cold, and there are no leaves on the trees, while others wait until it is almost summer," said Rap, as they walked down a narrow lane toward the river. There were bushes lining the path on each side, and from the singing you would think that every bush had a bird on each twig. In fact, there were so many birds in sight that Nat did not know which to ask about first, and so kept looking instead of talking.

"The birds who are Citizens are usually the first to build," answered the Doctor. "They merely roved about during the winter months, and had no long journey to make before they reached the home trees again, and then the hardy seed-eating birds can return from the South much earlier than their frailer kin."

"Last year," said Rap, "when the men were chopping trees in the great wood beyond the lake, the miller went up one day to hunt coons and took me with him. It was the beginning of March and terribly cold; there were long icicles hanging on the trees, and we were glad enough to go in by the fire in the lumbermen's camp. But what do you think?—if there wasn't an Owl's nest, up in a pine tree, with two eggs in it! It was in a very lonely place, and the miller said the Owl had borrowed an old Crow's nest and fixed it up a little."

"I should think the eggs would have frozen hard and been spoiled," said Nat.

"No, the old Owl sat on them ever so tight and would hardly budge to let the miller see them. We didn't stay long, for the Owl was a savage big thing, nearly two feet high, with yellow eyes and long feathers sticking up on its head like horns."

"A Great Horned Owl," said the Doctor. "I only wonder that it let the miller go near it at all; they are generally very wild and fierce."

THE BIRD'S NEST 51

"This one was sort of friends with the lumbermen," continued Rap, "for they used to hang lumps of raw meat on the bushes for it, and they said it kept the rats and mice away from the camp and was good company for them. It frightened me when I heard it first; it gave an awful scream, like a hurt person. After a while another one began to bark like a dog with a cold, just like this—'who-o-o-o—hoo—hoo—hoo.' And, Doctor, one of the lumbermen told me that with Owls and Hawks the female is mostly bigger than the male. Do you think that is so? Because with singing birds the male is the largest."

"Among cannibal birds the female is usually the largest," answered the Doctor, who was pleased to see that Rap so often had a "because" for his questions. "These birds do a great deal of fighting, both in catching their living prey and holding their own against enemies; and as the female stays most at home, being the chief protector of the nest, she needs more strength."

"Some singing birds are real plucky too," said Rap. "That same year I found a Robin's nest in April, when the water-pail by the well froze every night, and a Woodcock's nest in the brushwood. It's hard to see a Woodcock on the nest, they look so like dead leaves. It snowed a little that afternoon, and the poor bird's back was all white, but there she sat. It made me feel so sorry, and I was so afraid she might freeze, that I made a little roof over her of hemlock branches. And she liked that and didn't move at all; so then I wiped the snow off her back, and she seemed real comfortable.[1] I used to go back every day after that to see her; we grew to be quite friends before the four eggs hatched, and I've seen them do queer little tricks; but I never told anybody where she lived, though, because lots of people don't seem to understand anything about birds but shooting or teasing them."

"Some day you shall tell us about what the Woodcock did, my lad. You must tell us a great many stories, for you know what you have seen yourself. That is the best knowledge of all, and it will encourage Nat to hear you," and Dr. Hunter put his arm affectionately around the shoulders of each boy.

"Hush! Wait a moment and listen to that Thrasher," said the Doctor, stopping behind some thick bushes; "he is wooing his mate!"

"What is wooing?" whispered Nat.

---

[1] This story of Rap's—particularly the detail about wiping the snow off a wild bird's back—provoked incredulity in at least one reviewer, who noted that it was one of the few instances in *Citizen Bird* where the authors diverged from a realistic depiction of the natural world. (See Clinton Hart Merriam's [C.H.M.] review of *Citizen Bird* in appendix 1.)

"Asking her to marry him and come and build a cosy home in one of these nice bushes. Listen! See! There he is, up on the very top of that young birch, with his head thrown back, singing as if his throat would split." As the children looked up they saw a fine bird with a curved beak, rusty-brown back, and light breast streaked with black, who was clinging to a slender spray, jerking his long tail while he sang.

"It seems as if I could almost hear the words he says," said Rap.

"Birds sing in many different tones," said the Doctor. "The Thrasher's song is like some one talking cheerfully; the Meadowlark's is flute-like; the Oriole's is more like clarion notes; the Bobolink bubbles over like a babbling brook; while the dear little brown striped Song Sparrow, who is with us in hedge and garden all the year, sings pleasant home-like ballads."

"There are some birds that Olive told me can't sing a bit," said Nat, "but only call and squeak. How do they ask their mates to marry them?"

"All birds have alarm cries, and a call-note that serves the same purpose as a song, although it may not seem at all musical to us. We are naturally more interested in that order of birds whose voices are the most perfectly developed. These not only sing when they are courting, but all the time their mates are sitting upon the eggs, and until the young are ready to fly."

"Why do birds always build nests in spring?" asked Nat.

"I think because there is more for them to feed the little ones with, than when it gets to be hot and dry," said Rap, "and it gives them time to grow big and strong before winter comes, when they must go away."

"Quite right, Rap, and it also gives the parents a chance to shed the old feathers that have been worn by rubbing on the nest, grow a new, thick, warm coat for winter, and rest themselves before they set out on their autumn journey. Do you remember what I told you that rainy day in my study about this moulting or changing of feathers?"

"Yes, I do," said Rap and Nat together. "Most birds have two coats a year, and the male's is the brighter," continued Nat eagerly, proud to show that he remembered. "The one that comes out in the spring is the gayest, so that his mate shall admire him and when this coat comes he sings his very best and—"

"Stop and take breath, my boy," laughed the Doctor; "there is plenty of time. Why do we think that the male has the gayest feathers—do you remember that also?"

"No, I've forgotten," said Nat.

"I remember," cried Rap; "it is to please the female and because she sits so much on the nest that if her feathers were as bright as the male's her enemies would see her quicker, and when the little birds hatch out they are mostly in plain colors too, like their mother."

"Oh, I remember that now," said Nat. "And after the young are hatched and the old birds need new coats, they keep rather still while they shed their feathers, because they feel weak and can't fly well."

"Then when the new feathers come they are sometimes quite different from the old ones, and seldom quite so bright—why is this, Nat?" asked the Doctor. But Nat could not think, and Rap answered: "Because in the autumn when they make the long journeys the leaves are falling from the trees, and if they were very bright the cannibal birds would see them too quickly."

"Have I told you about the Bluebird, and how, though he only sheds his feathers once a year, yet his winter coat is rusty and not bright clear blue as it is in spring?"

"I think not," answered Nat.

"Well, the outside edges of its feathers are blue, but a little deeper in the feather is brownish. So when they have worn the same feathers many months, and rubbed in and out of their little houses and bathed a great deal and cleaned their feathers off every day in the dust, as birds always do, the blue ends wear off and the rusty parts show. It is quite worth while to tell little people things when they have the patience to listen and the interest to remember."

"Yes, uncle, but it's the way you tell us about birds that makes us remember. You talk as if they were real people."

"Oh, oh, Nat!" laughed the Doctor, "if you flatter me so I shall have to hide my head in a bush like an Ostrich. Birds *are* people, though of another race from ours, and I am happy if I can make you think so. Ah! we must be near a Redwing's nest— what a commotion the colony is making!"

"Colony? I thought a colony was a lot of people who went off into a strange wild land and made a new home," said Nat.[2]

"That is one meaning of the word, but another one is when a number of people of the same race or trade live close to each other. A bird colony is a collection of the homes of many birds of the same family. After the nesting season almost all birds live in flocks of different sizes, each particular kind flocking by itself; but

---

[2] While the ostensible function of this moment is to reassert the naturalist definition of the world, this moment still reminds the reader of the dominant definition of "colony" and its association with imperialist expansion, something in which the United States was actively engaged at the time.

during the migrations great flocks are often made up of smaller flocks of various kinds of birds. During the nesting season it is quite different; the majority of birds prefer a quiet home life, each pair being independent of any others. Certain flocks, however, keep together, and all build their nests in a particular swamp or wood, and sometimes, it is said, male birds build nests to sleep in while the females are sitting. The Redwings nest in colonies; so do the Herons, who eat frogs and nest near water, and the little brown-cloaked Bank Swallows, who live in holes that they dig for themselves in high banks."

There were some twenty pairs of birds in this Redwing colony, who seemed to be much frightened by the approach of visitors.

"Here is a nest in this alder bush," said the Doctor; "step carefully on the grass hummocks, and look at it for a moment, Nat. See how neatly it is made of the dried leaves of flags and grasses, woven in and out between three upright stalks."

"Isn't it pretty?" said Nat; "so even and deep like a cup, and not at all ragged and mussy like a Robin's nest. There are a great many different kinds of nests, aren't there, uncle?"

"Yes, the nests of birds are almost as different as their songs and other habits, and the higher the order the brood belongs to the better built is the nest. The lower orders often only make a hollow in the ground or grass, but do not collect material and *build* in the true sense. None such can be called architects."[3]

"What is an architect?" asked Nat, who thought it was a pretty big name for any sort of a bird. "An architect, my boy," said the Doctor, "is anybody who knows how to build anything as it ought to be built, to look the best and be the most useful, whether it is a house or a nest."

"I wonder why nests are so different," said Rap, looking down the lane toward the river where the sun was streaming in and so many little birds were flying to and fro that they seemed like last year's leaves being blown about.

"Because, as the habits of the birds cause them to live in different places, and feed in various ways, so their homes must be suitable to their surroundings, and

---

[3] In comparing birds to architects, the authors reify the human-animal divide by explaining that birds do not build houses in the same careful way that human architects do. This type of comparison was common in the nineteenth century, as the study of animal behavior had not developed to the extent that scientists understood animals' reasoning or tool use, for example. A classic example comes from Karl Marx's descriptions of "species being" in *Capital: A Critique of Political Economy* (London: Penguin Books, 1867 [1990]: 283–284), when he compared human workers who think and plan to animals who merely follow instinct: "We presuppose labour in a form in which it is an exclusively human characteristic. A spider conducts operations which resemble those of the weaver, and a bee would put many a human architect to shame by the construction of its honeycomb cells. But what distinguishes the worst architect from the best of bees is that the architect builds the cell in his mind before he constructs it in wax."

be built in the best way to protect the young birds from harm—to keep them safe from House People, cannibal birds, and bad weather.

"The trim Thrushes and Sparrows, who are all brownish birds, and find their insect or seed food on or near the ground, build open nests low down in trees and bushes, or on the earth itself; but the gorgeous Baltimore Oriole, with his flaming feathers, makes a long pocket-shaped nest of string and strong plant fibres, which he swings high up in an elm tree, where it cannot be reached from below, and the leaves hide this cradle while the winds rock it. He knows that it would never do to trust his brilliant feathers down by the ground.

"The frail Hummingbird has no real strength to fight enemies bigger than its tiny self, but it has been given for protection the power of flying as quick as a whizzing bullet, and courage enough to attack even a Kingbird in defence of its nest, which is a tiny circle of down, covered with lichens, and is so fastened across a branch that it looks like a knot of the limb itself. The Woodcock you saw that snowy day, Rap, knows the protection of color and draws together for a nest a few leaves of the hue of her own feathers. This nest and the bird upon it are so blended together that few eyes could separate them."

"Some birds do not make any nests, but live in holes like squirrels and coons," said Rap. "Woodpeckers and all those."

"There again the home is suited to the occupation of the bird," said the Doctor; "for Woodpeckers are Tree Trappers, who find their food by creeping about trees and picking insects and grubs from the bark. What more natural than that they should have a house close at hand in some tree whose wood is soft enough to be hollowed out? You see they have a bill like a chisel for gouging out insects, and with this same tool they make their homes."

"Bluebirds and Wrens and Martins like to live in holes and boxes, though they can't make holes for themselves," said Rap.

"Yes, the habits of many birds have changed since the country has become civilized and House People are to be found in all parts of it.[4] Many birds, who have always been favorites with man, and have been protected by him, have gradually grown less wild, or almost tame, and now prefer living near houses and barns to building in wilder places. The Bluebird, Martin, and Wren are three very popular birds. They appreciate cosy homes and are grateful for the boxes built for them,

---

[4] The reference to birds changing their behaviors because of the encroachment of humans into previously wild territories is called behavioral adaptation. Here, the behavioral adaptation in nesting refers to cavity-nesting birds building nests in bird boxes, or birds building their nests in human-made structures, like buildings.

though we know that before they had such things they must have nested in tree holes."

"I wonder where the Chimney Swifts lived before there were any chimneys," said Rap, looking across the fields to where an old stone chimney stood—the only thing left standing of an old farmhouse. Above this chimney, Swifts were circling in shifting curves, now diving inside it, now disappearing afar in the air.

"We think they must have lived in hollow trees as the Tree Swallows do now," said the Doctor; "but when House People began to clear the land they naturally cut down the dead trees first, and so the birds moved to the chimneys."

"I used to call those birds Chimney 'Swallows,' but Olive says they are made more like Hummingbirds and Nighthawks than real Swallows," continued Rap.

"Nighthawks?" said Nat. "I thought Olive said Hawks were cannibal birds. How are they relations of Swallows?"

"That is a mistake a great many people make," said the Doctor; "for the Nighthawk is not a real Hawk, but a shy bird, who has a rapid hawk-like flight, though it eats nothing but beetles, moths, and other insects. Hark! Do you hear that cry high in the air?"

"As if something was saying 'shirk-shirk'?" said Nat.

"Yes; that is a Nighthawk on its way home. Look! he is over us now, and you can see two large white spots like holes in his wings. By these you can tell it from any of the real Hawks."

"Does he build high up in a tree?" asked Rap. "I have never found his nest."

"There is a good reason for that," said the Doctor. "There is no nest. Two eggs are laid on the bare ground, that is about the same color as the bird itself; and the eggs look too much like streaky pebbles to be easily seen. When the young are hatched they keep still until they are able to fly, and are colored so exactly like the place upon which they rest that it is almost impossible to see them, even if you know where they are."

"How much there is to learn!" sighed Nat. "I'm afraid you will have to make us a big book instead of a little one, Uncle Roy, to teach us all these things. Olive and Rap have such a start of us. Dodo and I don't know much of anything, and even what I thought I knew about birds isn't very true."

"Don't be discouraged, my boy; you do not need a big book—a little one will do for the present. What you need is patience, a pair of keen eyes, and a good memory. With these and a little help from Olive, Rap, and your old uncle, you can learn to know a hundred kinds of every-day birds—those that can be found easily, and have either the sweetest songs, the gayest plumage, or the most interesting habits. Some we shall find here in the lane and swamp meadow, or by the river. Others have made their home in my orchard for years. And I am going to put in the book more than a hundred beautiful pictures for you and Dodo, drawn so naturally that you can tell every one of the birds by them, and that will make it easier for you to understand what you read.

"For some of the water birds we must go up to the lake or in the summer make a trip over to the seashore. How do you like that? Yes, you too, Rap. By and by, when you know these hundred birds by name and by sight, you will be so far along on the road into Birdland that you can choose your own way, and branch off right and left on whatever path seems most attractive to you; but then you will need big books, and have to learn long hard Latin names."

"What birds will you begin with, please, Doctor Roy," said Rap, "the singers or the cannibals?"

"The singers, because they will interest Dodo and Nat the most easily, as they do you. Then we will talk about the birds that only croak and call; then the cannibal birds; next those that coo, and those that scratch for a living. Then we must leave dry land and go close to the water to find the birds that wade; and finally, we must go to the lake or sea itself for the birds that swim and dive."

"Why, here's Quick!" cried Nat, as the little fox-terrier came leaping down the lane, tracking them, nose to the ground. "How did you get out of the barn, sir?"

"I suspect that Dodo has discovered that we are missing and is looking for us," said the Doctor. "There is the breakfast bell. Do you realize, my lads, that we have been out two hours?"

"I often come out early in the morning," said Rap, "so it doesn't seem strange to me."

"I'm starving, Uncle Roy," said Nat, "though I am only beginning to feel it."

"Think how much worse you would have felt if you had not eaten some bread and milk before you started."

"Yes, indeed," said Nat. "Do many sicknesses come from not eating enough?"

"Not so many as come from eating too much!" laughed the Doctor. "Won't you come up to breakfast with us, Rap? There is always room at my table, you know, for children who love their Bird Brothers."

"I can't," said Rap regretfully; "you see it's Thursday and I have to mind clothes!"

There was a merry breakfast party that morning at Orchard Farm; Nat had so much to tell, and the Doctor said he felt twenty years younger after his walk with the boys. A letter had also arrived which made Nat and Dodo very happy; it was from their mother, who said: "We are delighted to hear that the Doctor is going to tell you bird stories this summer. Be sure to ask Olive to tell you all she knows about the flowers too. When we come home this autumn, perhaps your uncle will ask us to the Farm for a visit, and then we shall see your friend Rap."

"Uncle, uncle!" cried both the children, "will you ask mother and father to come here for a little? It will be lovely, and—and then we shan't have to go away so soon either."

"I have already asked them for a long visit, you little rogues," said the Doctor. "You seem to forget that your mother is my sister, whom I wish very much to see."

"And does Olive know all the flowers," chimed in Dodo, "and will you tell us about everything?"

"That would be a rash promise," said the Doctor, laughing; "but if you will stay long enough I will promise to teach you something about all the little wild beasts and bugs that live here, the flowers that bloom about us, the earth, moon, and perhaps even a star or two! Who knows? Is it a bargain?"

"Oh, *uncle!*" was all they said. But Dodo gave him a kiss on the end of his nose and Nat hugged Olive, who sat next to him. Just then Mammy Bun brought in a plate of steaming hot flannel cakes, and the Doctor said: "Now let us eat to the health of Birdland and a happy season at Orchard Farm! Olive, my love, please pass the maple syrup!"

CHAPTER 8

Beginning of the Bird Stories

WHEN THE DAY CAME for beginning the bird stories, warm spring showers were drenching the orchard, so that apple blossoms and raindrops fell to the ground together when the children gathered in the wonder room once more. This time there was no fire on the hearth; through the open window floated bits of birdsong and the fragrance of the lilacs—for there were lilac bushes all about Orchard Farm, close to the house, by the gate posts, and in a long hedge that ran down one side of the garden to the orchard itself. These tall bushes of purple and white lilacs were veritable music boxes, for almost every one held a Catbird's nest.[1]

"What bird do you think Uncle Roy will tell us about first?" said Nat to Rap, as they walked about the room, looking at the birds in the cases, while the Doctor was reading letters which Olive had brought in.

"I wish he would begin with that lovely fat bird, with all the red and green and blue feathers," said Dodo, pointing to a Wood Duck. "I wonder if it sings."

"No, that's a Duck and they don't sing," said Rap; "they gabble and squawk and swim in the water, but they can fly as quick as Swallows, for all they look so heavy."

"I wish he would begin with this little mite of a thing, that isn't much bigger than a bee," said Nat, showing Rap a Hummingbird.

"I don't care what bird he starts with," said Rap, "only I hope he will begin at the very beginning."

---

[1] Here, the authors tap into the conventions of nature writing in which seasonality is described by a variety of factors. Here, spring is not simply a time on the calendar, but rather it is when the apple trees and lilacs are blossoming, birds are singing, and there is no need for a fire in the fireplace. This holistic description also teaches children about what Stella Capek, in "Of Time, Space, and Birds" (2005), called "bird space" and "bird time." The lilac bushes are full of Catbird nests (bird space) during spring (bird time).

"That is a good idea, my boy," said the Doctor, who had finished his letters and was leaving his desk; "only what and where is the beginning?"

The children looked at each other in silence, and Olive said: "That is a very hard question for them to answer. No wonder they looked so puzzled, father."

Then the Doctor laughed and said: "The people who have studied the birds, bone by bone and feather by feather, have grouped these Citizens into orders and families to prevent confusion, so that we may easily tell the relationship between them. These lists sometimes begin with the lowest order, nearest to the crawling, reptile brethren,—the least interesting, far-away birds that have no song and cannot fly well, but swim and dive in the water,—and end with the beautiful singing birds that live in our gardens."[2]

"Couldn't you begin with the dear singing birds and end with the far-away clumsy diving ones?" asked Rap earnestly; "it's so much easier learning about things near home."

"You are right, my boy. In learning anything, whether of bird, insect, or flower, begin at home, and let this be the centre from which you work your way onward and outward. Then you will be sure of what you learn; and ever afterward, though you may follow strange birds all over the known world, you will come home again, to find that there are none more charming and lovable than those few whose acquaintance you will make this summer.

"I do not wish you to be confused by long words, so I shall give you their plain English names and divide these birds of our stories into six classes.[3] By and by,

---

[2] To contemporary birdwatchers, the order in which birds are presented in *Citizen Bird* will look haphazard. Most contemporary field guides begin with waterfowl like ducks and geese, moving on to birds of prey and woodland birds like woodpeckers and owls, and ending with the songbirds such as warblers, passerines, and finches. However, the order in which birds are presented in this volume makes sense in two ways. First, it follows the practice at the time of field guides and keys beginning with songbirds and ending with waterfowl, as both Wright and Coues did in their earlier field guides and keys. Second, it makes sense in terms of children's environmental education. A now-common children's environmental education strategy is to begin with the most common birds, so children can enjoy the excitement of learning birds they see most often. *Citizen Bird* presages this practice with its localized strategy, as when Dr. Hunter explains, "begin at home, and let this be the centre from which you work your way onward and outward." Wright explains these differences in order of presentation in her earlier field guide *Birdcraft*: "In modern science, classification follows the method of natural evolution, grading from the lowest forms to the highest. Under this system the Diving Water-birds should head the list, and the Thrush Family of Song-birds end it. Some time ago, a different system obtained, that of beginning with the highest orders and descending in the scale, and the birds in this book are so arranged. The reason for doing this is that it presents the Song-birds first, and it is to these that you will be first attracted, and, finding many of them familiar, you will be led by easy stages to the Birds of Prey and the Water-birds, which probably you have had less chance to know. If, however, you prefer to habituate yourself to the more modern method, all that you have to do is to begin at the end of the book and work backward" (p. 37).

[3] As noted in chapter 5, footnote 11, Wright used six categories to organize birds in *Birdcraft: A Field Book of Two Hundred Song, Game, and Water Birds* (London: Macmillan & Co., 1895). Coues's *Key to North American Birds* (Boston: Estes and Lauriat, 1872) included thirteen families and orders of birds. In *Citizen Bird*, these six categories are based on birds' behaviors and are called "guilds." While the names of the individual guilds do not necessarily emphasize

BEGINNING OF THE BIRD STORIES   61

when you have heard a few facts about them, we will group them into families; and I will tell you so much that, if you use your eyes well, you will be able to name any one of these birds when you see it out in the open air. You must always remember, children, when you see birds flying about, that you will not notice many little markings and bits of color that would be quite plain to you if you held the bird in your hand, or looked at it in a case, as you look at these stuffed ones now. A bird, whose breast is spotted may look striped when seen at a distance.

"When you are in doubt about the name of a bird that you have seen, you can come here and look for it; but very few children can do so. At best they can only look at pictures, and I do not wish you to depend upon the specimens in this room."

"No," said Rap, "because if our bird stories are printed, and other children read them, they may not have an uncle with a 'wonder room'; and so they must learn the names without."[4]

"That is another reason why we must have a great many pictures in our book, for these children," said the Doctor. "Now write the names of the six classes into which all our birds are to be gathered.

   I. The Birds that Sing.
  II. The Birds that Croak and Call.
 III. The Birds that are Cannibals.
 IV. The Birds that Coo and Scratch.
  V. The Birds that Wade and Paddle.
 VI. The Birds that Swim and Dive.

Squeak, squeak, went three pencils, two going fast and one toiling along as if it was lame and needed sharpening.

"Please, uncle, what birds are cannibals?" asked Dodo, as she finished writing this last word slowly, taking great pains. "I thought cannibals were people that ate each other."

"Well, my dear, so they are; and cannibal birds are those who *sometimes* eat each other."

---

birds' behavior as "good citizens," the term "guild" evokes the authors' emphasis on birds' labor, like the guild organizations of tradespeople in medieval times.

[4] Here is another explanation and justification for the printing and utility of *Citizen Bird*, including its illustrations, which makes explicit the authors' goal of bringing environmental education to children across the class spectrum, not just those who "have an uncle with a 'wonder room.'"

"If you please, Doctor, which of the birds that sing will you begin with?" asked Rap. "I wonder if we can guess it."

"You may all try," said the Doctor. "It is a bird that every one loves—the home bird who is so fond of House People that whenever we see one, we know that there is a house not far away."

"Then it must be the Bluebird!" cried Rap.

"You are right," said the Doctor; "and if you will come here by the window you can watch a pair who are flying in and out of the bird house, on top of the woodshed. Do you hear? Bluebirds have a call-note and a sweet warbling song. As I have told you before, all birds have some note or sound that they use to attract attention or call their mates; but it is only those whose voices are so highly developed that they can make really continuous musical sounds, that are called song birds.

"The male is the only real singer in Birdland. Many females have pretty musical notes that they give when about the nest, and some scraps of song; one or two are quite good musicians, but the great chorus comes from the males.

"These have their seasons for singing, and are not in equal voice during the entire year. They sing most persistently from the time they put on their spring coat, until after the nesting season, when they take it off. In early autumn some species sing for a time, and in warm climates there is more or less music all winter; but the great morning and evening chorus belongs to spring and the nesting season. It is as rare to hear the perfect song of a bird in autumn, as it is to see its perfect plumage. The young birds of the season are then swelling their little throats in trying to warble a few notes; and as their feathers are a mixture of those worn by their father and mother, such birds and their songs will both, most likely, confuse you.

"When you find a strange bird, try to see quickly a few of the things most necessary to naming him. I will make a measure of your middle finger for you such as Olive used to wear. Then you must try to answer the following questions:[5]

"How many inches long was he?

"What was his general color?

"Was his breast plain or speckled?

---

[5] The questions Dr. Hunter tells the children to ask themselves in order to identify a bird are still used as guiding questions in contemporary field guides. The Peterson's line of field guides instructs people to note the bird's size and shape, including the shape of its wings, bill, and tail. Then, it goes on to ask about its behaviors, including how it flies and whether it swims or wades, as well as other identifying features.

"What was he doing—feeding on the ground or in a tree?

"Did he walk with one foot after the other, or hop with both feet together?

"Did he sing or only call?

"At first you may only remember two or three of these questions, and they will probably be his size, color, and song, if he happens to be singing at the time.

"You may not think that a bird, who is hopping about in the grass or flitting among the branches of a tree, is doing anything in particular. But really he may be either collecting material for his nest, or searching for food of some particular kind, in a way which will tell you to what guild of the Bird Brotherhood he belongs.

"Everything in the daily life of a bird is interesting. You will find that every bird has its regular times for bathing, pluming, eating, sleeping, working, and playing, all in its own ways, just as you yourselves have. And everything he does is done cheerfully and promptly.

"I know that you think this a very long sermon, and that you would rather see a bird than be told how to see it. Only one word more. I am going to give you, as we go along, a few facts about the color and size of each bird, that you may write in your books; so that if you forget whether this bird or that one was striped or spotted you can look at your 'bird table' (not multiplication table) and see which it was. Now we will begin with our dear Bluebird."

CHAPTER 9

A Silver-Tongued Family

THE BLUEBIRD

"It will be difficult for you to mistake this little blue-coat for any other bird.[1] He is 'true blue,' which is as rare a color among birds as it is among flowers. He is the banner-bearer of Birdland also, and loyally floats the tricolor from our trees and telegraph wires; for, besides being blue, is he not also red and white?"

"To be sure, his breast is perhaps more brown than red, but when the spring sun shines on his new feathers, as he flits to and fro, it is quite bright enough to be called red. All sorts and conditions of people love and respect the Bluebird; all welcome him to their gardens and orchards. The crossest old farmer, with his back bent double by rheumatism, contrives to bore some auger holes in an old box and fasten it on the side of the barn, or set it up on the pole of his hayrick; while the thrifty villager provides a beautiful home for his blue-backed pets—a real summer hotel, mounted on a tall post above a flower-bed, with gables and little windows under the eaves.

"Why does this bird receive so much attention?[2] There are many others with gayer plumage and more brilliant songs. It is because the Bluebird is gentle, useful, brave, and faithful under adversity, while he and the Robin are the first two birds that children know by name. We must live in a very cold, windswept

---

[1] This is the first of the field guide chapters. From this point forward, the book follows this model of presenting a few birds at a time in the form of a story, with a more typical field guide description of each bird at the end of the chapter.

[2] The authors explain why the Eastern Bluebird and American Robin are the two first birds in this field guide: they are two of the most common birds that many American children already recognize and know by name. Also note the Bluebird is now called Eastern Bluebird, to distinguish it from Mountain Bluebirds and Western Bluebirds.

part of the country not to have some of these birds with us from March until Thanksgiving day, and then, when a week has passed and we have not seen a single one, we say winter has come in earnest. When weeks go by and our eyes grow tired of the glare of the snow, or our hearts discouraged at the sight of bare lifeless trees and stretches of brown meadow—suddenly, some morning, we hear a few liquid notes from an old tree in a sunny spot. All eagerness, we go out to see if our ears have deceived us. No, it is a Bluebird! He is peeping into an old Woodpecker's hole and acting as if he had serious thoughts of going to housekeeping there, and did not intend waiting to move in until May-day either. When you see him you may know that, though there is still ice on the water-trough and on the little streams, spring is only around the corner, waiting for her friend, the sun, to give her a little warmer invitation to join him in their old, old play of turning the sluggish sleeping brown earth into a wonderful green garden again.

Bluebird.

"As a Citizen the Bluebird is in every way a model. He works with the Ground Gleaners in searching the grass and low bushes for grasshoppers and crickets; he searches the trees for caterpillars in company with the Tree Trappers; and in eating blueberries, cranberries, wild grapes, and other fruits he works with the Seed Sowers also.

"So who would not welcome this bird, who pays his rent and taxes in so cheerful a manner, and thanks you with a song into the bargain? A very few straws are all that he asks for his housekeeping, and every time he promises a meal for his household, scores of creeping, crawling, hopping garden enemies are gobbled up. Then he, modest little fellow that he is, comes to the roof of the shed and murmurs his thanks for your hospitality, as if you and not he had done the favor; he continues to whisper and warble about it all the way down the meadow until, having caught another grasshopper, his mouth is too full for singing."

As the Doctor was speaking the shower cloud passed over, and the sun burst out full upon the Bluebirds that were building by the woodshed.

"Oh, they *are* red, white, and blue!" cried Dodo in great glee, "though the red is a little dirty,—not so fresh and bright as the color in our new flag."

"It is more the red of the ragged old flag they keep down in the Town Hall—the one that has seen service," said Rap thoughtfully.

SOME THINGS TO REMEMBER ABOUT THE BLUEBIRD

Length (from tip of beak over head to end of tail) seven inches.

Upper parts clear bright blue.

Throat and breast reddish earth color.

Belly white.

A Summer Citizen of the United States, and a Citizen of the milder parts of our
country.

A member of the guilds of Ground Gleaners, Tree Trappers, and Seed Sowers.

THE AMERICAN ROBIN

"Another home bird, first cousin to the Bluebird, coming with it in the spring, and often lingering through the winter in places that the Bluebird is obliged to leave—"

"The Robin a cousin of the Bluebird!" interrupted Nat; "why, they don't look one bit alike—how can it be, Uncle Roy?"

"I expected you to ask that question," said the Doctor. "The relationship of bird families, like that of other animals, is based upon a likeness in the formation of their bodies, and not upon mere size or color.[3] That sort of likeness proves that their ancestors of long ago were the same, so that they are descended from one pair of very great-great-grandparents; and that always makes cousins, you know. It runs in the blood; thus, a cat and a tiger are blood relations; the little coon and the great black bear are nearly akin. A tall broad-shouldered man, with black hair and a full beard, may have a cousin who is short and

American Robin.

---

[3] Here, the authors come close to explaining evolution as they describe the bird classification system in terms of "the formation of their bodies" and how "their ancestors of long ago were the same."

A SILVER-TONGUED FAMILY   67

thin, with yellow hair and no beard. You see nothing strange in this, because it is something to which you are accustomed. But with bird families it takes the trained eye of the student to see the likeness there really is between all birds who have had the same ancestors, though it may be hidden under many differences in their size, shape, color, voice, and habits.

"The Robin, like the Bluebird, is found in almost all parts of North America. In the far Southern States, like Florida, where they take refuge from winter storms, Robins begin to sing in chorus while the weather in the Middle and Northern States is still so cold that it would freeze the music before any one could hear it, even if the birds had courage to sing. But delightful as the climate is there, where it also provides a plentiful table of berries, these Robins break away from the land of plenty and begin their northern journey before the first shad dares venture up the rivers.

"On and on they go, this great army of Robins, flying in flocks of ten and hundreds. Here and there they meet with smaller flocks, which have been able to spend the winter in roving about not far from their nesting places, and then there is a great deal of talking; for the Robin has a great many ways of making remarks. Some of his numerous notes sound as if he were asking a long list of questions; others express discontent; then again he fumes and sputters with anger. It is easy to tell the plump, well-fed birds, just home from the South, from those who have been obliged to live on half rations during the northern winter.

"Before this flying army quite leaves the Southern States some of them halt for nest-building, and then the Robin sings the best of all his songs,—his happy, cheery melody,—all about the earth, the sky, the sun, the tree he and his mate have chosen to build in,—a song of the little brook where he means to get the water to wet the clay to plaster his nest,—a ballad of the blue eggs it will hold, and the greedy little Robins, all eyes and mouth, that will come out of them. But as he sings something frightens him; then he cries, 'quick! quick! quick!' and hurries away in a rather clumsy fashion. If any one could understand the meaning of all that the Robin says and put it into our words, we should be able to make a very good dictionary of the language of Birdland."

"I've noticed how different his songs are," said Rap eagerly, "and how some of his ways are like the Bluebird's, too. We had a Robin's nest last season in the grape vine over the back door, and I used to watch them all the time—" and then Rap hesitated in great confusion, for fear that he had been impolite in stopping the Doctor.

"Tell us about your Robins, my boy; we shall like to hear the story. Don't look so troubled, but say exactly what you saw them do."[4]

Rap wriggled about a little, then settled himself comfortably with his chin resting on the top of his crutch, and began: "It was the year that my leg was hurt. The miller was chopping a tree and it fell the wrong way on me and squeezed my leg so that it couldn't be mended; so I was around home all the time. It was a terribly cold day when the Robins came back, along in the first part of March. If it hadn't been for the Robins, anybody would have thought it was January. But in January we don't have big Robin flocks about here, only just twos and threes that pick round the alder bushes and old honeysuckles for berries. It was such a cold day that the clothes froze to the line so that mother couldn't take them off, and we didn't know what to do. Well, we were looking at them, mother and I, when a big Robin flew out of the pine trees and hopped along the clothes-line as if he wanted to speak to us. 'Maybe he's hungry,' said mother. 'I guess he is,' said I; 'the ground is too hard for worms to come out, so he can't get any of them. Can't I give him some of the dried huckleberries?' We always dry a lot every summer, so as to have pies in winter. Mother said I might, so I scattered some on the snow under the pine trees, and we went in the house and peeped out of the kitchen window. At first the Robins chattered and talked for a while, looking squint-eyed at the berries, but then the bird that came on the clothes-line started down and began to eat."

"How did you know that Robin from all the others?" asked Dodo.

"He had lost the two longest quills out of his right wing, and so he flew sort of lop-sided," said Rap readily. "As soon as he began the others came down and just gobbled; in two minutes all the berries were gone, but the birds stayed round all the same, hinting for more. We hadn't many berries left, so mother said, 'Try if they will eat meal.' I mixed some meal in a pan with hot water and spread it in little puddles on the snow. The Robins acted real mad at first, because it wasn't berries, but after a while one pecked at it and told the others it was all right, and then thirty Robins all sat in a row and ate that meal up, the same as if they were chickens." Here Rap paused and laughed at the thought of the strange sight.

---

[4] Rap's story about his close personal affinity with a Robin that, like him, is marked out from the rest of the flock by its injured limb veers close but ultimately stops short of the imaginative liberties taken by contemporary works such as Ernest Thompson Seton's *Wild Animals I Have Known* (New York: Charles Scribner's Sons, 1898), short stories about supposedly real encounters with animals there were derided as the products of "nature fakers." See Lutts (1990) *The Nature Fakers: Wildlife, Science, and Sentiment.*

A SILVER-TONGUED FAMILY   69

"Pretty soon after that the snow melted, and by April Robins were building around in our yard, in the maples by the road, and all through this orchard. One day I noticed some little twigs and a splash of mud on our back steps, and when I looked up I saw that something was building a nest in the crotch of the old grape vine. 'That's a queer place for a nest,' I said to myself, 'not a leaf on the vine and my window right on top. I wonder what silly bird is doing it.'

"Flap, and my Robin with the broken feathers came along with his mouth full of sticks; but when he saw me he dropped them and went over on the clothes-pole, and called and scolded like everything. Then I went up to my window and looked through the blind slats. Next day the nest was done. It wasn't a pretty nest—Robins' never are. They are heavy and lumpy, and often fall off the branches when a long rain wets them. This one seemed quite comfortable inside, and was lined with soft grass.

"Mrs. Robin looked like her husband, but I could tell the difference; for she didn't sit in the pines and sing, and her breast wasn't so red. When the nest was done, she laid a beautiful egg every day until there were four, and then one or the other of the birds sat on the eggs all the time. Robins' eggs are a queer color—not just blue or quite green, but something between, all of their own."

"Yes," said Olive, "it is their own color, and we give it a name; for it is called 'robin's-egg blue' in our books."

"The old birds had been sitting for ten days, and it was almost time for the little ones to come out, when one night there was a great wind and the grape vine, that was only fastened up with bits of leather and tacks, fell down in a heap. In the morning there was the nest all in a tangle of vine down on the ground. The vine must have swung down, for it hadn't tipped the nest over, and the mother bird was sitting on it still.

"'That will never do,' said my mother; 'the first cat that strays by will take the poor thing.' While I was looking at it mother went in the house and came back with a little tin pail. She picked some branches and tied them round it so that the tin didn't show. 'Now,' she said to the Robin, the same as if it understood our language, 'get up and let me see if I can't better you a bit.' Then the bird left the nest, making a great fuss, and crying 'quick! quick!' as if all the woods were afire.

"'Oh, mother!' I cried, 'the eggs will get cold. What are you taking the nest away for? It was better to chance the cats.'

"'Don't you fret, sonny,' said she; 'your mammy has some common sense if she don't trampoose all over creation watching birds.' And before I understood what she was doing she had put the nest in the top of the tin pail and hung it on a hook under the shed roof. 'Now,' she said, 'Mrs. Robin, try how you like that!'

"I watched and after a few minutes first one Robin flew under the shed and then the other, and the next thing one was sitting on the pail-nest as nice as you please!"

"Did the birds hatch?" asked Olive, Nat, and Dodo, almost in the same breath.

"Yes, they hatched all right; and then I noticed something funny. The backs and breasts of the little birds were almost naked when they were hatched, and their eyes closed tight; but when the feathers came they were spotted on their backs and breasts and not plain like their parents. Do you know," added Rap after a little pause, "that when Bluebirds are little, their backs and breasts are speckled too, though afterward they moult out plain? So there is something alike about Bluebirds and Robins that even a boy can see."

"You are quite right," said the Doctor; "the 'something alike, that even a boy can see,' is one of the things that shows these birds to be cousins, as I told you. Every one of the Silver-tongued Family is spotted when it gets its first feathers. It is strange," he added in an undertone, as if talking to himself, "how long it took some of us to find out what any bright boy can see."

THE AMERICAN ROBIN—REMEMBER THIS

Length ten inches.

Upper parts slate color with a tinge of brown.

Head black on top and sides, with white spots around the eyes. Tail black with white spots on the tips of some feathers.

Under parts brick-red, except the black and white streaked throat and under the tail.

A Citizen of the United States and Canada.

A Ground Gleaner, Tree Trapper, and Seed Sower.

THE WOOD THRUSH

One pleasant evening after tea, but before sunset, the Doctor sent Nat to ask Rap to come up to the Farm, as they were all going for a walk through the orchard and the river woods.

"What birds will you tell us about to-night?" asked Dodo, as they stood in the porch waiting for the boys.

"Cousins of the Bluebird—more cousins—but really the heads of the Silver-tongued Family. They wear much plainer clothes than the Bluebirds and Robins, on their olive or russet-brown backs and light-tinted, dark-spotted breasts, but have the most beautiful voices in all Birdland. The names of these wonderful singers, who make a musical quartette, are Wood Thrush, Hermit Thrush, Wilson's Thrush, and Olive-backed Thrush; but you will have to keep both your eyes and ears open to learn to tell them apart and name them rightly."

"There has been the beautifullest bird singing in the big elm on the lawn for more than an hour, but I don't know his name and I want to ever so much. Do you think he might be one of these Thrushes? He is singing now, Uncle Roy." And Dodo began tugging at the Doctor's hand, to lead him down the steps. They saw Nat and Rap coming along the road, and the Doctor motioned to them to walk quietly, so that Dodo's bird might continue his song.

"What is it? What are you waiting for?" whispered Nat. "A bird? Where?"

The bird answered Nat's question itself, telling him by its song in what part of the tree it was perching. "Hea-r-me, Hea-r-me," it called; and then followed a short song as if two musical instruments were playing together. The bird seemed well pleased with his performance, and perfectly unconscious of the group of House People who were listening to him; for he repeated the strain over and over again.

"It's almost as big as a Robin," said Dodo.

"But its breast is speckled in big spots," said Nat. "I wish I could see the top of it. There, it has flown to a lower branch, and its back is kind of rusty-brown. What is its name, Uncle Roy?"

"Rap knows, I'm sure," said the Doctor.

"It's a Wood Thrush," said Rap. "People call them Wood Robins, too, sometimes. I think that one, or his brother, has a nest in the spruce back of your house."

"Uoli-uoli, a-e-o-lee-lee!" sang the Thrush; and as the children became accustomed to the song they noticed that six or eight other Silver-tongues were singing the same tune in different parts of the orchard and garden. It sounded as if the evening breeze were stirring Aeolian harps.

"Why is he called the Wood Thrush?" asked Rap. "I've hardly ever seen him in the real woods—he loves to be in gardens and orchards. The trees round the miller's house are full of them."

"It is not easy to say why he was named so," said the Doctor, "unless it is because he builds his nest higher up in trees than most of his Thrush kin. I am very glad you have had a chance to hear and see him at the same time; for he is one of the home birds you must make a place for in your very inside heart, with the Bluebird

Wood Thrush.

and Robin, though he does not return from his winter outing until after these two have begun nesting."

"When he comes we are sure not only that it is Spring, but that Spring is in a pleasant, good-natured mood—that she is through with the tempers and crying fits she suffers from in March and April, and is kissing the buds of the early blossoms of May, coaxing them to open their eyes. When you see the first Wood Thrush hopping among last year's leaves, you may look for jack-in-the-pulpit's pointed nose and green and purple hood.

"As soon as this Thrush makes up his mind to settle in a certain place, he calls a mate to him with his thrilling song and begins house-building. From this time until he moults, late in July, every one in his vicinity may enjoy a free concert morning and evening, and at intervals during the day. Sometimes in cloudy weather he even sings at noon—a time when birds are most likely to be silent.

"In gratitude for what we owe him for his music and his work in the guilds, we must be patient with him when he secures the first ripe cherries from the top of the tree, before we House People know that they are even red. For every cherry and strawberry he bites, he pays ten times over by swallowing a hundred wicked hungry worms and bugs that eat everything and do no work in return. But House People are very blind about some things, and often act as if they had only one eye apiece, like the Cyclopes. We see one of these darling birds take a little fruit; we see more fruit with holes in it, and think that birds have done the damage, though a wasp or hornet may be the guilty party; and then we often say, 'What a nuisance those birds are!'

"But all the rest of the growing year, when these same birds toil from sunrise until sunset, to clear away insect pests and give us a better crop of fruit next year, we do not notice it. You children, however, will have no such excuse for keeping one eye shut when you know Citizen Bird as he really is."

A SILVER-TONGUED FAMILY   73

"How late at night does the Wood Thrush sing?" asked Nat. "Does he never sleep?"

"Oh, yes, he goes to sleep when it is really dark, but at this nesting season the night in Birdland is very short; some of the feathered people are stirring at three o'clock, and by four all thrifty birds have dressed themselves to go out marketing for breakfast."

"The Veeries are singing down by the river," said Olive to her father; "perhaps we had better go there before it grows dark."

"Veeries? Is that what you call those birds?" asked Rap. "I never knew their name, so I called them 'sunset birds,' to myself."

"Veeries, yes, but called Wilson's Thrush, too," said the Doctor; "because this kind of Thrush was named after Alexander Wilson, who wrote a description of it, and published a colored plate of it, seventy-five years ago.[5] But your name of 'sunset bird' is very good, my lad, for they sing best about twilight. We will go down to the river path and hear them, though you cannot see them very clearly now."

THE WOOD THRUSH

The largest of our Thrushes except the Robin—length about eight inches.

Upper parts warm brown, like ground cinnamon; brightest on the head, but a little greenish on the tail.

Under parts plain white in the middle, but boldly spotted with black all over the breast and along the sides.

Eye-ring whitish.

A Summer Citizen of the eastern United States, and a Ground Gleaner, Tree Trapper, and Seed Sower.

WILSON'S THRUSH

Commonly called VEERY from the sound of one of its notes

"How still it is here!" said Dodo, as they walked along the footpath that wound in and out among the trees toward the edge of the river. Swallows were skimming close to the water, which sang a little song to itself as it ran along.

---

[5] The Wilson's Thrush is now called the Veery.

Veery.

"What do you think those birds are doing, Rap," said Nat; "looking at themselves in the water or playing tag?"

"They are Barn Swallows, who catch flies and little gnats and things close down over the water. Hear them talking and laughing!" But the Swallows really seemed to be playing some sort of game as they circled about, every now and then turning sharply and giving little rippling cries.

The Doctor halted under a beech tree that spread its branches over a great mossy circle, seating himself on an old log that had been washed down the river and lay on the ground. For a minute the Veeries were silent; then from the tree over his head one sang a short tune—two sentences in a high key, then two a little lower and softer, like an echo.

"It is different from any other bird-song," said Olive, "and every spring when it comes it seems as lovely as the first time I heard it."

"Is that Veery only visiting here, or will he build a nest?" asked Nat.

"He will build; and though he is so shy that we do not see him as often as the Wood Thrush, his song makes him one of the best-known of the family. He makes his home from the Middle States, east and west, all over the country, up to the far North; but as insects are his chief food he does not come as early or stay as late in his summer home as the Hermit Thrush, and always tries to reach the warmer countries before the trees are wholly bare and there is danger of snow."

"Do they live up in the trees where they sing?" asked Dodo, after they had listened to the Veeries, who were then singing on both sides of the river.

"No, on the contrary, he is one of the Ground Thrushes, who builds his nest close to the ground in such places as that bit of brushwood opposite; and as he spends most of his time about home we seldom see him, even in places like this where many pairs live. But we do not need to see a Veery to know of his presence if we once learn his song by heart, because we shall remember it as long as our hearts beat."

The children sat silent for a long time, looking up through the trees at the coming of the night. Then Dodo nestled close to Olive and whispered, "I think that Veery is singing his prayers."

WILSON'S THRUSH—VEERY

Length seven and a half inches.

Upper parts warm brown all over, not so bright as the Wood Thrush is on the head, and not the least bit greenish on the tail.

Breast and throat deep cream color, finely specked with brown on the upper part. Belly white. No white ring around eye.

A Summer Citizen of the United States east of the plains.

A Ground Gleaner, Tree Trapper, and Seed Sower.

THE HERMIT THRUSH

"When we return to the house," said the Doctor, "I will show you the Veery and Hermit Thrush also; for whether or not you will hear the Hermit sing will depend very much upon what part of North America you live or travel in, and this bird's song is its chief claim to fame. Through all the southern and middle parts of the States he only pays visits during the fall, winter, and early spring. At these seasons he rarely sings, and spends his time in hopping about the underbrush, searching for insects. In spring and autumn you will see him about the magnolia trees in your yard or garden, or in the hedges along roads and the edges of light woods, where wild berries are plentiful. The name of Hermit would naturally make you expect to find a very shy bird, but he is not—only he likes his own company in secret places. When on his travels, unlike most birds, and like all good children in story books, he is oftener seen than heard. At this time you must look for him on or near the ground, for he is a famous Ground Gleaner.

Hermit Thrush.

"At first you may mistake him for a Wood Thrush. But look again—he is smaller; the spots on the breast are more joined together like stripes; the rump and tail are a very *reddish*-brown like ripe chestnuts, different from the *greenish*-brown on the back and head. You will be sure to notice this, for the Hermit jerks his tail about when he feeds on the ground, giving a little warning call that sounds like 'chek! chek!'"

"If you should happen to spend the summer among the mountains of New York, New England, or northern Michigan, and see the Hermit in his nesting home, you would find him quite another character, true to his name. There he is shy—or perhaps cautious would be a better word to describe the way in which he keeps the secrets of his precious nest. He loves the little moist valleys between the pine-clad mountains, where a bit of light woods is made an island by the soft bog-moss that surrounds it. There, feeling quite secure, he makes his nest upon the ground, of moss, leaves, pine-needles, and other such litter; and the eggs that it holds are very nearly the color of the Robin's, without any spots.

"He goes a little way from home, a bit up the mountain side, so that House People and squirrels, both of whom are sometimes cruel enough to steal eggs, may not know exactly where he lives; and then he begins to sing. His brother Thrushes have louder voices and know more brilliant songs; but when the Hermit reaches his high notes, that sound as clear as the music of a mountain brook, a strange feeling will suddenly come over you. You will forget that you belong to House People and that he is a bird; you will think he is telling you something in words that you understand—a message that makes you think about pure and holy things. The songs of some birds please the ear alone, but this little brown Hermit sings to your conscience. Some call him the Spirit of the Pines. If, however, you never hear his song you can remember that the Hermit is the brown bird with the rusty tail and speckled breast that hops among your bushes in spring and fall. You must be very kind to him, and tell your pet cat about him, warning her never to touch him."

THE HERMIT THRUSH

Length about seven inches.

Upper parts an even olive-brown, except the tail, which is rich reddish-brown, different from the rest.

Throat and breast light buff, with black spots that run together in chains.

Belly white. A yellowish ring around the eye.

A Summer Citizen of the northern parts of eastern North America, spending the winter south of its summer home.

A Ground Gleaner, Tree Trapper, and Seed Sower.

THE OLIVE-BACKED THRUSH

"Children who live where the Hermit Thrush sings will also have a good chance to hear the Olive-back give his rapid bubbling music; for, like the Hermit, he prefers a cool summer climate, and thinks that the mountains agree with his health much better than the seashore.[6] For this reason he makes his home all through the Northern States, from the Atlantic to the Pacific, following the mountains southward, and making long summer excursions to Labrador, Hudson Bay, and even Alaska."

"What stories of wild beasts he might tell us if he would! For he looks out of his nest of grass, moss, bark, and rootlets, to see moose browsing among the young trees, and hears black bears growling. His bird companions are Snowbirds, Horned Larks, Crossbills, and Pine Grosbeaks; and he trembles lest the Great Gray Owl shall find his nestlings.

"But much as he loves cool weather for nest-building, he tires of it when the first frost touches the valleys, and snow caps the tops of his favorite mountains; for then his insect food grows scarce. So he changes his summer habits; leaving the guild of Ground Gleaners, and becoming a Seed Sower, he follows the sun toward the tropics, where, likely enough, he tells the alligators long tales of northern lands and assures the water-moccasin that, big snake as he is, the mountain rattlesnake is quicker at biting.

Olive-backed Thrush.

"This Olive-backed Thrush you may *hear* more often than see—he is a will-o'-the-wisp for shyness, whether on his journeys or about home. But remember

---

[6] The Olive-backed Thrush is now called Swainson's Thrush.

three things about him: his back is evenly olive (if you do not know what this dark-greenish color is, look at the olives you have on the table, or that stand in the tall glass jars in the grocer's window, for if you wish to study birds you must learn to distinguish this color from brown or the bright green); he has a cream-yellow ring round his eye; and lastly, his black-speckled throat and breast are dull yellowish."

"Won't you let us go up to the wonder room now and see all these Thrush cousins in a row?" asked Nat, when the Doctor had finished describing them.

"We will go up to the house and you may take a look at them, but I want you to be also able to name them from what I tell you; for when you see a bird out of doors you will seldom be able to have a stuffed one with which to compare it.

"Now we will make a procession of these cousins," said the Doctor, as they reached his study. He then opened a glass case, took out six birds, and stood them on the window-sill. "See, this is the way they go arm in arm when they walk in the great procession of Bird families:

"The Bluebird and the Robin;

"The Wood Thrush and the Veery;

"The Hermit and the Olive-back.

"Rap, my boy, look at each one and see if you can remember some of the differences between them. Now shut your eyes and think.[7]

"What has the Bluebird?"

"A blue back and a red and white breast; it is the flag bird."

"The Robin?"

"A brick-red breast and dark back."

"The Wood Thrush?"

"A rusty-brown back, the brightest on the head, and a little greenish on the tail."

"The Veery?"

"An even light-brown back, the same from head to tail."

"The Hermit?"

"A greenish-brown back, much redder on the rump and tail, like a chestnut."

"The Olive-back?"

---

[7] Through this scene and others, the authors are modeling for adult readers a variety of pedagogical tactics used by contemporary educators to interest children in the study of birds. In the article "Bird-Studies for Children," published in a February 1899 edition of *Bird-Lore* (vol. 1, no. 1), the naturalist Isabel Eaton stresses the importance of having children close their eyes in order to "review" the birds they have learned, much like Rap is asked to do by the Doctor, and of engaging in the "conversational description" of birds, much like Dodo is asked to do a few pages later (p. 17).

A SILVER-TONGUED FAMILY   79

"An even greenish-brown back, the color of olives all over."

"And the under parts of the last four—what general color are they?"

"From white to buff, with different sized and shaped dark markings. The spots on the Wood Thrush are the roundest and blackest; those on the Veery are the smallest, lightest, and most on the throat; on the Hermit they are longer and run together more like stripes; and those on the Olive-back are most like the Hermit's."

THE OLIVE-BACKED THRUSH

Length about seven inches—the same as the Hermit.

Upper parts an even olive color all over.

Under parts cream-yellowish, whiter on the belly, the throat and breast spotted with black.

A yellowish eye-ring, like the creamy color of the breast.

A Summer Citizen of the mountains of the northern United States.

A Tree Trapper and Ground Gleaner.

CHAPTER 10

Peepers and Creepers

THE GOLDEN-CROWNED KINGLET

"We have been looking at some of the larger song birds; now try the sharpness of your eyes by finding a tiny little fellow—a veritable midget, who belongs to the guild of Tree Trappers. He is usually intent upon his work, continually hopping and peeping among little branches and twigs, and thinks it would be time wasted if he stayed still long enough to give you a chance to look at him. He is so small that there are very few North American birds to compare with him in littleness. The Hummingbird is smaller still, and the Winter Wren measures no more, only he is chunkier. But what of that? This Kinglet is as hardy and vigorous as the biggest Hawk or Owl. His body is padded with a thick feather overcoat that enables him to stay all winter, if he chooses, in all but the most northern States.

"Small as he is, however, every one knows him, for he disports himself at some time of the year in the North, South, East, and West. If you see a tiny bird, darting quick as a mouse in and out among the budded twigs of fruit trees in early spring, now and then showing a black stripe and a little gleam of red or yellow on its head, it is this Kinglet. If you see such a pygmy again in autumn, exploring the bare twigs, it is this Kinglet. When light snow is first powdering

Golden-crowned Kinglet.

the spruces and bending the delicate hemlock branches, dusky shapes flit out of the green cover. Are they dry leaves blown about by the gust? No, leaves do not climb about in the face of the wind, or pry and peep into every cone crevice, crying 'twe-zee, twe-zee, twe-zee!' They are not leaves, but a flock of Kinglets forcing the bark crevices to yield them a breakfast of the insects which had put themselves comfortably to bed for the winter. Think of the work that these birds do, who not only fight the insect army in summer, but in sleet and snow are as busy as ever destroying the eggs that would turn in another season to worms and eat the orchards!

"Though the Golden-crowned Kinglets rove about in flocks a great part of the year, they are extremely private in the nesting season. They go to northern and high places to hide their homes, putting them as far out of reach as does the Baltimore Oriole. This nest is made of moss and seems very large when compared with the size of the builder. It is partly hung from the concealing bough of an evergreen, sometimes quite near the ground, sometimes swinging far up out of sight."

"Does this Kinglet lay two little white eggs, like the Hummingbird?" asked Nat.

"No," said the Doctor, "this sturdy bird lays eight or ten white eggs with brown spots."

"Ten eggs!" cried Dodo. "How can it sit on them all at once and keep them warm enough to hatch?"

"Perhaps the birds stir the eggs up every day to give them all an even chance," said Rap.

"It is possible that they may," said the Doctor; "but that is one of many things about home life in Birdland that we do not know.

"There is one thing more that I must tell you here, lest you make a mistake about the Golden-crowned Kinglet. He has a twin brother, so much like himself that their own parents can hardly tell them apart without looking at the tops of their heads. The other twin's name is Ruby-crown, for he has a beautiful little crest of that color, half hidden in dark greenish; but not any of the black and yellow marks on the head that will always enable you to recognize the Golden-crown, if you can get a chance to see them while the little fellow is fidgeting about. It is a snug family that contains these two birdlets, for there is only one other member of it in all this part of the world, and you will not be likely to see him about Orchard Farm."

THE GOLDEN-CROWNED KINGLET

Length four inches.

Upper parts olive-green, browner on the wings and tail, which have some yellowish edgings.

A bright-red stripe on the crown, bordered by a yellow and then by a black line; but young birds and females have only the yellow and black stripes, without any red.

Under parts soiled white, without any marks.

A Citizen of the United States, and a Tree Trapper.

THE WHITE-BREASTED NUTHATCH

"'Yank! yank!' says the White-breasted Nuthatch, as he runs up tree-trunks and comes down again head foremost, quite as a matter of course.

White-breasted Nuthatch.

"At first, or from a distance, you may mistake him for his cousin the Chickadee, who wears clothes of much the same color and is seen in the same places; or perhaps for the little Downy Woodpecker, who also hammers his insect food out of the tree bark.

"But at a second glance you will find the Nuthatch is very different. He keeps his body very close to the tree and uses his feet to creep about like a mouse or chipmunk; he also goes upside down, in a way that Woodpeckers never do, clings to the under side of a branch as easily as a fly to the ceiling, and often roosts or takes a nap head downward on the side of a tree-trunk—a position that would seem likely to give him a severe headache, if birds ever have such things."

"This is the bird I saw the first day I went to the orchard with Olive; but why is he called a Nuthatch?" asked Nat.

"Because, besides liking to eat insects and their grubs or their eggs, he is also very fond of some kinds of nuts, like beech and chestnuts," said the Doctor, "and he may be obliged to live entirely upon them in winter, when insects fail him. Having no teeth to gnaw and crack them open as squirrels do, he takes a nut in his claws and either holding it thus, or jamming it tight into a crack in the bark, then uses his bill for a hatchet to split or hack the nut open. I have seen the bird crack

PEEPERS AND CREEPERS   83

hard nuts in this way, that it would take very strong teeth to break. People used to call him 'Nuthack' or 'Nuthacker'; these words mean exactly the same thing, but we always say 'Nuthatch' now."

"Then there are Nuthatches up in the hickory woods," said Rap, "but I never knew their real name until now; for the miller calls them 'white-bellied creepers.' Last summer I found one of their nests, when I wasn't looking for it either."

"Do they build here?" asked Olive. "I thought they only visited us in winter. I don't remember ever hearing one sing, or seeing one in late spring or summer."

"They live and nest everywhere in the eastern part of the country," said the Doctor; "but they are very silent and shy except in the autumn and winter. In fact, this Nuthatch keeps his nest a secret from everybody but his wife and the Dryad of the tree in which he places it; he will not even trust the little branches with his precious home, but makes it in the wood of the tree itself. You say, Rap, that you found one of these nests—won't you tell us about it?"

"It was this way," said Rap. "I was up in a hickory tree trying to look over into a Woodpecker's hole that was in another tree, when I stepped on a stumpy branch that was rotten and partly broke off; and there, inside, was a soft nest made of feathers, with, four very little birds in it. I was afraid they would fall out, but there was enough of the branch left to hold them in. While I was wondering what sort of birds they were, the father and mother came running along a branch above, and gave me a terrible scolding, so pretty soon I slid down and left them. How they did squeak!" and Rap laughed at the remembrance of it.

"They have not very musical voices at best," said the Doctor; "even their spring song is a rather husky performance."

"Isn't that a Nuthatch now?" asked Nat. "There—hanging to the end tassel of the big spruce; and a lot more above—do come and look, Olive."

"No, Nattie, they are the Chickadees that father said, a moment ago, you might mistake for Nuthatches."

"Chickadee-dee-dee!" said a bird, looking at the children with one eye.

THE WHITE-BREASTED NUTHATCH
Length about six inches.

Upper parts grayish-blue.

Top of head and back of neck black.

Some black and white marks on wings and tail.

Sides of face and whole breast white, turning rusty on belly.

Bill strong, straight, sharp-pointed, two-thirds of an inch long.

A Citizen of the eastern United States and Canada.

A Tree Trapper.

THE CHICKADEE

"I see them, I see them, *lots* of them!" almost screamed Dodo, growing so excited that Nat and Olive each grabbed one of her hands to keep her from clapping them, and so driving the Chickadees away.[1]

"I never saw a strange new bird so near by," explained Dodo, "and if my eye was only a photograph machine I could take his picture."

"You can make a word-picture instead, by telling us how the bird appears to you," said the Doctor in a low voice, "but you need not whisper, for whispering is an unnatural use of the voice; it makes birds and other people suspicious, and is more likely to attract attention than a quiet low tone."

"That is what mother said when she was sick last winter and the neighbors came in to sit with her. If they talked softly she stayed asleep and didn't mind, but if they whispered she said she dreamed that the room was full of geese hissing and always waked up frightened," said Nat.

The Chickadees did not mind the conversation in the least, but kept on flitting in and out of the spruces, swinging from the little pink buds that would grow into cones by and by, doing a dozen pretty tricks, and all the time calling "chickadee-dee-dee" as if they were repeating a joke among themselves.

Chickadee.

"They mean we shall know their name, anyway," said Nat. "Have they any other song?"

"Oh, yes, some nice little whistle-tunes like this—'whée-ewèe, whée-ewèe,'" said Rap, "and if you whistle back they'll answer. I've done it lots of times."

"Try now—do, Rap, and see if they will answer," begged Dodo.

"It's too open out here, but I will go back of the trees and perhaps they will answer. I heard one whistling in there a minute ago."

---

[1] Chickadees in the eastern United States are now split into two species, the Black-capped Chickadee and the Carolina Chickadee. This is most likely the Black-capped Chickadee, common in northern states like Connecticut, where Orchard Farm is set.

PEEPERS AND CREEPERS 85

The children listened, and presently "whée-ewèe, whée-ewèe," came two high notes from among the trees. They were answered by two others, very musical, but a little bit sad. So the duet went on, boy and bird, until Dodo and Nat lost count and could not tell which was which. Then the music stopped and Rap returned laughing, saying that when the Chickadee found out it was not another bird that he was calling to, he was vexed and flew away.

"Some Chickadees lived around our house all last winter," continued Rap, "and used to eat out of the chickens' dish. I watched them every day but one that was terribly windy, and then they stayed under the miller's cow-shed. Even strong winter birds don't like the wind much—do they, Doctor?"

"No, my lad, wind is one of the greatest enemies that a bird has. A hardy bird who has plenty to eat can endure bitter cold, but when the food-supply is scanty, as it often is in winter, and the trees are covered with snow and ice, life is a battle with the Bird People. Then if a high wind is added to all this discomfort their strength gives way, and they often die in great numbers.

"If people who own gardens and farms, where there are no evergreen trees or hayricks for birds to hide in, would put up each fall little shelters of brush and branches, they would save a great many bird-lives, and their orchards would be freer from insects in the spring.[2] But, Dodo, you are not painting the word-picture of the Chickadee. Haven't you watched them long enough to think it out?"

"Y-e-s, I believe I have," said Dodo slowly. "I see a dear little bird about as big as a Chippy Sparrow, only fatter, and he is nice soft gray on top, about the color of my chinchilla muff. He has a black cap on his head, that comes down behind where his ears ought to be, fastened with a wide black strap across his throat, and his face is a very clean white, and his breast, too. That is, it is white in the middle, but the sides and below are a warmer color—sort of rusty white. And that's all, except that he's as fidgety as ever he can be," ended Dodo, quite out of breath with her haste to tell all she could before the bird flew away.

"Do you think you will remember the Chickadee, while he is in the deep woods nesting this summer, so that you will know him again in the autumn?"

Dodo and Nat said they were quite sure they would, but Rap said: "I've known him ever so long, only the miller called him a 'black-capped titmouse.' Isn't he a relation of the Nuthatch, Doctor?"

---

[2] *Citizen Bird* also contains lessons for the adults reading the book with their children; here, adult readers are taught about landscaping for birds, something children typically would not be tasked with managing at home.

"Yes, a second cousin, and Black-capped Titmouse is one of his right names. They used to belong to the very same family, but they had a little falling out, and are not now so intimate as they were before each went his own way, and acquired some different habits."

"I thought they were alike in a good many things," said Rap, "and their nests are something alike, too."

THE CHICKADEE

Length about five inches.
Upper parts ashy gray.
Head, back of neck, and throat, shining black.
Cheeks pure white.
Middle of breast white; sides and belly buffy.
A Citizen of the eastern United States.
A Tree Trapper.

THE BROWN CREEPER

"Another bird that, like the Nuthatch, spends his days peeping into the cracks of tree bark in search of food. He is not a relation of the Nuthatch, but a lonely bird and the only one of his family in this part of the world.

"He does not advertise his whereabouts as freely as do the Woodpeckers and other tree-trunk birds, so you will have to keep a sharp lookout to find him. In the first place he is nearly the same color as the brown and gray bark upon which he creeps, the white under parts being quite hidden, and his call, which is the only note that is commonly heard, is only a little sharp squeaky 'screek, screek,' given as he winds his way up and around a tree-trunk, in the same way as a person would go up a circular staircase.

"You may catch sight of a brown object moving as swiftly as a mouse, and before you have made up your mind what it is he will have gone round the other side of the tree. But the Creeper has one habit that will some day give you a good chance to look at him. When he wishes to remain still a moment, he spreads his

Brown Creeper.

tail with its stiff pointed feathers and props himself by it against the tree. This is your opportunity."

"Does the Creeper stay here all summer?" asked Nat. "And doesn't he sing a song like the other birds when he makes his nest?"

"He is not a Citizen hereabouts; he likes a cooler climate and makes his home near and across the northern border of the United States. We shall see him in the autumn, when he has become a wanderer through the country. If the trees are not coated with ice, a little flock may stay here all winter, while others drift further south."

"Then we shan't hear him sing or see his nest—have you ever seen it, Uncle Roy?"

"Yes, my boy, and it was the beauty of his little song that made me stop one day, in going through an old pine wood, and search for the singer. The song was very strange and wild, unlike any other I had ever heard. As my eyes grew accustomed to the dim light, I saw that my old friend, the Brown Creeper, was the musician. At the same time he flew to one of the pine trees and seemed to disappear inside of it. I watched awhile until the bird flew out, and, climbing to the spot, saw that the nest was squeezed in a sort of pocket between the loose bark and the tree itself. You see, like the Chickadee and Nuthatch, he loves trees so well that he tries to creep as close to their hearts as he possibly can."

"Would you call this Creeper mostly a winter bird?" asked Dodo. "I'm going to remember the winter birds by themselves and write them in my book, because there will be fewer of them."

"Yes," said the Doctor, "at least a winter bird in places where we mostly see him; but you know that every bird must be a summer bird somewhere."

THE BROWN CREEPER

Length five and a half inches.

Upper parts mixed brown, white, and buff.

A plain brown tail, and a light-buff band on the wings.

Under parts white, without any marks.

Bill very sharp and slender, curved like a surgeon's needle.

A Summer Citizen of northern North America.

A Tree Trapper.

CHAPTER 11

Mockers and Scolders

THE SAGE THRASHER

"I thought that more tree-trunk birds, such as Woodpeckers, would come next," said Rap.

"We are still taking the Birds that Sing," said the Doctor. "Woodpeckers have no real song; they belong to the Birds that Croak and Call; but the Nuthatch, Chickadee, and Brown Creeper each has a little tune of its own, as you have heard."

"Of course—I don't see why I said that, for I know Woodpeckers only hammer and croak," said Rap.

"The family of Mockers, Thrashers, and Wrens is one of the most interesting that we shall meet in our Birdland excursions, for all its members are bright intelligent birds and great talkers. They have something to say for themselves and say it so cleverly that we do not care if their feathers are of sober grays and browns. This family should be very proud of itself, but it does not show any false pride or exclusiveness; its different members are as sociable and friendly as possible, building their nests in bushes not far from the ground, and taking every occasion to chat confidentially with House People.[1] Some of these friendly birds are the Sage Thrasher, the Mockingbird, the Catbird, the Brown Thrasher, the Rock Wren, the House Wren, and the Long-billed Marsh Wren, the last being the only really shy bird among the seven I am going to tell you about."

---

[1] Here, we see how the persistent anthropomorphizing of the birds extends even to how the characteristics of different species are rendered. Thus, Mockingbirds, Thrashers, and Wrens, all of which are very vocal birds, are described as "sociable and friendly," frequently "chatting" with people.

"Do Wrens and Mockingbirds belong to the same family?" asked Nat. "One so little and one so big! Mother had a Mockingbird in a cage once, but it got out and flew away to live in the park, she thought."

"They are cousins and belong to the same large family, though to different households, like House People.

"The Sage Thrasher belongs only to the West, just as its relative the Brown Thrasher belongs to the eastern part of the country. When your Cousin Olive and I lived one summer here and there, from Colorado westward, it was this bird that made us feel at home by its sweet sociable music.

"Everywhere in that mountainous region the sagebrush, with its blue flower spikes, spreads over the ground, making a silvery greenness where other plants could not grow. In and out of the sage, nests and scratches and hops this Thrasher, taking its name from the plant. He also ventures up on the mountain sides, giving his inquisitive, questioning, mocking notes, and so earns a second name in those places, where he is called the Mountain Mockingbird.

Sage Thrasher.

"Though he is a good deal smaller than the true Mockingbird of the South, they have many points in common. They can both imitate almost any sound that strikes their fancy, such as the songs of other birds, whistle various tunes of their own, and almost mock the peculiarities of human speech. Not that they all do it—oh, no, many have only their own beautiful natural song; every Mockingbird has not the power of imitation, but certain members of the tribe acquire a knack of mockery of which they seem quite conscious.

"The Sage Thrasher, though gentle and sociable in its wild state, does not thrive in cages as well as the true Mocker. It seems to miss the broad expanse of plain and mountain to which it has been used, and seldom lives long in confinement.

"Read what you have written about the size and color of this Thrasher," said the Doctor to Rap.

THE SAGE THRASHER

Length eight inches.

Upper parts gray, tinged with brown.

Under parts white shaded to buff, and spotted thickly on the breast with very dark
brown, almost black.

Two white bands on each wing, and white spots on the end of the tail.

A Summer Citizen of the western United States.

A Ground Gleaner, Tree Trapper, and Seed Sower.

THE MOCKINGBIRD

"Mammy Bun knows about Mockingbirds," said Dodo. "She says the bushes were full of them down in Louisiana where she was born, and that sometimes they used to sit on the top of the cabins and sing so loud at night, when the moon shone, that the children couldn't go to sleep, and they had to throw sticks and things at them."

"Did the children throw sticks at the birds, or the birds pelt the children?" laughed the Doctor—for poor Dodo was famous for mixing up her sentences.

"No, no, Uncle Roy, neither; the children's *mothers* threw the sticks at the Mockers."

"What else did Mammy Bun tell you?"

"Lots and lots of things, and a song, too, that her people used to sing about the Mockers, only I can't tell it as she does because you know she has a sort of language all her own."[2]

"Suppose we ask mammy to come and tell us about the Mockingbirds herself," said Olive, "May we, father?"

"Certainly, if you can coax her."

The children followed Olive to the house and soon returned leading mammy, who was chuckling and out of breath, but evidently very much pleased to be

---

[2] Following in the footsteps of white authors like Harriet Beecher Stowe in *Uncle Tom's Cabin* (1852), Joel Chandler Harris in *Uncle Remus: His Songs and Sayings* (1880), and Mark Twain in *Adventures of Huckleberry Finn* (1884), Wright and Coues here made the decision to have Mammy Bun speak in what they imagined to be Black vernacular speech in the Deep South, which they attempted to convey through the use of "eye dialect" (the deliberate use of misspellings to convey nonstandard pronunciations of words). Often used for comic effect, this type of literary minstrelsy was very common in the second half of the nineteenth century and contributed to the proliferation of racist stereotypes of nonwhite Americans, particularly African Americans. The chapter is being included in this teaching edition unedited, with the exception of racial slurs, which have been expurgated, in keeping with best practices and Rutgers University Press's publishing policies. Likewise, in keeping with best practices for teaching, we strongly recommend against reading this chapter out loud in class. For readers who would prefer not to read this chapter at all in its original form, the editors have included in appendix 1 a standardized version of Mammy Bun's bird story regarding the Mockingbird. For more on blackface minstrelsy in nineteenth-century American literature, see Toll, *Blacking Up: The Minstrel Show in Nineteenth Century America* (New York: Oxford University Press, 1974), and Richards, *Imitation Nation: Red, White, and Blackface in Early and Antebellum American Literature* (Charlottesville: University of Virginia Press, 2017).

asked. She could not be persuaded to try the apple-tree perch, so they made her a sort of throne at the foot of the tree and sat respectfully in a row in front of her. Mammy wore a dark-blue print dress with white figures on it, but as she was one of the good old sort, she had a plaid handkerchief tied turban fashion round her head. As she talked she rolled her eyes and waved her hands a good deal, and her words had a soft comfortable sound like molasses pouring out of a big stone jug.

"Does I know de mockin'bird, I reck'n so—'bout de fust t'ing I did know, 'cept how ter suck sugar-cane. Sugar-cane am good eatin' long in de 'arly fall, but de Mocker ain't doin' much singin' dese yer times, least not 'less he's in a cage in a good sunshiny place. He am a kind ob a peart gray bird, darker in some places, lighter in oders, and clean as a parson. But come 'long spring and time for droppin' de cottin seed, de Mocker he know mighty well what's a-doin'. 'Long in March he comes inter de bushes and orange scrub round de field a-makin' a fuss and tellin' folks to git along to work, or dere won't be no cottin, and he keep it straight up all de day long till cottin's out o' bloom. All de day long kind o' chatterin' and hurryin' de n— up when dere a-droppin' de seed in de line, and scoldin' and hurryin' all de day long, when dere a-hoein' down de weeds. Den when it come night, de she-bird keep close onter de nest, and de he-bird go in de scrub or de redwoods or de gin'gos, nigh de clarin', maybe right on de cabin roof, and he say to hisself— 'Now dem n— done dere work, I'll gib 'em a tune ter courage 'em like.' Den he jes' let hisself onter his singin'. Sometime he sing brave and bold, like he say big words like missis and de folks dat lib in de big house. Den he whisper soft an' low widout any words, jes' like a mammy was a-singin' to her baby. Den agin he sing kin' o' long and soft and wheedlesome, like Sambo when he come a-courtin' o' me. Sho, now! come to t'ink o' Sambo, he didn't nebber like Mockers, a'ter one time he 'spicioned a Mocker tole tales on him. Massa Branscome—he were a mighty fine man and your gran'dad, Miss Olive—he say he wouldn't have no puss'n to rob de nests o' Mockers, not anywheres on his 'states. Dey did eat a pile o' fruit, but dat was nuffin'. Fus' place he jes' loved ter hear 'em sing, an' den he 'lowed dat dey was powerful fond o' cottin worms, what was mighty bad some years.

"Now lots o' [slaves] dey uster steal de youn' Mockers jes' afore dey lef' de nest and sell 'em to white trash dat ud tote 'em down the ribber an' sell 'em agin in N'Orleans, to be fetched off in ships. And I'se hear tell dat dere ain't any sech birds in oder countries, and dat de kings and queens jes' gib dere gold crowns offen dere heads t' have a cage o' Mockers.

"Dem [slaves] nebber got no gold crowns, howsumever. What dey got was mos'ly a quarter foh free he-birds. Now Sambo he was a-courtin' an' wanted a banjo powerful bad, an' he didn't want no common truck, so he 'lowed to get one up from N'Orleans. So he 'greed to pay for it in Mockers, an' he to'ht he know'd where he'd get 'em foh sure. Mockers don' nes' in de woods and wild places, dey allus keeps roun' de plantations near where folks libs.

"He know'd he war doin' wrong and he felt mighty uncomfoh'ble; but he done took de youn' Mockers on our plantation right under massa's nose. He war crafty like and on'y took one outen each nes' and at night de ole birds never miss 'em. When he got de banjo 'bout paid foh, dat time he took a whole nes'ful to onc't an' de birds what it b'longed to saw what he war a-doin' an' gib him a piece o' dere mind, an' folled him 'round all day an' sat on de roof ob his quarters an' talked all night, 'an tole him to bring back dem Mockers or dey'd tell; an' Sambo war skeered an' wanted to put de birds back an' den he didn't like to. Nex' day, he 'lowed de he-Mocker wen' to de big house, an' tole massa 'bout it, an' he an' Miss Jessamine— dat was your ma—dey come down to de quarters an' tole Sambo he done took Mockers an' ask him what had he done wid all on 'em. An' he mos' turn' white an' he say, 'I sol' 'em down de ribber'; an' massa say, 'I'se a great mind to sell you down de ribber, too'—but he nebber sol' nuffin'— gib us all our freedom. Now, no n— want' to be sol' down de ribber, an' Sambo say, 'Oh, Miss Jessamine, dere's f'ree I didn' sell, an' I'll gib 'em back to dat he-bird, an' ax his pardin.' Massa he laff and say, 'If dat he-bird will 'scuse you, I will.' So Sambo put 'em back an' de he-bird act' s'if he know'd an' talk' a lot o' good advice to Sambo, but I'se shore 't war anoder n— w'at tole on Sam.

"Dey uster have a song 'bout de Mockers roun' de cabins, an' a dance went wid it, 'cause it was a berry long song; but aftah dat Sambo done change it some when he uster sing it."

Mammy then chanted a verse, keeping time by beating her hands on her knees.

Mockingbird.

"De sugar-cane hits pushin' in de bottoms,
    De rice hits a-sproutin' now fo' shore!
De cotton hits a-greenin' in de furrer,
    An' honey I'se a-waitin' at de door!

"Did I tole you dat I know'd whar dere's a possum?
    Did I tole you dat I know'd whar dere's a coon?
Oh, mah lady, come out soon!
Oh, mah honey, come out soon!
    While de Mocker, while de Mocker
    Am a-singin' to de moon!"

Suddenly mammy jumped up, and waving the children off, started for the house as fast as she could trot, muttering to herself.

"What *is* the matter?" called Olive; "has a bee stung you?"

"No, nope chile, but t'inkin' 'bout dem times I done forgit I lef' a big pan o' buns a-risin' foh yoh lunch. Like's not dey's rised till dey's bust an' popped over!" And mammy disappeared amid a chorus of laughter.

"What mammy has said about the Mockingbird in his summer home is true.[3] As a visitor who sometimes stays and builds, he strays east and north as far as Massachusetts, and westward to Colorado and California. If he were not a hardy bird who sometimes raises three broods a year, I'm afraid the race would come to an end, because so many nestlings are taken each year and sold for cage birds."

THE MOCKINGBIRD

Length about ten inches.

Upper parts gray, but dusky-brownish on the wings, which have a large white spot.
    Three white feathers on each side of the tail, which is blackish. The males, who
    sing, have more white on the wings and tail than the females, who are songless.
Under parts whitish.

Sings his own true song, a rapid, sweet melody, heard best after twilight; but has
    many comic songs of whatever nonsense comes into his head.

A Citizen of the southern United States, often straying northward to New England.

A Ground Gleaner, Tree Trapper, and Seed Sower.

---

[3] The Mockingbird is now called the Northern Mockingbird.

THE CATBIRD

When the Doctor said "Catbird" the children began to imitate the various calls this famous garden bird utters, for by this time they were familiar with all his tricks and manners. Some of the imitations were very good indeed, if not musical. "Miou! Zeay! Zeay!"

"That is all very well in its way," said the Doctor, "but which one of you can imitate his song?"

"I've often tried," said Rap, "but somehow he always gets ahead of me, and I lose the place."

"Listen! There is one singing now in the grape arbor, and he has a nest somewhere in the syringa bushes," said Olive.

The Catbird was not alarmed when he saw that five pairs of eyes were turned upon him. He seemed to know that the secret of his nest was in safe keeping, flew out to the pointed top of a clothes-pole, and continued his song, jerking his tail up and down and showing the rusty feathers beneath, as if this motion had something to do with the force of his music. "I can hear the words as plain as anything," said Nat; "if I only understood his language!"

"That is the difficulty," said the Doctor; "if some kind bird would write a dictionary for us we should soon learn a great many strange things."

"Roger, the gardener, says that Catbirds are bad things and if he had his way he would shoot them. He says they bite the strawberries and grapes and things, even when he is looking at them," said Dodo.

"There is some truth in what Roger says," replied the Doctor, "but on the other hand, the Catbird, besides being a merry garden neighbor and musician, which in itself is enough to pay his rent, belongs as a citizen to the Tree Trappers and Ground Gleaners, and is also a great sower of wild fruits. Though he does provoke us at times by taking a bite from the largest berries in the bed, yet he really prefers wild fruits if he can find them. So it is better for us to protect our grape arbors and strawberry beds with nets and bits of bright tin strung on twine to frighten him away from them, than to lose him as a friend and insect destroyer.

"Surely his song is worth a few handfuls of cherries. Then he is such a quick-witted, sympathetic bird, always willing to help his neighbors when they have trouble with Crows or squirrels. And when half a dozen pairs of Catbirds choose the garden for their home, you may be sure that they will furnish fun as well as music."

"Why does he jerk his tail so?" asked Dodo.

"It is a trick that all the family have," said the Doctor, "from which some of them are supposed to have taken the name of Thrasher, but that is doubtful. The Mockingbird thrashes about in his cage; the Brown Thrasher on the ground under the bushes; the House Wren does the same, and the tiny Winter Wren gives his tail a jerk instead, for it is not long enough to really thrash."

"There is a bright-brown bird beating with his tail, down under the quince bushes now," said Dodo. "Is that some kind of a cousin?"

"It's a Song Thrush," said Rap.

"Or rather what the Wise Men call a Brown Thrasher," said the Doctor; "the very bird of which I was speaking."

"Who are the Wise Men?" asked Rap.

"A society of House People who study American birds and decide by what name it is best to call each species, so that each may be known everywhere by the same name. This Brown Thrasher is sometimes called Song Thrush, Brown Thrush, Brown Mockingbird, and Mavis—though the first and the last of these four names belong only to a kind of European Thrush that is never found in this country. You see how confusing this is, and how much better it is for the Wise Men, who know him intimately, to give him one name you can be sure is right."

Catbird.

THE CATBIRD
Length between eight and nine inches.

Upper parts slate color.

Crown, bill, feet, and tail black.

Under parts lighter grayish-slate color, except a chestnut-red patch under the tail.

A Summer Citizen of the United States.

A Ground Gleaner, Tree Trapper, and Seed Sower.

THE BROWN THRASHER

"As I told you a moment ago, this handsome clean-built bird with keen eyes, curved bill, and long graceful tail that opens and shuts like a fan, has several names besides that of Brown Thrasher, which seems the most suitable for him."

"He looks redder than brown, for we called the Wood Thrush 'brown,'" said Nat.

"Yes, his back is a much brighter brown than that of any Thrush, and this will show you the need in studying birds of being able to distinguish between several shades of the same color. There are words to represent these different grades of color, such as 'rufous' for reddish-brown and 'fuscous' for dusky-brown; these you must learn later on, for some of them are pretty hard ones. Now it is better for you to use words whose meaning is perfectly familiar to you.

"The brown of this Thrasher, you see, is brighter than that of the Wood Thrush; it is a ruddy brown, with a faint brassy glint, something like a polished doorknob, particularly when the sun strikes his back."

"How he scratches round upon the ground," said Dodo; "just like a hen. Why doesn't he belong to the Birds that Scratch?"

"Because, for one reason, his feet have the three toes in front and the one behind, all on the same level; this makes him a perching bird."

"Don't all birds sit on a perch when they go to sleep?" asked Dodo.

"By no means. The perching birds grasp a twig firmly with their very limber toes and sharp claws, and put their head under their wing; but many others, like tame Geese and Ducks, sleep standing on the ground on one foot or sometimes floating on the water.

"The Thrasher is a Ground Gleaner, who spends most of his time in the underbrush, having a great appetite for the wicked May beetle; but he does not live near the ground only, mounting high in a tree when he wishes to sing, as if he needed the pure high air in order to breathe well, and he never sings from the heart of a thick bush, as the Catbird does so frequently.

"But I am wrong in saying that he *only* goes up into trees to sing, for there is no denying that he visits cherry trees to pick cherries, in spite of the fact that he is neither invited nor welcome. Yet we must remember that if he does like fruit for dessert he has also first eaten caterpillar-soup and beetle-stew, and so has certainly earned some cherries."

"Hush!" whispered Olive; "our Thrasher is singing now in the birch tree, where you can both see and hear him."

MOCKERS AND SCOLDERS   97

"That's a sure sign his nest is not very near," said Rap; "for they never sing close by their nests." This Thrasher was clinging to the end of a slender branch, one claw above the other, so that his head, which was thrown back, looked straight up to the sky. He seemed to be half talking and half singing, as if giving directions to some unseen performer, then following these by two or three clear notes.

"What is he saying?" said Dodo.

"He is telling you who he is, and what he sees from the tree-top," said the Doctor. "Olive, dear, I am going to repeat to the children the jingle you made about the Thrasher." Though Olive then blushed and said it was only nonsense, the children were delighted with it.

"My creamy breast is speckled
(Perhaps you'd call it freckled)
Black and brown.

"My pliant russet tail
Beats like a frantic flail,
Up and down.

"In the top branch of a tree
You may chance to glance at me,
When I sing.

"But I'm very, *very* shy,
When I silently float by,
On the wing.

"*Whew* there! *Hi* there! Such a clatter!
What's the matter—what's the matter?
Really, really?

"Digging, delving, raking, sowing,
Corn is sprouting, corn is growing!
   Plant it, plant it!
   Gather it, gather it!
   Thresh it, thresh it!
   Hide it, hide it, do!
   (I see it—and you.)

Brown Thrasher.

Oh!—I'm that famous scratcher,
H-a-r-p-o-r-h-y-n-c-h-u-s r-u-f-u-s—Thrasher—
Cloaked in brown."

THE BROWN THRASHER

Length eleven inches.
Above bright reddish-brown, with two light bands on each wing.
Beneath yellowish-white, spotted with very dark brown on the breast and the sides.
Very long tail—about five inches—fan-shaped.
A Summer Citizen of the United States east of the Rocky Mountains.
A famous Ground Gleaner and Seed Sower.

THE ROCK WREN

When the children had finished applauding Olive's poetry—or was it really the Thrasher's own performance?—the Doctor went on:

"We have seen that the West has one sort of a Thrasher in the sage-brush, and the East another, in our own gardens. I also told you that these birds were a kind of overgrown Wren; and before we call upon Mrs. Jenny Wren, I want to tell you about a bigger relative of hers that Olive and I knew when we were in the Rocky Mountains. He is called the Rock Wren—"

"Oh! I know—because he lives in the Rocky Mountains," said Dodo, clapping her hands at this discovery.

"Yes, that is partly the reason," resumed the Doctor, after this interruption, "but those mountains are very many, and varied in appearance, like most others: covered in most places with pine trees, but including in their recesses grassy meadows and silvery lakes. Some parts of those mountains are the home of the Rock Wren, but the little fellow is quite as well satisfied anywhere else in the western parts of the United States, if he can find heaps of stones to play hide-and-seek in with his mate, or great smooth boulders to skip up to the top of and sing. So you see the mountains and the Wrens are both named for the rocks."

"Do these Wrens look like our kind and act that way?" asked Nat. "Ours always make me think of mice."

"All kinds of Wrens are much alike," answered the Doctor. "They are small brownish birds with cocked up tails, not at all shy about showing themselves off, when they choose, but they must have some hiding-place to duck into the moment anything frightens them, and some odd, out-of-the-way nook or cranny for their big rubbishy nests. Some prefer to hide in marshes among the thickest reeds, some live in dry brush heaps, and some, like the Rock Wren, choose piles of stones. Their wings are not very strong, and they seldom venture far from their favorite retreats, except when they are migrating.

"When your cousin Olive and I were in Colorado we climbed a mountain one day above the timber-line"—[4]

"Do *all* the trees out there grow in straight lines?" asked Dodo anxiously.

"No, my dear little girl, trees don't grow in straight lines anywhere," said the Doctor, laughing—"except when they are planted so. The 'timber-line' of a mountain is the edge of the woods, above which no trees grow, and we see nothing but bare rocks, and the few low plants that cling to the cracks among them. Well, we had hardly rested long enough to get our breath after such a

---

[4] Most field guides include birds only of a specific area, such as Eastern North America. While most of the birds featured in *Citizen Bird* can be found in the eastern United States, Coues made a late addition of several western birds he had previously studied and discovered, as explained in the introduction. Thus, while the Rock Wren would not be found in a field guide to birds found in Connecticut, the narrative frame allows for the story about Dr. Hunter and Olive visiting Colorado, as a way to introduce a bird that these children would never see at Orchard Farm.

Rock Wren.

climb, when we heard a rich ringing song, something like a House Wren's, but louder and stronger, and very quick, as if the bird were in a great hurry to get through. But he wasn't, for he kept saying the same thing over and over again. Presently we spied him, on the tiptop of a pile of stones, standing quite still, with his head thrown back and his bill pointing straight up. He looked gray, dusted over with pepper-and-salt dots on the back, and his bill was very straight and sharp—almost an inch long, it looked. This was a Rock Wren."

"He must have had a nest somewhere in those rocks," said Rap. "Wrens most always have nests near where they sing."

"No doubt he had, as it was the nesting season—June," answered the Doctor; "but it was growing late in the day, we had a long scramble down the mountain before us, and could not wait to hunt for it. Most likely, too, if we had found the very place where it was, we should not have been able to see it, for probably it was tucked away too far in a crooked passage under a shelving rock.

"When we were half-way down the mountain we passed a miner's cabin. He was at home, and we sat down on a bench by the door to rest. Thinking he might know about the nest of the Rock Wren,—for an old miner knows a great many things he never thinks of making a book about,—I asked him if there were any Wrens around there.

"'Wall, I should smile, stranger! Lots on 'em—more'n one kind, too—but mostly not the reg'lar kind they have where you tenderfoots live—bigger, and pickeder in front, and make more fuss. When they fust come, 'long about May, or nigh onter June, they act kinder shy like, but they get uster to yer, soon's they find nobody ain't goin' to bother with 'em, and stay around altogether, mostly in the rocks. Last y'ar there was two on 'em come nigh chinking up this shebang with trash they hauled in for a nest, afore they got it fixed to suit 'em, and had it chuck full o' speckled eggs. Then one of these yere blamed pack-rats tore it all up, and they had to start in to hauling more trash.'

"So you see, children, this miner knew a Rock Wren—do you know a Jenny Wren?"

THE ROCK WREN

Length nearly six inches.

Back gray, with fine black-and-white dots.

Under parts no particular color.

Some of the tail-feathers with black bars and cinnamon-brown tips.

A Citizen of the United States from the Rocky Mountains to the Pacific Ocean.

A Ground Gleaner

THE HOUSE WREN

"We all know Jenny Wren!" cried the children. "The Farm is full of Jennies and Johnnies!"

"They build in bird-boxes," said Dodo.

"And in old tin cans, and water pots, and anything they find," said Rap.

"And Jenny does most of the work; if the can is very large she fills it full of sticks until there is only a cosy little corner left for the nest, for she is a very neat bird," said the Doctor, when he could be heard. "She keeps her house nice and clean, and is very industrious too, making a fresh nest for every new brood, which means a great deal of work, for Wrens often raise three families a season."

"But Johnny Wren works too, doesn't he?" asked Nat; "he is always taking home bugs and things, and he sings as if he would split."

"Wrens live in woodpiles in winter," said Rap.

The Doctor laughed heartily at the hurry with which the children told their knowledge.

"Everybody has a bowing acquaintance with the House Wren," he said, "for they are seen everywhere through the United States, those that are citizens of the West being a trifle paler in color and more sharply barred than their easterly brothers, but all having the same habits; even the Rock Wren is as jolly and sociable as his house-loving cousins.

"But the Wren that Rap says lives in the woodpile in the winter is not our House Wren, but another member of the same family—the smallest of all, called the Winter Wren.

"He is a citizen of the far North, whence he follows the mountains down to Carolina, and he is chiefly seen when he visits the Eastern States in the winter—hence his name. But few who see him then have heard his ripple-song—one of the sweetest bits of our bird music."

House Wren.

"Hear Johnny Wren singing on the trellis, and his wife scolding at him all the time, too. I wonder why she does it?" said Nat.

"She is only making believe scold," said the Doctor, "because she has a quick temper and wants to say something, and cannot exactly sing. Johnny and Jenny make a great fuss, but they are really very fond of each other and make the very best of citizens, eating no fruits and being officers in the guilds of Ground Gleaners and Tree Trappers."

"Look!" said Dodo, "Jenny is scolding and dancing about, and Johnny is singing away again. What is the matter with them, Uncle Roy?"

"Did you never hear the 'Wrens' duet'? That is what they are singing now. Listen, and I will tell you what they say in House People's language:

Johnny (keeping time with his wings):
I'm jolly Johnny Wren,
The busiest of men;
For I sing and I clean house, too.
Though wife is such a bustler,
'Tis I that am the hustler,
For *I work* when there's *nothing to do*!
   And *I* don't care to talk,
   And *I* daren't take a walk,
  For Jenny's such a jealous, j-e-a-l-o-u-s She!

Jenny (keeping time with her head):
I'm thrifty Jenny Wren.
The foolish, lazy men
Think they work if they sing all day.
If husband is a martyr,
I'm a great deal, great deal smarter,
For I *talk* when I've *nothing to say*!
   And though I mind my work,
   I also prink and perk,

For Johnny's such a *f-a-s-cin-a-ting* He!
Both (beating time with all four wings):
(*She*) Though you don't care to talk—
(*He*) We might both take a walk—
(*Both*) For we are such a captivating WE!

Exeunt, dancing on tiptoe along the trellis."

THE HOUSE WREN

Length five inches.
Upper parts dark brown finely barred with black.
Under parts gray, washed with brown and very faintly banded.
Tail rather long (for a Wren's), full of light and dark bars, mostly held cocked up.
A fidgety little bird with a very merry song.
A Summer Citizen east of Indiana, and a Citizen south from the middle districts.
A Ground Gleaner and Tree Trapper.

THE LONG-BILLED MARSH WREN

"You must always wear your rubber boots when you go to look for the Marsh Wren," said the Doctor; "and you must be careful where you step, for this Wren knows where to put his nest safely out of the way of both House People and cats.[5] He chooses a bunch of reeds, or a bush that is surrounded either by water or the treacherous green grass of bogs, and there weaves an oblong or globular nest from coarse grass and leaves, with a little hole on one side for a door. This done, he goes to a short distance and appoints himself day watchman to his home. If a footstep touches the grass ever so lightly, he tells his mate of it and they flit off; and if any one thinks that by following the birds they will find the nest, they will be very much disappointed. Mr. and Mrs. Long-bill will lead them a will-o'-the-wisp dance; and when the House People are tired, bewildered, and very wet in the shoes, the clever birds will return home by a secret way, chuckling to themselves.

Long-billed Marsh Wren.

---

[5] The Long-billed Marsh Wren is now called Marsh Wren.

You will know this little bird by his nervous Wren-like ways and jerking tail, even if you are not near enough to see his markings and long curving bill."

"But there are no marshy places near the Farm, so I'm afraid we shall never see him, except in the wonder room," said Nat.

"By and by when we go to the beach, where our river meets the sea, I will show you some nests. I speak of this Marsh Wren now so that you may remember it with the rest of this family of Mockers and Scolders."

THE LONG-BILLED MARSH WREN

Length about five inches.

Upper parts clear brown, with a long light line over the eye, and a patch of black-and-white streaks on the back; light and dark brown bars on tail and wings.

Under parts white, tinged with brown on the sides.

A long slender bill, with more of a curve than a House Wren's.

Song something like a House Wren's, but more bubbling and gurgling.

A Citizen of the eastern United States.

A Ground Gleaner.

CHAPTER 12

Woodland Warblers

"Now you may be introduced to a family of American birds, many of them brightly colored and none of them large, who have no cousins or relations in any other country. You must not expect them to come and peep in the window like the Catbird, or feed on the lawn like the Thrush and Robin; for they are birds of woodland and brushland. Yet they often come for a time in their journeys to gardens and orchards, for they are among the greatest travellers."

"Why do they travel so much, if they are only American birds?" asked Nat. "I shouldn't think they would have to go far if they always live in America."

"America is a very large country, my boy, and you must not forget it includes South as well as North America—the Western Hemisphere of the whole globe. Warblers are insect-eating Citizens and cannot live long on anything else. Now, as many of them nest far North, when the early frosts lock the country they must often make long journeys at short notice, until they find their insect food again."

"Why don't we see swarms and swarms of them flying by?" asked Dodo.

"You mean flocks," said Olive; "we only say 'swarms' when we mean bees or other insects."

"They make their journeys mostly by night," continued the Doctor, "for darkness protects their bright colors from the cannibal birds and various other enemies. One day there will not be a single Warbler in the river woods, and the next the trees will be bright with them.

"Another reason that we do not commonly see these Warblers is, that the greatest number do not come from the South until the trees are in leaf, and they pass back again through the middle portions of the States before the trees are bare in autumn, so that they easily hide from us."

"Are there no bright-colored birds that live all winter where the trees are bare?" asked Rap.

"Yes, three—the Cardinal, the Crossbill, and the Pine Grosbeak. They are seed-eating birds, and all belong to the Sparrow family. Most of the very showy birds belong to tropical countries, where the trees are always in leaf and there are quantities of orchids and other conspicuous flowers to attract the eye from the birds themselves.

"This habit of travelling by night has caused a great many of these beautiful Warblers to lose their lives, for they often fly against telegraph wires, high stee-ples, and lighthouse towers, and are killed. Another danger also besets them— they may come from the South with a bit of early mild weather, and nearing the Great Lakes meet a storm from the North, and the food-supply being very scanty, the icy winds overcome their strength.

"A friend of mine who lives in Wisconsin," continued the Doctor, "has a gar-den that slopes down to Geneva Lake. Late one April there came a windstorm from the northwest, and the next morning the lawn was strewn with the bodies of hundreds of little Warblers who had become confused in the darkness and unable to reach shelter.

"You see how many troubles and risks Citizen Bird has to endure at best, so that we House People should do everything we can to protect him and make his life among us happy.

"You will have more use for your eyes than your ears, in naming the Warblers. Their plumage is almost always striking, but their voices are rather lisping than musical, though they sing pretty little snatches in the woods; but many of their call-notes sound more like the squeaks and buzzings of insects and tree-toads than like the voices of birds, and it will take time and practice before you can distinguish them apart. I have chosen only half a dozen species to tell you of, from the half-hundred that rove about the United States. The first, and one that you are the most likely to see, is the Black-and-white Warbler."

THE BLACK-AND-WHITE WARBLER

"There are exceptions to everything," said the Doctor, as he pointed to an old willow tree on the edge of the river woods, where he had taken the children to look for Warblers. "And the exception among the shy Warblers of these woods is that sociable little black-and-white fellow over there, who is creeping and swinging about the branches as if he was own brother to the Brown Creeper himself. This Black-and-white Warbler hides his nest in an overturned stump, or on the ground, and you may try for days in vain to find one. But at the same time he spends his time running merrily through the orchard trees, even whispering his husky 'weachy-weachy-twee-twee, tweet' to the old queen apple by the study window."

"Is that bird a Warbler?" asked Nat. "I thought he was some kind of a Nuthatch or a Woodpecker—he was with a whole lot of them up by the house last week."

"I used to think so too," said Rap; "but now I see a difference. The body and bill of the Nuthatch is stouter, and not such a pretty shape, and his bill almost turns up. This Warbler is thinner, with a slender bill that curves a little down, like the Brown Creeper's. Then too, he has smaller and finer stripes than any Woodpecker."

"What guild does he belong to?" asked Dodo.

"To the Tree Trappers; most of the Warblers belong to this, while some have joined the Sky Sweepers, and a few the Ground Gleaners and Seed Sowers."

Black-and-white Warbler.

"Look!" said Nat. "He has spent a long time on one twig and he doesn't seem to have cleaned off all the insects yet; he must have pretty good eyes."

"Yes, and more than that," said the Doctor, "his eyes magnify much more than ours do, so that all objects appear far larger to a bird than they do to us, and they can see insects that we never notice."

"I wonder if that little Warbler thinks spiders are crabs and flies chickens," said Dodo, so soberly that all the others laughed heartily.

THE BLACK-AND-WHITE WARBLER

Length five inches.

Upper parts striped everywhere with black and white.

Under parts white in the middle, with many black stripes on the sides.

Has a weak and wheezy voice.

From its habit of scrambling about tree-trunks and branches, it may be mistaken for a real Creeper, or a Nuthatch, or even a little Woodpecker.

A Summer Citizen of the United States, east of the plains; in winter from Florida southward.

A Tree Trapper.

THE YELLOW WARBLER

(Or Summer Yellowbird)

"I know this Warbler by sight already," said Dodo; "there is one in the low case in the wonder room—the pretty bird sitting on a fuzzy nest; it looks like a Canary."

"You may think that he looks like a Canary at a little distance, but not when you are near by," said the Doctor. "The Canary has a short, thick, cone-shaped bill suited to cracking seeds, while the Yellow Warbler has the slender bill necessary for prying into small cracks and crannies for insects. This Warbler also has light rusty streaks on his yellow breast. Do you remember having ever seen a Canary with such markings?"

Nat and Dodo thought for a moment, and then said they never had.

"It really may not be like a Canary," said Rap, "and it hasn't much of a song, but it has so many cute little ways that it seems like one. I know a boy who always says it's a wild Canary, but it can't be that, I see. A pair of these Warblers have a nest in one of the elder bushes by our fence, and they wouldn't mind a bit if we went to look at them. Would it be too far for you to come, sir?" he inquired timidly of the Doctor, evidently proud of having something to show.

"We shall be glad to see the nest, my boy. How is it that you have so many birds about your house?"

"I think it's partly for the same reason that you have birds here—for we don't keep cats either—and it's partly because we have four big old mulberry trees."

"What have mulberry trees to do with birds?" asked Nat, without stopping to think.

"Everything," said the Doctor. "The mulberry is one of the most attractive fruits to our familiar birds, and at least twenty-five species feed upon it greedily.

Yellow Warbler.

WOODLAND WARBLERS 109

"Whoever plants a mulberry tree in his garden sends a public invitation through Birdland for its people to come and live with him. The invitation is always accepted, and the birds appreciate the kindness so much that when they find mulberries they leave the cherries and strawberries in that garden in peace. This should teach us to plant wild fruits and berries for the birds, who prefer them to garden fruits."

As the children turned from the road into Rap's garden they saw that it held a great many birds. The bushes and trees were all untrimmed, and the old house with its shingled sides and coast-backed roof was covered with a trumpet-creeper and some grape vines.

"What a lovely place for Hummingbirds!" cried Olive.

"And Martins," added the Doctor, pointing to a bird-box with ten or twelve divisions in it, that was fastened under the eaves.

"The Warbler's nest is here," said Rap, leading the way to a back fence and feeling very proud at the admiration his home was receiving.

The children tiptoed up and each took a peep into the cup-shaped nest. The little gold and olive mother, trusting Rap from past experience, gave a quick flip of her wings, and perched on a wild blackberry bush near by. The outside of the nest looked as if it were made of silvery-gray linen floss. There were some horsehairs woven in the lining, and here and there something that looked like sponge peeped out between the strands which held the nest firmly in the crotch of the elder stem.

"What is that soft stuff?" whispered Dodo.

"It is wool scraped from the stalks of young ferns," said the Doctor; "the soft brown wool that is wrapped round the leaves to keep them warm in their winter sleep until they stretch out of the ground and feel the warmth of the sun. The little Warblers gather it in their beaks and mat it into a sort of felt."

"There is something else in the nest-lining that looks like feathers," said Nat.

"That is dandelion down."

"Don't you think, Doctor, that this nest is very thick underneath?" asked Rap. "It is twice as high as the one they built here last summer."

The Doctor felt of the bottom of the nest very gently with one finger and said, "I thought so! You have sharp eyes, Rap; it is very thick, and for a good reason—it is a two-storied nest!"

"A two-storied nest! Are there such things?" clamored the children together.

"The mother-bird is worrying; come over under the mulberry tree and I will tell you about this wonderful nest.

"There are some very ill-mannered shiftless Citizens in Birdland, called Cow-birds," began the Doctor; "you will learn about them when we come to the family to which they belong.[1] They build no nests, but have the habit of laying their eggs in the nests of other birds, just as the equally bad-behaved Cuckoos do in Europe. Some birds do not seem to know the difference between these strange eggs and their own, and so let them remain until they are hatched. Others are wise enough to know their own eggs, and chief among such sharp-eyed ones is this little Yellow Warbler.

"Coming home some morning after taking exercise for the good of her health, Mrs. Warbler finds a great white egg spotted with brown, crowded in among her own small pale blue eggs, that have their brown spots mostly arranged like a wreath around the larger end.

"Being disgusted and very angry to find her house invaded, she and her mate have a talk about the matter. Why they do not simply push the strange egg out, we do not know, but instead of that they often fly off for milkweed fibres and silk to make a new nest right on top of the first one, shutting the hateful egg out of sight underneath. Then they begin housekeeping anew, in a two-storied nest like this one, living in the upper story, and keeping the Cowbird's egg locked up in the basement, where no warmth from their bodies can reach it; and so it never hatches. If a second Cowbird's egg is laid, in the new upper story of the nest, the Warblers generally abandon their home in despair, and choose a new nesting place; but sometimes they build a third story over the other two, and thus defeat the evil designs of both their enemies without giving up their home.

"This nest of Rap's is a two-storied one, and when I touched the bottom I could feel that there was an egg in the lower story. By and by, when the birds have flown, we will take the nest apart and you can see for yourselves how ingeniously it is made."

"To think of all the ways birds have," said Rap; "going to such a heap of trouble for something they could fix with one good push."

"What happens when the Cowbird's egg stays in the nest and hatches out? Aren't the other little birds squeezed and uncomfortable?" asked Dodo.

---

[1] Here, the authors introduce the Brown-headed Cowbirds as "bad citizens" because of their brood parasitism behavior (laying their eggs in other birds' nests). The authors discuss Cowbirds in more detail in chapter 17, "A Midsummer Excursion," but they included a short discussion of them in this chapter, as the Cowbirds' parasitism affects primarily smaller songbirds like warblers. (See chapter 17 for more information.)

"Yes, they are very uncomfortable indeed, and often starve to death; but you must wait to hear about that until we come to the Cowbird himself."

"What family does he train with?" asked Nat.

"With the Blackbirds and Orioles," said the Doctor.

Then the male Yellow Warbler flew out along a branch above their heads, gave his lisping song, that sounded like "sweet, sweet, sweet, sweeter," seized an insect, and went across the garden toward his nest.

"I'm going to watch that nest," said Rap, "and if a Cowbird lays in it any more I'll take the wicked old egg away."

"Sweet, sweet, sweet," called the Warbler from the bushes.

"Maybe he understood you," said Dodo. "I'd believe most anything about birds."

THE YELLOW WARBLER

(Or Summer Yellowbird)

Length about five inches.

Upper parts rich olive-yellow, brightest on the rump and crown, but dark brown on wings and tail, with the inside half of each tail-feather yellow, and some yellow edgings on the wing-feathers.

Under parts bright yellow, in the male streaked with rich brownish-red.

A Summer Citizen of the greater part of North America, nesting in orchards and bushes, and going to the tropics in winter.

Belongs to the guilds of Tree Trappers and Sky Sweepers.

THE YELLOW-RUMPED WARBLER

(Or Myrtlebird)

"This Warbler does not sing much of a song, even in nesting-time; but you will know him on the wing by the bright yellow spot on the rump, and if he perches near by perhaps you will also see the crown of gold on the head and a spot of yellow on each side of the breast. They say there was once a great king named Midas, whose touch turned everything to gold, he was such an avaricious old miser. If that be true he must have put his finger on the Myrtlebird in four different places. Unlike most of his family the Yellow-rump is fond of seeds and berries; and so he is able to live further north in winter than any of his brothers. Unless you are spending the summer near the Canadian border you will not see him in his own home. But when they are on their journeys in spring and autumn you will meet them almost everywhere, travelling in sociable flocks."

"It must be that dark-backed bird with a yellow spot on his tail, that gobbles all the bayberries—and eats the poison-ivy berries too," said Rap.

"Yes, I see that you know him; 'that dark-backed bird with a yellow spot on his tail' is not a bad description of the Myrtle Warbler," said the Doctor; "at least, as you generally see it, in autumn or winter, when that particular spot is the only one of the four which shows off well."

"But why is he called *Myrtle* Warbler?" asked Nat. "Does he build his nest in myrtle? I thought myrtle was that shiny-leaved plant down on the ground, that doesn't have berries."

Yellow-rumped Warbler.

"No, my boy, the bird is not named from that sort of creeping flowering myrtle; his name comes from a Latin word for 'bayberry,' because the bird feeds upon its fruit, as Rap told you."

"And bayberry is that low sweet-smelling shrub that we gather in the rocky pasture, to fill the great jar in the fireplace," said Olive. "Some call it candleberry, and others wax-myrtle."

"Yes," said Rap, "and these Warblers stay round that pasture in winter as long as there is a berry left."

THE YELLOW-RUMPED WARBLER

(Or Myrtlebird)

Length about five and a half inches.

Upper parts dark gray, streaked with black; two white bars on each wing; large white spots on some of the tail-feathers. *A yellow patch on the rump and crown.*

Under parts white, streaked with black on the breast and sides. A yellow patch on each side of the breast.

A Summer Citizen of the northern United States and northward. Much less common in the West than the East. Travels south, and spends the winter everywhere from southern New England to Panama.

A great Seed Sower and a Tree Trapper.

THE OVENBIRD

"I will show you a 'skin' of the Ovenbird, because it may be some time before you will see this Ground Warbler at home in the deep woods."[2]

"'*Skin!*' What is that?" asked Rap, as the Doctor took from his pocket what looked merely like a dead bird.

"A 'bird-skin,' so called, is the bird preserved and prepared for stuffing, with all its feathers on, but without glass eyes and not mounted in a natural position. You see that it takes up much less room than the birds that are set up in my cases, and is more easily carried about."

Ovenbird.

"He looks like a little Thrush," said Olive, "except that he is too green on the back, and the stripe on his head is of a dingy gold color. That is why he is often called the 'Golden-crowned Thrush,' though he is not a Thrush at all, but one of the American Warblers, and the crown is more the color of copper, than like the gold on the Golden-crowned Kinglet's head. Perhaps the Kinglet is called after new, clean gold, and this 'Thrush' after old dusty gold."

All this time Rap had been looking intently at the Warbler without saying a word; then he said suddenly: "Why, it's the bird that builds the little house-nest on the ground in the river woods! The nest that is roofed all over and has a round hole in one side for a door! I'm so glad I know his name, for it isn't in my part of the Nuttall book and the miller doesn't know what he is called. Is he named Ovenbird because he has a door in one side of his nest like an oven?"

"Yes, Rap, the nest is shaped like the kind of oven that Indians used. Tell us about the one you found."

"I was sitting on the bank where it goes down a little to the river, and the ground there was humpy with bunches of grass. A little bird like this Warbler

---

[2] Here, Dr. Hunter explains the difference between "bird skins," also called "study skins," and taxidermized birds mounted and displayed in a lifelike pose. As an ornithologist, Dr. Hunter would have both types of birds in his collection. See the introduction for more information on the killing of wild birds for study skins, which accounted for a great deal of wild bird deaths at the time of *Citizen Bird*'s publication.

ran from between two of the grass humps and picked about on the ground for a minute and then ran back. I thought he had gone into a hole, but pretty soon he came out again and flew up through the bushes to a tall tree a little way off. He went out to the end of a long branch and began to call—soft at first and then very loud, as if his throat would split before he ended. It was a very big noise for such a little bird."

"Did he seem to say '*Teacher*, TEACHER, TEACHER'?" asked the Doctor, who knew John Burroughs very well.[3]

"Yes, he kept calling exactly that way. Then when he stopped, I looked for the hole in the ground where he came from. I felt round a little, and then I lay down on the bank and looked up hill at the place to try if I could find it that way. Then I saw a place where the grass and leaves were made into a sort of roof between the grass humps, and in the middle of this was a smooth round hole. I put my finger in and another bird, just like the first, flew out, and I saw that there were eggs there; so I drove a stick in the ground to mark the place, and went away.

"The miller said it must be a field-mouse's nest that some birds had stolen. But in the fall I took the nest home and I saw it was a real bird's nest, all woven round of strong grass with finer kinds for a lining; and there were dead leaves on the outside, so that the top looked like all the rest of the ground. I had often heard that loud singing before, but this was the first time I had a good look at the bird and his nest, and the miller won't believe now that it's a bird's nest either."

"What trade does the Ovenbird belong to?" asked Dodo. "He ought to be a baker if he lives in an oven."

"He is a Ground Gleaner and a Tree Trapper," said the Doctor, while the children laughed merrily at Dodo's idea of a baker bird.

THE OVENBIRD

Length about six inches.

Upper parts frog green, with a rusty-yellow streak between two black lines on the crown.

---

[3] Here, the authors refer to naturalist and nature writer John Burroughs. Among many other accolades, he is credited for coining the mnemonic "teacher teacher teacher" to describe the Ovenbird's song in his 1871 collection of essays on birds, *Wake Robin*. After the 1897 publication of *Citizen Bird*, Burroughs and Louis Agassiz Fuertes both joined Edward Harriman's 1899 expedition to Alaska, alongside other prominent conservation figures such as John Muir, C. Hart Merriam, and George Bird Grinnell.

Lower parts white, with black streaks on the breast and sides.

A Summer Citizen as far west as Kansas and north to Alaska, wintering far south.

THE MARYLAND YELLOW-THROAT

"Now we come to three very jolly Warblers with bright feathers and perfectly distinct ways of their own.[4] They are the Maryland Yellow-throat, the Yellow-breasted Chat, and the American Redstart. The Maryland Yellow-throat is the merry little bird who puts his head on one side to peep at you through his black mask, and then flits further along to a thicket or clump of bushes, calling persuasively—'Follow me-é, follow me-é, follow!' He is trying to coax you into a game of hide-and-seek; but if you play with him you will soon find that you must do all the seeking, for he intends to do the hiding himself.

"Does he wish to show you his deep narrow nest, made of grape-vine bark, old leaves, and grass? Not he; being crammed full of good spirits he simply wants you to share them and have a race. Sometimes he will stop a moment quite near and call—'I-spy-it, I-spy-it,' and then fly off and challenge you to a new chase. Or sometimes, if two or three call at once, you will stray away from your path without knowing it.

Top: Male. *Bottom*: Female. Maryland Yellow-throat.

"They are very gentle, lovable little birds too, and sing all through the summer when many of the better singers have grown silent."

"The Yellow-throat must be what I've called the Black-faced Yellowbird," said Rap. "Please, Doctor, does he sometimes fly right up in the air to sing a little bit and then go back into the bushes as if he had changed his mind?"

---

[4] The Maryland Yellow-throat is now called the Common Yellowthroat.

"Yes, Rap, that is one of the Yellow-throat's habits in late summer, but one that very few people notice."

THE MARYLAND YELLOW-THROAT

Length about five and a half inches.

Upper parts olive-green, in the male with a black mask reaching along each side of the head, and behind this an ashy-white border; but the female wears no mask.

Under parts bright yellow, growing white on belly.

A Summer Citizen of the United States from Georgia to Canada.

When he lives west of the Mississippi River he is called the Western Yellow-throat.

A Tree Trapper and occasionally a Sky Sweeper; a beautiful and familiar bird of the brush and tangles.

THE YELLOW-BREASTED CHAT

"The Chat, besides being a very handsome bird, is a ventriloquist and a great joker."

"Please, Uncle Roy, what is a ventroquist?" asked Dodo.

"I should have remembered not to use such a long word," laughed the Doctor. "A ven-tril-o-quist is a person who can not only imitate sounds, but makes it seem as if they came from his stomach, or even in a different direction from where he is himself. The Mockingbird can imitate many sounds, but all these come directly from the bird; while the Chat can perch on a twig above your head and give a whistle that seems to come from a bush across the road.

Yellow-breasted Chat.

"This is what enables him to play tricks on birds, House People, and various other animals. He will whistle until he has set a dog tearing through the bushes to find his supposed master. Another time he will give such a soft strange series of notes that a bird-lover will immediately begin to search through a tangle of briers, after what he imagines to be a strange bird. Then he indulges in a fit of merriment at his own jokes—'chatter-chatter-chat-chat-chat-chat-chat' he says, calling his own name as he slips away to the security of a catbrier or barberry bush. Large and vigorous and strong of beak as he is, this practical joker is wise, and does not often show his conspicuous yellow breast in open places.

"Some day in the nesting season you may see the Chat fly up in the air and hear him sing his courting song, which is very sweet, different from all his jests and jeers. You will say, if you are near enough to take a long look—'Why, that Chat has forgotten to fold up his legs, they are hanging straight down.' He has not forgotten, however; it is merely one of his odd habits at this season to cut all sorts of capers in the air, with his legs and wings and tail let loose, while his mate is quietly house-keeping in some thick bush near by. The nest is something like a Catbird's, not very tidy outside, but snug inside, and easy to find if you look in the right place. If you find it at the right time you will see that it holds four or five well-rounded eggs of a crystal-white color, with plenty of bright reddish-brown spots all over them."

THE YELLOW-BREASTED CHAT

Length seven and a half inches—much more than any other Warbler measures.

Upper parts bright olive-green, even all over.

Lower parts very bright yellow on the throat, breast, and wing-linings, but the belly
  pure white.

A strong dark-colored beak, with some dark and light marks between it and the eyes.

A Summer Citizen of the United States east of the plains and south of Ontario and
  Minnesota; travels far south in winter. When he is found west of the plains his tail
  is somewhat longer, and he is called the Long-tailed Chat.

Chiefly a Tree Trapper, but also a Seed Sower.

THE AMERICAN REDSTART

"The Redstart is the dancing Warbler, just as the Chat is the joker. He never flies along in a sober, earnest fashion, as if his business was of real importance. When on the ground he skips and hops, then takes a few short steps and a little dance backward. In the trees, where he also feeds and where in some crotch he lashes his pretty nest of leaf-stalks, moss, and horse-hair, he moves about as suddenly as can be imagined, and he has a way of flying up and backward at the same time that makes him a very confusing bird to watch. In flitting among the branches, or darting into the air for gnats, his colors make him look like a tiny Oriole."

"Oh, uncle! Uncle Roy!" cried Dodo, who had been looking along the path, "there are two of the dearest little birds down there, and one of them is red and black as you say the Redstart is, and the other is shaped like it but has brown and yellow feathers, and they move along as if the wind was blowing them!"

Before Dodo stopped speaking the whole party were looking where she pointed, Olive using the field-glass.

"Those are a pair of Redstarts," she said, "and they are picking up ants. I saw a number of little anthills there yesterday."

"A pair?" queried Nat. "They aren't the same color—one has yellow spots where the other is red."

"I guess the one with the brown and yellow feathers must be the female," said Rap; "you know the Doctor told us, way back, that when the male bird wore very bright feathers, the female was oftenest plain, so that House People and cannibal birds shouldn't see her so easily when she sat on the nest."

"You are right, my boy," said the Doctor, who always let the children answer each other's questions, if they could. "Madam Redstart, you see, wears an olive-brown cloak trimmed with yellow, and even her boys wear clothes like their mother's for a couple of seasons; for Heart of Nature does not allow them to come out in their red and black uniforms until they are three years old, and know the ways of the world."

"Learning to name birds is harder than I thought it would be," said Nat. "Some wear different feathers in spring and fall, a lot more pairs are different to begin with, and the young ones are mixed up at first. It's worse than arithmetic"—and poor Nat looked quite discouraged.

"You certainly have to remember the laws of Birdland, as well as their exceptions," answered the Doctor; "but when you have once recognized and named a bird you will carry its picture always in your

Top: Male. *Bottom*: Female.
American Redstart.

WOODLAND WARBLERS 119

mind, for the Redstarts that you will see when you are very old men and women, will be like the one that is dancing along the walk now."

"Why do they call this Warbler a 'Redstart'?" asked Dodo.

"Because it has a lot of red on it, and it's always starting up in a hurry," ventured Rap.

"That is not the real reason," said the Doctor. "The name comes from a German word that means 'red tail,' and rightly belongs to a bird of Europe that is never found in this country. Our bird has some red on the tail, but I really think that Rap's answer is the better one."

THE AMERICAN REDSTART

Length about five and a half inches.

Upper parts shining black, marked on the wings and tail with rich salmon-red.

Under parts shining black on the neck and breast, bright salmon-red on the sides, and pinkish-white on the belly.

In the *female* all the parts which are black in her mate are light greenish-gray, and she is clear yellow where he is red.

A useful Summer Citizen of eastern North America, from Kansas to Labrador. Winters in the tropics.

A Ground Gleaner, Tree Trapper, and Sky Sweeper.

CHAPTER 13

Around the Old Barn

THIS DAY THE BIRD LOVERS from Orchard Farm were having a picnic in the hickory and oak woods back of the fields. It was a charming place for such a day's outing, for on the edge of the woods stood an old two-storied hay barn, which was empty in early June and a capital place in which to play "I spy" and "feet above water." On the other side of the wood was an old swampy meadow full of saplings and tangled bushes, such as birds love for nesting places.

The Doctor had set Rap, Nat, and Dodo roaming about to look for birds, and promised to tell them something of their habits when each child had written down the description of two birds.

The children divided their hunting ground, so that they might not interfere with each other. Dodo chose the woods, because she wanted to stay near Olive, who was making a sketch of some ferns; Rap took the old barn and a bit of bushy pasture near it, and Nat went down to the swampy meadow with its border of cedar trees. While they tramped about the Doctor sat with his back against the side of the barn, looking over the beautiful scene and thinking.

The children did not return until after Mammy Bun had spread out a delicious luncheon in the barn, and then they were divided between hunger and the wish to tell about their birds.

"I have two nice birds all written down," said Dodo, between mouthfuls. "One was rather little and sort of green on top and white underneath, and he kept going up and down all the branches of an oak tree as if he couldn't keep still a moment, and he talked all the while as if he was asking me why I watched him and then scolding me for doing it."

"That is the Red-eyed Vireo," said the Doctor.

"Maybe he did have red eyes," said Dodo, "but he moved so quick I couldn't see them. But my other bird was splendid! Very bright red all over, except his wings and tail—they were black, and I'm sure he has a nest high up on an oak branch."

"That is the Scarlet Tanager. What did you see, Nat?"

"I crept in among the cedar trees, and there was a whole lot of rather big gray birds sitting in a row on a branch; they had black around their beaks and their head feathers stuck up in front. They didn't seem to be building nests, but were only whispering to each other."

"Those were Cedar Waxwings."

"Then," continued Nat, "when I was coming back I saw a flock of the prettiest, jolliest little birds flying round the old grass, and hanging on to some stalks of weeds. They were mostly yellow with some black, and they sang something like Canaries, and when they flew they sort of jerked along."

"Those were American Goldfinches. And now for yours, Rap."

"I was looking at the Barn Swallows most of the time," he answered, "and thinking there must be a good many different cousins in their family; then I went down to the pasture and saw a bird I never noticed before, who flew over from the potato field and went into a thorn bush. He was bigger than a Robin and had a thick head and beak. He was black and white on top, but when he went by I saw he had a beautiful spot on the breast like a shield—sort of pink red, the color of raspberries, you know."

"That was the Rose-breasted Grosbeak," said the Doctor. "Now, we have pockets full of material for bird stories,—enough to last a week. By the time you have heard about these six birds and some of their near relations, such as the Butcher Bird, you will have been introduced to the chief of the Birds that Sing and be on the way to those that only Croak and Call. We will begin with Dodo's 'Talking Bird.'"

THE RED-EYED VIREO

(The Talker)

"This bird is the most popular member of his family—and he has twenty brothers, all living in North America."

"Isn't he a Warbler?" asked Rap. "I always thought he was one, for he fusses round the trees the same as they do, though of course he has much more of a song."

Red-eyed Vireo.

"He belongs to a family of his own, but yours was an easy mistake to make, for the difference is not readily seen except in the beak, and you have to look at that very closely to see it. The Warblers mostly have smooth slender beaks, but the Vireos have stouter ones, with a little hooked point that enables them to pick out and secure a great variety of insects. The Chat is our only Warbler with a very stout beak, even stouter than a Vireo's, but it has no hook at the end. The Redstart's has a hooked point, but the rest of the beak is very broad and flat, with a row of stiff bristles at each corner of the mouth, to keep insects from kicking free when they are caught."

"You say his eyes are red. But why is his name 'Vireo'—does that mean anything?"

"'Vireo' comes from the Latin word meaning 'green,' and because all of this family have greenish backs one of their common names is 'Greenlet.' Besides being very pretty to look at, this little red-eyed bird is a great worker and does whatever he undertakes in a most complete manner. When he starts his tree trapping in the morning he does not flit carelessly from one tree to another, but after selecting his feeding ground, goes all over one branch, never leaving it for another until he has searched every crack and leaf.

"Meanwhile he carries on a rapid sing-song conversation, sometimes for his own benefit and sometimes to cheer his mate on the nest, for this Vireo is one of the few birds who talk too freely about their homes. These homes of theirs are another proof of industry; they are beautifully woven of a dozen kinds of stuff—grass, bark-strips, seed-vessels, fine shavings, and sometimes bits of colored paper and worsted, and half hang from the crotch of a small branch with a nice little umbrella of leaves to cover Madam's head. There she sits peeping out, not a bit shy if she feels that your intentions toward her are kindly. I have often found these nests in the orchard, on branches only a few feet from the ground, and I have also found them high up in the maples by the attic window.

"The Vireo does not stop work at noon when the field hands lie under the apple trees, with their dinner pails beside them. No, he only works and talks faster, keeping one eye on the home branch, and this is what he says, stopping

AROUND THE OLD BARN 123

between every sentence: 'I know it—I made it—Would you think it?—Mustn't touch it—Shouldn't like it—If you do it—I'll know it—You'll rue it!'"

"He was talking exactly like that this morning," said Dodo. "Will the nests last after they are empty, Uncle Roy, so we can find some?"

"Yes, surely; these nests are very strong and firm, often lasting a whole year."

"I know it—I made it!—Would you think it?" called a musical voice from the wood.

"Why, he is at it yet," said Rap; "I think 'The Talker' would be a fine name for him."

"So it would—and more polite than 'The Preacher,' as some call him who think he is a trifle too prosy in his remarks. One of his brothers, whose eyes are white instead of red, and who lives in the bushes instead of high woods, is called 'The Politician' from his fondness for newspapers—not that he can read them, of course, but he likes to paper his nest with clippings from them, which is his way of making a scrap-book."

THE RED-EYED VIREO

Length about six inches.

Upper parts olive-green, with a white line over the eye, and gray cap with a black border.

Under parts white, shaded with greenish on the sides.

A Summer Citizen of North America east of the Pacific States, and a hard-working
member of the guild of Tree Trappers.

THE GREAT NORTHERN SHRIKE

(Or Butcher Bird)

"I thought you would tell about my beautiful red bird next," interrupted Dodo. "Why do we want to hear about this bird if he lives so far north?"

"Your bird will come later on, little girl. Nat and Rap must each have their turn before it comes to you again; besides, this Shrike is a sort of cousin to the Vireos by right of his hooked beak, and you know I am trying to place our birds somewhat in their regular family order."

Poor Dodo felt ashamed to have seemed selfish and interrupted unnecessarily.

"Some winter or early spring day, when the woods are bare and birds are very scarce, you will look into a small tree and wonder what that gray and black bird, who is sitting there so motionless, can be. He is too small for a Hawk, though there

Northern Shrike.

is something hawk-like about his head. He is altogether too large for a Chickadee; not the right shape for a Woodpecker; and after thus thinking over the most familiar winter birds, you will find that you only know what he is *not*.

"Suddenly he spreads his wings and swoops down, seizing something on or near the ground—a mouse perhaps, or a small bird—let us hope one of the detestable English Sparrows. Or else you may see this same bird, in the gray and black uniform, peep cautiously out of a bush and then skim along close above the ground, to secure the field-mouse he has been watching; for the guild of Wise Watchers catch their prey in both of these ways, and most of them are cannibal birds."

"What is a cannibal bird?" asked Dodo. "I forget. I know that real cannibals are people that eat other people. Do these birds eat people?"

"They eat birds and other small animals," said Rap. "Don't you remember?"

"Why, of course I do," said Dodo. "But if Shrikes eat birds, aren't they very bad Citizens?"

"I do not wonder that you think so, my lassie; and so they would be if they ate birds only; but the Shrike earns his right to be thought a good Citizen by devouring mice and many kinds of insects, like beetles, which injure orchards and gardens. The comparatively few birds that he destroys are mostly seed-eaters—not the most valuable kinds to the farmer.

"In fact, the Shrike is especially useful in helping us to drive out the greedy, quarrelsome English Sparrow. This disreputable tramp not only does no work for his taxes—he hates honest work, like all vagrants—but destroys the buds of trees and plants, devours our grain crops, and drives away the industrious native birds who are good Citizens; so the Wise Men, who have tried the Sparrow's case, say that he is a very bad bird, who ought to suffer the extreme penalty of the law.[1]

---

[1] As noted in several earlier annotations, the English Sparrow (House Sparrow) is depicted as a "bad bird" throughout the text. Here, the English Sparrow is counterposed with the Northern Shrike, who is a "good bird" despite eating other birds, because the Shrike also performs valuable ecological duties for humans. In contrast, the English

AROUND THE OLD BARN 125

"For this reason we must forgive the Shrike if he takes a few other birds when he is hungry and in a hurry. He has a strange habit which has earned for him the name of Butcher Bird. If at any time he secures more food than he needs for his immediate use, he puts it by to keep in 'cold storage' by hanging it on the frozen twigs of a tree or thorn bush. Heart of Nature has doubtless taught him this habit through hard experience. Where the Shrike spends his winters, the food-supply is variable; it may snow for days and days, when he can find nothing to eat; so he has learned to store up provisions when the hunting is good, and of course such a thrifty bird may sometimes save up more than he really needs.

"You may know this Shrike on sight without hearing him sing—and perhaps you do not expect a cannibal bird to be a singer. But in late March and early April, when he is about to take his homeward journey to the North, he often warbles beautifully, and even brings in some mocking notes, until you would think that a Catbird, Thrasher, or Mockingbird must have wandered from the South too soon; and if you ever happen to see a Shrike and a Mocker close together, you may mistake one for the other, they look so much alike at a little distance."

"I never knew that there were nice birds around in winter," said Nat. "I thought all the country was good for then, was for coasting and skating! I wish I could stay here a whole year, Uncle Roy."

"Stranger things have happened," said the Doctor, looking at Olive with a twinkle in his eye that the children did not see.

THE GREAT NORTHERN SHRIKE
Length about ten inches.[2]

Upper parts bluish-gray, with a broad black stripe along the side of the head to behind the eye. Black wings with a large white spot on each. Black tail with white tips to the outside feathers.

Lower parts grayish-white, faintly barred with darker. A great strong beak, hooked like a Hawk's.

Sparrow does no such work, as he is a "disreputable tramp" who "hates honest work, like all vagrants" and worse, "drives away the industrious native birds who are good Citizens." The reference to the Wise Men saying the English Sparrow "ought to suffer the extreme penalty of the law" is prescient; the Migratory Bird Treaty Act of 1918 protects all migratory birds from being killed or hunted for food, feathers, or sport, but it does not include invasive, nonnative birds such as the English Sparrow under its protection.

[2] The Great Northern Shrike is now called the Northern Shrike.

Only a Winter Visitor in the United States—a Summer Citizen of the far North. Belongs both to the Ground Gleaners and the Wise Watchers.

THE CEDAR WAXWING

(The Polite Bird)

"This is the bird, Nat, that you saw in the cedar tree, where you said it was 'sitting about doing nothing,'" continued the Doctor.

"The reason of this seeming idleness is, that he belongs to the small group of birds who do not nest until June, and hereabouts rarely begin their homes before the middle of that month. Waxwings are very gentle, affectionate birds; before the nesting season, and after their families are able to take care of themselves, they wander about in flocks of sometimes thirty or forty, keeping close together, both when they fly and when they take their seats. They spend most of the time in the trees where they feed, whispering to one another in their quiet way, and you will very seldom see them on the ground.

"Your best chance to watch them is either before the leaves are out or after they have fallen, when a flock will sometimes sit for half an hour in a bare tree, exchanging civilities, stroking each other's feathers, and passing food around. This trait has given them the reputation of being the most polite birds in all Birdland. One will find a dainty morsel and offer it to his next neighbor, who passes it on—hunt-the-slipper fashion—until some one makes up his mind to eat it, or returns it to its original owner. All the while such a pleasant lunch is going on, the amiable birds make complimentary remarks to one another about their dress—how very handsome is one's long pointed topknot, what a becoming yellow border another's tail has, and how particularly fine are the coral-red bangles on the wings of a third—which is much better than if they should pick each other to pieces and talk about 'frumps' under their breath.

Cedar Waxwing.

"Some people have complained that the Cedar Waxwing eats cherries, and have given him the name of 'Cherry Bird'; but the Wise Men say that he really eats very few cherries or other garden fruits, more than half of his food being wild berries, such as those of the evergreen juniper we commonly call 'cedar.'

"He may be called one of the best of neighbors; for, besides feeding his young on many different kinds of destructive insects, he eats cutworms and the wicked beetles which destroy so many grand old elm trees. And you know it is always nice to have polite neighbors."

THE CEDAR WAXWING

Length about seven inches.

Upper parts quiet Quaker brown, very smooth and satiny, with a fine long, pointed crest on the head.

Rich velvety black about the beak and in a line through the eye.

A yellow band across end of tail, and some little points like red sealing-wax on the inner wing-feathers, from which it takes the name "Waxwing."

A Citizen of North America from the Fur Countries southward, visiting all but the most southern of the United States.

Belonging both to the Tree Trappers and Fruit Sowers.

CHAPTER 14

The Swallows

"'Rap has been watching the Barn Swallows," continued the Doctor, after the children had been over to the cedar belt to see if the flock of polite birds were there still. "He thinks there are a great many cousins in the Swallow family, but can't tell them apart.

"There are ten species of North American Swallows, four of which are very familiar birds in all parts of the United States. These are the Purple Martin; Barn Swallow; Tree Swallow; and Bank Swallow.

"As a family it is easy to name the Swallows from their way of flying. All are officers who rank high in the guild of Sky Sweepers, being constantly in the air seizing their insect food on the wing; thus they kill all sorts of flies, flying ants, small winged beetles, midges, and mosquitoes. They have lithe and shapely bodies, strong, slender wings, wide mouths, and flat, broad bills coming to a sharp point, which makes it easy for them to secure whatever they meet in the air. So swift and sure is their flight that they can feed their newly flown nestlings in mid air; but their feet are small and weak, so that in perching they usually choose something small and easy to grasp, like a telegraph wire.

"Though they nest in all parts of the country, some species going to the Fur Countries, as far north as any trees grow, yet they all seek a very warm climate for their winter home, because it is only in such places that the insects of the air are found.[1] The distance, therefore, between the summer and winter homes

---

[1] By "the fur countries," the authors are most likely referring to the parts of the United States and Canada associated with the North American fur trade.

of the Swallow family is very great, and these brave little birds are wonderful travellers.

"They are so swift on the wing that they do not fear to fly in the day-time, and so escape a great many of the accidents that overtake birds who travel by night. They come to the middle parts of the United States during the month of April, and start on their southward journey during late September and early October.

"After mating they either choose separate nesting places, or keep together in colonies. In early autumn they gather in great flocks along the borders of rivers, ponds, and lakes, often also on sea beaches, where they fly to and fro, as if strengthening their wings for the long flight they intend to take. It has been recently discovered by the Wise Men that these birds, who had been supposed to eat nothing but insects, feed at this time upon the same bayberries of which the Yellow-rumped Warbler is so fond; and that is one reason why they stay by the sandy wastes where these bushes grow. But no doubt Rap could have told us that, if we had asked him about it. Another reason for lingering near water is, that winged insects fly about wet places later in the season than they do in dry ones."

"But you have left out the Chimney Swallow," said Nat; "and there are plenty of them all about everywhere."

"I have not left him out. Have you forgotten that he does not belong to the Swallow family? Though he looks like a Swallow and flies like one, the Wise Men know that he is not a song bird, and have put him where he belongs—with the Birds that Croak and Call, next to the Hummingbird and Nighthawk. They call him the Chimney Swift, because he flies so fast, and you must always give him his right name.

"If you write very carefully in your little books the description of our four common Swallows, you will not find it difficult to name them when you see them. We will begin with the largest—the Purple Martin."

"Why is it called 'Martin'?" asked Rap. "Did somebody named Martin find it, as Mr. Wilson found the Thrush they named after him?"

"No, my boy, the name comes from a Latin word, meaning 'warlike' or 'martial,' because in the Old World certain Swallows there called Martins were considered good fighters, and very brave in driving away Hawks and other cannibal birds. Don't you remember that Mars was the God of War in classic mythology, and haven't you heard soldiers complimented on their fine *martial* appearance?"

THE PURPLE MARTIN

Length seven and a half inches.

Upper parts shining blue-black, not quite so glossy on the wings and forked tail.

Under parts the same as the upper in the male, but grayish-white in the female and young ones.

Song rich and musical, of two or three flute-like notes. Nest made of a few leaves or straws, in a bird-box when it is provided—otherwise in a hollow tree. Eggs white, without any spots.

A good Summer Citizen and a favorite everywhere; but for many reasons it is growing scarcer every year. The English Sparrow is one of its greatest enemies, and not only drives it from its nesting-boxes, but attacks the young birds.

A member of the guild of Sky Sweepers.

Top: Male. *Bottom*: Female. Purple Martin.

THE BARN SWALLOW

Length six to seven inches.

Upper parts shining steel-blue, but the face buff.

Under parts rich buff, brick-red on the throat, where there is also a steel-blue collar.

Tail very long and deeply forked, with the side-feathers narrow, and some white spots on them.

Song a musical laugh, heard when the birds fly low over meadows and ponds.

Nest a sort of bracket, made of little mud balls and straw stuck on a beam in a hayloft. Eggs white, with plenty of reddish-brown spots.

A Summer Citizen in most of the United States.

A Sky Sweeper of the very first rank.

Barn Swallow.

"Barney is a charming neighbor, who should be welcome in every home—sociable, musical, and very useful in destroying the flies and gnats that worry horses and cattle. Though it builds its first nest in May, it often brings out its last brood in August; thus during its long nesting season consuming a very large share of insects, and proving itself a kind friend to the cows at a time when flies are most persistent."

Tree Swallow.

THE TREE SWALLOW

(Or White-bellied Swallow)

Length six inches.

Upper parts sparkling green, with darker wings and tail, the latter but little forked.

Under parts snow-white.

A sweet, twittering song.

Nests in the hollows of dead trees, usually in old Woodpeckers' holes, but occasionally in bird-boxes. Eggs pure white.

A good Citizen of the United States, but more shy than the Martin and Barn Swallow; these two often return, year after year, to some favorite nesting place, but the Tree Swallow is not so reliable.

A Sky Sweeper.

THE BANK SWALLOW

(Or Sand Martin)

The smallest Swallow, only five inches long.

Upper parts dusty brown, darker on the wings, and tail forked a little, like the Tree Swallow's. Under parts white, with a brown band across the breast.

Song a sort of giggle—like some little girl's we know.

Nests many together in holes in a clay or loamy bank, lined with feathers and straw. Eggs pure white.

A Citizen of most parts of the world—northerly in summer, southerly in winter.

A Sky Sweeper.

Bank Swallow.

"Bankey is a sociable, useful little bird, living usually in great colonies. I have seen a hundred of their holes in a single bank, all dug by these industrious little Swallows with no other tools than their feeble beaks and claws. When the young from these nests are learning to fly the old birds are darting to and fro all day long to teach them how to use their wings, and the bank seems like a bustling village; every bird has something to do and say, and they always try to do both at once. If any one asks you why House People should love and protect Swallows, even if you have forgotten the names of many of the insects they destroy, remember to answer—'Swallows eat mosquitoes!'"

CHAPTER 15

A Brilliant Pair

THE SCARLET TANAGER

"That is my beautiful red bird!" cried Dodo, clapping her hands. "I never shall forget the looks of his bright red coat with black sleeves and tails. I saw a sort of green bird in the same tree, but it was so different I never thought it could be his wife, till I came to think—for the green one stayed near the nest when I came nearer and looked up, but the red bird flew away and hid behind some leaves."

"You are quite lucky to have seen a Scarlet Tanager in his home woods," said the Doctor, "for he is a shy bird who does not often venture to show his tropical colors in open places. He knows enough not to make himself a target for cannibal birds or House People either. Except in his journeys to and from his winter home he lives in the shelter of the tallest forest trees, where it is very difficult to see him, showy as he is in his flashing colors, and even if you know by his song that he is there. He may say, as some people think he does, 'Pshaw! wait—wait—wait for me, wait!' but he does not wait a moment if he thinks he is seen.

Scarlet Tanager.

"He is very fond of water, both for bathing and drinking, and seldom nests far from it. Whether he uses the quiet ponds and smooth streams also for a looking-glass to comb his hair and arrange his gay coat by, we cannot be sure, but he always looks as trig as if he had some such aid.

"The Tanager children are curious things. Sometimes they wear coats of many colors, like Joseph's."

"Why is that?" asked Nat.

"The reason is this. You remember I told you that young birds usually wear plain feathers like their mothers?"

"Oh, yes," said Rap; "so that it is hard to see them until they have sense enough to take care of themselves."

"Precisely! Now, Mother Tanager is greenish and yellow, and Father Tanager is scarlet and black. The young ones come from the nest looking like their mother, but as they shed their baby clothes and gain new feathers, bits of red and black appear here and there on the little boys, until they look as if they had on a crazy-quilt of red, yellow, green, and black. You need not wonder that little Tommy Tanager does not care to be seen in such patched clothes, but prefers to stay in the deep woods or travel away until his fine red spring jacket is complete. Father Tanager also changes his scarlet coat after the nesting. About the time he counts his children and starts on his southward trip, he puts on a greenish coat like his wife's gown; but he keeps his black tail and wings, so that the children need not mistake him for their mother. It is lucky for her that he and the boys have sense enough to put on their own clothes, or such a very dressy family would keep her busy looking after their toilets."

"These Tanagers aren't very plenty about here—are they, Doctor?" asked Rap.

"Not now, my boy; their scarlet feathers are very handsome, and thoughtless, greedy people have shot so many in the nesting season, to sell for bonnet trimmings, that the family is growing small. But I hope that, by making laws to protect birds and teaching children everywhere what good neighbors and Citizens they are, these beautifully plumed families may increase once more.[1]

"The Scarlet Tanager is the brightest red bird that you will find in the eastern half of the United States, but even he is not as showy as his western cousin, the Louisiana Tanager."

---

[1] As discussed in the introduction, the use of bird feathers in hats was one of the inciting factors for the resurgence of the Audubon Society in the late nineteenth century. This passage also demonstrates another lesson for adults, as the authors exhort their adult readers to create laws to protect birds.

THE SCARLET TANAGER

Length about seven inches.

Male: bright scarlet with black wings and tail.

Female: light olive-green above, dull yellow below, with dusky wings and tail.

A good Summer Citizen of North America east of the plains and north of Virginia.

Belonging to the guilds of Tree Trappers and Seed Sowers.

THE LOUISIANA TANAGER

"Isn't this the one I saw in your glass case, Doctor?" asked Rap with great eagerness; "I mean that one like a Scarlet Tanager, but not so red, more of a rose-pink all over, wings and tail too."[2]

"No," said the Doctor pleasantly. "That is a Summer Tanager—the only one I ever saw in this neighborhood. It is so rare here that I shot it to make sure there was no mistake, and you probably never saw one alive, for the Summer Tanager is a tender bird, who seldom strays so far north as this. But see—what do you think of this—isn't it a beauty?"

So saying, the Doctor took out of his pocket a bird-skin he had provided for the occasion, and the children could not restrain their glee at the sight.

"Oh! oh!" exclaimed Dodo, clapping her hands as she always did when excited; "it's all gold and ruby and jet. Where did you get it, Uncle Roy?"

"A friend of mine sent it to me from Oregon," answered the Doctor; "he thought I would like to have it for my collection, because it came from the very region where this kind of Tanager was discovered almost a hundred years ago."

"I thought you said it was a Louisiana Tanager," said Rap and Nat, almost in the same breath.

"So it is, boys; but it does not live in the State of Louisiana you are thinking about, down by the mouth of the Mississippi River. I shall have to explain how it got its name by giving you a little lesson in the history and geography of our country.[3] A great many years ago there was a King of France called Louis

---

[2] The Louisiana Tanager is now called the Western Tanager. This represents yet another bird from the West that would never be found in Connecticut, but that Coues inserted later in the writing process, as a way of including some of his expertise as a Western frontier ornithologist. This inclusion is less surprising given Coues's history with the bird, described in more detail in the following footnote.

[3] Here, the authors include the history of the Lewis and Clark expedition as part of the Louisiana (Western) Tanager's origin story. Lewis and Clark were the first Western explorers to formally describe the bird in their 1804–1806 expedition. The Lewis and Clark expedition was close to Coues's heart, for in 1893, he edited a new edition of the official account of the Lewis and Clark Expedition, originally written by Nicholas Biddle and Paul

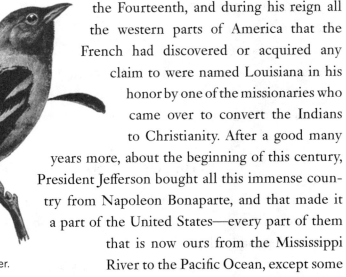
Louisiana Tanager.

the Fourteenth, and during his reign all the western parts of America that the French had discovered or acquired any claim to were named Louisiana in his honor by one of the missionaries who came over to convert the Indians to Christianity. After a good many years more, about the beginning of this century, President Jefferson bought all this immense country from Napoleon Bonaparte, and that made it a part of the United States—every part of them that is now ours from the Mississippi River to the Pacific Ocean, except some that we afterward took from Mexico.

President Jefferson was a very wise man, and as soon as he had bought all this land he wanted to know about it. So he sent an expedition to explore it, under two brave captains named Lewis and Clark. They were gone almost three years; and one day,—I remember now, it was the sixth of June, 1806,—when they were camping in what is now Idaho, near the border of Oregon, they found this lovely bird, and wrote a description of it in their note-books—just as you did with your Scarlet Tanager, Dodo, only theirs was the first one anybody ever wrote. They also saved the specimen and afterward gave it to Alexander Wilson, who painted the first picture of it, and named it the Louisiana Tanager in his book."

"Did you ever see one alive, Uncle Roy?" asked Nat; "what does it look like flying?"

"I can answer that question," said Olive; "don't you remember, father, when we were in Colorado, the same year we found the Sage Thrasher and Rock Wren, that I thought the first one we saw was a Scarlet Tanager in one of its patch-work plumages, till you told me about it—though it did seem to be too bright yellow, and the middle of the back was black. But it looked the same size, and flew just the same. How beautiful it looked, as it flashed its golden feathers through the dark-green pine trees!" added Olive, her face lighting up at the recollection.

Allen and published in 1814. Coues's reprint of the *History of the Expedition Under the Command of Lewis and Clark* included copious annotations, many of which drew on his knowledge as an ornithologist, as the original journals and field notebooks include numerous references to the bird-life encountered on the expedition.

"Yes, I remember," answered the Doctor. "All the Tanagers of our country have pretty much the same habits. Even if we had found the nest we might have mistaken it for a Scarlet Tanager's. Those I have seen in the Museum are quite similar, built of twigs and pliant stems, and lined with fine rootlets. The position of the nest, saddled as it is on the horizontal limb of a tree, is very similar, and you could hardly tell the eggs apart.

"But come, children, you must be tired by this time, and hungry too. Let us go to supper, and see what Mammy Bun has cooked for us this evening. You stay too, Rap."

THE LOUISIANA TANAGER

Length about seven inches.

Adult male: rich yellow, with black wings, tail, and middle of the back; the wings with two white or yellow bars on each; the whole head crimson.

Female: not very different from the female Scarlet Tanager.

A handsome and useful Summer Citizen of nearly all that great part of the United States which was once called Louisiana.

A member of the same guilds as the Scarlet Tanager.

CHAPTER 16

A Tribe of Weed Warriors

(Containing both Soldiers and Quakers)

"A NEW FAMILY? Soldiers and Quakers? What does that mean?" asked Nat. "I thought my jolly yellow bird with the black cap came next."

"His family does come next—the Finch family. You must hear a little about that first, and let your American Goldfinch take his turn with his brothers and cousins, for Rap's Rose-breasted Grosbeak belongs also in this family."

"You say my bird is called American Goldfinch. He is such a bright yellow that gold is a good name for him, but what does 'Finch' mean?"

"Finch, as I said, is the name of the great family to which he belongs. It is the very largest family in Birdland, and members of it live in almost all parts of the world. All kinds of Finches and Sparrows belong to it, and so do Grosbeaks and Buntings, as well as the Canaries that we keep for pets. There are about five hundred and fifty different kinds of them.

"The birds that you have been studying thus far, from the Bluebird, Robin, and Wood Thrush to the Tanagers, belong to several different families and are chiefly insect-eaters, taking various fruits and berries in season, it is true, but making insects their regular diet. Insects are not hard for any bird to eat, and so the bills of these birds do not have to be very stout or thick—some, indeed, are very thin and weak, like the Brown Creeper's.

"But the habits of the Finch family are quite different, and their beaks also. They are true seed-eating birds, and their beaks are short, stout, and thick—cone-shaped it is called, like that of the White-throated Sparrow you learned about one day. This enables them to crack the various seeds upon which they live at all times except in the nesting season, when few seeds are ripe. During this time they eat a variety of insects, and feed them to the young birds; for young birds must grow so rapidly, in order to be strong enough for the autumn journey, that they require more nourishing food than seeds.

"The Finch family being able to live so well upon seed food do not have to make such long autumn journeys; for even in very cold places there are plenty of seeds to be had all through the winter."

"Do you mean berries, please, uncle?" said Dodo; "because if it was very cold wouldn't berries freeze as hard as pebbles?"

"They eat berries, but only as Weed Warriors,—for the seeds that are in the berries,—not for the juicy, fruity part, as the Seed Sowers do.

"The Robin, Thrush, and Catbird eat fruits and berries for the juicy, pulpy part. They swallow this, and the seeds or pits pass out with the wastage of their bodies; this is what makes them Seed Sowers. But when one of the Finch family eats berries, it is for the seed or pit inside the pulp. His strong beak cracks the seed and his stomach digests its kernel. So these birds do not *sow* the seeds they eat, but *destroy* them. This is why I call them Weed Warriors. A warrior is any one who goes to war, and fights against enemies; we have enemies among plants, and these birds fight for us against them. There are hundreds of different kinds of plants, whose flowers have no beauty, and for which we have not as yet found any use; so we call them weeds. All such seeds would be blown about, take root, and sprout everywhere, thus filling the place of useful plants, if they were not held in check by these seed-eating birds."

"Isn't it wise the ways things are fixed?" said Rap. "Some birds to eat the insects and sow wild fruits and berries; some birds to eat weed seeds and prevent them from being sown. I think some people would do better if they didn't think themselves so smart and mix things all up!"

"You are right, my boy! We should not interfere with Heart of Nature by foolishly trying to aid him unless we are perfectly sure that he wishes and needs our help.

"There is one member of this Finch family, the European Sparrow, that we know by the name of English Sparrow. In his native country he eats both insects and seeds, and also does some good by eating certain tree-worms. A number of years ago the trees in our cities were being eaten by canker-worms, and some one said—'Let us bring over some of these Sparrows to live in the cities and eat the canker-worms.' This person meant well, but he did not know enough about what he was doing.[1]

"The birds were brought, and for a while they ate the worms and stayed near cities. But soon the change in climate also changed their liking for insects, and they became almost wholly seed and vegetable eaters, devouring the young buds on vines and trees, grass-seed, oats, rye, wheat, and other grains.

"Worse than this, they increased very fast and spread everywhere, quarrelling with and driving out the good citizens, who belong to the regular Birdland guilds, taking their homes and making themselves nuisances. The Wise Men protested against bringing these Sparrows, but no one heeded their warning until it was too late. Now it is decided that these Sparrows are bad Citizens and criminals; so they are condemned by every one. All this trouble came because one man, as Rap says, 'thought he was so smart and mixed things up.'"

"It was those Sparrows in the city that made me think all wild birds must be ugly; but that was because *I* was too smart and didn't know anything about other birds," said Nat frankly.

"I think we are getting way off from Nat's yellow bird," said Dodo; "and now I see lots more of Rap's Rose-breasted Grosbeaks, over on the fence. I want to know what they are doing in the potato field. I hope they don't dig up the little potatoes."

"No, you need not worry about that," said the Doctor, "and you must wait a bit yet, for the Rose-breast does not come until nearly the end of his family."

"There must be a great many different-looking birds in this Finch family," said Rap, "if plain Sparrows and yellow Goldfinches both belong to it."

"Indeed there are! Did I not say that there were both Quakers and soldiers in it?" said the Doctor. "For in addition to the Goldfinch there is a bright-blue cousin and a red one."

"What are their names, and shall we see them here?" cried Dodo.

"You will learn their names very soon. The blue one now has a nest across the meadow, and the red one makes us a visit every autumn; but you must stop asking questions if you want to hear about them to-day.

---

[1] This segment describes the introduction of English Sparrows (House Sparrows) to the United States from Europe. The American Acclimatization Society, among other organizations, brought over English Sparrows to help eat pest insects on farms. Although English Sparrows are omnivorous, they eat vastly more grains than bugs, and thus their utility to humans (or "citizenship") was put into question.

"The first of the Finch family is a bird you will only see in the winter, and not even then if you are living further south than the middle range of States. It is called the Pine Grosbeak."

THE PINE GROSBEAK

"This bird has a great heavy beak, that makes him look rather stupid; in fact, this beak gives him the name of Gros-beak, which means the same as Great-beak.[2] He loves the pine woods of Canada and builds his nest among them, only a little way above the snow that still covers the ground at the early season when this bird begins housekeeping.

"When the northern winter is very severe, Pine Grosbeaks gather in flocks and scatter through the States. But you must not expect to see a whole flock of beautiful strawberry-red birds, for only the old males are red; the females are dull gray and yellowish, while the young males look like their mothers, and do not wear their gay coats until they are two years old. You will not be likely to hear these birds sing, though they sometimes do so on their winter trips. Their usual call-note is a whistle which they give when flying.

Pine Grosbeak.

"Some day this winter when you are taking a walk you may see them on the ground under chestnut and beech trees, and in old pastures where the red sumach berries are the only bright things left above the snow. You will think it a very cheerful sight—red birds and red berries together. You will also have time to take a good look at them, for they move slowly, and be glad to know the names of your friends who are hardy enough to brave the cold.

"Though this Grosbeak seems rather dull and stupid out of doors, he is a charming cage pet, growing tame and singing a delightful warbling song. I picked up one with a broken wing when I was a boy, and kept him for many years; the hurt wing was soon healed, and the bird was always tame and happy

---

[2] The Pine Grosbeak is another bird not typically found in Connecticut, but it was not one of the birds Coues added toward the end of the writing of *Citizen Bird*, the full list of which can be found in the introduction.

after that, though he soon lost his bright feathers. But I would never advise any one to make a cage pet of a bird who has been born wild and once known liberty. No matter if he lives and thrives: he will sometimes remember the days when he was free, and be very sad."

"My Canary is never sad," said Nat: "he is always singing."

"For very many years Canaries have been bred in cages, to be pets, and as these have never been wild they are used to cage life. They are the best birds for pets, because they are seed-eaters, and it is easy to supply the food they like.[3]

"Some winter day, or even late in autumn, you may see on your walks, another red bird—a near relation of the Pine Grosbeak; in fact, the two often flock together. This bird is called the American Crossbill."

THE PINE GROSBEAK

Length about nine inches.

General color of adult male strawberry-red, the wings and tail dark, with some light-brown and white edgings; the tail forked a little.

The female and young male gray, tinged here and there with saffron-yellow.

A Summer Citizen as far north from the States as trees grow, roving in winter about the northerly and middle States.

A fine, large Weed Warrior, with a very stout beak, almost like a Parrot's.

THE AMERICAN CROSSBILL

(The Cone Wrencher)

"When it is winter in the northern parts of North America, and the Great Snow Owls have scattered on their southward journey—when heavy snows have beaten down and covered the seed-stalks of weeds and well-nigh walled the little fur-bearing beasts into their holes—then in regions where March brings only storms of sleet to coat the tree-trunks and lock up insect food, a pair of strange birds are already building their nest.

"These two birds, though alike in shape, are as different in color as Mr. and Mrs. Scarlet Tanager. But there is one point about them by which you may tell

---

[3] The differentiation between formerly wild animals bred for captivity, such as the Canary, and still-wild animals, such as the Pine Grosbeak, exemplifies the social construction of nature (discussed in earlier footnotes). Readers of *Citizen Bird* are encouraged to think about wild birds and caged birds differently, in a way that justifies humans' breeding of canaries for captivity.

them from any others. Their curving bills are *crossed at the tip*, which strange arrangement gives them their name of Crossbill.[4] At a little distance you might mistake them for Paroquets, but only the upper half of a Paroquet's beak is curved, and it closes over the under half; while both parts of the Crossbill's beak are curved, and they cross each other at the tip like a pair of scissors that do not close properly.

"How and where do you think these birds build their nests in such a cold season?"

"Make a burrow in the snow, perhaps," said Dodo.

"Go into a haystack or under a shed," said Nat.

"Or a hole in a tree," added Rap.

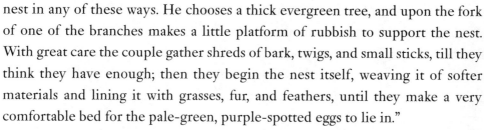

American Crossbill.

"No, the Crossbill does not place his nest in any of these ways. He chooses a thick evergreen tree, and upon the fork of one of the branches makes a little platform of rubbish to support the nest. With great care the couple gather shreds of bark, twigs, and small sticks, till they think they have enough; then they begin the nest itself, weaving it of softer materials and lining it with grasses, fur, and feathers, until they make a very comfortable bed for the pale-green, purple-spotted eggs to lie in."

"How cold the poor birds' toes must be while they are working," said Dodo with a shiver; "and I should think the eggs would freeze instead of hatching."

"But what do they find to eat when everything is frozen stiff?" asked Rap. "Are they cannibal birds that can eat other birds and mice?"

"These two questions can be answered together," said the Doctor. "The nests are usually built in evergreens, which are cone-bearing or coniferous trees. You all know what a cone is like, I think?"

"Yes, I do!" cried Rap. "It is a long seed pod that grows on evergreens. In summer it is green and sticky, but by and by it grows dry and brown, and divides into little rows of scales like shingles on a house, and there is a seed hidden under each scale. Each kind of an evergreen has a different-shaped cone; some are long

---

[4] The American Crossbill is now called the Red Crossbill.

and smooth like sausages, and some are thick and pointed like a top. The squirrels often pick the cones off the spruces over at the miller's and shell out the scales, just as you shell corn off the cob, to get the seeds."

"Very good, my boy," said the Doctor. "I see you know something about trees as well as birds. The Crossbills build in evergreens, and all around their nests hang the cones with spicy seeds stored away under the scales, ready for the birds to eat. So they do not have to go far from home for their marketing."

"But their beaks are so crooked that I don't see how they can pick out the cone seeds," said Nat.

"These curiously twisted bills, like pincers, are made expressly for the purpose of wrenching the scales from the cones, so that the seeds are laid bare."

"It's very funny," said Nat; "whenever we think a bird is queer or awkward and would be better in some other way, it is sure to be made the very best way, only we don't know it."[5]

"By and by, when the eggs are laid and the young are hatched," continued the Doctor, "Crossbills make the most devoted parents; they would let themselves be lifted from the nest rather than leave their family.

"And when it is midsummer the old and young Crossbills form into flocks. Then the parents begin to think that the young people need a change of air for their health, and a few months of travel to finish their education. So they wander southward through the States without any method or plan, sometimes going as far as New Orleans before winter really begins; and it is on these journeys that we see them.

"Some frosty morning in October, if you hear a sound coming from the sky, like the tinkling of little bells—'Tlink-link-link-link'—you may be sure there is a flock of Crossbills near, and soon you will see them climbing about an evergreen, or quietly picking seeds on a birch or beech. The moment before they move to another tree they begin to call; this is the only note you will be likely to hear from them, and one which they often keep up during flight.

"They are capricious birds when on their travels, sometimes letting you come very near them without showing a sign of fear, then suddenly taking flight and dashing about in a distracted way. They are also tardy in getting back to their

---

[5] This section gives the authors an opportunity to instruct readers on how to understand different elements of birds' features, such as how different bills serve different functions (see also chapter 4, "The Building of a Bird"). Nat's comment about birds' seemingly odd features being "made in the very best way, only we don't know it" also harkens back to Osgood Wright's concept of the "Heart of Nature," or how nature works. (See also chapter 4, footnote 3.)

A TRIBE OF WEED WARRIORS 145

piney homes sometimes, and choose their mates on the journey, unlike most birds. Very often a thoughtless couple are obliged to camp out and build a home wherever they happen to be, so that their nests have been found in several of the New England States."

"Is there only one kind of Crossbill in North America?" asked Rap.

"No, this Red Crossbill has two cousins; one with two white bars on each wing, called the White-winged Crossbill, who sometimes travels with him, but is rarer; and another who lives in Mexico."

THE AMERICAN CROSSBILL

Length about six inches.

Beak crossed at the tips, but looking like a Parrot's if you do not notice how the points cross.

Male: general color Indian red, with dark wings and tail.

Female: general color dull olive-green, with wings and tail like the male's.

A Citizen of the North, making winter excursions all through the United States.

THE AMERICAN GOLDFINCH

(The Jolly Bird, or Thistle Bird)

"This must be my other bird," said Nat, "the yellow one from the wild grass meadow, who had what looked like a little black velvet cap tipped down over his eyes. They are such jolly little chaps that it made me laugh when I watched them swinging on the ends of the tall grass. Once in a while one would play he was angry and try to look cross; but he couldn't keep it up long, because he really felt so good natured."

"I believe every one knows Goldfinches," said Olive. "I remember them longer than any birds, but the Robin and Bluebird."

"Yes, for even I know them a little bit," said Dodo, "but not by their right name, for when I saw some in the Park last summer somebody said they were wild Canaries that had flown out of cages."

"What do they eat, cones or little seeds?" asked Nat.

"They eat grass-seeds, and the seeds of weeds—the most fly-away weeds too, that blow everywhere and

American Goldfinch.

spread ever so fast," said Rap. "Look, quick! There's a flock coming by now, and they are calling 'Come *talk* to me! Come *talk* to me!' See—they have settled on the long grass by the fence and are gobbling seeds like everything," continued Rap in a whisper.

As he spoke a flock of twenty or more birds flew over; some were the bright-yellow males and others the more plainly colored females. They did not fly straight, but in a jerky way, constantly dropping down and then lifting up again, and calling out "wait for me" on every down-grade curve, until by common consent they alighted among some wild grasses, where the early yellow thistles were already going to seed.

"Watch and listen," said the Doctor, as he handed the field-glass to the children in turn.

There was a perfect babel of bird-talk, the jaunty blond males all making pretty speeches to the gentle brown-haired females, who laughed merry little bird-laughs in return.

"It is like the noise in the store where they sell Canaries," whispered Nat, after taking a long look; "first they all sing together and then a few sing so much louder that the others stop. I wonder what they are saying?"

"They are talking about housekeeping," said the Doctor. "Some of the ladies say they prefer high apartments in a tree-top, while others like one-story bushes the best; but all agree that the ground floor is too damp for the health of their families. In a few days, or a week at most, this merry flock will have parted company, and two by two the birds will begin housekeeping."

"Why, they are pulling off the thistle-down, and gobbling it up. I should think it would choke them," said Dodo.

"Those are some of the fly-away seeds that Rap spoke of a moment ago. The fluff is not the seed, but a sort of sail to which the seed is fastened, that the wind may blow it away to another place to grow. If you look carefully you will see that the birds do not eat thistle-down, but only the seed; they will soon use the down to line their pretty round cup-shaped nests."

"Oh, yes," said Dodo, "there are lots of fluffy seeds, and they mostly belong to very bad weeds. Olive has been telling us about them, Uncle Roy, and so of course the Goldies do heaps of good by eating them. If they eat those weed-seeds and do not need insects they can live here all winter—can't they, uncle?"

"Certainly; they gather in flocks after their nesting-time, which you see is very late. Then the males shed their bright-yellow feathers, and look exactly like

A TRIBE OF WEED WARRIORS   147

their wives and children. Still, they make a merry party flying about in the garden and field edges, where the composite flowers have left them food, whispering and giggling all day long—even singing merrily now and then. They often have hard times in winter, and when I am here at the Farm I always scatter canary seed on the snow for them."

"What is a com-pos-ite flower?" asked Dodo.

"A kind of flower which has a great many little blossoms crowded together in a bunch, so that they look like one big flower—such as a dandelion, thistle, or sunflower. Olive will tell you more about them to-morrow. She is the Flower Lady, you know—I am only your Bird Uncle, and if I mix up flowers with birds I shall be apt to confuse you."

"They eat sunflower seeds," said Rap. "We grow these seeds for our hens and the Goldies always get their share."

"I wonder if that is why they are such a beautiful yellow," said Dodo. "'Flying Sunflower' would be a nice name for them. No, you needn't laugh at me, Nat; the man in the bird store said he gave Canaries red pepper to make them red, so I don't see why the seed of yellow sunflowers shouldn't make birds yellow!" But in spite of her argument Nat and Rap continued to laugh.

"It must be hard to tell them when they lose their yellow feathers," said Nat finally.

"No; Goldfinches keep up a habit by which you can always tell them, old or young, male or female, in summer or winter. Can you guess what it is?"

"I know! Oh, I know!" cried Rap. "They always fly with a dip and a jerk."

THE AMERICAN GOLDFINCH

Length about five inches.

Male in summer: bright clear yellow, with a black cap, and the wings and tail black with some white on both.

Female at all times, and male in winter: light flaxen brown, the wings and tail as before, but less distinctly marked with white, and no black cap.

A Citizen of temperate North America, and a good neighbor.

Belongs to the guild of Weed Warriors, and is very useful.

THE SNOWFLAKE

(The Autumn Leaf)

"It is a very warm day to talk about snowstorms and winter birds, but several of these birds belong to the Finch family," said the Doctor, a few mornings later, as the children went through the old pasture down to the river woods in search of a cool quiet place to spend the morning. The sun was hot, and most of the birds were hiding in the shade trees. "But as the Snowflake will walk next to the Goldfinch in the procession of Bird Families I am going to show you after a while, we must have him now."[6]

"I think a cool bird will be very nice for a warm day," said Dodo. "Something like soda water and ice cream. That makes me think—Mammy Bun was cracking ice this morning, and I wonder what for!"

Snowflake.

"I wonder!" said Olive, laughing.

"I know," said Nat, who was a tease; "it must be to bake a cake with!"

"Here is a nice place for us," said the Doctor, who had walked on ahead, "where we can see over the fields and into the woods by only turning our heads, and the moss is so dry that we may sit anywhere we please.

"The trees are in full leaf now," he continued, looking up as he leaned comfortably against the trunk of an oak that spread its high root ridges on each side of him like the arms of a chair. "The spring flowers are gone, strawberries are ripe, and there is plenty of food and shelter for birds here. But if we were to travel northward, beyond the United States and up through Canada, we should find that the trees were different; that there were more pines and spruces. Then if we went still further north, even these would begin to grow more scanty and stunted, until the low pines in which the Grosbeak nests would be the only trees seen. Then beyond this parallel of latitude comes the 'tree limit'—"

---

[6] The Snowflake is now called the Snow Bunting.

A TRIBE OF WEED WARRIORS   149

"Oh, I know what a 'parallel of latitude' is, because I learned it in my geography," said Dodo, who had been pouting since Nat teased her about the cracked ice; "it's a make-believe line that runs all round the world like the equator. But what is a 'tree limit'?"

"Don't you remember, little girl," answered the Doctor, "what I told you about the timber-line on a mountain—the height beyond which no trees grow, because it gets too cold for them up there? It is just the same if you go northward on flat ground like Orchard Farm; for when you have gone far enough there are no more trees to be seen. In that northern country the winter is so long and cold, and summer is so short, that only scrubby bushes can grow there. Next beyond these we should find merely the rough, curling grass of the Barren Grounds, which would tell us we were approaching the arctic circle, and already near the place where wise men think it is best to turn homeward; for it is close to the Land of the Polar Bear and the Northern Lights—the region of perpetual snow. But dreary as this would seem to us, nest building is going on there this June day, as well as here.

"Running lightly over uneven hummocks of grass are plump, roly-poly, black-and-white birds, with soft musical voices and the gentlest possible manners. They may have already brought out one brood in thick, deep grassy nests, well lined with rabbit fur or Snow Owl feathers, that they know so well how to tuck under a protecting ledge of rock or bunch of grass. Now and then a male Snowflake will take a little flight and sing as merrily as his cousin the Goldfinch, but he never stays long away from the ground where seeds are to be found.

"The white feathers of these birds are as soft as their friend the snow, of which they seem a part. They have more white about them than any other color, and this snowy plumage marks them distinctly from all their Sparrow cousins. After the moult, when a warm brown hue veils the white feathers, and the short northern summer has ended, the birds flock together for their travels. When they will visit us no one can say; they come and go, as if driven by the wind.

"A soft clinging December snowstorm begins, and suddenly you will wonder at a cloud of brown, snow-edged leaves that settle on a bare spot in the road, then whirl up and, clearing the high fence, drop into the shelter of the barnyard.

"'How very strange,' you will say; 'these leaves act as if they were bewitched.' You look again, and rub your eyes; for these same whirling winter leaves are now walking about the yard, picking up grass-seed and grain under the very nose of the cross old rooster himself! Then you discover that they are not leaves at all, but plump little birds who, if they could speak, would say how very much obliged they are for the food.

"When the snow melts they fly away. By the time they have got home again, weather and travel have worn the brown edges of their feathers away, so that the black parts show; and thus, without a second moulting, they are black-and-white birds again.

"When you search for them look in the air, or on the shed-top, or about the haystack, or on the ground; for they seldom perch in trees."

"Why is that?" asked Rap. "I should think it would be warmer for them in the thick evergreens."

"They nest on the ground, and as they also gather their food there, are unused to large trees."

"Why don't they nest in trees up North?" asked Nat.

"For the same reason," laughed Olive, "that Simple Simon didn't catch a whale in the water pail! There are no trees where the Snowflake nests!"

THE SNOWFLAKE

Length seven inches.

In summer snow-white, with black on the back, wings, and tail.

In winter wears a warm brown cloak, with black stripes, fastened with a brown collar, and a brown and white vest.

A Citizen of the North, travelling southward in snowstorms as far sometimes as Georgia.

A member of the guild of Weed Warriors, eating seeds at all seasons.

THE VESPER SPARROW

(The Grass Finch)

"Please, uncle, before you tell us about this Sparrow, will you look at a sort of a striped, dull-brown bird that has been fidgeting over there under the bushes ever since we have been here?"

"I have been watching him too," said Rap; "a minute ago, when he flew over the stone fence, I saw he had white feathers outside on his tail—now he is back again."

"How very kind that bird is to come when he is wanted, and save my time—it is the Vesper Sparrow himself. I suspect that we are nearer to his nest than he cares to have us, he is so uneasy."

"Where would the nest most likely be?" asked Nat; "in a tree or a bush?"

"Most Sparrow nests are near the ground," said Rap.

"A little lower yet, Rap; the Vesper Sparrow sinks his deep nest either in thick grass or in the ground itself; but though it is thus supported on all sides it is as nicely woven as if it were a tree nest."

"It isn't a very pretty bird," said Dodo. "Does it sing well? Why is it called the Vesper Sparrow—what does Vesper mean, Uncle Roy?"

"Vesper means evening. This plainly clothed little bird has a beautiful voice, and sings in the morning chorus with his brothers; but he is fond of continuing his song late into the twilight, after most others have gone to bed. Then in the stillness his voice sounds sweet and clear, and the words of the song are: 'Chewee, chewee, chewee lira, lira, lira lee.' That is the way he says his evening prayers: you know that in some of the churches there is a beautiful service called Vespers. Ah, if we only knew bird language!"

Vesper Sparrow.

"Do you remember," said Olive, "last night when you were going to bed you asked me if it wasn't a very rare bird that was singing so late down in the garden, and I told you that it was a Sparrow? It was the Vesper Bird, perhaps the very one who is over there in the bushes, wondering if the giant House People will find his nest. You can easily tell him when he flits in front of you by the roadside, because he always shows two white feathers, one on each side of his tail."

THE VESPER SPARROW

Length six inches.

Upper parts brown, streaked with dusky; some bright bay on the wings, but no yellow anywhere, and two white tail-feathers.

Under parts dull-white, striped on breast and sides with brown.

A Citizen of North America from Canada southward, nesting north of the Middle States.

A regular member of the guild of Weed Warriors, and in summer belonging also to the Seed Sowers and Ground Gleaners.

WHITE-THROATED SPARROW

(The Peabody Bird)

"The White-throat is another bird that you will not see in his summer home, unless you look for him in the Northern States.[7] You may find him nesting about the White Mountains, on or near the ground, with the Olive-backed Thrush and Winter Wren. In other places he may be seen as a visitor any time in spring and autumn, or may even linger about the whole winter. You remember the dead one Nat found, that we used when I was teaching you something about birds in general that rainy day, before I began to tell you the particular bird stories.

"If you think of Sparrows only as a sober, dusty-colored family, you may be surprised to learn that this large, handsome bird, with the white throat, the head striped with black and white, a yellow spot over the eye, and richly variegated brown feathers, is a member of that group."

"It bothered me dreadfully at first," said Rap, "until one fall some sportsmen, who came through the upper fields looking for Quail, whistled his song and told me about him. There were lots of them here early this spring by the mill, but the miller didn't like them because they pitched into his new-sown pasture and gobbled the grass-seed."

White-throated Sparrow.

"Yes, of course they eat grass-seed in spring, when the old weed seeds of autumn are well scattered; but surely we must give a Citizen Bird some good valuable food, not treating him like a pauper whom we expect to live always on refuse.

"Some morning in early spring, when the Chickadees who have wintered about the Farm are growing restless, and about ready to go to a more secluded spot to nest, you will hear a sweet persuasive whistling song coming from a clump of bushes. What is it? Not a Bluebird, or a Robin. The notes are too short and simple for a Song Sparrow or a Thrush, too plaintive for a Wren, and too clear for a lisping Wood Warbler.

"Presently several White-throats fly down to a bit of newly seeded lawn or patch of wild grass, where they feed industriously for a few minutes, giving

---

[7] The subheading "The Peabody Bird" refers to the White-throated Sparrow's song, which is sometimes transcribed as a mnemonic "Old Sam Peabody Peabody."

only a few little call-notes—'t'sip, t'sip'—by way of conversation. Then one flies up into a bush and sings in a high key. What does he say—for the song of two short bars surely has words? One person understands it one way, and thinks the bird says 'all-day whittling, whittling, whittling!' Some one else hears 'pe-a—peabody—peabody—peabody!' While to me the White-throat always says '*I* work—cleverly, cleverly, cleverly—poòr mè—cleverly, cleverly, cleverly!'"

As the Doctor paused a moment, Rap whistled an imitation of the song, throwing the sound far from him after a fashion that the Chat has, so that it seemed to come from the trees, completely deceiving Dodo. "Uncle, uncle!" she whispered, creeping softly up to him, "one of the White-throats must have stayed until now, for that bird says 'cleverly! cleverly! cleverly!'"

Rap was delighted at the success of his imitation, and Nat and Dodo tried to whistle with him, Dodo being the most successful.

"Oh! oh! what happens to whistling girls?" said Nat, who was a little provoked at her success.

"Nothing at all," said Olive, "when they only whistle bird-songs. I've whistled to birds ever since I could pucker up my lips, and father taught me how—didn't you, father dear? Only you used to say, 'Never whistle in public places.'"[8]

"I believe I did; and Rap shall teach you, Dodo, so you can call a bird close to you by imitating its song."

THE WHITE-THROATED SPARROW

Length about six and a half inches.

Striped on the back with bay, black, and gray; two white crossbars on each wing, the edge of which is yellow; two white stripes on the black crown, and a yellow spot before the eye.

Gray below, more slate-colored on the breast, with a pure white throat, which is bounded by little black streaks.

A Summer Citizen of the Northern States and beyond. Spends the winter in the Middle and Southern States.

Belongs to the guild of Weed Warriors, and is a bright, cheerful, useful bird.

---

[8] At the time it was considered "unladylike" for girls and women to whistle.

THE CHIPPING SPARROW

(The Chippy. The Sociable Bird)

"I know a Chippy now, when I see it, before you tell us anything about it!" said Dodo gleefully. "There were three or four dear little ones yesterday on the grass, near the dining-room window. They had velvety brown caps on, and said 'chip, chip, chip' as they hopped along, and as they didn't seem afraid of me I threw out some bread-crumbs and they picked them up. Then I knew, to begin with, that they must be seed-eating birds."

"How did you know that?" asked Nat. "Bread-crumbs aren't seeds!"

"No, but bread is made of ground-up wheat-seed! Don't you remember Olive said so last week when she told us about all the grains?"

"Yes," said Nat reluctantly.

"Birds that won't eat seeds won't eat bread-crumbs either," continued Dodo earnestly; "'cause I tried Wood Thrushes with bread-crumbs last week and they simply turned up their noses at them."

Chipping Sparrow.

Rap and Nat laughed at the idea of birds turning up their noses, but the Doctor said: "Very good indeed, Miss Dodo, you are learning to use your eyes and your reason at the same time. Tell us some more about your Chippies."

"At first I didn't know what they were, and then they seemed like some kind of Sparrows; so I went to the wonder room and looked at some of the books that you left out on the low shelf for us. I couldn't find any picture that matched, but then I began to read about Sparrows, and when I came to Chippy Sparrow I was sure it matched; for the book said it was a clever little fellow with a jaunty red cap that came with his mate to the very door and that children make the Chippy's acquaintance and hunt in the vines on the piazza or in a bush for its nest and that the nest is very neat and made of horsehair—" Here Dodo stopped to get her breath.

"Bravo! bravo!" called the Doctor. "I see that I shall soon have to resign my place as Bird Man if this young lady takes to bird hunting and reading also. Is there more to come, little one?"

"Yes, Uncle Roy, just a little bit more. Because the book said children looked for Chippies' nests I went right away to see if I could find one. First I hunted in all the bushes, and the Catbirds scolded me and the Brown Thrasher in the barberry bush was very mad and a Robin in the low crotch of the bell-pear tree nearly tipped his nest over, he flew away in such a hurry. I thought I had better stop, but by this time I was way down in the garden and all at once I saw a Chippy fly straight into the big rose bush at the beginning of our arbor. I looked in and there about as high up as my chin was the loveliest little nest like a nice grass cup, with pretty rosebuds all around it for a trimming, and on it sat a Chippy—and do you know it never flew away when I stroked its back with my finger! It was so cute and friendly I thought I would give it a little mite of a kiss on top of its head. But I guess it misunderstood and thought I meant to bite, for it flew off a little way and I saw three speckled blue eggs and—then I thought I'd better come away."

"Did you hear it sing?" asked Nat.

"No—it only said 'chip—chippy—chip.'"

"Chippies have two songs," said the Doctor. "One is a kind of chirp or trill like an insect's note—'trr-r-r-r-r.' They give this usually when they first wake up in the morning. The other is a pretty little melody, but is less frequently heard."

"If they eat seed, why don't they stay here all winter?" asked Rap; "yet I'm sure they don't."

"They are not as hardy as some of their brothers, and do not like our winter weather; but even in autumn you may mistake them for some other Sparrow, for then Mr. Chippy takes off his brown velvet cap, and his dainty little head is stripped."

THE CHIPPING SPARROW

Length about five inches.

A dark chestnut cap, a light stripe over the eye, and a dark stripe behind the eye; forehead and bill black; back streaked with black, brown, and buff; rump slate-gray; wings and tail dusky.

Under parts plain light gray, almost white on throat and belly, darker on breast.

A Citizen of North America, nesting from the Gulf of Mexico to Canada, wintering in the Southern States and beyond.

A Weed Warrior and a member of the Tree Trappers and Ground Gleaners in nesting-time.

THE SLATE-COLORED JUNCO
(The Snowbird)

"Here we have a northern winter bird—or, at least, one that we associate with winter and call the Snowbird; for everybody sees him on his autumn and winter travels, and knows his Sparrow-like call-note, while his summer home is so far north or so high on mountains that few visit him in the tangled woodlands where he sings a pretty trilling song to his mate.

Slate-colored Junco.

"When I was a boy here at the Farm, these white-vested Juncos were my winter pets. A flock was always sure to come in October and stay until the last of April, or even into May if the season was cold. One winter, when the snow came at Thanksgiving and did not leave the ground until March, the birds had a hard time of it, I can tell you. The Robins and Bluebirds soon grew discouraged, and left one by one. The Chickadees retreated to the shelter of some hemlock woods, and I thought the Winter Wrens were frozen into the woodpile, for I did not see any for weeks. The only cannibal birds that seemed to be about were a pair of Cat Owls that spent most of the time in our hay-barn, where they paid for their lodgings by catching rats and mice.

"But my flock of Juncos were determined to brave all weathers. First they ate the seeds of all the weeds and tall grasses that reached above the snow, then they cleaned the honeysuckles of their watery black berries. When these were nearly gone, I began to feed them every day with crumbs, and they soon grew very tame. At Christmas an ice storm came, and after that the cold was bitter indeed. For two days I did not see my birds; but on the third day in the afternoon, when I was feeding the hens in the barnyard, a party of feeble, half-starved Juncos, hardly able to fly, settled down around me and began to pick at the chicken food.

"I knew at a glance that after a few hours' more exposure all the poor little birds would be dead. So I shut up the hens and opened the door of the straw-barn very wide, scattered a quantity of meal and cracked corn in a line on the floor, and crept behind the door to watch. First one bird hopped in and tasted the food; he found it very good and evidently called his brothers, for in a minute they all went in and I closed the door upon them. And I slept better that night because I knew that my birds were comfortable.

"'They may go in once, but you will never catch them so again,' said my father, when he heard about it. I had an idea, however, that the birds trusted me; for though they flew out very gladly the next morning, they did not seem afraid.

"Sure enough, in the afternoon they came back again! I kept them at night in this way for several weeks, and one afternoon several Snowflakes came in with them. Later on this same winter five thin starving Quails came to the barn-yard and fed with the hens. I tried several times to lure or drive them into the barn with the Juncos, but they would not go. Finally, one evening when I shut the chickens up, what did these Quails do but run into the hen-house with the others and remain as the guests of our good-natured Cochins until spring!

"I well remember how happy I was when grandmother gave me half a dollar and told me to go over to the mill and buy a bag of grain sweepings for my 'boarders'; how angry I was with the miller when he said, 'Those Quails'll be good eatin' when they're fat'; and how he laughed when I shouted, 'It's only cannibals that eat up their visitors!'"

THE SLATE-COLORED JUNCO
Length about six inches.

Dark slate color; throat and breast slate-gray; belly and side tail-feathers white; beak pinkish-white.

A Citizen of North America, nesting in the northern tier of States and northward, and also on high mountains as far south as Georgia.

A Tree Trapper, Seed Sower, and Weed Warrior, according to season.

THE SONG SPARROW

(Every One's Darling)

"This Sparrow, who guides you to his name by the dark spot on the breast as clearly as the Peabody-bird does by his white cravat, is every one's bird and every one's darling," said the Doctor, as if he were speaking of a dear friend.

Song Sparrow.

"When you have learned his many songs, his pretty sociable ways, and have seen his cheerfulness and patience in hard times, you will, I know, agree with me that all possible good bird qualities are packed into this little streaked Sparrow.

"Constancy is his first good point. If we live in southern New England or westward to Illinois, we shall probably have him with us all the year, wearing the same colored feathers after the moult as before, not shedding his sweet temper and song with his spring coat. Now there are a great many birds, as you will see, that wear full-dress suits and sing wonderful songs in spring and early summer, while the weather is warm, food plentiful, and everything full of promise; but whose music and color vanish from the garden and roadside when frost comes. Yet the Song Sparrow sings throughout the year, except in the storms of February and March—not always the varied spring song, but still a sweet little tune.

"The Song Sparrow is humble and retiring about the location of his nest, usually putting it on or near the ground; though of course some pairs may have ideas of their own about nest-building, and choose a bird-box or even a hole in a tree. One thing you must remember about birds and their ways: Nature has fixed a few important laws that must not be changed, but has given birds and other animals liberty to follow their own tastes in all other matters.

"Wherever the thick nest is placed, it is cleverly hidden. If in a low shrub, it is in the crotch where the branches spread above the root. If on the ground, it is against an old stump with a tuft of grass on each side, or in a little hollow between bushes. Our Sparrow likes to live in the garden hedges and about the orchard, and to cultivate the acquaintance of House People in a shy sort of way.

"He never flies directly to and from his home like the Chippy, Wren, and Robin, but slips off the nest and runs along the ground as nimbly as a Thrush, till he reaches a bush, well away from his house, when he hops into it and flies away.

A TRIBE OF WEED WARRIORS 159

"'Chek! chek! chek!' is the call-note of the Song Sparrows, who also have a short, sweet song, which every bird varies and lengthens to please himself or his mate. 'Maids, maids, maids, hang on your tea-kettle-ettle-ettle,' some people fancy the bird says, and the short song fits these words very well. But when this Sparrow sings his best music, all trembling with love and joy, he forgets about such a simple thing as the tea-kettle! Now it is a grand banquet he tells you of, with flowers and music; then he stops suddenly, remembering that he is only a little brown bird, and sings to his favorite alder bush by the brook a soft apology for having forgotten himself. This Sparrow even dreams music in the spring, when you will often hear his notes in the darkest hours of the night.

"The eggs are as varied as the songs, being light blue or whitish, with every imaginable sort of brown marking—no two sets are exactly alike. Birds' eggs often vary in color, like their plumage, and the different hues seem fitted to hide the eggs; for those of birds that nest in holes and need no concealing are usually plain white.

"If you ever make a bird calendar at Orchard Farm, you may be able to write this Sparrow's name in every month of the year. Another good thing about this happy faithful bird is, that his tribe increases in Birdland, in spite of all dangers."

"My mother loves Song Sparrows," said Rap. "She says they are a great deal of company for her when she is doing her washing out under the trees. She thinks they tell her that people can be happy, even if they wear plain clothes and have to be snowed up in the country half the winter. She is right, too; the Song Sparrows only tell her what happens to themselves."

THE SONG SPARROW

Length about six inches.

Head and back all streaked with gray and brown, and a brown stripe on each side of throat. Under parts whitish, all striped with dark brown, the heaviest stripes making a large blackish spot on the breast.

A Citizen of the United States east of the plains, nesting from Virginia northward to the Fur Countries.

A Ground Gleaner as well as a Weed Warrior, and a constant joyful songster.

THE TOWHEE

(Joree. Chewink. Ground Robin.)

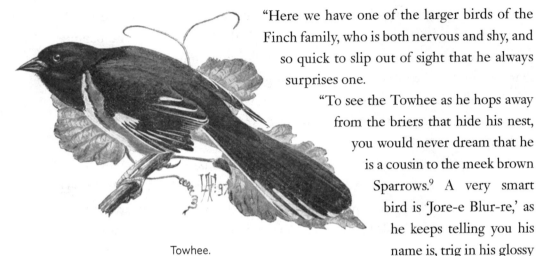

Towhee.

"Here we have one of the larger birds of the Finch family, who is both nervous and shy, and so quick to slip out of sight that he always surprises one.

"To see the Towhee as he hops away from the briers that hide his nest, you would never dream that he is a cousin to the meek brown Sparrows.[9] A very smart bird is 'Jore-e Blur-re,' as he keeps telling you his name is, trig in his glossy black long-tailed coat, his vest with reddish side facings, white trousers, and light-brown shoes and stockings. A knowing glance has he in the ruby-red eyes that sparkle in his coal-black head, while inside that little head are very wise thoughts."

"How are his eyes red, Uncle Roy?" asked Dodo. "Are they all plain red or only red in a ring around the seeing part where mine are blue?"

"They are 'red in a ring,' as you say; we call this ring the *iris*, and the 'seeing part' the *pupil*."

"Please, what does iris mean? Iris is the name of one of the lily flowers that grow in the garden."

"Iris is a word that means rainbow, which as you know is a belt of beautiful colors, made by the sun shining through rain. The iris of the eye is a film of color covering the watery inside part of the eyeball, and the pupil is a round hole in the iris that lets the light into the back of the eye. This opening expands and contracts according to whether the eye needs much or little light. I tell you this now, but you will need to remember it when we come to the Owls, who have curious ways of keeping too much light from their eyes.

"The iris in birds, as in House People, may be of many different colors—red, as in the Vireo I told you about, and as you now know it is with the Towhee.

---

[9] The Towhee is now called the Eastern Towhee.

A TRIBE OF WEED WARRIORS   161

Each has a brother with white eyes. You remember the White-eyed Vireo, and in Florida there is a Towhee who has white eyes; but this is so unusual that it makes the bird look to you as if it were blind, until you understand that it is the natural color. Most birds' eyes are brown of some shade, or perfectly black; a few have blue or green eyes. But where did I leave Mr. Jore-e Blur-re?"

"You were saying that he is wise," answered Rap.

"Well, he is wise enough never to fly either straight to or from his nest, which is a rather poor affair, down on the ground, within reach of every weasel or snake that cares to rob it.

"He does not sing on the ground, but moves silently among the leaves and litter of old ferns, such as are found near ponds and streams. A stick will crackle perhaps, and thus draw your attention to him. When he knows that he is seen, he will flip his wings and flirt his tail, like suddenly opening and shutting a fan, as he flits on before you with his head on one side, giving the pert call 'Towhee! towhee!' that is one of his names. Some people think he says 'Chewink! chewink!' and call him by that name; while some who have noticed where he lives, and seen that the color of his sides is like the reddish breast of the Robin, call him the Ground Robin, though he is no relation of the Thrush family.

"Meanwhile his wife stays quietly on the nest, where her brown back matches the dead leaves of which it is made outside, keeping her quite safe from sight.

"In the afternoon, when the work of the day is almost over, and her mate is tired of scratching about for food, he takes a little rest and goes up high in a tree to boldly declare his whereabouts.

"'Jore-e Blur-re, Jore-e Blur-re, willy-nilly, willy-nilly!' he calls defiantly, as if he did not like having to keep quiet all day, and meant to tell his name at last.

"In early autumn the Joree family grow sociable enough to come into the garden, but they seldom linger late; vigorous as they are, they hurry southward before any hard frosts come."

THE TOWHEE

Length about eight and a half inches.

Male: black with chestnut sides, white belly, tan-colored under the tail, the side feathers of which are white-tipped.

Female: reddish-brown where the male is black.

A Summer Citizen of the United States east of the plains, and along the southern border of Canada. Nests northward from Georgia. Winters south of the Middle States. A Ground Gleaner, Seed Sower, and Weed Warrior.

THE CARDINAL

(The Cardinal Grosbeak)

"There is a legend about this Cardinal—the soldier with a red uniform," said the Doctor; "one of Mammy Bun's strange stories that came from the Indians to the negroes, always growing larger and stranger.[10]

"There were two Indian warriors of the southwest that hated each other. One had an only daughter and the other a son. While their fathers were at war, this boy and girl met in the green forest. The old women of their tribes told them that they must never speak to each other, or their fathers would surely kill them. But the children said, 'There is no war or hate in our forest; the birds meet—why may not we?' One summer evening they stayed too long, watching the fish swim in the river and floating little sticks for canoes. The two warriors returned suddenly to their villages, missed their children, and then some one told them tales.

Cardinal.

"The wind whispered to the trees, 'Trouble, trouble! These warriors hate each other more than they love their children. Hide them, O trees!' Then the trees whispered to the birds, 'Help the poor children—help, help!' And the birds said, 'They shall be turned into birds and escape, if you will make a little fire, O wind, to delay the warriors and give us time.'

---

[10] An instance in a long tradition of white American authors claiming Indigenous origins for their fictions, this purportedly Native American legend is actually the invention of the authors. Wright was a devoted reader of the poems of Henry Wadsworth Longfellow, including his immensely popular *The Song of Hiawatha* (1855), which contributed to the romanticization of Native American folklore in nineteenth-century American popular culture. Wright's *Wabeno the Magician* (1899), the sequel to *Tommy-Anne and the Three Hearts*, borrowed from Longfellow's *Hiawatha* more substantially, using several names that Longfellow gave to his Native American characters and telling its tales about the natural world in the form of faux-Indigenous myths.

A TRIBE OF WEED WARRIORS   163

"So the trees told the fireflies to light the dead leaves that covered the ground; the wind breathed on the fire, and soon the wood was all aflame!

"'What birds do you choose to be, that you may always live in the forest together?' asked the Bird Brothers of the children. 'Answer quickly, for the time is short.'

"'I will be a large brown Sparrow,' said the girl; 'then none will trap me for my feathers.'

"'And I too,' said the boy.

"Suddenly they were no longer children. But there was confusion, as the fire burned nearer and nearer. "'Fly! fly!' cried the Bird Brothers. 'You have wings—do not look at the earth, lest you grieve to leave it.'

"Gonda, being obedient, made an effort to fly above the flame, which only tinged some of her feathers red. But Towai, loath to leave the earth, lingered so long that his feathers became all red from the flames, and the soot blackened his face.

"Though these two birds and their children still belong to the dull-brown Sparrow family, they have little peace in the forest where they live. Towai wears a splendid red robe and is called the Cardinal, but there is a price upon his head because of his beauty.

"This is one of the legends that explains why this bird is classed with Sparrows. The Tanager is more fiery red, and the Oriole carries flame on his back; but there is something strange about the Cardinal—he seems out of place and lonely with us. He should belong to a tropical country and have orchids and palms for companions—but instead, where do we find him?"

"Please, Doctor," said Rap, who thought he could answer that question, "the miller's wife has a pair in a cage, but they aren't very pretty, 'cause they've scraped most of the feathers off their heads and rumpled their tails, trying to get out. The miller caught three of them down there last winter, only one died and the other two aren't a bit happy; the male doesn't sing and the female has a cough. The miller's wife doesn't care much for them; they're a bother to feed, she says—have to have meal-worms, and rice with the hulls on, and all that."

"Why doesn't she let them out?" asked Olive.

"'Cause she thinks that maybe some of the people that come fishing will buy them."

"How much does she ask for them?" said the Doctor.

"She said if they ever moulted out and got any decent feathers she could ask three dollars for them, but the way they were looking a dollar was all she could expect."

"Children, shall we have a Liberty Festival this morning? How would you like for me to buy these birds and bring them here, so that you can see them, then— then what?"

"Open the cage and let them out and see what they will do!" screamed Dodo, jumping up and down.[11]

"May I go down to buy them?" begged Nat.

"You will have to take me, too," said Olive.

"Can I open the door?" asked Dodo.

"Here is the dollar—now go, all together," said the Doctor, putting his hands over his ears; "but if you make so much noise the birds in the river woods will mistake your kind intentions and think you are a family of wildcats."

In less than half an hour the party returned, Nat carrying the cage, which was only a box with a bit of wire netting over the front.

"No wonder poor Mrs. Cardinal has a cough, living in this dirty box," said Olive. "See, father, only one perch—and I don't believe the poor things have ever had a bath given them."

"That is the saddest part of caging wild birds," said the Doctor. "Not one person in fifty is willing to give them the care they need. Put the cage under those bushes, Nat.

"I began by asking, Where do we find this bird? Living in Florida in sunshine, among the shady redwoods of Kentucky, and in all the bitterness of our northern winters. He varies his habits to suit his surroundings, and roves about after the nesting season; in mild climates he sings for six months of the year—from March until August. But one of the strangest things about him is that he wanders most when the trees are bare and he can be so easily seen that hundreds of his kind are shot for their gay feathers, or trapped to sell alive for cage birds. When snow is on the ground he is very conspicuous."

"Why doesn't he get into evergreens or cedar bushes?" asked Rap.

"He does when he can and often sings when so hidden; but he is not a very quick-witted bird and seems to move awkwardly, as if his topknot were as heavy as a drum major's bearskin.

---

[11] This section provides another lesson against caging wild birds. This time, the authors focus on the harm captivity does to wild birds, rather than on highlighting that some birds are "bred for captivity." Additionally, the Cardinals are sold for one dollar, which is $38 in today's money.

"But no one can find fault with his song; it first rings out loud like a shout, then ends as clearly as the bubbling of the stream near which he likes best to live—'Cheo-cheo-chehoo-cheo-qr-qr-qrr-r-r.'"

"Isn't it time to let them out?" whispered Dodo. "Mrs. Cardinal is coughing again dreadfully!"

"In a moment. Turn the cage sideways, Nat, so that we can watch them through the bushes—so, and please keep quite still. Now, Dodo, open the little door—carefully."

For two or three minutes there was perfect silence. Four young people squeezed behind a tree, and a Wise Man down on his hands and knees behind a stump—all watching two forlorn birds, who did not understand that liberty was theirs for the taking.

Mrs. Cardinal put out her head, then took a step and hopped along the ground into a cornel bush; where, after looking around a moment, she began to smooth her poor feather's. Another minute and Mr. Cardinal followed, giving a sharp chip like a loud Sparrow call. They both hopped off as if they were not half sure their freedom was real.

"I think they might have sung to us," whispered Dodo.

"Too soon," said the Doctor; "but I'm sure that we have not seen or heard the last of our Cardinals."

"Hist!" said Nat, "they are taking a bath in the brook this side of the stepping-stones." And so they were.

THE CARDINAL

Length eight and a quarter inches.

Male: splendid cardinal-red, with a black throat and band about the coral-red bill, and a fine long crest, like a Cedar Waxwing's.

Female: yellowish-brown with a little red in her crest, wings, and tail, and her face not so black as her mate's.

A Citizen of the eastern United States to the plains and from Florida to the Great Lakes, nesting wherever found.

A Tree Trapper, Ground Gleaner, Seed Sower, and Weed Warrior, besides being a fine singer.

THE ROSE-BREASTED GROSBEAK

(The Potato-Bug Bird)

Rose-breasted Grosbeak.

"This must be the bird I saw the other day in the brush lot by the old barn," said Rap; "and there were two more this morning in our own potato patch. Why do they go there, Doctor?"

"Because this bird, besides wearing a beautiful rosy shield on his breast, and singing at morning and evening more beautifully even than the very best Robin, is a very industrious and useful bird. He earns his living by helping farmers clear their fields of potato-bugs. If you go quietly over to the large potato lot on the north side of the Farm, you will find these birds at work any morning. I saw them myself to-day, and am going to trust my crop entirely to their keeping this season. They are nesting in the young growth near these very river woods, and I will show you one of their homes presently. You see that protecting birds, and leaving suitable bits of woodland and brush for them to build in, is practical as well as sentimental.

"This Grosbeak dares not trust its brilliant colors in large trees or open places, and so nests where it may hide in a maze of bushes. When it finds the right spot, it is not very particular about nest-building. A jumble of weeds, twigs, roots, and sometimes rags or bits of paper, serves to hold its light-blue eggs with brown markings.

"If it be ever right to cage a wild bird, you may make a prisoner of this Grosbeak; but remember, you must take a young male before it has known the joys of freedom, and give at least a half-hour every day to taking care of him. Then he will grow to love you and be a charming pet, living happily and singing gladly;

but under any other circumstances it is less cruel to shoot one than to make it a prisoner."

THE ROSE-BREASTED GROSBEAK

Length about eight inches.

Male: black on the head, back, wings, and tail; the belly, rump, several spots on the wings, and three outer tail-feathers, white; rose-colored breast and wing-linings; bill white and very heavy.

Female: streaked brownish above and below, without any rosy color, but orange-yellow under the wings; she looks like an overgrown Sparrow with a swelled face.

A Summer Citizen of the eastern United States from Kansas and the Carolina mountains to Canada, travelling south of the United States in winter.

A Tree Trapper, Ground Gleaner, Weed Warrior, and Seed Sower. Rather naughty once in a while about picking tree-buds, but on the whole a good neighbor.

THE INDIGO BIRD

(The Blue Canary)

"Blue birds and blue flowers are both rare; you can count our really blue birds on the fingers of one hand, and a Blue Canary is even stranger than a green rose or a black tulip.

"The Indigo Bird has many of the Canary's gentle ways, and though his music is not so fine or varied as that of the Goldfinch or Song Sparrow, he sings a sweet little tune to his brown mate on her nest in the bushy pasture.[12]

"She is fortunate in having a dull dress; for, if she were as splendidly blue as her husband, nesting would be a very anxious occupation for her. Indeed, her poor mate has anything but an easy time; his color is so

Indigo Bird.

---

[12] The Indigo Bird is now called the Indigo Bunting.

bright that everybody can see him at a glance, and when he picks up grass-seed in the streaming sunlight, his feathers glisten like sapphires."

"We saw an Indigo Bird yesterday!" cried Nat and Dodo together. "It was in the geraniums by the dining-room window, eating the seed I tipped out of my Canary's cage when I cleaned it," continued Dodo. "Mammy Bun said it was a Blue Canary, but Nat said it couldn't be, and I forgot to ask about it."

"Are you going to tell us about many more birds in the Finch family, Uncle Roy?"

"Not now. You have heard about those that will be most likely to attract your attention, and when you can name them, they will introduce you to all the rest of their relations."

"It is a great family," said Rap, who was sitting thinking. "Big birds and little, plain gray and brown, or red, blue, and yellow—some like warm weather and some want it cold."

"Speaking of cold, I wonder what became of the ice that Dodo saw Mammy Bun cracking this morning?" asked the Doctor, looking at Olive. "The very word has a pleasant sound, for it seems to me to be growing warmer and warmer."

"Toot! toot! t-o-o-t!" squeaked a tin horn across the field from the direction of the farmhouse.

"What's that?" said Nat, jumping up; "it's the dinner horn, and it can't be dinner-time."

"Not more than eleven o'clock," said Rap, looking at the sun after the fashion of those who spend much time out of doors.

"I know what the horn means," said Olive. "It means that the cake, that Nat said Mammy Bun was going to bake with the ice, is done!"

"But that was only nonsense, you know," said Nat. "Ice won't bake anything!"

"Perhaps not, but ice can freeze something, if you mix salt with it, even on this warm day, and the horn means that mammy has a tin pail full of ice cream, waiting for some one to eat it! Ice cream, made with fresh strawberries! Don't break your neck, Nat!" For Nat had dashed off so quickly that it was no use for Dodo and Rap to try to keep up with him.

"Why do you mostly have something nice for us to eat on bird-days?" asked Dodo, cuddling into the bend of her uncle's arm.

"For two reasons, girlie. When I was a boy, being out of doors made me so hungry that it always seemed a long time between breakfast and dinner. I know that little brains remember best when the stomachs that nourish them are not empty. Neither Bird Children nor House Children should go too long hungry; it is as bad as nibbling all day."

"I've noticed since I came here I haven't needed even to peep in the cooky box between times. Aren't you one of the seven Wise Men of—of—I-forget-where?" asked Dodo, hugging him.

"Greece," answered the Doctor; "no, fortunately, I am not, for they are all dead."

"What's that?" whispered Rap, pointing toward the river, whence a strong, rapid, musical song came, ending before you could catch the syllables, and then being repeated two or three times.

"It is the Cardinal," said the Doctor, in some surprise—for the bird was singing almost at noon. "I can see his red liberty cap near the top of the tallest hemlock!"

"Che-o—hoo—hoo," called the Cardinal, and then the ice-cream pail arrived, escorted by Nat.

"This is a festival for us as well as for the Cardinal," said Rap.

THE INDIGO BIRD

Length five and a half inches.

Male: bright blue, of a greener tint than the Bluebird; wings and tail dusky.

Female: plain brown above and whitey brown below, with a few streaks, including a sharp black one under her beak.

A pleasant neighbor and good Citizen, belonging to the southern branch of the Finch family.

A Tree Trapper and a Weed Warrior.

A Summer Citizen of the eastern United States, west to Kansas and north to Canada.

From Kansas to the Pacific Ocean he is replaced by his brother, the Lazuli Bunting.

CHAPTER 17

A Midsummer Excursion

IT WAS THAT WONDERFUL WEEK after the middle of June. The week that holds the best of everything; the longest days of the whole fly-away year; the biggest strawberries and the sweetest roses. Everything at its height; birds in full song; bees in the flowers; children in hammocks under the trees, and a Wise Man humming happily to himself as he breathed it all in.

"I don't think that anything nicer than this can happen," said Nat, swinging so hard in his hammock that he rolled out into the long grass.

"It doesn't seem as if it *could*," answered Dodo; "only here at Orchard Farm there is so much niceness you never can tell what is the very nicest."

The Wise Man laughed to himself, and then whistled an imitation of the White-throated Sparrow's call—at which sound Dodo promptly rolled out of her hammock and bumped into Nat, who was still lying in the grass; then both the children sat up and listened.

"All day—whittling—whittling—whittling," whistled the notes.

"You ought to be further north building your nest," said Nat. "Don't you know that, Mr. Peabody?"

"It's Uncle Roy!" cried Dodo, spying him back of the apple-tree perch.

"How would you like to go down to the seashore to-morrow, little folks?"[1]

"There!" exclaimed Dodo; "you see there is more niceness yet!"

---

[1] The seashore referenced here are the beaches along the Connecticut coastline that are a part of the Long Island Sound, a tidal estuary consisting of both saltwater and freshwater.

A MIDSUMMER EXCURSION 171

"I suppose by that you mean 'yes,'" laughed the Doctor. "Olive and I have planned to take the six-seated surrey, with a hamper of good things to eat, and drive down to the sandy shore where the river broadens into salt water. There is a house on the bay where we can have our dinner, and the meadows and marshes are full of birds—don't quite smother me, Dodo! Then in the cool of the afternoon we can return and have a picnic supper at some pretty place on the way, for to-morrow night the moon is full!"

"Can Rap go with us—for he hardly ever gets down to the shore?"

"Certainly!"

"How far is it?" asked Nat.

"About fifteen miles by the road, though not more than ten in a straight line."

"Are the birds different down there?"

"Some of them are; there is a great colony of Blackbirds I want you to see, for our next family is a very interesting one. It contains a harlequin, a tramp, a soldier, a tent-maker, a hammock-maker, and a basket-maker; and we shall probably see them all, sooner or later, but certainly one or two of them to-morrow.

"No, I won't tell you a word about them now. But go down and invite Rap, and tell him we will call for him by half-past six o'clock in the morning, because we must have time to drive slowly, stop where we please, and use our eyes." Early next morning the party set out. Five happy children—the youngest eight and the oldest fifty-eight—started from Orchard Farm behind a pair of comfortable white horses that never wore blinkers or check-reins. These big members of the party were human enough to look around as the children scrambled into the surrey, and then prick up their ears as if they knew the difference between a picnic and a plough, and were happy accordingly.

They trotted down the turnpike a mile, and then turned into a cross-road bordered by hay-fields almost ready for cutting. Olive was driving, for she loved the old white horses. Rap, Nat, and Dodo sat in the middle seat, and the Doctor behind.

"Please, Doctor, what is the name of the Bird family we are going to visit?" asked Rap.

"The family of the Blackbirds and Orioles; but it has a Latin name, *Icteridae*, when it walks in the procession."

"Listen! listen!" cried Dodo. "Oh, Olive, do stop; there's some kind of a bird on top of those bars that is singing as if he had started and couldn't stop, and I'm sure his voice will fly away from him in a minute!"

Olive said "whoa" immediately.

"It's only a Bobolink!" said Rap, as the bird spread his wings and soared into the air still singing, leaving a little stream of music behind him, as a dancing canoe leaves a train of ripples in the water.

"It is a Bobolink, surely," said the Doctor, "and not 'only a Bobolink,' but the very bird we should be most glad to see—the first of the Blackbird and Oriole family—the harlequin in his summer livery."[2]

THE BOBOLINK

(The Reed Bird. The Rice Bird)

"Why do you call the Bobolink a 'harlequin,' Uncle Roy? What is a harlequin?" asked Dodo.

Bobolink.

"Don't you remember that Harlequin was the name of the man in the pantomime we saw last winter, who wore clothes of all sorts of colors, changed from one thing to another, and was always dancing about as if he could not possibly keep still?"

"Y-e-s, I remember," said Dodo, "but I don't think he was a bit like this Bobolink; for that harlequin didn't say a word, only made signs, and the Bobolink sings faster than any bird I ever heard before."

"Yes, he sings now; but it is only for a short time. Next month he will be dumb, and before you know it his beautiful shining black coat, with the white and buff trimmings, will have dropped off. Then he will be changed to dull brown like his wife, and keep as quiet as poor Cinderella sitting in the ashes.

---

[2] When Rap says, "It's only a Bobolink!" and Dr. Hunter responds, "and not only a Bobolink, but the very bird we should be most glad to see," Dr. Hunter is teaching the children how to appreciate common birds. (See also chapter 1, footnote 10.)

"Do you see any birds in that meadow of long grass?" asked the Doctor.

"I don't see any in the grass," said Rap; "but there are some Bobolinks all about in the trees along the edges, and more of them up in the air. Where are their nests, Doctor? I've never found a Bobolink's nest!"

"Their nests are hidden in that long grass, and their mates also. Whoever would find them must have the patience of an Indian, the eyes of a bird, and the cunning of a fox.

"Mrs. Bobolink finds a little hollow in the ground where the roots grow, and rounds up a nest from the grass stalks with finer grass tops inside. Then she so arranges the weeds and stems above her home that there is no trace of a break in the meadow; and when she leaves the nest she never goes boldly out by the front door or bangs it behind her, but steals off through a by-path in the grass. When she flies out of shelter at last, she has already run a good way off, so that, instead of telling the watcher where her home is, she tells him exactly where it is not.

"Bob earns his living these days by singing and going to market for the family, but he does both in a tearing hurry; for his housekeeping, like his honeymoon, is short. He must lead his children out of the grass before the mowers overtake him, or the summer days grow short; for then he will have to spend some time at his tailor's before he can follow the warm weather down South again.

"Twice a year Bob has to make the most complete change of plumage that falls to the lot of any bird. His summer toilet is so tiresome and discouraging that he retires into the thickest reeds to make it. Out he comes in August, leaving his lovely voice behind with his cast-off clothes, dressed like his wife, with hardly a word to say for himself, as he joins the flock into which various families have united. He even loses his name, and is called Reedbird, after his hiding-place. He grows reckless and says to his brothers, 'What do we care? If we can't sing any more, we can eat—let us eat and be merry still!' So they eat all they can, and wax exceedingly fat; the gunners know this, and come after them.

"Meanwhile, in southern lowlands the rice-fields, that have been hoed and flooded with water all the season to make the grain grow, are covered with tall stalks of rice, whose grains are not quite ripe, but soft and milky like green corn.

"Some morning there is a great commotion on the plantation. 'The Ricebirds have come!' is the cry—this being only another name for the Bobolink.

"Out fly the field-hands, men, women, and children, waving sticks, blowing horns, and firing off guns, to frighten the invaders away. Fires are lighted by night to scare them, for the birds travel both night and day. The Bobolinks do not stop for all this noise, though of course a great many are shot, ending their lives inside a pot-pie, or being roasted in rows of six on a skewer. But the rest fly on when they are ready, leaving the United States behind them, and go through Florida to Brazil and the West Indies.

"In spring, on the northward journey, the rice-fields suffer again. The males are jolly minstrels once more, all black, white, and buff, hurrying home to their nesting grounds. They think that rice newly sown and sprouting is good for the voice, and stop to gobble it up in spite of all objections.

"Their song is not easy to express in words. 'Bobolink,' from which they take their name, is the sound most frequently heard in it; but every bird-lover has tried to give it words, and some have written it down in rhyming nonsense verses, like poetry. I think Mr. Lowell's are the best.[3]

"'Ha! ha! ha! I must have my fun, Miss Silverthimble, thimble, thimble, if I break every heart in the meadow. See! see! see!' is one translation."[4]

"That does sound exactly like a Bobolink," laughed Dodo; "and here is one now, right over in that tree, so crazy to sing that he doesn't mind us a bit."

"Kick your slipper! Kick your slipper! Temperance! Temperance!" said Bob, as the white horses turned into the road again. "Temperance! take a drink! go to grass, all of you!"

THE BOBOLINK
Length about seven inches.

Male in spring and summer: jet black with ashy-white rump and shoulders; some light edgings on the back, wings, and tail-feathers, and a buff patch on the back of the neck, like a cream-puff baked just right.

Female: brownish and streaky like a big Sparrow, with sharp-pointed tail-feathers; two dark-brown stripes on the crown. Brown above, with some black and yellowish streaks. Plain yellowish below.

---

[3] The American poet James Russell Lowell references Bobolinks in a number of his works and even wrote a poem called "The Bobolink," which celebrates the bird as "Anacreon of the meadow / Drunk with the joy of spring!" (*A Year's Life* [Boston: C. C. Little and J. Brown, 1841], p. 24). Lowell's mnemonic for the Bobolink, however, comes from his book *My Garden Acquaintance* (Boston: Houghton Mifflin, 1871): "[The Bobolink] had the volubility of an Italian charlatan at a fair, and, like him, appeared to be proclaiming the merits of some quack remedy. *Opodeldoc-opodeldoc—try-Doctor-Lincoln's-opodeldoc!* he seemed to repeat over and over again, with a rapidity that would have distanced the deftest-tongued Figaro that ever rattled" (33).

[4] This second mnemonic for the Bobolink is attributable to the naturalist John Burroughs; it is found in full in his *Birds and Poets* (New York: Hurd and Houghton, 1877): "Ha! ha! ha! I must have my fun, Miss Silverthimble, thimble, thimble, if I break every heart in the meadow, see, see, see!" (31).

A MIDSUMMER EXCURSION 175

In autumn and winter both sexes alike.

A Summer Citizen of the northern United States and southern Canada. Visits all the
Southern States in its journeys, but winters south of them.

A member of the guilds of Ground Gleaners and Tree Trappers, and a good Citizen in
its nesting haunts. But on its travels through the South a mischievous bird, who
eats sprouting rice in spring and ripening rice grains in fall.

THE ORCHARD ORIOLE

(The Basket-Maker)

The sun was now well above the trees. The children laughed and talked happily,
now seeing a bird they knew, then some of the flowers that their dear flower lady,
Olive, had shown them about the Farm.

"When we know some flowers and birds, shan't we learn about the bugs and
things the birds eat, and the bees and butterflies that carry the flower messages,
Uncle Roy?"

"Yes, to be sure; and by that time there will be something else for you to wonder
about."

"Why!" cried Dodo gleefully, "if we
stay here till we know all we want it will
be so long that Rap will have a beard like you,
uncle, and I shall have my hair stuck up with
hairpins, and wear the long skirts that tangle
people up"—and at this they all laughed.

"What was that?" asked Nat, as a bird
darted by, flashing with orange and black.

"That's an Oriole," said Rap.

"Yes, an Oriole; but do you know
what kind?" said the Doctor.

"I didn't know there was but one
kind," answered Rap. "Anyway, this one
makes a long nest hanging from the end
of a branch; he is a good fighter if any one
touches it, and can keep away squirrels
and chipmunks like a little man."

Top: Male. *Bottom*: Female.
Orchard Oriole.

"There are seven different species of North American Orioles," said the Doctor; "but you are only likely to see two of them—the hammock-maker and the basket-maker. This one, the hammock-maker, who has just flown by, is called the Baltimore Oriole, because George Calvert, Lord Baltimore, on landing in this country in 1628, is said to have admired the colors of the bird and adopted them for his coat of arms. Some called him Fire-bird, because he is so flaming orange on some parts, and others Hang-nest, from the way he slings his hammock.

"The plainer black and chestnut bird, who now has a nest in our own Orchard, is the Basket-maker. As these two belong to the Blackbird and Oriole family, we may as well have them now, though in the regular family procession the 'tramp' walks next to the Bobolink, who is such a vagrant himself.

"This Oriole takes his name because he was once supposed to hang his nest chiefly in the branches of orchard trees; but he is as likely to be found in the maples by the garden fence as anywhere else.

"He has a cheerful rolling song, as varied in its different tunes as that of the Song Sparrow. It is not like a Robin's, or a Thrush's, or even like Brother Baltimore's; it is perfectly original, and before these birds leave the Orchard you must listen, to hear it for yourselves.

"Mrs. O. Oriole is a famous weaver; her grass nest, hung from a crotch, is one of the tidiest bits of basket-making in Birdland, and would do credit to human hands. Yet she has only a beak for a shuttle or darning-needle—whichever you please to call it. I think it is most like the needle of a sewing-machine, with the eye at the point, so that it pokes the thread through as it goes into the cloth, instead of pulling it through with the other end."

THE ORCHARD ORIOLE

Length seven inches.

Male: black; the rump, breast, belly, and lesser wing-coverts chestnut. Round black tail with whitish tips, and some whitish on the wings.

Female: grayish-green on the upper parts, greener on the tail, with paler bars on the wings; dull yellow on all the under parts.

The young male is like the female the first year, but a little browner on the back; next year he has a black throat; then he patches up his clothes till he looks like his father, all black and chestnut.

A Summer Citizen of the United States, west to the plains, north to some parts of the Northern States and Canada, travelling entirely south of the United States to spend the winter.

A pleasant though shy neighbor, and very good Citizen, belonging to the Ground Gleaners, Tree Trappers, and Seed Sowers. Eats a little cultivated fruit for dessert, and should be welcome to it.

THE BALTIMORE ORIOLE

(The Hammock-Maker)

Baltimore Oriole.

"The Baltimore Oriole is not so shy as his brother, and rather relies on keeping his nest out of sight than himself out of mind. His home is a sort of hempen hammock, only deeper and more pocket-shaped, to keep the babies from falling out, as Nat and Dodo both did out of our hammock yesterday."

"This nest Mrs. B. Oriole twines herself, from plant fibres, adding strings of cotton or worsted when she has a chance to find any. She secures it to the end of a strong supple twig, usually at a good height from the ground, and she likes an elm tree best of all, because it is not easy for cats or House People to climb far out on the slender swaying branches. Up there the eggs and young are safely rocked by the wind and sheltered by leaves. A cat may look at a king, and also at an Oriole's nest, but the looking will not do her much good in either case.

"Mamma Oriole sits on the nest, which is almost closed over her head, and keeps all safe. Though she does not sing to House People, how do we know but what she whispers a little lullaby like this, on stormy nights, to her nestlings?

"Rains beat! Winds blow!
Safe the nest in the elm tree.
    Days come! Nights go!
    Birds at rest in the elm tree.
To-and-fro, to-a-n-d-fro,
Safe are we from every foe—
    Orioles in the elm tree.
Cats come! Cats go!
Lullaby in the elm tree!

"Meanwhile B. Oriole does a great deal of work, for he is a tireless member of the guilds of Tree Trappers and Ground Gleaners, eating hosts of caterpillars, wireworms, and beetles. When he is very thirsty he does, now and then, take a sip of the fruit he has helped to save, and once in a while he may eat a few green peas. But would any one refuse a mess of peas to a neighbor in the next house? Then why should you begrudge a few to neighbor B. Oriole? He doubtless paid you for them before he took them, or will do so before long.[5]

"B. Oriole comes north before his mate to be, and spends a few days in fretting until she arrives. Then he sings a gladsome song, to tell her of his pleasure, and she answers, I am sorry to say, in rather a complaining tone; but the match is soon made. Though they are not the sweetest-tempered birds possible, they are as quick to aid as to quarrel with their neighbors.

"Their bright colors seem rather out of place in the family which contains also our sombre Blackbirds, but before the leaves have fallen both kinds of Orioles and their families start for Mexico and Central America, where such tropical hues seem more in keeping, and where many members of the family are quite as brilliant as those we see here."

"There goes another Oriole!" cried Nat. "What a beauty, too! I suppose he has a nest high up in one of these elms over the road."

"Very likely, for in autumn, when the trees are bare, I have sometimes counted a dozen Orioles' nests in this very row of elms."

"Look, Uncle Roy! Look over in that pasture! What are all those black and brown birds walking round after the cows, just as chickens do?" said Dodo.

---

[5] Here, the Baltimore Oriole provides an excellent example of how the ecological benefits of birds are framed in terms of citizenship, which is tied to the Protestant work ethic. Orioles "pay for" any fruits they eat by virtue of eating insects that harm farmers' crops.

"Those are members of the Blackbird family called Cowbirds, because they follow the cows as they feed, in order to pick up worms and bugs that are shaken out of the grass. But I am sorry to say that these birds are the vagabonds of Birdland—the tramps I told you of."

THE BALTIMORE ORIOLE

Length seven and a half inches.

Male: orange flame-color, the head, neck, and upper half of back black; wings black, edged with white; tail black and orange, about half and half.

Female: not clear orange and black, but the former color much duller, and the latter mixed up with gray, olive, and brown.

A Summer Citizen of the United States east of the Rocky Mountains, north to Canada, travelling to Central America for the winter.

A worthy Citizen, fine musician, and a good neighbor. Belongs to the guilds of Ground Gleaners, Tree Trappers, and Seed Sowers.

THE COWBIRD

(The Tramp)

"Cluck-see! cluck-see!" called a Cowbird, flying over the wall to join the others in the pasture.[6]

"What a hoarse ugly cry!" said Nat.

"Yes, but not more disagreeable than the bird's habits. I will tell you what happens every season to some poor Warbler, Sparrow, or Vireo, on account of this strange bird.

"A Song Sparrow builds her nest in the grass; an egg is laid, the bird looks proudly at it, and may perhaps fly off for a few minutes. Meanwhile, peeping and spying, along comes a Cowbird. She wants to lay an egg, too, but has no home, because she is too lazy and shiftless to build one. She sees the Sparrow's nest and thinks, 'Ah, hah! that bird is smaller than I am, and cannot push my egg out; I will leave it there!' This she does very quickly, and slips away again.

---

[6] The Cowbird is now called the Brown-headed Cowbird. The subheading "The Tramp" refers to the authors' disdain for Cowbirds, calling them "the vagabonds of Birdland—the tramps I told you of." Their reasons for disliking Cowbirds are ornithological, not personal, and are discussed extensively in the introduction. For example, the authors anthropomorphize Cowbirds as "bad citizens" for their nest parasitism (the practice of laying their eggs in other birds' nests).

Cowbird.

"When the Sparrow comes home she may wonder at the strange egg, and perhaps be able to push it out of the nest; but more likely she takes no notice of it, as it is so much like her own, and lets it stay. If she does this, that egg is only the beginning of trouble. It is larger than her own, so it gets more warmth and hatches more quickly. Then the young Cowbird grows so fast that it squeezes the little Sparrows dreadfully, sometimes quite out of the nest, and eats so much that they are half or wholly starved. The poor Sparrow and her mate must sometimes think what a big child it is; but they feed it kindly until it can fly— sometimes even after it leaves the nest. Then it goes back to join the flock its tramp parents belong to, without so much as saying 'thank you' to its foster parents.

"A Cowbird lays only one egg in each nest, but sometimes several visit the same nest in succession; and then the poor Sparrow has a hard time, indeed.

"The Yellow Warbler is one of the clever birds who will not always be imposed upon—you remember the two-storied nest we found; and some of the larger birds push out the strange egg. But Cowbirds are very crafty, and usually select their victims from among the small, feeble, and helpless."

"Does this hateful Cowbird ever sing?" asked Dodo.

"Sometimes in spring he tries to; he squeaks a few notes, and makes faces, struggling, choking, wheezing, as if he had swallowed a beetle with hooks on its legs and was in great pain. It is a most startling noise, but it certainly is not musical, though perhaps it pleases the Cowbird ladies; for if they have such bad taste in other ways, they doubtless like such harsh and inharmonious sounds."

"I don't see what makes them act so," said Rap. "I thought birds had to build nests, or have a hole or a bit of ground or rock of their own—that it was a law."

"So it is, my boy; but the Cowbird is one of the exceptions I told you about; and I am glad to say there are very few."

THE COWBIRD

Length about seven and a half inches.

Male: very glossy black, excepting the head and neck, which are shiny dark brown like burnt coffee.

Female: dusky brown, the lower parts lighter than the upper.

A Citizen of the entire United States.

A Ground Gleaner and a Weed Warrior, to some extent, but a bad neighbor, a worse parent, a homeless vagabond, and an outlaw in Birdland.

ON AGAIN

The road crept down hill, passed through a village, and then into the woods once more. The children saw a great many bird friends—Swallows, Goldfinches, a beautiful Blue Jay, which was new to them, and some Yellow Warblers. They stopped for half an hour in the wooded lane, where a Chat whistled to them, a Scarlet Tanager flew hastily overhead, and the Doctor showed them a Towhee rambling among the leaves, while a little brownish bird kept flitting into the air and back to his perch, calling "pewee—pe-a-r!" in a sad voice.

"What's that?" asked Rap; "it's a bird I often see near the mill, catching flies on the wing."

"It is called the Wood Pewee," said the Doctor; "when we come back this afternoon we will stop, and I will try to find its nest to show you. We must go on now." As soon as they drove out of the wood, the smell of the salt marsh came to them, and they saw that the road led between low meadows, with wooded knolls here and there. By and by the trees grew thinner and the grass coarser.

"Oh, I see the water!" cried Dodo, "and the little house where we are going! Oh, look at the black birds flying over those bushes! Are those Cowbirds too? And there are more black birds, very big ones too, going over to the water, and more yet coming out of those stumpy little pines, and there are some yellow pigeons down in the grass! Do stop quick, Olive! I think there is going to be a bird clambake or a picnic down here!" And Dodo nearly fell out of the surrey in her excitement.

"Not exactly a picnic," said the Doctor, "but what I have brought you purposely to see. The birds flying over the alders are Red-winged Blackbirds; those coming from the pines are Purple Grackles; the big black ones flying overhead are Crows; and the yellow-breasted fellows walking in the grass are Meadowlarks. We must first make the horses comfortable, and then we can spend the day with the birds among these marshes and meadows."

When they reached the beach the wagon track led through a hedge of bar-berry bushes to a shed covered with pine boughs at the back of the fisherman's house.

The fisherman himself came out to help them with the horses. He was a Finlander, Olaf Neilsen, who kept boats in summer, fished, and tended two buoy lights at the river entrance for a living.[7] His hut stood on a point, with the sandy beach of the bay in front of it, and the steeper bank where the river ran on the left. All the time the water was rushing out, out, out of the river and creeping down on the sand to make low tide.

The children did not know it then, but they were to spend many happy days on this beach, in company with their uncle and Olaf, during the next two years.

The Doctor whispered something mysterious to Olaf about clams, hoes, and "dead low water"; then he told the children to rest awhile under the pine shelter, and hear about the Blackbirds before they went out to see them in the meadows.

THE RED-WINGED BLACKBIRD

(The Hussar)

"This handsome Blackbird comes early and stays late in places where he does not linger all the year. He loves wet places, and his note is moist and juicy, to match his nesting haunts. 'Oncher-la-ree!' he calls, either in flying or as he walks along the ground after the fashion of his brethren—for Blackbirds never hop, like most birds, with both feet together, but move one after the other, just as we do.

"The Redwings are sociable birds, nesting in small colonies, and when once settled they never seem to stray far from home. The nest is a thick pocket hung either between reeds over the water, or fixed to the upright stems of a bush, quite near the ground, if the place is very marshy.

"The Redwings place their nests where it would seem very easy to reach them; but really the bushes are either surrounded by a little creek, hidden deep in the reeds, or the ground is so marshy that neither man nor beast can come near. That is the one reason why the males fly about so boldly, showing their glossy uniforms with the red and gold epaulets. When we try to visit that group of alders, where the colony lives, you will see for yourselves how nicely it is protected.

---

[7] For more on the character of Olaf Neilsen, the Finnish lighthouse keeper, please see the introduction.

"We welcome this Blackbird in the spring, because his is one of the earliest bird-notes. In autumn, when he leaves the marsh and brings his flock to the grain-fields, we do not like him quite so well; but the Wise Men say that even then he is a good fairy in disguise, eating cut-worms, army-worms, and other injurious kinds; even when stealing a bit of green corn, they think he clears away the worms that bore under the husks."

THE RED-WINGED BLACKBIRD

Length nine and a half inches.

Male: glossy black, except the scarlet shoulders, edged with buff. Female: mixed rusty black and buff, with dull reddish-orange shoulders—not conspicuous.

A Citizen of North America in general.

A member of the guilds of Ground Gleaners and Tree Trappers.

Red-winged Blackbird.

THE PURPLE GRACKLE

(The Crow Blackbird. Rusty Hinge.)

"What a noise those Blackbirds are making!" said Nat.

"That's nothing to the way they do early in the spring, or in autumn, after they are through nesting," said Rap. "You should hear them. They come to a big chestnut across the road from our house, more than a hundred of them at once, and they creak and crackle and squeak till all of a sudden down they go on the ground, and walk about awhile to feed."

"Yes," said the Doctor, "I call them Rusty Hinges, for their voices sound like the creaking of a door that needs oiling on the hinges. But in spite of this they try to sing to their mates in spring, and very funny is the sight and sound of their devotion. To judge only by their notes, they should belong to the Croaking Birds, and not to the Singers at all; but they have a regular music-box in the throat, only it is out of order, and won't play tunes. Like the Redwings, they also nest in colonies, either in old orchards, cedar thickets, or among pines; the rest of the year, too, they keep in flocks. Except in the most northerly States Crow Blackbirds stay all winter, like Crows themselves. They are not particularly likable birds, though you will find they have very interesting habits, if you take time to watch them."

"I wonder if you fed them with cod-liver oil and licorice lozenges if their voices would be better?" asked Dodo, who had suffered from a hoarse cold the winter before.

"I don't know what that treatment might do for them," laughed the Doctor; "but if you will agree to feed them I will give you the oil and licorice!" And then Dodo laughed at herself.

THE PURPLE GRACKLE

Length twelve to thirteen and a half inches.

Male: glossy black, with soap-bubble tints on the head, back, tail, and wings, and yellow iris. A long tail that does not lie flat and smooth like that of most birds.

Female: dull blackish and smaller—not over twelve inches.

A Citizen of the Atlantic States from Florida to Massachusetts.

A good Citizen, if there are not too many in one place to eat too much grain.

A Ground Gleaner and Tree Trapper, clearing grubs and beetles from ploughed land.

Purple Grackle.

THE MEADOWLARK

"In early March the Meadowlark comes to the places that he was obliged to leave in the winter, and cries, 'Spring o' the year! Spring o' the y-e-a-r!' to the brown fields and icy brooks.[8] They hear the call and immediately begin to stir themselves.

"Then the Meadowlark begins to earn his living, and pay his taxes at the same time, by searching the fields and pastures first for weed seeds and then, as the

---

[8] The Meadowlark is now split into various regional species and subspecies; the one depicted here is likely the one now called the Eastern Meadowlark.

ground softens, for the various grubs and beetles that meant to do mischief as soon as they could get a chance. By the middle of May, when the grass has grown high enough to protect him, this gentle bird thinks he has earned a right to a home in one of the meadows he has freed from their insect enemies, and sets about to make it. A little colony may settle in this same field, or a single pair have a corner all to themselves.

"A loose grass nest is arranged in a suitable spot, usually where the grass is long enough to be drawn together over the nest like a sort of tent. Here the mother tends the eggs and nestlings, the father always keeping near to help her, and continually singing at his daily toil of providing for his family as charmingly as if he were still a gay bachelor; for Meadowlarks are very affectionate both toward each other and their young. It is really distressing to hear the sadness of the song of one who has lost his mate. He seems to be crying, 'Where are you, dear?' and beseeching her to come.

Meadowlark.

"Though we frequently hear their song in the marsh meadows in autumn, they are shyer then, and keep in flocks. At that season they grow fat, and gunners continually worry them; but I do not think that sportsmen often shoot these song birds. They are chiefly the victims of thoughtless boys or greedy pot-hunters. The true sportsman is one of the first to preserve all song birds, and give even game birds a fair chance for life; he is thus very different from the cruel man who, simply because he owns a gun, shoots everything, from a Robin to a Quail, and even in the nesting season."

"Please, what is a pot-hunter?" asked Dodo.

"A pot-hunter is one who kills birds and other game at any time, regardless of the law, merely for the sake of money-making."

"Is there a law about killing birds?" asked Nat.

"Certainly. All really civilized States have their game-laws, and I hope the time is near when all our States will unite in this matter.[9] Where there is a good law no wild bird or beast, even those which are suitable and intended for food, may be killed in its nesting or breeding season, or for some time afterward. Also, these creatures must only be killed by fair hunting, not with snares or traps or by any foul means; and even fishes are thus protected against wanton or excessive destruction."

"But if there is a law in some places and not in others, why don't the birds that travel get shot when they go about?" asked Rap.

"They do, my boy, and that is the pity of it. Some people seem to think there are so many birds in this great country that they cannot be killed out; and others are brutal, or do not think at all, but kill for the sake of killing. The worst of it is that little or no protection is given the poor birds in the warm countries where they spend the winter. Thrushes are shot for pot-pie, all the gayly colored birds are killed for their feathers, and flocks of doves are slain to see how many a man can hit in a day!

"Olaf says the Meadowlarks are raising their second brood now and he can find you some empty nests, if you go with him, so you can see how they are made; he will show you the Redwings' nests, too. You boys may take off your shoes and stockings; and Miss Dodo, being a girl, shall ride on Olaf's shoulder."

"Please, can't I have my shoes off too?" begged Dodo. "I love to wade like the boys!"

"By and by, on the beach; but what if a frog or an eel should touch your foot, or a sharp straw stick in it—are you enough of a boy not to scream?"

Dodo was not sure, and thought she would begin by riding.

THE MEADOWLARK

Length ten to eleven inches.

Upper parts marked with brown, bay, gray, and black; head striped, with a yellow spot
in front of the eye; wing-feathers nearest the body, and most of the tail-feathers,
scalloped with black and gray, but the outside tail-feathers white.

---

[9] Here, the authors lament the lack of a federal game law protecting birds. The Lacey Act, the first national game law in the United States, was passed by Congress three years after the publication of this book, in 1900. This law prohibited market hunters from selling poached game (wild animals or birds) across state lines. Before the Lacey Act, game laws existed (or not) on a state-by-state basis. For more information on state- and federal-level conservation laws, see the introduction.

A MIDSUMMER EXCURSION   187

Under parts nearly all yellow, with a black crescent on the breast, but further back flaxen-brown, with dark stripes.

Bill stout where it runs up on the forehead, but tapering to the point.

A Citizen of the United States and Canada.

A good and useful neighbor. A famous member of the guild of Ground Gleaners, its chief work being to kill bad insects which eat the grass-roots in pastures and hay-fields.

A beautiful bird and charming songster.

CHAPTER 18

Crows and Their Cousins

In half an hour the children were back again, all talking eagerly together.

"The Redwings scolded us like everything!" said Dodo, "and Rap stepped right into an empty Meadowlark's nest, without seeing it. A little way back there are lots of Bobolinks, too, singing and singing, but we couldn't find a single nest."

"It was pretty warm out there," said Nat, fanning himself with a wide haymaker's hat, such as both he and Dodo had worn since they came to the Farm.

"Come under the shelter and rest until Olaf has dinner ready. Where is Olive?"

"She is down by the water looking for seaweeds, for her album."

"Have we used up all the Blackbird family?" asked Dodo, as they sat on the sand and began to dig holes with their hands.

"Oh, no; there is the biggest of all—the Crow," said Nat.

"Strange as it is," replied the Doctor, "though the Crow is the blackest of all our birds he does not belong to the Blackbird family, but to a separate one of his own—the family of Crows, Jays, and Magpies."

"How is that, Uncle Roy? You said that beautiful blue and gray bird we saw in the woods was a Jay," said Nat.

"Yes, but that is no stranger, as far as looks go, than to find a flaming Oriole in the Blackbird family, is it? You remember that I told you the relationship of birds depends upon their likeness in the bones and the rest of their inwards, not upon the color of their feathers."

"See! there are a great many Crows on that sandbar! They are picking up mussels! Some are bigger than others!" said Rap, who had been taking a look through the field-glass. "Are the small ones the females, or are there two kinds of Crows?"

"There are several kinds of Crows in the United States, besides Ravens and Magpies, who are cousins to the Crow. About here we usually only see two of them—the two that are now down on the bar—the American Crow and the Fish Crow. The Fish Crow is the smaller of the two, lives along the coast, and does not often go further north than Connecticut. It takes its name from its habit of catching fish in shallow pools and bays.

"The larger Crow is the bird that every one knows and most people dislike, because it has always been called a corn thief, though the Wise Men say it is rather a useful bird after all.

"The Crow is certainly a black, gloomy-looking bird, with a disagreeable voice. If several pairs make up their minds to build in the cedars or tall pines in one's grounds, anywhere near the house, the noise they make early in the morning is very tiresome. 'Ka—Ka—Ka-a-a-ah!' they call and quaver, at the first peep of day. Then they begin to look about for breakfast. If there is a Robin's or Dove's nest at hand, they think it is foolish to look further, and help themselves to fresh eggs or squabs. This makes us very angry, and we have the great Crow's nest—a peck or two of sticks, lined with the bark of cedars and grape vines—pulled from the tree-top where the crafty bird had hidden it.

"It is perfectly right to do so, from our point of view. I, for one, do not wish Crows in my garden or about the Farm, where I see only the bad side of their characters. So we chase them away, and put scarecrows in the corn-fields. Do the Crows care? Not a bit! They laugh and talk about us behind our

American Crow.

backs, and before our faces too. They pretend to be afraid, and fly away if a man appears a quarter of a mile off; but merely to settle down in another part of the field until their watcher tells them to move away again.

"There is a watcher for every flock, who gives the order to fly, and warns the troop at every approach of danger.

"Of course we must remember that for many months of the year the Crow eats grasshoppers, grubs, and even mice; but it is easy to forget this when one discovers that half a dozen Crows have eaten all the young Robins in the orchard, in a single morning."

"Did they ever do that in our Orchard?" asked Dodo.

"Yes—not once, but many times; and that is the reason why I do not allow Crows to nest anywhere on the Farm. In great open farming districts, where other birds are few, they may do much more good than evil; but not in well-settled places or about gardens and pleasure grounds."

THE AMERICAN CROW

Length from eighteen to twenty inches.

Glossy black from the tip of its beak to the end of its toes.

A Citizen of North America from the Fur Countries to Mexico.

A dismal and noisy neighbor for three months in the year, making itself hateful by
destroying grain, and the eggs and young of song birds; but for the other nine a good
citizen, working in the guilds of Ground Gleaners and Wise Watchers.

THE BLUE JAY

"This Jay is accused of the same bad tricks as the Crow—pulling up sprouting corn, eating ripe corn, and going birds'-nesting, to suck the eggs and eat the helpless young. But we must not judge the whole tribe by what we have seen a pair or two do in the Orchard or home woods in the mating season.

"The Blue Jay is the third of our really familiar blue birds and is certainly very handsome. Do you remember who the other two are?"

"The Bluebird!" said Dodo quickly. "And the Blue Sparrow!" cried Nat.

"You mean the Indigo Bird," laughed Rap. "The Blue Jay is a queer bird, who can twist himself into all sorts of shapes. He sits one way when he sings, another when he is watching out for danger, and when he calls he is too funny for anything—he humps himself up and drops his tail as if he was falling apart, and then squawks!"

"I see that you know this bird very well," said the Doctor. "Have you seen his nest?"

"Once. It was in the miller's woods, half-way up in a chestnut tree, and built just like a Crow's, only much smaller. That season one of the Jays whistled and carried on till I thought there were ever so many birds together, and then laughed at me! They come round the mill for sweepings in winter, but they are almost as shy as Crows."

When Olaf came with a basket and some short-handled hoes, the Doctor told Dodo she might take off her shoes and stockings and go down on the sandbar with Nat and Olaf, to dig clams for the chowder for dinner.

"More niceness!" screamed Dodo. "Olaf! Olaf! do clams grow in hills like potatoes? I thought they swam like fish! Aren't you coming, uncle, and Rap too, to tell us about clams?"

"No; you must talk to Olaf. We are going to help Olive with her seaweeds."

Blue Jay.

THE BLUE JAY

Length nearly twelve inches.

A fine blue and black crest on the head, very tall and pointed.

Upper parts blue, brighter on the wings and tail, which have many black bars and some white tips.

Under parts grayish-white, with a black collar.

A Citizen of eastern North America from the Fur Countries to Florida.

Belonging to the guild of Ground Gleaners, his special work being to kill grasshoppers and caterpillars; but often eats young birds and sucks eggs, like a cannibal bird.

CHAPTER 19

A Feathered Fisherman

THE OSPREY

Before the day was over the children were so in love with Olaf—with the beach where crabs were living, with the sea over which water birds were soaring—and wished to know so many things, that the Doctor told them the only way to satisfy them would be to camp on the shore in August, when the water would be warm enough for bathing; for to answer all the questions they asked would take a month.

"And then you can tell us another bookful about water and fish, and crabs and sky," said Dodo. "So we shall have a bird book, and a butterfly book, and Olive's flower book!"

"Yes, and a beast book, too!" said Nat, "about coons and bears, and squirrels and foxes, you know! Rap has seen foxes right on our Farm!"

"I wish I knew something about the stars—and the rocks too," said Rap very earnestly. "Was this earth ever young, Doctor?"[1]

"Yes, my boy, everything that Heart of Nature guides had a beginning and was once young."

---

[1] Wright had envisioned *Citizen Bird* as the first in a series of nature books for children, which she called the "Heart of Nature" or the "Orchard Farm" series, Orchard Farm being the setting of *Citizen Bird*. Each book she planned to publish in partnership with a famous naturalist, such as Frank Chapman of the American Museum of Natural History. "When the Earth Was Young" was her working title for the fifth book in the series, which would cover, as she put it in an outline in her correspondence with her publisher, "Mineral—Vegetable—Animal Kingdoms, Geology—Physical Geography—Astronomy."

Osprey.

"What is that? An Eagle?" cried Dodo suddenly, pointing up to a very large bird, with a white breast and brown-barred tail, who flew over the bay and dived into the water.

"It's the Fisherman Bird," said Olaf. "Some call it the Fish Hawk and others the Osprey. They say it lives all over North America, but it goes far south in winter, and when it comes back in spring we know the fish are running again; for it lives on the fish it catches, and won't come until they are plenty."

"How does it catch fish?" asked Dodo.

"It hovers overhead until it sees, with its sharp eye, a fish ripple the water; then it pounces down like a flash, and grabs the fish with its long claws, that are made like grappling-irons. If the fish is small the Osprey carries it home easily; but if it is a big one there may be a fight. Sometimes, if the Osprey's claws get caught in a fish too large to fly away with, the Fisherman Bird is dragged under water and drowned."

"Do they still nest on Round Island?" asked the Doctor. "There were a dozen pairs of them there when I was a boy."

"Yes, sir! But there is only one pair now. It's a great rack of sticks, half as big as a haystack; for they mend it every season, and so it keeps growing until now it is almost ready to fall out of the old tree that holds it. And, do you know, sir, that

Purple Grackles have stuck their own nests into the sides of it, until it is as full of birds as a great summer hotel is of people."

"Oh, we must see it!" said Olive, who had finished putting her seaweeds to press; "for as yet I have only read about such a nest."

"What does the Osprey look like near to?" asked Rap.

"Like a large Hawk," answered the Doctor. "You would know him to be a Hawk by his hooked beak and claws. He walks in the procession of bird families along with the cannibal birds among whom he belongs, and who come after the Birds that only Croak and Call. But he is not a real cannibal, because he lives on fish, and never eats birds. So I will give you a description of him now."

THE OSPREY

Length about two feet.

Upper parts dark brown with some white on the head and neck.

Under parts white with some dark spots.

Feet very large and scaly, with long sharp claws, to hold the slippery fishes he catches.

A Citizen of North America.

A very industrious fisherman who minds his own business and does nobody any harm.

CHAPTER 20

Some Sky Sweepers

About four o'clock, after a long rest, the party started for home, because they wanted to have plenty of time to stop in the wood lane on the way.

The first bird that Nat spied after they left the meadows was perching on the topmost wire of a fence by the roadside. Every once in a while he darted into the air, snapped up an insect, and returned to the same perch on the wire whence he had started. He was a very smart-looking bird, with a flaming crest that he raised and lowered to suit himself; and every time he flew into the air he cried "Kyrie—kyrie!"

"That is a Kingbird," said the Doctor; "it is very kind of him to show himself, for he is the bird I most wished to see. We have finished with the true song birds now, and the next order is that of the Songless Perching Birds—birds that have call-notes, some of them quite musical, but no true song. So we will name them the Birds that only Croak and Call.

"The crowing of a Rooster, the screech of a Night Owl, the Hawk's harsh scream, the laughing and hammering of a Woodpecker, all answer the same good purpose as a song.

"The first family of Songless Perching Birds is that of the Tyrant Flycatchers, and the first of these birds with which we have to do is the one you have just seen. He belongs to the guild of Sky Sweepers.

"But do not try to write anything down while we are driving over this rough road; the surrey jolts too much. You need only listen now, and Olive will help you with your note-books to-morrow."

THE KINGBIRD

"How the winged insects must hate a Kingbird, who is a real tyrant over them, and must seem very cruel!" continued the Doctor.[1] "He sits on a rail or wire, and suddenly—flip, snap! a fly is caught—flip, snap! a wasp dies. All day long he is waging war, and helping us in our never-ending battle with the bugs.

"If he happens to fancy a rose-bug or juicy ant, he dashes to the leaf or grass-blade on which the insect is crawling, hovers a moment in the air to take aim, and then snatches the bug off. So clever is he that when he eats bees, as he some-times does, he seldom takes the honey-makers, but mainly the drones; perhaps he is afraid of being stung."

"What is a drone, Uncle Roy?" asked Dodo.

"A bee which does not work for its living and cannot sting."

"The Kingbird is proud of his nest, which he often confines to a maple on the edge of a garden, or to your pet pear tree. But let Hawks and Crows beware even of thinking about a Kingbird's nest! For he loves his home, and hates those who would injure it; and what is more, he is not one bit afraid of them. If they come in sight he attacks them bravely, and drives them far away, even if they are so big and fierce that he has to call his friends to help him; so that the robber Crow or cannibal bird is lucky if he does not lose an eye before he escapes.

"But the Kingbird is not quarrelsome—simply very lively; he is the very picture of dash and daring in defending his home, and when he is teaching his youngsters how to fly.

Kingbird.

"Like other insect-eaters, he leaves the northerly States before cold weather and journeys beyond the United States for the winter. We always miss him when he has swooped along the fence rail for the last time and joined his brethren in the tree-tops, where the flocks form for their long flight."

THE KINGBIRD

Length eight inches—about the size of a Wood Thrush.

Upper parts slate-colored, with black head, wings, and tail; a white band at the end of the tail, and a flaming orange spot on the crown.

---

[1] The Kingbird is now called the Eastern Kingbird.

Under parts pure white, a little grayish on the breast.

A Summer Citizen of the United States and Canada, travelling to Central and South America for the winter.

One of the best neighbors, and a brave soldier. An officer of the guild of Sky Sweepers, also a Ground Gleaner and Tree Trapper, killing robber-flies, ants, beetles, and rose-bugs. A good friend to horses and cattle, because he kills the terrible gadflies. Eats a little fruit, but chiefly wild varieties, and only now and then a bee.

THE PHOEBE

(The Water Pewee)

"Smaller, but not a whit less active than the Kingbird is the Phoebe or Water Pewee—the small Flycatcher who is almost as familiar about the farm and roadside as the Robin himself.[2] Look about the woodshed or cow-shed. Is there a beam or little nook of any sort that will hold a nest? If so, in early May you will see a pair of nervous brown birds, heaping up a mound of moss and mud. When they have made it large enough to suit them, they line it with soft grass and horsehairs; the nest is then ready for the white eggs, which once in a while are varied with a few brown spots.

"Sometimes Phoebes build under a bridge, or in a rocky pocket above a stream; for they love water and are great bathers. Then they make the outside of the nest to match the rock by covering it with lichens.

"The Phoebe, like all other Flycatchers, sits motionless upon a dead twig, fence rail, or often the clothesline, waiting for insects to come by. Then he darts out, seizes one, and returns to the same perch, flipping the tail, raising the little crest, and calling 'Phoebe—p-h-o-e-b-e,' in a very anxious voice.

"Phoebe is a hardy Flycatcher, who journeys north in March to tell us spring is coming, and it takes a hard frost to send him away again. Even then he does not hurry off toward the tropics like the ardent Kingbird, but lingers all winter in the Southern States."

Phoebe.

---

[2] The Phoebe is now called the Eastern Phoebe. (Older names included Water Peewee or Bridge Peewee.)

THE PHOEBE

Length seven inches. Wings hardly any longer than the tail.

Upper parts deep olive-brown, darkest on the head; bill and feet black.

Under parts dull white, with a grayish or yellowish tinge.

A Citizen of North America east of the plains and north to Canada, nesting from South Carolina northward, and wintering in the Southern States.

A useful and pleasant neighbor, who likes our society, often nesting in sheds and under porches.

A member of the guild of Sky Sweepers, who also works with the Tree Trappers.

THE WOOD PEWEE

"Among all the other Flycatchers, big, little, and least, I can only tell you of one more, and will choose the Wood Pewee as being the one most likely to interest you.

"This morning in the wood lane I saw a pair that were surely nest-building, and I wondered if they were not the great-great-grandchildren of those who lived there when I was a boy. The Pewee's nest is very pretty—almost as dainty as the Hummingbird's. I will try to find it for you as we go back this afternoon."

"Then the Wood Pewee builds late, like the Cedar Waxwing and Goldfinch?" said Rap.

"Yes, rather late; about the first or second week in June. He is a lazy traveller; and then, perhaps, he thinks his nest is so frail that he needs to have the trees in full leaf to protect it. The Wood Pewee takes his name from his liking for the woods and his call-note; yet he is quite as fond of our Orchard and the lower side of the garden.

Wood Pewee.

"When you have once met him face to face and heard his sad cry—'pewee—pewee—pee-eer—weer!'—you will probably find half a dozen pairs about home.

"It is usual to call the notes of this bird sad; but it only seems so from our point of view; for he is a happy, fussy little bird, and I dare say that when he calls he is only saying 'peek-a-boo!' to his mate on the other side of the tree."

"Wouldn't it be nice if we knew all that the animals and birds do, and could see what they see, besides being ourselves?" said Nat.

"I think we should be too wise and proud," said Rap.

"No, my lads," said the Doctor, "we should probably be more humble than we are now, and realize how very little House People really know about the wonderful lives of those creatures we commonly call 'dumb animals.'"

"You haven't given us any table for the Wood Pewee," said Dodo, who always took great pleasure in writing in her little book. "I like to hear it, though I can't write it now."

THE WOOD PEWEE

Length six and a half inches. Wings much longer than the tail, and feet very small.

Upper parts dark brown with an olive shade, and light bars on the wings; top of the head not darker than the back, and under side of the beak not black.

Under parts yellowish-white with a tinge of dark gray along the sides and across the breast.

Looks very much like the Phoebe, but you can tell them apart if you attend carefully to the tables.

A Citizen of North America from Florida to Canada and west to the plains. Travels beyond the United States for the winter.

A good Citizen and shy neighbor. A member of the guild of Sky Sweepers.

CHAPTER 21

Hummers and Chimney Sweeps

THE RUBY-THROATED HUMMINGBIRD

"It won't be dark for a long time yet," said Dodo, after they had driven silently for a couple of miles, watching the clouds against the tree-tops and the Swallows that were out in full force, sky-sweeping for their evening meal.

"Are you growing sleepy?" asked Olive.

Ruby-throated Hummingbird.

"No, only *terribly hungry*," whispered Dodo, as if rather ashamed of the fact; "and do you know, Olive, after dinner to-day I told Olaf I never should be hungry again, because I ate so much chowder. After we had driven awhile I thought to myself, 'I shan't want supper to-night anyway.' Then pretty soon I thought, 'I *shall* want supper,' and now I want it *right away!*" The Doctor laughed and looked at the cows that were pasturing in the roadside fields, for they were passing a farming village.

"I don't see any Cowbirds this afternoon," said Nat, thinking the Doctor was looking for them.

"This time I am looking at the cows themselves! Those over there are beautiful creatures, and there is a clear spring of water in the corner of the pasture. When we come to the farmhouse where they belong, we will stop to buy some milk, and Miss Dodo shall have supper; for even Mammy's buns, when they have been travelling about all day in a basket, would be rather dry without milk."

"But wouldn't the milk be good if the cows were not pretty, and there was no spring in the pasture?" asked Nat, who must have a reason for everything.

"It is not a question of pretty cows; it is whether they are clean and healthy or not, that makes the milk good or bad. And good pure water to drink, from a spring that is not near any barnyard or outbuilding, is one of the best things for keeping cows in good health."

Meanwhile they had driven up to a farmhouse, almost as large as their own, and the mistress, who was arranging her pans for the evening milking, said they might have cold milk then, or fresh warm milk if they would wait a little while until the cows came home.

Under the back porch was a cage with a little Owl in it, and the woman said it belonged to her boy. Joe, for that was his name, was about Rap's age, and soon made friends with them.[1] They told him where they had been spending the day, and about their uncle's wonder room, and the birds at Orchard Farm. "Have you got a Hummingbird's nest on your farm, and a Swaller chimney?" Joe asked anxiously.

"No, not exactly," said Nat, hesitating. "There are some birds in Uncle Roy's chimney, but we haven't found a Hummingbird's nest yet, though there are lots of the birds about the garden."

"Well, there's a Hummingbird's nest in our crab-apple tree, and we own the biggest Swaller chimney there is in the county! Pa says so, and he knows," said Joe proudly. "If you'll come with me and not grab the nest, I'll show it to you. It's a widow Hummingbird, too. I've never seen her mate since she began to set, but before that he was always flyin' round the honeysuckles and laylocks, so I'm sure he is dead."

"May I come too?" asked the Doctor.

"Pleased to have you, sir," said Joe, making a stiff little bow. "I'd have asked you, only most men folks don't set much store by birds 'nless they are the kind they go gunnin' for. Only pa does. He likes any kind o' bird, whether it sings or not, and he's powerful fond of the Swallers in our chimney. He says they eat the flies and things that tease the cows down in the pasture, and since those

---

[1] Like Rap, Joe, the son of dairy farmers, is depicted as closer to nature and thus appreciative and protective of the bird life that surrounds him on the farm.

Swallers came to our chimney we haven't had to put fly-sheets on the oxen when they are in the pasture—not once."

"Now, children, you see what good the Sky Sweepers do," said the Doctor.

"Sky Sweepers! We don't call 'em that! We call 'em Chimney Swallers!"

Then the children told Joe about the Bird Brotherhoods.

"Stand on this box," said Joe to Dodo, "and look hard at that small slantways branch, with the little bunch on it!"

"The little round bunch that looks like soft green moss?"

"Yes. Well, that's the Hummer's nest!"

"Oh! oh!" cried Dodo, forgetting to whisper, "I see a mite of a tail and a sharp needle beak sticking over the edge!"

This was too much for Mrs. Hummer, who flew off with a whirr like an angry little spinning-wheel—if such a proper Puritan thing is ever angry; and there in the nest were two tiny eggs, like white beans.

"Come back by the fence and watch," said Joe. "She doesn't like to leave the nest much when it is toward night."

"It's a pity her mate is dead. How lonely she must be!" said Dodo, who had a tender little heart.

"I do not think her mate is dead," said the Doctor; "he is merely staying away, after a custom of his family. The bird whose nest we see there is called the Ruby-throated Hummingbird, because he has a patch of glittering ruby-red feathers under his chin, at the top of his buttoned-up vest that hardly shows any white shirt-front. He wears a beautiful golden-green dress-coat, with its dark purplish tails deeply forked. His wife looks very much like him, only she has no ruby jewels to wear.

"Bold as this bird is in darting about and chasing larger ones, he is less than four inches long—only about the size of one of the hawk-moths that come out to feed, just as this valiant pygmy lancer leaves the flowers for the night.

"These Hummingbirds live on honey and very small insects, and dread the cold so that they spend the winter southward from Florida. But as soon as real spring warmth comes, they spread over the United States, east of the plains, and north even to the Fur Countries. They are the only kind found in the eastern half of North America, though there are more than a dozen other species in the West, most of them near the Mexican borders of the United States.

"When the Hummers arrive here, early in May, we see the brilliant males darting about—sometimes, I am sorry to say, quarrelling with their rivals and giving shrill cries like the squeaking of young mice. The last of May the dainty nest is made of plant-down and lichen scales. Then the male goes off by himself and sulks. You may see him feeding, but he keeps away from the nest—selfish bird that he is—until the little ones are ready to fly.

"Meanwhile the mother takes all the care and trouble herself, feeding her little Hummers in a peculiar way. She swallows tiny insects, and when they have remained a little while in her crop she opens her beak, into which the young bird puts its own and sucks the softened food, as a baby does milk from its bottle."[2]

"I was wondering this very morning," said Joe, "how the old bird was going to feed her young ones when those two eggs hatched, without any mate to help her. I'm real glad you came along to explain it, sir. Somehow the reasons lots of folk give for things aren't reasonable at all."

"Now, children," said the Doctor, "write the Hummingbird table before the twilight comes on."

THE RUBY-THROATED HUMMINGBIRD

Length less than four inches.

Male: shining golden-green above, with dark purplish wings and tail, the latter forked; glittering ruby-red throat; other under parts grayish, with some white on the breast and greenish on the sides.

Female: lacks the ruby throat, and has the tail not forked, but some of its feathers white-tipped.

A Summer Citizen of the eastern United States from Florida to Canada.

Though songless, a jewel of a bird, belonging to the guild of Tree Trappers. Nest a tiny round cup of moss and plant-down stuccoed with lichens; eggs only two, white.

THE CHIMNEY SWIFT

"Now, wouldn't you like to see the big chimney?" asked Joe. "The birds go in and out a good deal this time o' day. It's across the road there, where the old house used to be. The house is all gone, but the chimney is as strong as ever—I can climb up top and look down at the nests inside. See! there it is now!" Looking over the fence,

---

[2] Here, the authors present a partially incorrect description of how mother birds feed their young. Rather than the baby bird eating from the mother's bill, the mother bird inserts her bill into the baby's mouth and regurgitates the food. The inaccuracy is likely a purposeful depiction to anthropomorphize the birds, as both Wright and Coues accurately described the process in their birding books written for adult audiences.

they saw a tall stack of worn gray stones, that looked more like a tower than a chimney. Small blackish birds kept streaming from the top, circling high in the air and darting down again, all twittering as they dropped one after another out of sight, inside the weather-beaten pile.

"Look, children!" said the Doctor. "These are Chimney Swifts, usually called Chimney Swallows: and their color is like soot, to match the places they live in."

"Aren't they any relations of Swallows?" asked Rap.

"No, my boy; they look like Swallows, but as I think Olive told you once, the Swifts are a family all by themselves. This one lives in the eastern half of the country in summer, and goes far south for the winter. When he lives in a wild region, he chooses a hollow tree for his nesting place, as his ancestors always did before there were any houses or chimneys.

Chimney Swift.

"The flight of the Swift is so rapid that at times it is almost impossible for the quickest eye to follow him; his wings are very strong, and almost as long as all the rest of his body. Short and blunt as his tail looks when he flies, each feather ends in a hard sharp point which sticks out beyond the soft part. They feed on insects which they catch as they dash through the air, and can also break off dry twigs for nest-building without stopping—sometimes seizing the little sticks in their bills and sometimes in their claws, which are much stronger than those of Swallows."

"How do they make the sticks stay in the chimney? What do they set them on, and how do they perch while they are building?" asked Nat, all in one breath.

"Do you remember how the little Brown Creeper propped himself against the tree when he looked for insects?"

"Yes," said Rap; "he stuck his sharp tail-feathers into the bark and made a bracket of himself."

"The Swift does this also when he fastens twigs together for a nest. They are glued together into a little openwork basket, and gummed to the wall of the chimney, with a sticky fluid which comes from his own mouth."

"I've got a lot of old nests that fell down the chimney after a storm last winter that wet the glue and made them come unstuck," said Joe; "and I'll give you each one. If you look up the hole where the kitchen fireplace was, you can see the new nests quite plain; for the birds don't build them very near the top."

"Be careful of loose stones!" called the Doctor; but in a flash four young heads had disappeared in the ruins of the great fireplace, where three pairs of trousers and a short brown linen skirt alone were visible.

In a little while they had some milk and strawberries; and before they drove on Joe's father promised to take him up to Orchard Farm to see the birds in the Doctor's wonder room, as soon as haying should be over. To the children's astonishment they found it was half-past six o'clock; they had been at the farm an hour and a half, and could not stop again until they reached the wood lane where their uncle had promised to look for the Pewee's nest.

"Stay here, little people, and ask all the questions you like of Olive," said the Doctor, when they had reached the lane; "for I shall be able to find the nest more easily if you do not frighten the birds by talking."

"Pewee, pewee, pe-e-er!" cried a little voice.

"There he is, crying 'peek-a-boo' again," said Dodo. "Please, Olive, won't you tell us the table for the Chimney Swift now?"

"Certainly; and there is plenty of light yet if you wish to write it down."

THE CHIMNEY SWIFT

Length five and a half inches.

Sooty brown. Sharply pointed tail-feathers.

A Summer Citizen of eastern North America from Florida to the Fur Countries.

An excellent neighbor—a friend of the farmer and his cattle. An officer in the guild of
 Sky Sweepers, who shoots through the air in the shape of a bow and arrow.

"Come softly," said the Doctor, returning to the roadside; "I have found the Pewee's nest; it is quite new, and has no eggs in it as yet. This way—up along this ledge of rocks, and you can almost look into it." They moved quietly over the rocks until they reached a pepperidge tree, when the Doctor motioned them to stop and pointed to one of its branches which stretched over the rock. There was a flat nest with an evenly rounded edge, all covered with lichen scales outside.

"It is just like a Hummingbird's nest," whispered Nat.

"Only flatter, more like a saucer than a cup," said Rap. "Is it made of plant-down, too?"

"No—of fine grasses, rootlets, and bits of bark," said the Doctor; "and in a few days it will hold three or four creamy-white eggs, prettily wreathed around one end with dark-brown spots."

"Pewee, pewee, pe-e-er!" cried the nest owner very sadly.

"We are going home, so you needn't worry, dear," said Dodo. "Good-night."

CHAPTER 22

Two Winged Mysteries

THE NIGHTHAWK

THE SUN WAS QUITE LOW when the party drove out of the lane; the birds were singing their very best, and Olive stopped the horses on top of the next hill, that they might all look at the beautiful twilight picture around them.

"How quickly the sun slides when it once begins to go!" said Nat. "It looks as if it were going into a cage with the striped clouds for bars."

"Shirk—shirk—boom!" A large bird that had been sailing about overhead dropped through the air till it was almost over the surrey, then turned suddenly and darted upward again.

"What is that?" cried Nat and Dodo.

"That's a Nighthawk—don't you remember the bird we heard early one morning in the river woods? He's looking for small birds to eat," answered Rap.[1]

"He is called the Nighthawk, but never eats anything except beetles, flies, and other insects," said the Doctor, "for he is not a real Hawk. He takes his name from the fact that he dashes about at twilight and in cloudy weather like a Hawk; but his broad, shallow mouth is only suitable for insect-eating, like his cousin's, the Chimney Swift's, and the beak is equally small and feeble, not at all like the strong hooked one of a cannibal bird. Look overhead!"

"There are two light spots like holes through his wings," said Rap. "Ah yes! now I remember about him—we can always tell him from a real Hawk."

---

[1] The Nighthawk is now called the Common Nighthawk.

Nighthawk.

"How does he make that queer noise?" asked Nat. "It sounds like when I hit the telegraph wires with stones, or blow in the bunghole of a barrel."

"Watch him when he drops," said the Doctor; "do you not see that he does so with open wings? The air rushes between the long wing-quills and makes the vibrating noise. Now he is up and away again, but you see he keeps circling in the sky."

"Does he build in chimneys?" asked Dodo.

"The Nighthawk does not build any nest; the eggs are laid on bare ground or rock in an open field—occasionally on a house-top. Strange as this seems, the parent birds are so near the color of earth and rock that it is very difficult to find them when they are sitting, the young when hatched are equally invisible, and the eggs themselves look like two little stones—for there are never more than two. I will show you a Nighthawk in my cabinet, and you will see for yourselves how nicely the colors match ground and rocks."

"He looks like a pretty big bird," said Dodo. "How long is he? Is there only one in his family?"

"He has a brother called the Whip-poor-will, that we should meet very soon."

THE NIGHTHAWK

Length ten inches.

Mottled black and rusty above. Barred on the under parts with black and white or buff. A white collar on the throat, a white spot going entirely through the wing, and a white band across the tail.

A Summer Citizen of eastern North America, from the Gulf of Mexico to Canada, travelling far south for the winter.

A shy neighbor but a valuable Citizen, belonging to the Ground Gleaners as well as Sky Sweepers.

THE WHIP-POOR-WILL

"This mysterious bird is also a dweller in lonely places, feeding at night in the woods, having no nest, and laying the eggs in a hollow in the ground or on a stump or log. He is so nearly of the color of wood, earth, and rock, that you may pass near him a hundred times and never see him. Then too, when he perches in the day-time, he does not sit across a branch like other birds, but lengthwise, so that House People and cats cannot see him from below or cannibal birds from above. He is an insect-eater and so goes southward before hard frosts."

"Does this bird make any noise, and why is he called the Whip-poor-will?" asked Nat; "that is such a funny name."

Rap was about to answer when the Doctor signed to him and he stopped.

"Whip-poor-wills call their own name after dark, and I think you will hear them when we pass the miller's woods in a few minutes; for some reason they seldom come about the Farm."

"I believe I—am—growing—sleepy," murmured Dodo, trying to be polite and swallow a little yawn, but not wholly succeeding.

Whip-poor-will.

"I am very sure that *I* am," said Olive. "I don't think any of us will sit up much later than the birds to-night!"

"I hear a Veery," said Rap, "and a Phoebe too."

"Whip-poor-will! Whip-poor-will! Church!" cried a loud voice close by, and something like a long-winged Owl almost struck Olive with its wing as it flitted past.

"Oh, my!" cried Dodo, waking suddenly, "that must be a Whip-poor-will, for he called his own name as plain as the Chickadee does; and listen! there are more of them all up the hill."

Soon they passed Rap's house and left him at the gate. When the good old white horses trotted in the gate at Orchard Farm, Quick ran out, barking joyfully to tell them all that had happened during the day, and how he had guarded everything safely; but Dodo was fast asleep with her head on her uncle's arm.

"De deah lamb," said Mammy Bun, who came out to help them unload; "don' you go to wake her up, Massa Nat—ole mammy'll tote her up to bed. Dese am powerful healthy days for you chillens! And Massa Doctor and Miss Olive—if they ain' more'n half gone, too! 'Scursions am terrible sleepy things—least when dere all ober!"

THE WHIP-POOR-WILL

Length nearly ten inches.

A very large mouth, fringed with long bristles, useful as an insect trap.

Plumage all mottled with gray, buff, and black, but the end half of three outside tail-feathers white, and a white breast-band.

A Summer Citizen of the United States and Canada east of the plains; in winter from Florida southward.

A member of the guilds of Sky Sweepers and Ground Gleaners.

CHAPTER 23

A Laughing Family

When the children had their uncle with them, and could listen to his stories, it seemed very easy to name the birds. But when they were alone it was quite a different matter. The birds had a way of moving on, at exactly the wrong moment. Of course they made some very funny mistakes, and at times grew quite discouraged.

"I thought we could learn a hundred birds in no time," said Nat to Olive, one morning; "but I'm only pop sure of ten when they fly in a hurry, and about ten more when they sit still and let me take a good look at them."

"I think that is doing very well, indeed, for watching live birds is not a bit like learning rules and figures by heart. Though your tables give you some facts about birds' colors and habits, every bird has some little ways and tricks of his very own that are always a surprise; and then, you see, a bird in the hand looks very different from a bird in the bush!"[1]

"I suppose that is why uncle wants us to go out to see for ourselves, instead of telling us stories every day. This morning, when I was over in the miller's woods, where we heard the Whip-poor-will, I saw the queerest bird, running up a tree; he let me come close to him, without being frightened.

"At first I thought he was a Black-and-white Creeper, for he was all black and white. Then I saw he was much bigger, and the beak was square at the end, as if it was cut off instead of being sharp-pointed. He had the strangest feet, two

---

[1] This section emphasizes the authors' focus on experiential learning, that children should learn birds through observation in the wild and not through only studying books or dead specimens ("a bird in the hand").

Downy Woodpecker.

toes behind and two in front, and when he came down near where I stood, I saw a bright-red spot on the head. When I went a step nearer, he didn't like it, and then laughed out loud at me—'Quip! Cher, cher, cher, cher! Ha! ha! ha! ha!' I thought he might be some kind of a Woodpecker, but those in uncle's room are a great deal bigger."

"A very good description of the Downy Woodpecker," said the Doctor, coming up under the porch where they were sitting. "This bird belongs not only to a different family from any you have heard about, but to a different order also.

"You have seen that Perching Birds all have three toes in front, and one behind on the same level, so that they may easily grasp a perch and keep their balance. But Woodpeckers do not perch in the true sense—they rest either against a tree-trunk or on a limb, and even sleep in these positions. They almost all have four toes, two in front and two behind, and the strong pair of hind toes prop them up when they climb the trunks of trees, or when they stop to bore for their food. They also have stiff, pointed tail-feathers that they press against the upright trunks of trees to keep themselves in place, the same as Swifts do inside chimneys, or Brown Creepers scrambling about trees. So they make brackets of themselves, as Rap says. Their bills are strong and straight, like chisels, so that they may cut and gouge hard wood without breaking them. Besides all this, they have curious long fleshy tongues, with horny barbed tips, which they can thrust far out of their mouths, to spear their insect food from holes and crannies."

"Can any of them sing?" asked Nat.

"They belong to an entirely songless group, but have several ways of calling and signalling to each other. One of these is to beat rapidly on a tree with the beak, which makes a rolling noise, each different species doing his drumming in his own way. Besides this, they all have jolly laughing notes, in spite of the fact that most of them are rather shy birds. Hence they are often called the Laughing Family!"

"Are there many kinds of Woodpeckers in North America?"

"More than twenty, but you are likely to notice only a few of them. I am sure, however, that you will be good friends with four kinds before snowfall—the Downy Woodpecker that you saw this morning; the beautiful golden-winged

Flicker; the gay Red-headed Woodpecker, so glossy blue-black and white; and the mischievous spotted Sapsucker who visits us in autumn. You will find them very different in looks and habits, in spite of their being cousins."

"Uncle! Uncle Roy!" cried Dodo, running through the Orchard in a great state of excitement. "There is a very handsome, rare, wonderful kind of a Meadow-lark walking on the lawn by the front steps. It's brown speckled with black and has a black patch on the breast and red on the head and when he flies you can see a white spot over the tail. Do you think he has come out of a cage?"

"No, missy, that is not a Meadowlark, is not rare or wonderful, and has not been in a cage; that is an every-day sort of a Woodpecker, having many names. Some think he is called the Flicker because he has a way of flicking his wings, and the Yellow Hammer because he hammers on trees with the beak and has fine golden wing-linings. The nest of the one you saw is in a hole, high up in the old sassafras by the side fence, and some say that this is why another of his names is High-hole. But it received all three of those names for other reasons you need not bother your head about just now.

"There are young birds in the nest now, and if you tap on the trunk with a stick you will hear them making a noise. This seems to be Woodpecker day, for Nat has seen the little Downy in the woods, you have seen the Flicker on the lawn, and I was telling him about two others; so you are just in time *not* to be too late. Now write the table for Nat's Downy, first, and then we will have the rest of the Woodpeckers."

THE DOWNY WOODPECKER

The smallest North American Woodpecker—hardly seven inches long.

Upper parts black, with a long white patch on middle of back; wings spotted with
   black and white. Some black and white bars on the outside tail-feathers. Red band
   on back of head of the male, but not of the female.

Under parts all white.

A Citizen of the eastern half of North America, where he stays all the year round.

A good and useful neighbor—one of the best. Does not bore holes in trees to injure
   them or eat the sap, but to get at the hurtful grubs which live under the bark, and
   the sharp, barbed tongue is especially fitted to pick them out of the holes which
   are dug with the stout chisel-like beak.

Eats a little fruit, chiefly wild berries, and is a hard-working member of the guilds of
   Tree Trappers and Ground Gleaners, as he eats not only grubs, but ants, beetles,

bugs, caterpillars, and spiders. He is also a Seed Sower, though in being so he and his brothers, without intentional mischief, scatter the seeds from the watery white berries of the poison ivy. He always digs for himself a nest in some partly decayed tree, and never takes long journeys, but moves about only in search of food.

THE RED-HEADED WOODPECKER

"There, that will do for the Downy," continued the Doctor, as the children finished the table; "only I ought to tell you that I have a friend who calls him the Flying Checker-board, because he looks when he flies as if he were checkered all over in squares of two colors—black and white. The Red-head is a much gayer bird, with three colors—ha! there goes one now! This is Woodpecker day indeed, and we are in luck."

A very handsome bird, glittering in the sun, had come looping swiftly past, and swung himself up to the broken-off top of a tall tree, where he rattled a loud rataplan, as much as to say, "Am I not a fine fellow?"

"Yes, I know him," said Rap eagerly; "there's a pair that have a nest in our orchard, the same I guess that were there last year, when they raised a brood, only when the young ones came out they had gray heads instead of red ones, and their wings were not clear white like this one's, nor their backs so shiny black—is that right, Doctor?"

"Yes, my boy, and it shows you know how to use your eyes, for young Red-heads look very different from their parents till they get a new suit. You remember that we called the Bluebird the Flag Bird, on account of his three colors. But this Woodpecker has the red of the head much brighter than a Bluebird's breast, and shows purer white as he flies, in large spaces on his back and wings; though his blue is not so bright—it is what we call blue-black, very dark and glossy, like polished steel."

"Do they stay around all the year?" asked Nat.

"Some of them do, but not many. They are very common in summer, but not as hardy as the Downies, and most of them go off south for the winter. They are very merry, frolicsome birds, with all sorts of tricks and manners—even Dodo's Flickers are no jollier members of the Laughing Family."

Red-headed Woodpecker.

A LAUGHING FAMILY   215

"Do they work when they are through playing?" asked Nat; "and do any good?"

"Yes, indeed," answered the Doctor; "all kinds of Woodpeckers are industrious workers, and all of them except the Sapsuckers are very useful to us in destroying hurtful insects."

"What kind of eggs do they lay?" asked Dodo; "it must be hard to get a look at them in such deep holes so high up."

"Very pretty ones indeed," replied the Doctor. "They are not very easy to reach, though you can readily see the rounded hole that leads into the nest, for it is almost always bored in a bare, dead part of the tree. I can show you some Woodpecker's eggs in my cabinet. They are all alike, except in size—more round than most birds' eggs are, very smooth and glossy, like porcelain, and pure white. But now write your table while that Red-head is still in sight. It is a very easy one; his colors are plain, and you can guess pretty nearly how long he is."

THE RED-HEADED WOODPECKER

Length about nine inches.

Head and neck crimson-red all around; back and most of wings and tail glossy blueblack; all the rest snow-white, except a little red tinge on the belly.

Young ones gray where the old ones are red, and not so pure black and white in other places.

A Citizen of the eastern half of the United States and some parts of Canada, but mostly going to the Southern States for the winter.

A good neighbor and useful member of the guilds of Tree Trappers and Ground Gleaners; he takes some of our fruits now and then, but is welcome to them for the good he does in destroying insects which would injure and perhaps kill our fruit trees if he did not eat his full share of them; and he has to work very hard to dig them out of the places where they lurk under the bark.

THE FLICKER

"The Flicker's beak is more slender and curving than those of his brethren, and he has an extremely long, barbed tongue, which he uses to probe ant-hills. The sticky substance in the bird's mouth covers the little barbs on its tongue, and thus he is able to catch a great many ants at a time. He is one of our best ant-eaters."

"Are ants very bad things if they don't get into the sugar?" asked Dodo.

"There are a great many kinds of ants; though all may not be harmful, some of them do great damage by destroying timber or ripe fruit, and helping to spread lice about the roots of all sorts of plants.

"The Flicker has a jolly laughing call that sounds like 'Wick-wick-wick-wick!' repeated very quickly, and he also hammers away on a tree in fine style when he wishes to call his mate or let her know his whereabouts. Like other Woodpeckers, he hollows out a soft spot in a tree until he has made quite a deep hole, which, with a few chips in the bottom for bedding, serves as his nest. Most little Woodpeckers climb up to the hole-edge to be fed; but young Flickers are fed in the same way as little Hummingbirds, the parent swallowing food and when it is softened bringing it back from the crop by pressing on it with the beak."

"What is the crop?" asked Dodo.

"It is an elastic pouch in the gullet of a bird, where food that has been swallowed is kept for a while before it goes further down into the stomach. You have seen this crop in the necks of Chickens and Pigeons."

Flicker.

"Oh, yes, a round swelled-up place; but what is the good of it?" persisted Dodo.

"It is a resting-place for food, where it may swell, soften, and be partly ground up. All birds are fond of eating sand and gravel."

"Oh, yes! My Canary picks up lots of little bits every time I put fresh sand in his cage."

"This gravel mixes with the food and helps to grind it up. You can understand how necessary this is when you remember that some birds, like Pigeons, swallow hard grains of corn entirely whole."

"Yes, and I saw Mammy Bun clean a Chicken yesterday," said Nat; "there was a lot of sand and corn in a lump in its throat—and so that's called a crop?"

"To return to the Flickers: they live in flocks in autumn, and when a number are feeding on the ground at a little distance they might be taken for Meadowlarks—so you see that you did not make such a dreadful mistake after all, little girl."

"Won't you come over to the miller's woods with us, uncle, and perhaps we can find the Downy's nest hole," said Nat.

"Yes, I will come and tell you about the fourth Woodpecker on the way—the one called the Yellow-bellied Sapsucker. Though very handsome, this is not a bird that you would care to have come in great numbers to your garden or orchard. For this bird makes holes in the tree bark and eats the sap that leaks out, from this habit gaining the name of Sapsucker. Of course you see that this is a very bad thing for the trees; for when a great many holes have been bored near together the bark loosens and peels off, so that the tree is likely to die. The Sapsucker also does harm by eating the soft inner bark which is between the rough outside bark and the hard heart-wood of the tree; for this soft bark is where the sap flows to nourish the tree.

Yellow-bellied Sapsucker.

"When the bird bores the holes and the sap oozes out, a great many insects gather to feed on it—hornets, wasps, spiders, beetles, flies, and other kinds. These the Sapsucker also eats, sweeping them up in the sap with his tongue, which is not barbed like that of other Woodpeckers, but has a little brush on the end of it, shaped something like those we use for cleaning lamp chimneys. In this way he can easily lick up great quantities of both sap and insects. You will not probably see him before autumn, for he nests northward from Massachusetts; but you can write down his table now, and then be on the watch for him."

THE YELLOW-BELLIED SAPSUCKER

Length about eight and a half inches.

Upper parts mixed black, white, and dull yellowish; wings and tail black, with much white on both; crown scarlet in the male.

Under parts light yellow on the belly, scarlet on the throat, black on the breast, and with black marks on the sides.

A Citizen of eastern North America, roving further north than most Woodpeckers
and wintering as far south as Central America. A useful bird in wild places, but
unwelcome in gardens and orchards, and not a good neighbor.

A member only of the guild of Tree Trappers.

"I wonder if I shall see the little Downy," said Dodo, as she skipped down the road to the woods between her uncle and Nat.

"Don't hop so," said Nat; "it doesn't do at all when you are bird-hunting. Rap says you must go quietly, and not swing your arms either, for it frightens birds more than even a scarecrow."

"It is very hard to keep still when you are bursting with hurry to get somewhere," answered Dodo very meekly, but not wholly able to resist an occasional jump.

"I'll show you the way," said Nat. "The little Downy's tree was beside the footpath on top of the river bank. But the bird has gone!"

THE FLICKER

Length twelve inches.

Upper parts brown barred with black; the rump snow-white; the head gray with a
scarlet band on the back of it.

Under parts crowded with round black spots; a large black patch on the breast; throat
lilac; the male with a pair of black moustaches, which, of course, the female does
not have.

Under side of wings and tail almost all golden-yellow, even the shafts of the feathers
being of this rich color.

A Citizen of eastern North America, west sometimes to the Pacific Ocean. Spends the
winter in the southern half of his range.

This Woodpecker is not only a beautiful, but a useful, Citizen, doing almost as much
work in the guild of Ground Gleaners as the Meadowlark, besides being a Tree
Trapper and Seed Sower.

CHAPTER 24

Two Odd Fellows

"Kuk—kuk—kuk! Crock—c-r-o-c-k—c-r-o-c-k!" cried a harsh voice from the wood edge.

"Tr-r-r-at-tat-tat!" rattled another bird from over the river bank.

"Those must both be Woodpeckers," said the children; "for both noises are like hammering."

"Yes," continued Nat, "and I see the one who made the rattle. It is a Woodpecker with a very big head and bob tail, and sort of gray with black straps in front. See, uncle! He is on a branch of that dead tree, right over the river—there, he has fallen off into the water!"

The Doctor smiled as he said: "Here is another case of mistaken identity—very much like Dodo with her rare Meadowlark! This bird is a Kingfisher, who did not fall into the water, but dived in after the fish for which he sat watching."

"So some wood birds eat fish, as well as the Osprey that we saw at the beach; but how do they chew them, Uncle Roy?"

"They do not chew them. If the fish is not too large, they swallow it whole, and very funny faces they make sometimes in doing so. If it is too large, they beat it against a branch and tear it before eating. As they live on fish, they make their home near water, and only travel south when the rivers freeze."

"Do they build nests in trees?" asked Dodo.

"No; they burrow tunnels in the earth of river banks, and put their nests at the end of them, just as the Bank Swallow does; only the Kingfisher's tunnel is much larger, and his nest is not nicely lined with feathers—the young often have no softer bed than a few fish-bones."

THE BELTED KINGFISHER

Length about thirteen inches.

A long, bristling crest; bill longer than head, stout, straight, and sharp.

Leaden-blue above, with many white bands and spots on the short, square tail and long, pointed wings.

Below white, with a blue belt across the breast, and the female with a brown belt also.

A Citizen of North America.

Belonging to no useful guild, but a rather startling, amusing neighbor, who always minds his own business and is an industrious fisherman.

Belted Kingfisher.

"What was the other bird, who cried, 'kuk kuk!' on the outside of the woods? There, it is calling again! I'm sure that it is a Woodpecker!"

"Wrong again—it is a Cuckoo; the Yellow-billed one, I think, for the voice is louder and harsher than that of his Black-billed brother."

"What! a little blue and white bird like the one that bobs out of mother's carved clock at home? Oh, do let us try to find it! But this bird didn't say 'cuckoo'; it only cackled something like a Hen when she is tired of sitting."

"The clock Cuckoo is an imitation of the merry, heedless English bird, who lays her eggs in the wrong nests, as our Cowbird does. The Yellow-billed Cuckoo is quite different, being long, slender, and graceful, and a very patient parent—even though the nest she builds is rather a poor thing, made of a few twigs piled so loosely in a bush that the pale-green eggs sometimes drop out.[1]

"Let us go over to the brush hedge where the bird seemed to be. Hush! there he sits upon the limb of a maple. No—look a little higher up. He is perfectly still, and

---

[1] The Yellow-billed Cuckoo depicted here is not a nest parasite and is therefore a "good citizen," as opposed to the Common Cuckoo of Europe, that "heedless English bird."

acts as if he was half asleep. See what a powerful bill he has! With that he tears away the ugly webs of tent-caterpillars from the fruit trees, and sometimes eats more than forty caterpillars without stopping—he is so fond of them. Look at him through the glass, and see if the following description fits him."

Yellow-billed Cuckoo.

THE YELLOW-BILLED CUCKOO
Length about twelve inches.
Upper parts olive-gray or Quaker color all over, smooth and shiny; wings tinged with bright cinnamon, and most of the tail-feathers black, with large white spots at the ends.
Under parts pure white. Under half of bill yellow.
A Summer Citizen of temperate North America west to the plains. Travels south for the winter to the West Indies and South America.
A very valuable neighbor, and an officer of high rank in the guild of Tree Trappers.
His brother—the Black-billed Cuckoo—is very much like him, except that the tail is not black, its spots are smaller, and he has no yellow on the bill, but a red ring round the eye.

"Kuk-kuk-kuk—couk—co-uk—co-uk!" cried the bird, as he spread his wings and sailed off, giving the children a fine chance to see his long, rounded, black tail with the white spots. "Are there any Owls in these woods, Uncle Roy?" asked Nat. "You know we haven't seen an Owl yet, though we hear one almost every night."

"Doubtless there are; but the best place to find Owls is in the old wood, far up by the lake, where the lumbermen have their camp. The Great Horned Owl nests there, and many Hawks besides. I will take you all there some day, and, if you do not find the birds themselves, you can see the wild places where they like to nest."

"Couldn't we go very soon, uncle? Next week, perhaps?" urged Dodo.

"Fourth of July comes next week," said Nat, "and uncle said we could go down to the shore again, and take our fire-crackers! It will be such fun to stick them in rows in the sand and make them sizzle—more fun even than Owls! Don't you think so, Dodo?" he asked anxiously.

"Oh, yes; and then it wouldn't be polite either not to have fire-crackers on the Fourth of July. I think the American Eagle or the President or somebody expects children to have fire-crackers. Mammy Bun says the first American Eagle was hatched on the Fourth of July, you know," said Dodo earnestly. "Do you think he was, uncle?"

"No; it was the United States that were hatched on the Fourth of July, seventeen—seventy—six," said Nat, hesitating a little over the date.

"You are both right in a way," laughed the Doctor; "but you need not give up the Owls in order to celebrate the Eagle's birthday. We will have an Eagle's birthday party at the beach on the Fourth; and on the eighth—which is Dodo's birthday, if I am not mistaken—we will have an Owl party up at the lake!"

"Oh! oh, how lovely!" cried Dodo, giving her uncle such a sudden hug and kiss that his hat flew off. "And the lake is a long way off, so first we go in the cars, and then in a big hay wagon with straw in the bottom—at least, that is the way Olive said she went the last time!"

CHAPTER 25

Cannibals in Court

Dodo's birthday and a disappointment came together on the eighth, and the disappointment took the shape of a rainy day. Not an early morning shower, with promise of warmth and clear weather; for it was one of the cold, northeasterly storms that are very trying at any time of the year, but doubly so when they come in July, and seem, for the time, to turn summer into autumn.

Dodo, Nat, Rap, and Olive stood under the shelter of the porch, the children vainly hoping that it might clear up before nine o'clock—the hour the train left—and Olive racking her brain for something that would soothe their feelings. "We might ask mammy to let us go into the kitchen and make candy," she said. "The weather is too damp and sticky for molasses candy, but butter-scotch will harden if we put it in the dairy." Even this did not seem to be very tempting to little people who had expected to go to the real Owl woods, and Quick barked and yelped as if he, too, felt cheated out of an expected excursion.

Presently the Doctor came out and saw the forlorn group, which, being quite heedless of the sharp slant of the rain, was rather wet and limp.

"Poor little bird-hunters!" he said—rather too cheerfully, they thought—"you look as unhappy as the party of astronomers who went all the way to Africa to photograph an eclipse of the sun, and when the time came were so excited that they forgot to open the camera, and so took no pictures.[1] Come into the

---

[1] A possible reference to the total solar eclipse on December 22, 1889, which was the subject of an extended U.S. scientific expedition to West Africa, a record of which by astronomer Eben J. Loomis was published under the title *An Eclipse Party in Africa* in 1896.

224 CITIZEN BIRD

hall and I will tell you about a plan I have. Catching cold isn't a nice game for a birthday party.

"You expected to hear something about the cannibal birds to-day, and see the woods where a great many of them live and make their nests, didn't you?"

"Yes," said Dodo; "we wanted to know why they are cannibals, and see where the wicked things live that eat little Chickens and song birds."

"Very well. Now do you know that though all Hawks and Owls sometimes eat other birds and help themselves to poultry from the barnyards, yet at the same time most of them are the farmer's best friends?"

"No," said Rap; "I thought they were all bad, evil birds, and that the Government often gave money to people for killing them; besides, I am sure that a Hawk took eleven of our little Chickens this very spring!"[2]

"The Wise Men have been looking up the records of these cannibals—or Birds of Prey, as they are usually called—and find that very few of them—only two or three kinds, perhaps—should be condemned to death. The others belong to the secret guild of the Wise Watchers who, sitting silently in the shadows of the woods, or perching in the trees around the edges of fields, wait for rats, mice, moles, rabbits, gophers, beetles, cutworms, and many other creatures which destroy vegetable life. The Wise Watchers kill these hurtful creatures, and so become the guardians of the fields."

"Oh, do tell us which ones do this and which took Rap's Chickens," said Dodo, forgetting her disappointment for the time.

"I am going to make a play for you. Some of the Owls and Hawks shall speak for themselves, and tell you about their own habits and customs. In fact, the most familiar of these cannibals shall have a hearing this morning in the wonder room. The American Eagle is to be the judge, and I think that, as you cannot go to the woods, you will like to come into my room to hear what they have to say."

"Birds talking about themselves in the wonder room!" said Dodo in a puzzled way.

"What is a hearing?" asked Nat.

[2] This statement is likely referring to state officials offering bounties for killing wild animals that were believed to kill farm animals and sportsmen's prey. Beginning in 1875, Delaware was the first state that enacted a bounty on birds of prey. Other states subsequently passed such bounty laws, including Colorado, Virginia, West Virginia, New Hampshire, Ohio, and Indiana. The most egregious and perhaps best-known example was Pennsylvania's "Scalp Act of 1885," which offered bounties for killing weasels, foxes, hawks, and owls. The act was repealed in 1887, due to its incredible expense and lack of evidence of its utility to the farmers. In fact, many of the birds of prey targeted under this act were found to help farmers by eating animals such as mice. By 1890, many states had repealed their bounty laws, and by 1899, eight states had enacted laws protecting select species of birds of prey.

"I know what a hearing is," said Rap. "It is where people are accused of doing something wrong and they go down to the courthouse, and the judge hears what they have to say about it; and, if he thinks they have done the things, he binds them over for trial. They often have hearings down in the town hall in the East Village."

"You are quite right, my boy; and at this hearing of ours, as the birds are stuffed and cannot speak, I shall speak for them. Even if they could talk, we could not understand them, unless we borrowed Tommy-Anne's magic spectacles.[3] Now, if you will come into the study, you will find them all ready."

The children did not wait to be asked twice; Nat and Dodo rushed along the hall, followed by Rap.

In the study two tables were put together, making a sort of platform at the end of the room. On this platform a dozen stuffed birds sat in solemn silence. The Owls were on one side, with a row of Hawks facing them on the other. A big Golden Eagle was at the foot, and a White-headed American Eagle held the place of honor at the head, on a pile of books. Each bird was mounted on a wooden perch; and, as they were all set up in very natural positions, the effect was quite startling to the children.

"Where did all these big birds come from?" asked Nat. "They were not in the glass cases."

"No, they were in the attic. You must excuse them if their feathers look a little shabby, for it is a long time since they flew about in the woods, and took a bath or plumed themselves."

"The judge ought to wear spectacles! May I cut him a pair out of paper?" asked Dodo. "See how wise he looks," she said, as she put the make-believe glasses on the Eagle's nose.

"Order!" called the Doctor, rapping on the table with his knuckles. "The American Eagle makes the first speech, which I will translate to you."

Golden Eagle.

---

[3] Here the authors allude to Wright's previous work of children's literature, *Tommy-Anne and the Three Hearts* (1896).

The Eagle looked very fierce as he sat there. His head, neck, and tail were white, but the rest of his body was dark brown. The upper part of his great yellow beak was hooked; his yellow feet were bare and scaly; and his four sharp claws, or talons as they are often called, were black. He was nearly three feet tall, and if he had spread his powerful wings he would have measured seven feet from tip to tip.

The Golden Eagle, who sat at the foot of the table, was about the same size and an equally handsome bird. He held his golden-brown head proudly erect, and his black wings folded tightly. He too had some white feathers in the tail, though none on the head; his hooked beak was black, and he wore dark leggings almost down to his powerful claws.

These two Eagles, though not exactly friends, are not enemies; for the Baldheaded one ranges over all of North America, especially in open places near the water, while his Golden brother keeps more to the western parts, and loves the loneliness of cold northern mountains.

"We Birds of Prey," said the Eagle, "who bow to no one and even sleep sitting erect—we, whose females are larger than the males for the better protection of our nests, are accused of eating not only our smaller brethren, but also four-footed animals which are of service to man. I deny that we do this as a tribe, except when we are pressed for food, and Heart of Nature says to us all, 'Take what ye need to eat!'

"Now, you are all in honor bound to speak the truth at this hearing, and you shall be heard first, Brothers of the Darkness—you, with strange voices and feathered eye-circles—you, who have three eyelids and whose eggs are whiter even than moonlight.

"Brother Screech Owl, whose day is my night, tell us about yourself—how and where you live."

There were two Screech Owls perched side by side on one stump. They were not ten inches long, and had feathery ear-tufts standing up like horns an inch long. One Owl was mottled gray and black; the other was rusty-red; and the toes of both peeped out of holes in their thin stockings. The gray one gave a little quavering wail and said:

Screech Owl.

"I am everywhere a well-known Owl; though I say it myself, I am a good, hard-working Citizen, and in this the Wise Men agree.

CANNIBALS IN COURT   227

"All day I stay by my nest hole in some old tree; but when others go to sleep I awake, and steal noiselessly on my rounds through barn, field, and garden. What for? For mice, moles, bats, and beetles. Sometimes I go a-fishing; sometimes I snatch a frog with my sharp claws—the hunting weapons of my family. Do I catch birds? Sometimes, but they are few compared to the mice I kill. When I think of mice, I become a feathered cat! Do mice run fast? I fly faster! Winter or summer I always hear when a mouse squeaks or a chipmunk chatters. When I swallow bones, fur, and feathers, they never give me any pain—no, never! I understand the science of digestion. Instead of making my poor little stomach grind up all the things I swallow, I just roll up what I do not care to digest into little pellets, and spit them up. If you look on the ground under my home tree, you will find these little balls, and by them judge of what I eat.

"My family are also distinguished by two other odd habits. Having two sets of eyelids, an inner and an outer, we can close one or both at will. The inner one is a thin skin that we blink with, and draw across our eyes in the day-time when the light annoys us, just as House People pull down a curtain to shut out the sun. The outer lids we close only in sleep, when we put up the shutters after a night's work, and at last in death—for birds alone among all animals are able to close their own eyes when they die. The other habit is the trick of turning our heads entirely round from front to back, without wringing our necks or choking to death. This we do to enable us to see in every direction, as we cannot roll our eyes about as freely as most birds do.

"Come to think of it, I am very fond of eating one bird that, so the Wise Men say, is as bad as a mouse for mischief. I eat English Sparrows!

"One thing I wish the Wise Men would tell me. Why am I, without season or reason, sometimes rusty-red and sometimes mottled gray? It confuses my brain so that I hardly know my own face in the pond."

"Acquitted!" said Judge Eagle. "Long-eared Owl, what have you to say?"[4]

The Long-eared Owl was about fifteen inches high. He had, as his name implied, long ear-tufts that stood up very straight over his yellow eyes, and thick tawny stockings on his feet and legs. He was finely mottled above with brown, black, and dark orange, had long brown streaks on his buff breast, and dark-brown bands on his wings and tail. He gave a hoot and spoke very quickly.

---

[4] The illustration for the Long-eared Owl appears at the end of the introduction, as it served as the frontispiece of the original publication of *Citizen Bird*.

"I'm a good Citizen, too. I do not eat many birds, and those I do eat are not the useful ones who kill insects; moles, mice, rats, and beetles are my daily food. But House People do not know this, and limit me until I am almost discouraged; for though I am a Night Owl I do not live in such wild places as some of my brethren, and so I am more easily caught. I live and nest anywhere I like, from the Atlantic to the Pacific. I rear my young equally well in an old Crow's nest in a high tree, or one I build for myself in a bush. I mean well and am a Wise Watcher. I know my voice frightens House People, but let them pity me and point their guns at something else."

"Short and to the point! Acquitted!" said the Eagle. "Snowy Owl, it is your turn."

This beautiful white Owl, marked here and there with black bars and spots, had a smooth round head like a snowball, great yellow eyes, and thickly feathered feet; his bill and claws were black, but you could hardly see them for the thickness of the feathers in which they were muffled up. He winked with each eye, clicked his bill once or twice, and thus began:

"I'm a very good-looking bird, as you see—fatally beautiful, in fact; for House People shoot me, not on account of my sins, but because I can be stuffed and sold for an ornament.[5] I do not stay long enough in the parts of the country where they live, to do much harm, even were I a wicked Owl. My home is in Arctic regions, where my feather-lined nest rests on the ground, and even in winter I come into the United States only when driven by snowstorms from the North.

Snowy Owl.

---

[5] In an ad in the February 1900 issue of *The Oologist*, a periodical devoted to "oology, ornithology, and taxidermy," a stuffed and mounted Snowy Owl was priced at $8.00 ($300 today), compared to $1.25 ($47 today) for a Screech Owl and $3.00 ($112 today) for a Great Horned Owl, which suggests not just its comparative rarity as an ornithological specimen but also its popularity as an ornament.

"At home I live chiefly on lemmings, which are a sort of clumsy, short-tailed field-mice, not good for anything but to be eaten. When I go visiting I may take a little feathered game, but oftener I live on my favorite mice, or go a-fishing in creeks that are not frozen; for I am a day Owl, and can see quite well in the sunlight. You never see me except in winter, for I am a thing of cold and snow, whose acquaintance you can seldom cultivate; but if you knew me well you would find me gentle, kind, and willing to be friends with you—if you do not believe me, ask the Wise Men."

"Acquitted! You see we are proving our innocence," said the Eagle proudly. But he hesitated a moment before calling upon the Great Horned Owl, as if he himself doubted the honesty of this savage bird.

He was large, nearly two feet high, with very long ear-tufts and great staring yellow eyes in the middle of his large flat face. He was mottled on the back and wings with buff and black, had on a white cravat, and his vest was barred with black, white, and buff; his sharp black talons were almost hidden by feathers, but not so much so as the Snowy Owl's.

"None of you like me because you are afraid of me, and so you would rather condemn me than not," began the Horned Owl fiercely. "But I am not afraid of anything or anybody. I am a liberal parent and heap my nest up with food, like all the Owl and Hawk Brotherhood. If I wish a Hen or a Goose or a Turkey I take it, though I may only care to eat the head; for I am very dainty, and any one is welcome to what I leave. I also like wild game—Ruffed Grouse particularly; but I eat rabbits and rats enough too, I warrant you. I could give you a long list of the evil-minded rodents I kill in every one of the States where I live; but I won't, for you might think I wished to prove myself no

Great Horned Owl.

cannibal. I don't care what you think of me; for I am able to take care of myself, and quite independent.

"I do not even have to build my own nest. In February, when I need a home, there is always an old Crow's or Hawk's nest ready for me; and as for my young, they are hardy and need no pampering! Whooo-ooo-hooo—ooo! Hands off, Bird and House People! The Great Horned Owl knows how to use both beak and claws!"

"Bound over for trial," said the Eagle, "and you are lucky not to be committed for contempt of court."

"He is a very cross bird to talk so, even if he does some good," whispered Dodo to Rap; for the Doctor had given the Owl's hoot so cleverly it all seemed real to the children. Then Judge Eagle spoke again:

"Now for my brothers whose keen eyes can look at the sun himself—you who strike with the claws and rend with the beak in open daylight—it is your turn to speak. Marsh Hawk, where and how do you live?"[6]

The Marsh Hawk was nineteen inches in length, with a long tail, pointed wings, and Owl-like face. At first glance he seemed to be a bluish-gray bird, but on close inspection one could see that his under parts were white, mottled with brown, and there was also a large white patch on his rump. He spoke very clearly and said:

"I roam all over North America, wherever there is open country and free flying, and make my nest on the ground wherever I find tufted grass or reeds to hide it. Marsh lands please me best, and so I am called the Marsh Hawk. The voices of the Hawk Brotherhood are like the voices of the winds, far-reaching, but not to be put in words. Mine is one of the softest of the cries of the Wise Watchers. Some brothers take their pastime in the skies, but I keep near the ground, in search of the things I harry—mice and other small gnawing animals, insects, lizards, and frogs. Sometimes I take a stray Chicken or some other bird, but very few compared to the countless rodents I destroy. House People do not realize that those gnawers are the

Marsh Hawk.

---

[6] The Marsh Hawk is now called the Northern Harrier.

greatest enemies that the Wise Watchers keep in check. Day and night these vermin gnaw at the grain, the roots of things, the fruits, the tree bark, even the eggs and young of useful birds. I am their chief Harrier; by chance only, not choice, am I a cannibal."

"A very honest statement," said the Eagle. "Acquitted! Sharp-shinned Hawk, it is your turn."

This little Hawk, only a foot long, was bluish-gray above and had a black tail barred with ashy; his white breast was banded with reddish-brown, and he had a keen, fierce eye.

"I have very little to say for myself," he began. "Everywhere in North America I am a cannibal. I know I am small, but I can kill a bird bigger than myself, and I have a big brother who is a regular Chicken and Hen Hawk. I hide my nest in the lengths of thick evergreens, or on a rocky ledge, and all the year round I take my own wherever I find it. I prefer to prey on birds—Dove or Sparrow, Robin or Thrush, song bird or Croaker—all are alike to me. I consider myself a true sportsman, and I do not like such tame game as mice or frogs.

Sharp-shinned Hawk.

I pounce or dart according to my pleasure; I can fly faster than any one of you, and few small birds escape my clutches. Sometimes in winter I make my home near a colony of English Sparrows and eat them all for a change, just to see how it feels to be of some use to House People; but in spite of this I am a bold, bad bird, and as every one knows it I may as well say that I take pride in my reputation, and do not intend to reform!"

"Guilty!" said the Eagle solemnly. "Red-shouldered Hawk next."

Red-shouldered Hawk.

The Red-shouldered Hawk held up his head proudly and returned the Eagle's gaze without flinching. He was a fine muscular bird, standing a little under two feet high, with deep rusty-red shoulders and reddish-brown back, while his head, neck, and under parts were spotted and cross-barred with rusty and white. He had a black tail crossed by half a dozen white bars.

"I am a Hawk of eastern North America, living from the great plains to the Atlantic coast, going northward to the British lands and southward to the warm-watered Gulf of Mexico. I am often called Hen Hawk by those who speak without thinking, but in truth I am not much of a bird-thief, for a good reason. I am a thoughtful bird, with the deliberate flight of a Night Owl, rather than the dash of my daylight brethren. I clear the fields of mice and other gnawers, besides spiders, grasshoppers, and snails; while as a frog-lover, I am a veritable Frenchman.

"I am a faithful Hawk besides, and when I am protected will nest for a lifetime in the same woodland, if there is a marsh or spring near by to furnish my daily frogs. I am faithful also to my mate through life. I help her build the nest and rear our young. If House People are kind to me, I can be a gentle friend to them, even in the trials of captivity; but if I suspect a stranger, he must look at me only at long range, heavy though my flight appears.

"So I say boldly that I am a useful bird and a good Citizen. If you think a Hawk has stolen a pet Hen, look well before you shoot; and if he has rusty-red shoulders count yourself mistaken—and let him go."

"A true account," said the Eagle; "you stand acquitted. Sparrow Hawk, your turn."[7]

This charming little Hawk, about the size of a Shrike, had all the beauty of shape and color of a song bird, combined with Hawk-like dash. His wings were narrow and pointed. His back was reddish-brown with a few black bars, and there was a broad one on the end of his tail; his wings were partly bluish. Underneath he was white, shading to cream color and spotted with black. His head was bluish with black markings on the sides and a red spot on the top. He was not at all embarrassed at being in such grand company, for he was used to the best society, having come of noble ancestry in the Hawk line.

"You all know me," he said in a clear voice. "Since Sparrow-killing is ordered by the Wise Men, you should think well of me—especially you House People, who love song birds. I will tell you a secret—I am thinking of eating no birds but English Sparrows in future!"

---

[7] The Sparrow Hawk is now called the Kestrel.

"So you *have* been eating other birds?" said Dodo.

"Y-e-s, I have, but not many more than the Shrike takes, and mostly seed-eaters—hardly ever an insect-eating song bird. Do you know how many bad insects I eat?" The little Hawk rattled off a long list, beginning with grasshoppers and ending with beetles; but he spoke so fast that the children could not remember half the names he mentioned.

"Where do I live? All over North America, though I leave the colder parts in winter, for I like to be comfortable. I make my nest in some snug hole that a Woodpecker has kindly left. Sometimes, for a joke, I kill Sparrows and take their nest! Or make myself a home in a dove-cote—only I never seem to stay there long, for the Doves tell tales about me. I can sing a little, too; I have a high soprano voice and I——"

Sparrow Hawk.

"That will do," interrupted the Eagle. "For a small bird you are a great talker. But you are acquitted! Who comes next? Brother Osprey?"

The children recognized the Fish Hawk they had seen the first day they went to the sea-shore.

"The Osprey is a fisherman like myself, so we need not question him about his habits," continued the Eagle, who had his own private reasons for not caring to hear all the Osprey might say, remembering that he had sometimes stolen fish the Osprey had caught; "but I should like to tell the House Children that he is one of the long-lived birds who mate for life after the manner of true Eagles, many of whom have lived a hundred years, and also very industrious. Golden Eagle, what is your bill of fare?"

"The food of a wild bird of the mountains, far from the homes of men. I seize Wild Ducks and other game birds, hares, rabbits, fawns—yes, and young calves also, if House People make their dwellings near me and bring cattle into my fortress; but if they keep away from me, I never molest them."

"Humph!" said the Bald Eagle; "you and I are somewhat alike, for though I chiefly fish for a living I also kill the young of large animals, and even eat carrion when game is scarce. But as it is unusual for a judge to condemn himself, I think

Bald Eagle.

I must go free; and as there are not very many of either of us, it really doesn't matter much."

"How many did you condemn as really bad cannibals?" asked Nat, speaking to the Eagle. "The Sharp-shinned Hawk, and the Great Horned Owl are held over for further trial!" answered Judge Eagle.[8] "These two are the only ones who have been brought before this court, though accusations have been made against that big brother of his whom the Sharp-shin spoke of, and also against a still bigger relative he did not mention. The names of these two offenders are Cooper's Hawk and the Goshawk, who will both be brought to the bar of justice at our next session. This court is now adjourned!"

After the children had spent some time in looking at the Hawks and Owls, Nat asked, "What are the 'game birds,' uncle, that those cannibals sometimes eat?"

"That is not an easy question to answer, my boy; but as we are coming to these birds next, you will learn about them separately. Game birds as a whole are those chiefly useful as food, and the hunting of them is the occupation of sportsmen. These birds may belong to the working guilds, and all have habits interesting to bird-lovers; but as regards their value to the world, it is mostly in the shape of food for House People."

"Then it isn't wrong for people to kill these birds for food?"

"No, not if it is done fairly, in a true sportsmanlike spirit, and not with traps or snares, or in the nesting season, when no bird should be molested. The true sportsman never shoots a bird out of season, or a song bird at any time, and it is owing to his care that laws are made to stop the pot-hunters."

"Are the game birds tree birds, or what?" asked Dodo.

"There are many kinds," said the Doctor. "Some of them have cooing notes and build their nests in trees; these belong to the Pigeon family. Some scratch

---

[8] Even though game birds may earn the title of a "good citizen" by virtue of belonging to a working guild, the authors create symbolic boundaries between different types of birds and socially construct the notion that game birds' primary value to people is as food.

CANNIBALS IN COURT   235

about and feed on the ground, where they also nest, like our barnyard poultry. Others run along the banks of rivers or on the sea-beaches, where they wade in shallow water to pick up their food, like Snipes and Plovers; while others swim with their webbed feet and take their food from deep water, like Geese and Ducks. There are a few game birds in this glass case—some Pigeons and Grouse; suppose we finish the morning in their company?

"We will call Pigeons the Birds that Coo; and Grouse are some of the Birds that Scratch, so called because they all have much the same habit as our domestic fowls of scratching the ground for food and to raise a dust in which they take a sort of bath. See, this Cooer is called the Passenger Pigeon."

CHAPTER 26

A Cooing Pair

THE PASSENGER PIGEON AND
THE MOURNING DOVE

"You all know the Pigeons that are kept about stables and barnyards. You have often seen them walking with dainty steps to pick up their food, and have heard the soft crooning 'coo-oo' they give when talking to each other. They all belong to the Birds that Coo. Their food is taken into the crop, which can be plainly seen when it is quite full. These birds feed their young in the same way Hummingbirds and Flickers do; for they give the little ones softened food from the crop, mixed with a sort of milky fluid that also comes from the crop. One habit that Pigeons and Doves have, all their own, is that in drinking they do not raise the head to swallow like other birds, but keep the beak in the water until they are through.

"Our domestic Pigeons have beautiful and varied plumage, but to my mind many wild species surpass them. The two best-known wild species are the Passenger Pigeon of the Northwest, and the Mourning Dove, which may be found nesting everywhere in temperate North America.[1]

"Here are the two birds"—and the Doctor set them upon the table. "At first glance you may think them much alike, and if you should see them on the wing you would surely be confused.

---

[1] The Passenger Pigeon is one of the most famous examples of anthropogenic extinction. At the time of the writing of *Citizen Bird* in 1897, the Passenger Pigeon had already been in rapid decline for well over two decades. The Passenger Pigeon was considered extinct in the wild after the last recorded bird was shot in the wild in 1900. Attempts to breed Passenger Pigeons in captivity failed, and Martha, the last known Passenger Pigeon, died in the Cincinnati Zoo in 1914.

"Rap, you may describe the Passenger Pigeon, and Nat shall take the Dove; let me see if you can do it clearly enough for your written tables."

Rap looked at the Pigeon for some time. "It isn't an easy bird to describe—all the colors run together so. It has bluish-gray upper parts, and underneath it is a sort of pinky brown with white under the tail. The sides of the neck are shiny with soap-bubble colors. The outside tail-feathers are bluish and fade off white at the tips, but the middle ones are all dark; the beak is black, and the feet are red. But see here," he added, as he looked sharply at the bird's tail again, "there are some chestnut and black spots at the roots of the side feathers."

"Very good, my boy. How long do you think it is?"

Rap measured with his finger and said he thought about fourteen inches.

"You are almost right, though these Pigeons vary in length, because some have longer tails than others. I think this one measured about sixteen inches when it was stretched out straight; but it looks shorter now, because it is set up in a natural position.

Passenger Pigeon.

"The life history of this beautiful Pigeon should teach every one the necessity of protecting birds by law. Up to fifty years ago the Passenger Pigeon was extremely plentiful everywhere east of the great plains—there were many millions in a single flock sometimes. It was a most valuable bird, its flesh being particularly well-flavored and tender. It nested in large colonies that often stretched unbroken for many miles in the woods, and was both hardy and prolific. If it had been protected in the breeding season and hunted fairly as an article of food at other times, we should still be enjoying Pigeon pie as freely as we did in my boyhood. But as the population of the country increased, these great flocks were cruelly slaughtered, for the mere greed of killing them; thousands were often left to decay upon the ground, and now I do not believe that any one of you has ever seen a wild Pigeon before to-day."

"We have Pigeon pie at home in the winter," said Dodo.

"Yes, tame Pigeon pie," said the Doctor.

"It might have been tame pie and it was very good! But, Uncle Roy, why did people want to kill these good, food birds when they didn't care to eat them?"

"It is difficult to say exactly, little girl. People living in what we call a state of nature, like African savages, or as our American Indians once did, seem to follow Heart of Nature's law: 'Kill *only* what ye need for food.' But many people that are called civilized never think of natural law at all, and having a coarse streak in their natures desire to kill wild things merely for the sake of killing. It is against such people that laws must be made by those who have more intelligence.[2]

"Now for your Dove, Nat—called the Mourning Dove from his mournful 'coo-o-coo-o!'"

"At first," said Nat, "when I saw it in the glass case it looked sort of bluish-brown. But near by it is greenish-brown and gray on top, and its head and neck have bright colors, like what you see on silver that has not been cleaned for some time or the spoon with which you have been eating boiled eggs."

"We call those colors metallic tints," interrupted the Doctor, to help Nat out.

"Thank you; that is what I was trying to say. It is just like what Rap called soap-bubble colors on the Pigeon's neck, but this Dove has got black specks like velvet on the neck too, and a black band on the tail with white tips

Mourning Dove.

to the feathers; underneath it is dull purple and sort of buff, and its feet are red, and it's about a foot long."

"That is a fairly good description of a bird whose colors it is almost impossible to put into words. Do you know anything about this Dove, Rap?"

"I only know it builds such a poor nest that you would think the eggs would drop through the bottom, only they don't seem to. There was a nest in the miller's woods last year, with two white eggs like tame Pigeons', only smaller, and when they hatched I took one of the squabs home for a pet. It became very tame, but I had to let it fly because it grew too big and dirty,—it was like keeping a Chicken in the house.

---

[2] If children are described throughout *Citizen Bird* as closer to the natural world, here we see the problematic application of this Romantic idea to the representation of non-European cultures, which are assumed to be "savage" or child-like, living in a "state of nature" compared to "civilized" white Americans and Europeans. Even in celebrating Indigenous Americans and Africans as stewards of the environment, the Doctor is espousing something quite close to Adam Smith's stadial theory, the belief that every society passes through discrete stages of development linked to their mode of subsistence, from hunting (seen as less "civilized") through commerce (seen as more "civilized").

"The miller said they were mischievous birds, and ate so many oats that he had to sow his field twice over. Is that true, Doctor, or do they belong to some good guild?"

"They do not eat insects, though they may do a little work as Weed Warriors, and as they are fond of grain they may have helped themselves to some of the miller's oats; but usually when they feed on the ground they are Gleaners, and they never disturb grain in the ear. They have many pretty ways, and even though their love-song is sad they are cheerful and happy. Their 'coo-oo' sounds very gentle in the morning chorus, and though the Dove often nests in open woods and gardens, it seems most at home in a quiet place near water; for it is very fond of drinking and bathing."

CHAPTER 27

Three Famous Game Birds

"If any one should ask you which are the most famous American game birds, you may answer without hesitation, 'Bob White, Ruffed Grouse, and Woodcock'—the whistler, the drummer, and the sky dancer—all three good Citizens and handsome, interesting birds.

"Bob White is the most familiar, because in spring, when he feels quite sure that the law will protect his pretty head, he comes out of the thick bushes to the rail fence by the roadside and calls his own name—'Bob—white, bob—white!'—so that the shy mate he desires shall know where to find him. Then if she is hard-hearted and a long time coming he will say—'Bob-white, *poor* bob-white!' as if craving for pity.

"The last of May the nesting begins, and from then until autumn Bob White tells his name and whereabouts to no one; for it is a very busy season with him. The nest of leaves on the ground may yield during the summer twenty or thirty little Bobs, whom he must help supply with food and teach to walk about and care for themselves.

"In autumn each one of these Quail families—for Mr. Bob White is a kind of Quail—is called a 'covey.' They take to thick brush for winter food and shelter, being very clever at hiding from the sportsman, and only flying from shelter when nosed out by his dog.

"The Ruffed Grouse is also a bird of woods and brushy places, but at all seasons is more fond of trees than Bob White. It is much larger than Bob, and if seen among the underbrush looks like a small, brown, speckled Hen. Watch one in the spring-time, when he is roaming the woods in search of a mate, and you will see that he is every inch a game bird—a king of game birds too. In early May this Grouse mounts a fallen tree, or the rail of an old fence, and swells his breast proudly till the long feathers on each side of his neck rise into a beautiful shining black ruffle or tippet, such as you can see in some old-fashioned portraits of the times when Elizabeth was queen of England. He droops his wings and spreads his tail to a brown and gray banded fan, which he holds straight up as a Turkey does his when he is strutting and gobbling. Next he raises his wings and begins to beat the air—slowly at first, and then faster and faster. 'Boom—boom—boom'—the hollow sound comes rolling with a noise like beating a bass drum.

Bob White.

"Thus does the Ruffed Grouse drum up his mate, as the Woodpecker hammers or the Thrush sings. You remember the booming sound made by the wings of the Nighthawk, when the air whizzed through them? When Bob White and his Grouse brother fly, their wings make a whirring noise that is equally startling."

"And does his mate understand that the drumming is meant to call her?"

"Yes, surely; and soon there is a nest of dry leaves somewhere about the roots of a tree, or under a fallen log. Father Grouse then becomes selfish and takes himself off with some men friends, leaving mamma alone to hatch the eggs and feed the babies. But this is not so dreadful as it seems, because the young ones are fully covered with down like Chickens when they first leave the egg, and able to follow their mother; besides, they are the most obedient little things imaginable.

"If she but gives one cluck of alarm, they vanish, under the leaves or twigs, and do not stir again until they hear her say the danger is over. And that patient watchful Mother Grouse has as many ways of leading an enemy away from her nest as any House Mother could devise if her children were in danger.

Ruffed Grouse.

"This Grouse is a Ground Gleaner, a Seed Sower, and a Weed Warrior also in autumn. When snow covers all other food, he nips buds from low plants. Sometimes he burrows in deep snow for shelter from the cold, and then is liable to be caught by a sleet storm and frozen in his hiding-place. So you see his life is not altogether an easy one.

"The young Grouse stay with their parents until they are old enough to choose mates for themselves; but the flocks are never as large as the covey Bob White musters about him.

"The American Woodcock, the last of the trio, and the most wary of all, belongs to a family of shore birds who patter about the water's edge; but he does not often go in wading, and prefers seclusion in the woods that border swamps. He is a worm and grub eater who, by the aid of his long straight bill, which has a sensitive tip like your finger, can feel his food when it is out of sight, and is able to probe the soft mud for things to eat that other birds cannot find. The strangest thing about his bill is, that the upper half of it can be bent at the end, almost as much as you can crook the last joint of your fingers. Such a bill is of the greatest assistance to him, as his eyes are set so far in the back of his head that he cannot see what he eats."

"How queer!" said Nat; "what is the reason for that? I suppose there must be a reason!"

"This is it. By being placed far back in his head his eyes become like two watch-towers, from which he can scan the country behind as well as in front, and be on the alert for enemies. Woodcocks are very cautious birds, keeping well hidden by day and feeding only during the twilight hours or at night.

"They do not pass the winter in the colder parts of the country, and so escape the suffering that often overtakes Bob White and the Ruffed Grouse. They must be able to brave snowstorms, however, at the latter end of the cold season; for sometimes, when they begin to lay in early April, winter changes its mind and comes back to give them a snow blanket."

"You said that they are dancing birds," said Dodo. "When do they dance?"

"They dance in the sky in spring and summer!" cried Rap, unable to keep still any longer. "I saw a pair of them doing it this year, when I was out with the miller, looking for his colt that had strayed into the big woods beyond the pond. He said he knew there must be a Woodcock about, because he saw the little round holes in the mud, where they had been boring for earthworms, and that is the way he knows where to find them in the fall when he wants to go hunting."

"Yes, but how did they dance?" persisted Dodo.

"Oh! like crazy things with wings! First one ran around a little and whistled; then one jumped right off into the air, making a whirring with his wings until he was way up out of sight, and then after a little while he came pitching down zig-zag, like a kite that has lost its tail, whistling something like the way a Swallow twitters, and making a queer twanging noise. The other one stayed on the ground and jigged about all the time. I would have liked to watch longer, but we had to find the colt, you know."

American Woodcock.

"Now write your tables," said the Doctor, "for it is nearly dinner-time."

BOB WHITE

Length ten inches.

Upper parts mixed reddish-brown, buff, gray, and black, with a white line over the eye and a row of buff streaks on the inside wing-feathers.

Under parts white, black, and chestnut, the breast quite black and the throat pure white in the male, but buff in the female, and other markings much mixed up.

A Citizen of the greater part of temperate North America, and a very valuable one, the prince of the game birds of its family. The bill is stout for crushing seeds, the head has a slight crest, and the feet have no feathers on the scaly part that goes from the drumstick down to the roots of the toes.

THE RUFFED GROUSE

Length about seventeen inches.

Upper parts mottled with reddish-brown, black, gray, buff, and whitish, in different blended patterns; on each side of the neck a tuft of long glossy greenish-black feathers in the male, much shorter and not so dark in the female; the tail in both sexes gray or brownish with black bars or mottling, especially one broad bar near the end, and gray tip of the feathers.

Lower parts light buff or whitish with many dark-brown or blackish bars, best marked on the sides.

A Citizen of eastern North America, and a valuable game bird. It lives on the ground and looks like a small Hen, but has a longer and handsomer tail that spreads round like a fan. The bill is stout and the head crested, like the Bob White's; but the feet have little feathers part way down from the drumstick to the toes.

The Ruffed Grouse, like the Bob White, belongs to the Birds that Scratch.

THE AMERICAN WOODCOCK

Length ten to twelve inches—female larger than male.

Upper parts variegated with brown, tawny, and black.

Under parts plain warm brown.

A Summer Citizen of eastern North America, wintering in southern parts of its range, and a famous game bird. A ground bird of marshy woods and near-by fields, though he belongs to the same family as the Snipe, and is therefore classed among the Birds that Wade. He has a plump body, with short legs, neck, tail, and wings, a big head with the eyes set in its back upper corners, a very long bill which is soft, sensitive, and can be bent a little; and the three outside feathers in each wing are very much narrower than the rest.

The dinner bell rang as the children wrote the last words.

"You see," said the Doctor, "that though it is still raining and blowing, the morning has gone in a twinkling, and I now suspect the birthday cake is waiting to be cut."

"Yes," said Dodo, "I've been smelling the flowers and candles that go with a birthday cake for ever so long! And after dinner we can accept Olive's invitation and make candy—can't we, Uncle Roy?"

"I suppose so; and as nothing is too good for a rainy birthday, I will add something more to the feast. I will tell you a birthday secret—or, rather, what has been a secret until now.

THREE FAMOUS GAME BIRDS   245

"Next month we are all going to the sea-shore to spend a few weeks in Olaf's little cabin, to bathe in the salt water, and sail in his sharpie.[3] Then you can ask all the questions you please about the marsh and water birds. You will learn how the tides ebb and flow, and see the moon come up out of the water.

"There! Don't all talk at once! Yes, Rap is coming with us—and his mother also, to help take care of you children, for Mammy Bun must stay here. She does not like to camp out—says she is afraid of getting break-bone fever.[4]

"Come, dinner first, and then talking, or the candles will burn out all alone!"

---

[3] A sharpie is a type of flat-bottomed sailboat, traditionally used for oystering and associated with the New Haven, Connecticut, area of the Long Island Sound.

[4] Break-bone fever is another name for Dengue fever.

CHAPTER 28

On the Shore

By the first of August, bird housekeeping was over at Orchard Farm. The Barn Swallow had guided her last brood through the hayloft window, without having it closed upon her as she had feared. The friendly Robins had left the Orchard and lawn, to moult in the quiet of the woods. The Thrashers, and Catbirds too, were quite silent and invisible; of all the voices that had made the last three months so musical, the Red-eyed Vireo and the Song Sparrow alone persisted in singing, aided by a few Wood Thrushes.

"Rap says that August is a poor month for birds about here," said Nat to his uncle; "do you think there will be more of them down at the shore?"

"That we cannot tell until we go there, but we are likely to meet some of the Wading and Swimming Birds who have nested in the far North, and are on their southward journey. If the weather is pleasant, they often pass by far out at sea; but if it is foggy or stormy, they may stop awhile to rest and feed."

"Do many of these birds nest near our beach?"

"A few, but the greater number breed further north. Olaf will show us Herons in the island woods, and where the Rails nest in the reeds, near the Marsh Wrens, a mile or two up the river. Some day when it is calm, we will sail over to Great Gull Island, where many water birds lay their eggs on the bare sand.[1] There will be enough for you to see and do, I promise you."

---

[1] In the same way that Orchard Farm is a stand-in for Wright's home, Mosswood, so are the beaches and islands referenced here all based on those around the nearby Connecticut coastline or, in the case of Great Gull Island, farther out in the Long Island Sound.

ON THE SHORE 247

The next day they all went to the shore. Mr. Wolf looked after them very sadly from the door of his kennel, where he was chained, and barked a gruff good-bye; but Quick informed them that he intended going also, took matters into his own hands, and started to run down the road ahead of the wagon.

After much arranging, talking, and laughing, two wagon-loads of people, rubber boots, fishing tackle, and other things, started toward the shore, a farm hand going with each team to drive the horses back.

"Miss Olive, honey!" called Mammy Bun as they were starting, "don' you let de chillen eat too many o' dem clams what has de long necks; dey is powerful full o' cramps." And Olive promised that she would be very careful.

When they reached the shore, they found everything ready for them. Olaf's little home, which contained four tiny rooms, was as clean and compact as a ship's cabin. There was a kitchen, one room for Olive and Dodo, one for the Doctor, and another for Rap's mother; while Olaf, Nat, and Rap were to sleep close by in a tent made of poles, canvas, and pine boughs. Several boats were drawn up on the beach, by a creel of nets and some lobster pots, while Olaf's sharpie was anchored in deep water a little way offshore.

It was late when the horses turned homeward after leaving their loads; it had been a beautiful afternoon, neither too warm nor too cool. "Oh!" exclaimed Dodo, "now that the horses have gone, the good time will begin; for we can't go back even if we want to."

The children amused themselves for some time in looking at their new quarters, and then in watching Olaf row out to light the beacon lamps.[2] When it grew dusk they had supper, wondering at the strange stillness of the evening; for, though it was usually very quiet at the Farm, they had never before known the silence that falls with the twilight on a shore where the water does not rush and beat as on the ocean beaches, but simply laps lazily to and fro, like the swinging of a hammock.

Presently the stars began to give good-evening winks at the beacons—first one, then another and another, until the whole sky twinkled; while one evening star, the brightest of them all, hurried along the west as if it were trying to overtake the sun, and knew that it was fully half an hour behind the jolly god of day.

---

[2] Before lighthouses were automated in the twentieth century, keepers like Olaf would be responsible for maintaining the lights of the beacons and buoys.

"See how the tide is coming in," said Rap, when they returned to the beach. "When Olaf went out, he had to push his boat ever so far, and now the water is almost up to the line of seaweeds and shells."

"I wonder what makes the water go in and out?" questioned Dodo, half to herself.

"I don't exactly know," said Rap; "but I think it is because the earth goes round every day, making the water tip from one side to the other and then back again."

"Then why doesn't it all tip off into the sky?" persisted Dodo.

"I guess—because—that is, I don't know," stammered Rap.

"I must ask Uncle Roy to tell us, and why the earth down here on the shore stays sharp and gritty when it is wet; for when the earth up at the Farm is wet, it makes sticky mud," said Dodo.

"Yes," said Nat, "and why the stars are of such different sizes, and seem to stay quite still, except some that go along like that big bright one over there."

"Quok! Quok!" cried a strange voice from the marshes back of the beach. "Quok, quok, quok, quok!" answered other voices.

"What can that be?" said Nat; "it isn't a Whip-poor-will, or a Nighthawk—it must be one of the cannibal birds. Uncle Roy, what kind of birds are those calling away over in the marshes?" But the Doctor was not within hearing, and it was some time before they found him, sitting by the cabin door smoking his pet outdoor pipe, which was made of a corn-cob.

"Did you hear the Night Herons calling as you came up?" he asked.

"We heard a very queer squawky sound, and came to ask you what it was, for we couldn't guess," said Nat. "What is a Night Heron—a cousin of the Night-hawk, who lives near the water?"

"I don't think it's a water bird," said Rap, "because I have heard that same squawking up by the mill."

"But is not the mill close to the pond?" said the Doctor, smiling.

"Why, yes, to be sure—but I was thinking of salt water."

"That is a distinction that applies to few of our water birds; when we speak of the birds that wade, paddle, swim, and dive, we must remember that they may do so in lakes, rivers, bays, or the ocean, according to their individual habits. In fact, some members of a single family prefer fresh water, while their brothers are more fond of the salt sea. This is the case in the family of the Night Heron."

"Where does he belong?" asked Rap, "with the paddling birds or the swimming ones?"

"With the paddlers and waders."

"See, here comes the moon up out of the water and it makes a shiny path up to our feet and Olaf is rowing back right down it and the stars have stopped winking and are getting dim," said eager little Dodo, with an "and" wherever she ought to have stopped to breathe, as usual. "Hark! the Herons are squawking again—won't you tell us about them now, Uncle Roy?"

A LONG-NECKED FAMILY

"The long-necked, long-legged, long-billed Heron family, to which these squawkers belong, contains many marsh-loving birds. They are not exactly what we call shore birds, but live contentedly near any water, where they can wade and splash about pools and shallows for their food. For they eat meat, though they never kill birds, like the cannibals. Their taste is for frogs, lizards, snakes, snails, crabs, fish, and other small fry; they very seldom eat any warm-blooded animals. Herons are all rather large birds, the smallest of them being over a foot in length, while the largest stand fully four feet high."

Black-crowned Night Heron.

"Quok! Quok!" came the cry again, this time just over the cabin. Looking up, the children saw a dark body flying toward the wood belt; something like a long beak stuck out from its breast in front, and its long legs were stretched out stiff behind, but these were the only details that they could distinguish.

"I thought Herons had long necks," said Nat; "but this one doesn't seem to have any neck at all."

"Ah, but when it flies it folds its long neck, and thus draws its head down between its shoulders, while some of the Stork and Crane cousins poke out their heads in flying."

"Are Storks and Cranes cousins of the Herons?" asked Dodo. "I know about Storks—they are in my fairy book.[3] They live in the north country where little Tuk came from, and build their nests on roofs between chimneys, and stand a great deal on one leg in the water looking for frogs. Do Herons nest on roofs and stand on one leg, Uncle Roy?"

---

[3] "The Storks" and "Little Tuk" are both fairy tales by the Danish author Hans Christian Andersen.

"They do not nest on roofs, but they often stand on one leg when watching for food, and when sleeping—in fact, they stand so much in this way that one leg is often stronger than the other, and they most certainly belong to the guild of Wise Watchers. The Black-crowned Night Heron who has just flown over is the most familiar member of his family hereabouts, and quite a sociable bird. He prefers to live the hotel life of a colony, instead of having a quiet home of his own, and so do almost all other members of the Heron family. These Night Herons flock back from warm countries in April, and by early May have built their rough nests of sticks in trees near the water, or over a marshy place. There is a colony of twenty or thirty nests on Marsh Island, Olaf tells me; in my boyhood days there used to be hundreds of them.

"In nesting-time a heronry, as such a colony is called, is a very noisy, dirty place; for they do not keep their homes neat and nice, like the tidy land birds. Mr. and Mrs. Night Heron call hoarsely enough to each other, but imagine three or four baby Herons crying from every nest—truly the parents can have but little rest, for day and night they must go frogging or fishing, to fill the stomachs of their red-eyed awkward children.

"When the nesting season is over, however, this Heron again becomes the night watchman of the marshes. The tinkling of the bell on the home-going cow is his breakfast bell, and sunset the signal for him to leave his roost. Then beware! little fishes and lizards—those red eyes are glowing for you! That long spear-shaped beak is ready to stab you to death! Froggy 'who would a-wooing go,' return quickly to your mother, without making any impertinent remarks about 'gammon and spinach' on the way, or something much more savage than the 'lily-white duck' will surely gobble you up! Stay in doors patiently, until sunrise sends the rough-clawed prowler back to his heronry again."

"May we go to see the Herons some day? It would be so funny to go to a bird hotel and find everybody asleep, like the beauty in the wood," said Dodo. "You shall certainly pay them a visit, but I doubt that you will find them as sound asleep as you imagine."

The very next morning Olaf piloted the party across the meadows to the wood that was made an island by a little creek that threaded in and out among the reeds.

"I know somebody whose feet are wet already!" said Nat, pointing to Olive, who was slipping about uncertainly.

ON THE SHORE   251

"I know it was very foolish to come without my rubber boots, but they are so uncomfortable to wear in summer. Oh! please give me your hand—quick, father!" The Doctor caught her as she was sinking in what looked like a bit of good ground, but was really a bog tuft.

It took some time to work their way to the centre of the island. There the ground was drier in spots, between the little pools, and there were some high trees.

"Stop here," said Olaf cautiously, "and look well before."

They did so just as the crackling twigs startled some dusky shapes that flapped among the trees.

"The Herons!" exclaimed Rap, settling his crutch more firmly and preparing to watch closely.

As soon as their eyes became accustomed to the dim light, the party saw many large birds, some in the trees, some in the decaying underbrush, and others on the ground. Here and there among the trees were nests, looking like flat heaps of sticks. They were empty; but their sides, the trees, and the ground were all spattered and befouled with the chalky-white droppings of the careless colony. "Ugh!" shivered Dodo, who had a very keen nose, "what an ugly place to live in, and such a horrid smell! Please, uncle, don't these birds have dreadful headaches very often?"

"I think House People would have wretched headaches if they lived here—in fact, we must not stay very long; but it agrees with Herons, who are built to be the wardens of just such places."

"There are two kinds of Herons here," said Rap. "Some black and white, with a topknot, and some striped brown ones. Aren't the brown ones Bitterns? They look like one I saw in the miller's woods, and he called it a Bittern."

"The striped ones are the young birds, now wearing their first plumage. Bitterns prefer to live in freshwater meadows, or near ponds. They are solitary birds, keeping house in single pairs, and after nesting-time wander about entirely alone."

"Isn't it very hard to tell young Night Herons from Bitterns?" asked Nat.

"It would be easy for you to mistake them, but the habits of the two species are quite different. The Bittern nests on the ground, in a reedy bog, not in the woods, and may be seen flying in broad daylight, with his long legs trailing behind him. But in spite of this, he is a difficult bird to find; for if anything

American Bittern.

is 'remote, unfriendly, solitary, slow,' it is the American Bittern, who often stands motionless among the reeds for hours."[4]

"That is just what the Bittern did that the miller and I saw," said Rap. "We were hunting for a calf—the miller's things are always straying away, because he never mends his fences—and this Bittern was among some very tall grasses and dry flags; for it was along in the fall, when things were turning brown. I don't know how I ever came to see him; but when I did, he looked so queer that he almost scared me, and I said to the miller, 'Whatever is that?'

"For a minute he couldn't see anything, and then he said, 'Pshaw! that's only a Bittern; but I do wish I had my gun.'

"'Why doesn't he move?' said I. 'Look at the way he holds his head straight up, like a stick. I'm going round behind him to see what his back looks like.'

"'He's a stupid thing, and thinks we don't see him,' said the miller. I walked round and round until I began to get dizzy, but that bird was all front, and all I could see was his striped breast and neck. Then I saw the miller was laughing.

"'That bird isn't as stupid as he looks,' said he. 'He turns around just as fast as you walk, so you won't have a chance to get behind him.' Then we heard the calf low, and we went away."

"That was a sight worth seeing, my boy," said the Doctor; "for it is one of the best proofs that birds understand the value of protection of color. The Bittern and the old reeds blended their colors together, and by stretching up its neck the bird adapted his shape as much as possible to the straight, stiff lines of the reeds, while by keeping his front parts toward you, the curves of his back were concealed. You might have passed his hiding-place a hundred times without seeing him. But come—let us leave this Heron hotel, and find a way to the lane road."

The open air seemed doubly sweet and fresh, after the fishy smell of the Heronry. Dodo stopped under the first shade tree, and begged for her tables.

---

[4] Here we have a slightly misquoted allusion to the first lines of Oliver Goldsmith's "The Traveller": "Remote, unfriended, melancholy, slow, / Or by the lazy Scheld, or wandering Po" (1–2).

THE BLACK-CROWNED NIGHT HERON

(The Night Watchman)

Length about two feet.

Upper parts glossy greenish black in front, but ashy-gray behind and on the neck, wings, and tail; the forehead white, and two slender white plumes sticking out six or eight inches behind the head.

Under parts whitish, including the long throat or front of the whole neck.

Bill black, with greenish bare skin between it and the red eyes; legs yellow.

Sexes alike, but young very different, being grayish-brown above with many white or buff spots, and white below with black streaks.

A Summer Citizen of North America, useful in keeping down frogs and small reptiles, but too untidy to be a pleasant neighbor.

A member of the guild of Wise Watchers.

THE AMERICAN BITTERN

(The Stake-Driver or Thunder-Pumper)

Length from twenty-three to thirty-four inches, which is a very unusual difference in birds of the same species. Upper parts all freckled with brown, black, and tan color of various shades, as if sun-burnt, with a velvety black patch on each side of the neck, and the longest wing-feathers plain blackish with brown tips; top of head plain brown.

Under parts tawny whitish or pale buff, every feather with a dark streak, and the middle line of feathers along the whole throat white with brown streaks.

Bill blackish and yellowish; legs greenish; claws brown; eyes yellow.

A Citizen of temperate North America, but a very shy and solitary bird, who will not be neighborly and is oftener heard than seen in the bogs where he likes to live alone. He makes a loud noise that sounds like chopping wood with an axe or driving a stake in the ground with a mallet; so he is called the Stake-driver by some people, while others name him Thunder-pumper and Bog-bull. His body is about as big as a Hen's, and he is sometimes known as Indian Hen, though his very long beak, neck, and legs are not at all like those of a Hen.

A member of the guild of Wise Watchers, who keeps a sharp lookout for the reptiles and little fishes he spears with his strong pointed bill, and places his nest on the ground; the eggs are drab-colored, not pale green like those of most members of the Heron family.

A BONNET MARTYR AND A BLUE GIANT

"You promised to tell us about four Herons—please, who are the other two?" asked Dodo, when she had finished writing these tables, and had buttoned her book into the pocket of the long gray linen apron which the Doctor had taught both Olive and herself to wear on those excursions, whether they hunted birds, flowers, or butterflies.

"Boys have pockets—how I wish I was a boy!" Dodo had said, after she had been at Orchard Farm a couple of days.

Snowy Egret or Bonnet Martyr.

"So do I," had echoed Olive; "there is always something to carry, and everything seems either to fall out of girls' pockets, or to be smashed flat."

"If you will only promise not to turn into boys, I will furnish you with pockets," the Doctor had said, and he had kept his word as usual.

"Did I say four Herons?" he now asked. "Yes, to be sure; there are two more that will interest you—the Snowy Egret or Bonnet Martyr, and the Great Blue Heron or Blue Giant."

"Bonnet Martyr? What a strange name for a bird! Why do you call him that? Do they live about here?" asked Nat.

"They do not live so far north as this, though they sometimes stray through the Middle and Northern States. But in the Southern States, and Florida in particular, they used to live in vast colonies. Now they are being surely and quickly put out of the world by the cruelty and thoughtlessness of House People—the particular kind of House People who wear women's hats and bonnets.

"Once these Egrets covered the southern lowlands like drifting snow—for they are beautifully white. In the nesting season, when many birds are allowed some special attraction in the way of plumage, bunches of long, slender, graceful plumes grow on their backs between the shoulders and curl up over the tail.

"In an evil moment some woman, imitating the savages, used a bunch of these feathers to make a tuft upon her headgear. From that day the spotless bird was doomed to martyrdom. Egrets, as the plumes are called like the birds themselves, became a fashionable trimming for bonnets and have continued so to this day, in spite of law and argument; for many women seem to be savages still, notwithstanding their fine clothes and other signs of civilization.[5]

"These Herons only wear their beautiful plumes in the nesting season, when it is the height of cruelty to kill birds of any kind, and this is what happens: When the nests, which are built of sticks in bushes and trees above the lagoons, are filled with young, as yet too feeble to take care of themselves, and the beautiful parents are busy flying to and fro, attending to the wants of their helpless nestlings, the plume-hunters glide among them noiselessly, threading the watercourses in an Indian dug-out or canoe, and when once within the peaceful colony, show themselves with bold brutality. For well they know that the devoted parents will suffer death rather than leave their young in such danger.

"Shot upon shot rings out in repeated volleys, each followed in turn by the piteous cries of wounded birds, till the ground is strewn with hundreds of the dead and dying. Then the cruel hunters tear off the plume-tuft from the back of each victim, as the savage does a human scalp, and move on in search of another heronry, to repeat this inhuman slaughter of the innocents.

"But this is not all—what becomes of the young birds? They must either perish slowly of hunger, or be swallowed by the snakes that infest such places and are attracted to the nests by the clamoring of the starving orphans. Now do you wonder that I call this beautiful Snowy Egret the Bonnet Martyr?"

"I never, never will wear any kind of bird's feathers again," said Dodo; "and when I go back to school I am going to make a guild for people who will promise not to either. Are Ostriches killed for their feathers, Uncle Roy? Because my best winter hat has a curly row all round the crown."

"No. Ostrich plumes are a perfectly harmless decoration, for the bird earns his own and his master's living by growing them, without losing his life. They are the only kind of feathers that should ever be worn for ornament."

---

[5] See the introduction and chapter 26, footnote 2 for a discussion of the authors' problematic use of "savagery" to describe Indigenous peoples, and see the introduction for an extended discussion of the use of bird feathers in hats.

"Has the Great Blue Heron pretty feathers like a Bluebird?" asked Nat, who felt sorry for the fate of the Egrets, but did not like to show it and so tried to turn the subject.

"He is of a slate-gray color, which you might not think blue at all, and he too wears fine plumes, on his head, breast, and back. He is the largest bird of our hundred, being quite as tall as you are, Miss Dodo. If you ever see one of these birds standing on the edge of the mill pond, you will never forget it; for it does not seem like an American bird, but rather like a visitor from strange lands. You may imagine it to be an Egyptian princess in disguise, waiting for a barge to come down the river, rowed by black slaves and conveying a prince all glittering with jewels, who is bringing a ring cut with mystic letters to break the spell—as such things are managed in fairy tales.

Blue Heron.

"This Blue Heron, you will find, has no sweeter voice than his night-flying cousin, and, like the latter, nests in colonies in the trees; but afterward he travels about alone, as the Bittern does."

THE SNOWY EGRET
(The Bonnet Martyr)
Length about two feet.
Pure white all over, with a bunch of many long slender plumes growing between the
    shoulders, and shorter ones on the head and neck, in the nesting season. Feet and
    legs black. Toes yellow. Bill black and yellow.
A Citizen of temperate and tropical America.
A member of the guild of Wise Watchers, whose food and habits are the same as
    those of most other Herons, and who, if he does us no special good service, is

ON THE SHORE   257

perfectly innocent, and should never be butchered to make a woman's Easter
holiday bonnet.

He has a larger brother called the American White Egret, as pure white as himself,
but three feet or more instead of only two feet long, with the plumes hanging down
over his tail instead of curled up, and none growing on his head.

THE GREAT BLUE HERON

(Blue Giant)

Length about four feet.

Plumage mostly slate-gray or bluish-ash, but black and white on the head and each
side of the breast, and chestnut on the bend of the wing. A crest on the back of
the head, a fringe of long feathers at the root of the neck in front, and another
on the back in the breeding season. Feathers on upper part of the legs reddish-
brown, the bare scaly part black; bill yellow and greenish, with black on top; bare
skin between it and the eyes blue.

A Citizen of North America.

A member of the guild of Wise Watchers who is wise enough to mind his own business and do nobody any harm, though he is not inclined to be sociable with House
People.

"I think we had best be going toward the house," said Olaf, glancing at the
sky; "there's thunder-heads racing up." So the children, always ready for something new, started eagerly, and bewildered Olaf with questions about clouds and
weather signs all the way home.

CHAPTER 29

Up the River

THE THUNDER-CLOUDS thickened until the whole sky was black; the tide rose in great waves, and the children were glad to be in the house. But the storm played so many strange pranks that they could not keep away from the windows, asking a hundred questions about things that cannot be put in a bird book.

"If the water keeps up on end, as it is doing now," said Olaf, "it will be a week before I dare take you over to Gull Island; but I was talking to a man from up the river yesterday, and he says the reed shallows are full of Rails—maybe you'd like to see them."

"Rails, what are they?" asked Nat. "I thought rails were the steel things that cars run on, or else some kind of fence bars."

"The Rails that Olaf speaks of are marsh birds," said the Doctor. "Some are about as big as Robins, and some are bigger still, shaped like long-legged, long-necked, bob-tailed Hens, with long curved beaks. In fact, some members of the family are called Marsh Hens from this resemblance. Olaf often guides gunners through the waterways to find these birds; he shall take you also, and perhaps you may find some old Marsh Wrens' nests at the same time."

The next morning was clear and warm, and the children tumbled out in their flannel bathing-suits to have a dip before breakfast. Rap, by rolling over and over on the sand, was in the water as soon as Nat; but they did not venture out far, even though the tide was low, contenting themselves by splashing about in shallow places.

Presently Nat spied something on the stony end of the bar that stretched out at the right of the beach, and pointed it out to Rap, who said: "They are some sort of birds: you had better get the glass, for even if we could go nearer to them, they would be sure to see us and skip." Then Nat brought the glass and they each took a peep.

"The bodies are like speckled Pullets', but the heads are like Pigeons' and the legs are very thin," said Rap. "See! there is a different one, ever so much nearer over on this side, but I can't make him out very well. Here comes the Doctor, all ready to go in swimming; of course he can tell us."

Turnstone.

"Those mottled birds with red legs are Turnstones," said the Doctor, after looking a moment.[1] "They are wading shore birds, who run about the rock bars and sandy beaches, turning over small stones for the food that is hidden underneath. They very seldom come into bays like this, but keep more on the outer beaches. The other one, with black under parts and dark back finely speckled with yellow, is the Golden Plover, who often visits our beaches and marshy meadows."

"Do either of them ever nest up the river?" asked Dodo.

"No, indeed—you would have to travel many hundreds of miles to find the lonely Arctic beaches they both call home. They only come this way before they take the long fall journey to South America, where they winter; and in the springtime they are usually in too great a hurry to stop."

"What do they look like very near by?" asked Dodo, who always wanted details, while the boys took a more general sportsmanlike interest.

"The Turnstone is very trim and pretty when seen close at hand, and from the pattern of the feathers is often called Calico-bird. The Golden Plover is darker and not so conspicuously marked, especially at this season."

THE TURNSTONE

Length nine and a half inches.

In summer: Upper parts boldly variegated with black, white, and reddish-brown; tail black, with white base and tip. Under parts white, with large black marks on the breast. Bill and eyes black; feet orange, with a very small hind toe. In winter:

---

[1] The Turnstone is now called the Ruddy Turnstone.

American Golden Plover.

Without the bright, reddish-brown markings, which are gray; and with not so much black, which is also duller.

A Citizen of North America, making its summer home only in the Arctic regions, but at other seasons travelling almost all over the world; we see it mostly when it is migrating, in spring and fall, along the sea-coast.

A member of the guild of Ground Gleaners, who gleans its food industriously on beaches, and is very fond of the eggs of horseshoe-crabs.

THE AMERICAN GOLDEN PLOVER

Length ten and a half inches.

In summer: Upper parts blackish, all spangled with yellow of the tint of old gold, white forehead and a line over the eye. Under parts nearly all jet black, but sides of the breast pure white, and lining of the wings gray. Tail barred with white and gray. Bill and feet black. Only three toes, there being no sign of a hind toe, which almost all Plovers also lack. Bill shaped like a Pigeon's.

In winter: Without any pure black on the under parts, which are muddy whitish mixed and marbled with gray.

A Citizen of North America, whose summer home is with the Turnstone in the far North, and who travels to South America every fall and back again in the spring. We mostly see it in flocks on these journeys.

A member of the guild of Ground Gleaners, and a fine game bird, whose delicately flavored meat is a great luxury for invalids; it is therefore right for sportsmen to shoot Golden Plovers in the fall.

"Do tell us some more about paddling and wading birds," said Dodo, forgetting that she was in her sopping-wet bathing-dress.

"Break—fast! Break—fast! Come in—come in—come in!" called the big bell that Rap's mother was ringing at the cabin door. And the morning itself was hardly brighter than the smile on her face at the sight of her lame boy's happiness. "Hurry along and dress, you little Sandpipers, for by and by we are going up the river," said the Doctor.

"Why do you call us Sandpipers, Uncle Roy?" asked Nat.

"Because Sandpipers are long-legged little birds that run along the water's edge, where they patter about and whistle, but can't swim."

And they all raced laughing up to the cabin, Rap saying cheerfully, "Then I'm not a Sandpiper, for I hop like a Robin instead of running."

In the afternoon, Olaf had the sharpie (which is a flat sharp-nosed boat with two masts) ready with a little dingey tied on behind, and when the tide rose the party went aboard. First he headed well out into the bay, and then tacked to enter the river where the channel was deepest. The river, which was the same that ran through the woods above the Farm, was caught in a corner to make the mill-pond, and finally escaping, ran along for many miles until the bay opened its wide arms to receive it.

"What are those birds over there?" cried Nat, pointing toward the outer beacon. "Some look like white Crows, and the others go zigzag like big Barn Swallows. Are there any such things as water Swallows, Uncle Roy?"

"Not exactly—both the birds you see belong to the Swimmers. The larger ones are Herring Gulls, and the smaller ones are Terns. But your guess is not a bad one, for all Terns are also called Sea Swallows, because of their dashing flight. Both Gulls and Terns nest on Gull Island, where Olaf is going to take us some day when the water is smooth. The storm has driven some of them into the bay, where they do not usually come until later in the year; but in winter great flocks of Gulls live about our beach, clamming on the bar at every low tide."

"I guess we had better tie up yonder," said Olaf, when they had gone a couple of miles up the river. "And then I can put the children in the little boat and pole them in among the reeds."

So the Doctor and Olive went ashore, where the sharpie was tied to the end of what had once been a small wharf, while Dodo, Nat, and Rap crouched down in the dingey, obeying Olaf's order to keep very still and not make the boat tip.

The little reed-bordered creek that they entered was quite narrow, and soon grew to be only a thread of water, where they could touch the reeds on both sides. They heard many rustling sounds, but for some time could see nothing. Olaf, who was watching, suddenly laid down his pole, and seizing an oar gave the water two or three sharp slaps. Instantly half a dozen strange-looking birds started out, flapping and sprawling, with their legs dangling, one or two seeming to slide across the water, till they all disappeared among the flags again.

Virginia Rail.

"Oh! how funny they are!" cried Nat. "They have such foolish-looking faces, little perky tails like a Wren's, and such long, loose feet! Why didn't they fly instead of dodging about so—are their nests in the reeds?"

"They do nest here; but now that the season is over, they stay about picking up food from the mud until they shift southward a piece for the winter. These Rails fly well enough when they once get started, and go a long way without stopping. But they are lazy about it in their summer homes, where they only flap up and then dodge down again to hide; so they are easy shooting— too easy to be any sport. It's what I call killing, not hunting."

"What a strange note they have," said Rap. "Something like a Woodpecker's call."

"Yes, but you should hear the noise they make in spring, when there are crowds of birds along the river and back in the meadows. The Redwings and Meadowlarks sing all day long, the Marsh Wrens come along to join in, the Snipe begin to call, the Spotted Sandpipers whistle up, and we get a visit from the Wild Geese as they fly north. I tell you it is fine to be down here then. But in fall I'd rather be up at the lake by the lumber camp when the snow brings the foxes and other wild animals out."

"Do stop a minute, please, Olaf, and don't tell quite so fast," pleaded Dodo. "Uncle Roy never does. You have said the names of ever so many birds that we don't know, and when he does that he always stops and explains. Snipe and Spotted Sandpipers—please begin with those."

Olaf thought for a minute. He knew all the game and water birds—in fact, they were intimate friends of his; but it was not so easy for him to describe them.

"Did you ever see a Woodcock?" he began.

"Yes, oh yes!" cried Nat. "Uncle Roy showed us a stuffed one in the wonder room, and told us all about its long beak with a point like a finger to feel for its food in the mud because its eyes are too far back to see well in front, and all about its sky dance; and Rap has seen one sitting on its nest in a spring snowstorm."

"Well, the Snipe that comes about here belongs to the same family, and also pokes in the mud for its food; that is why it likes to live near fresh water like the Woodcock, where the mud is soft, rather than on the sea-shore, where the sand is gritty. It's a mighty shy bird and doesn't tell any one what it means to do. I've heard them come calling over the beach at night sometimes though, and I suspect they go to the muddy side of the bar to feed, but I've never seen them there. They mostly do their coming and going at night—and fly high too, even then.

"Sandpipers don't bore in the ground for their food, but just pick it up; so they keep along the shore of either fresh or salt water, some kinds choosing one place and some another. The Spotted Sandpiper is another of the little fellows who sometimes nests back in those meadows. He is not a bit shy, but runs about as tame as a Robin, and he isn't as big as a Robin either. Sometimes they lay their eggs in the meadow and sometimes among the tuft-grass back of the beach. They lay four eggs, very big at one end and peaked at the other, and put them in the nest with the pointed ends together in the middle, to take up less room; and they're sandy-colored, spotted all over. They hang about here all summer. We call them 'teeters' because they always tip up their tails and bob so when they run. They whistle like this, 'tweet-weet—tweet-weet!'

"There's another mite of a Sandpiper that comes around here late every summer, though it nests way up north. It is the very littlest of all, not bigger than a Sparrow, so pretty and innocent-looking that it ought to go with Singing Birds and never be shot for food. I've often had them run along in front of me on the beach, piping as sad as if they were telling me how little and helpless they were, and begging me to ask folks not to shoot them."

Then Olaf pushed up the creek a little further, hoping to be able to land or else reach some Marsh Wrens' nests from the boat. But one nest was all they could find—a ball of grasses fastened between two cat-tail flags. Olaf cut the

Wilson's Snipe.

stalks carefully and presented it to Dodo, much to her delight. Then he paddled back to the river, where they found Olive waiting with some beautiful pitcher-plants in her hands, while their uncle said that he had in his handkerchief a strange plant, that ate insects. But Dodo thought that he was joking, and as soon as they

Least Sandpiper.

were in the sharpie she whispered: "Uncle Roy, you must tell me four tables—Olaf knows the birds by sight, but he doesn't make them sound as distinct as you do in the telling."

"So missy is flattering her old bird man! Well, tell me the names, for I suppose you can remember them."

"Oh yes—but come to think of it, I don't think Olaf said what the Wise Men call these birds. One was a bob-tailed Rail—one was a Snipe with far-back eyes and a finger-beak like a Woodcock's—one was a Spotted Sandpiper that teeters and whistles 'tweet-weet'—and the other was a tiny little Sandpiper with a very sad cry. Now do you know them?"

"Famous!" laughed the Doctor; "of course I know them after that."

"Do they all belong to the same family?" persisted Dodo, whose little head was beginning to swim with all this new knowledge it had to hold.

"Not all of them. The Snipe and both the Sandpipers belong to one family, the same as that of the Woodcock; but the Rail belongs to a different family. So also does the Plover you learned this morning. The three families of Snipes, Plovers, and Rails are the largest ones of all the tribe of Birds that Paddle and Wade by the sea-shore. The Rails from their size and shape are sometimes called Marsh Hens. The Turnstone belongs to a fourth family, but it is a very small one. Now I will give you the tables of the four kinds of birds you have learned this afternoon."

Spotted Sandpiper.

WILSON'S SNIPE

Length about eleven inches, of which the very long and straight bill makes more than two inches.

Upper parts all mixed with black, brown, gray, buff, and white in very intricate patterns; long wing-feathers plain dusky with a white edge on the outside one; tail-feathers beautifully barred with black, white, and reddish.

Under parts white, but mottled with dusky on the breast, where it also tinged with
buff, and barred very distinctly on each side further back; under tail-coverts barred
with buff and black.

Eyes brown; feet and bill greenish-gray, the latter very soft and sensitive, the former
with a very small hind toe.

A Citizen of temperate North America, found at different seasons in marshy and
boggy places throughout the United States.

A member of the guild of Ground Gleaners, and, like the Woodcock and Golden Plover, a fine game bird, which it is right to shoot for food at the proper season.

THE SPOTTED SANDPIPER

Length seven and a half inches.

Upper parts a pretty Quaker color, like the Cuckoo's, but with many fine curved black
lines; tail regularly barred with black and white.

Under parts pure white, with many round black spots all over them; but young birds
do not have any spots.

Bill and feet flesh-colored, the former with a black tip, the latter with a very small hind
toe, and a little web at the roots of the front toes.

A Summer Citizen of most parts of the United States and Canada, also found in winter in some of the Southern States and far beyond.

A member of the guild of Ground Gleaners, and a very gentle, confiding little bird who
likes to be neighborly, and should never be shot, but encouraged to nest in our
fields.

THE LEAST SANDPIPER

Length only five and a half to six inches—the very least in size of all the Snipe family.
Upper parts black or blackish, in summer with rusty-red edgings and white tips of
many feathers, in winter these edgings gray, a light line over the eye and a dark line
from the bill to the eye.

Under parts white, tinged in summer with buff on the breast and at all seasons
mottled there with dusky.

Middle tail feathers blackish, the other ones plain gray with white edgings, but without any black cross-bars. Bill black; feet greenish-gray, with a small hind toe like
other Sandpipers', but no sign of any web at the roots of the front toes.

A Citizen of North America, nesting far north, beyond the United States, and travelling in large flocks in the fall to the West Indies and South America.

A member of the guild of Ground Gleaners. It belongs to a family of game birds, but it is a shame to shoot such a mite of a bird for the morsel of meat its tiny body affords—hardly one mouthful.

There is a brother of the Least Sandpiper, hardly any bigger, and so much like it that you can hardly tell them apart, unless you notice that this one has two little webs between the roots of the front toes. This is the Semipalmated Sandpiper, for *semipalmated* means "half-webbed," as its toes are. Both kinds are called "Peeps" by people who do not know the difference between them.

THE VIRGINIA RAIL

Length nine and half inches, of which the long, slender, curved bill makes an inch and a half.

Upper parts mixed blackish and brown, growing brighter reddish-brown on the wings, a light line over the eye and a dark one through the eye.

Under parts mostly cinnamon color, but distinctly barred with black and white on the sides behind and under the tail and wings, the chin whitish.

Feet big and clumsy, with very long toes in front—about as long as the bill.

A Citizen of temperate North America, nesting in the Northern States and wintering in some of the Southern States.

A member of the guild of Ground Gleaners, who does us no harm and not much good, though it is a sort of game bird whose flesh is palatable, and it may be shot in the fall. It is not neighborly and is seldom seen, as it lives only in the thickest reeds or herbage of marshy places, where it can run over the softest mud, or even floating plants, by means of its long spreading toes, which keep it from slumping in.

"To-morrow, when the tide begins to come in, we are going to fish for bluefish!" interrupted Nat joyfully. "Olaf says they are beginning to run, and there are lots of crabs to catch up in the creek too—only I'm afraid that there won't be half time enough for everything."

"How can fish run when they have no legs?" objected Dodo, who had not quite finished writing her tables and did not like to be hurried. And then, too, she was a little lady who took things literally, and liked to have them exactly right.

CHAPTER 30

Ducks and Drakes

Hooded Merganser.

IT WAS THE LAST WEEK of the children's stay at the shore before everything combined to make possible the sail to Gull Island. They had spent three glorious weeks, and were as ruddy brown as any of the little Indians who had once gathered wampum shells from the same beach in the long ago.[1] They were wiser also in many ways, for they had found out many things for themselves—which is the very best sort of wisdom. Now even Dodo could tell by the footprints on the sand whether a three-toed Plover or a four-toed Sandpiper had been pattering there.

When the right day came, without a sign of ugly squalls or of an equally unfortunate calm, Olaf borrowed a large cat-boat, and after stowing away the lunch hamper, that was always a 'must be' for an all-day trip, the boat almost flew out of the little bay and up the sound before the breeze that came with the morning tide.

---

[1] In point of fact, several Indigenous tribes occupied these coastal Connecticut lands before Fairfield was settled by the English in 1639 in the aftermath of the Pequot War.

"There are some more of your white Crows, Nat," said the Doctor, as they headed straight out after getting on the right tack. "The island where we are going is one of their famous nesting places."

"Their wings are very different from Crows' wings," said Rap, as he watched them overhead, now winnowing the air with steady wing-beats, or circling on motionless pinions—now poising in one spot for a minute by merely flapping the wings, and then dropping gracefully to float on the water. "Gulls' wings bend out more at the tip and are smooth-edged; Crows' look flatter and are saw-edged."

"Are there any other birds besides Gulls that nest on the island, Uncle Roy?" asked Nat.

"Yes, the Terns or Sea Swallows that you have seen about the reef nest there also; and this island, as well as the mainland near by, is a favorite stopping-place for all the shore and water birds in their journeys,—from Sandpipers to great flocks of Sea Ducks."

"I should think it would be a long swim for Ducks," said Nat; "it is as much as fifteen miles from shore."

"They don't swim—they fly there," said Olaf.

"Can Ducks fly?" exclaimed Dodo in amazement. "I'm sure the white Ducks at the Farm can only waddle on the ground, or swim and spatter along the water when Wolf or Quick chases them for fun. And anyway their legs are very stiff and queer and grow very far back, as if their bodies were too heavy and going to fall down front, and they had to hold up their heads very high to keep going."

"Our tame Ducks are very fat and lazy, for they have lived in captivity for many generations; yet they could fly very well with a little practice. The Mallard, which is a wild River Duck and a swift enduring flyer, is the one which has been domesticated and for hundreds of years kept as a barnyard Duck."

"River Ducks?" questioned Rap; "then are there different kinds of Ducks for rivers and lakes, and for salt water?"

"There are indeed many kinds of Ducks," said the Doctor, "all of which have easy marks of identification in the beauty-spot on the wings, and many other points about the plumage, as well as the different shapes of their heads, bills, and feet. Though all Wild Ducks, and Geese too, belong to one general family, they are divided into separate groups like cousins, instead of living in one household like brothers.

"Almost all Wild Ducks nest in the northern tier of States, or altogether north of them; the hardier species stay with us as winter visitors, but the others only stop to feed, as they follow the rivers and coasts in their migrations.

"There was a beautiful Duck that had a nest last year in a tree up near the logging camp; its feathers were as bright as if they had been painted. That is the Wood Duck—one of the exceptions to the rule that Wild Ducks nest on the ground like tame ones. Another kind, the Black Duck, nests as usual on the ground, on a wooded island not far from the one to which we are sailing."

"Will you please tell us why Ducks have such waddling legs?" begged Nat.

"Because the best legs to swim with are not the easiest to walk with."

At that moment the wind died down. The sails flapped once or twice, and then hung loose; and the boat, instead of dashing along, began to drift lazily, with an uncomfortable rolling motion, as the swell, borne in from the ocean many miles away, crept under it.

"If the water does that much more, I shall soon be hungry," said Dodo, looking a trifle sad and pressing her hands together over her waist.

"I quite agree with you," said Olive; "I know from having had the same feeling before, that unless we eat some of these little salt biscuits, and talk about something interesting, in a very few minutes you and I will be sea-sick—which is the hungriest, emptiest sickness possible."

"I thought the feeling was a little more puffy than real hungriness," said Dodo, chewing her biscuit in great haste and having some trouble in swallowing it.

"May not we men have some too?" asked the Doctor, looking drolly at the boys, who were glancing longingly at the biscuits, but were too proud to confess their feelings. "Not that we feel ill—oh, no! Merely for company, you know.

"Now while you munch away, I will talk Duck to amuse you; eating and Duck talk go very well together, for the Duck is chiefly to be considered as food. You all know what a well-rounded, compact body a Duck has; do you remember having seen one carved, and how very hard it was to cut off its legs?"

"Yes, I do," said Nat. "Sometimes the Duck almost bounces off the dish, and then, father says things—at least, I mean, he says he wishes that people who go shooting and send him presents of Wild Ducks would send a carving map and a good sharp knife with them; but I never understood what he wanted the map for."

"To find the joints, my boy," laughed the Doctor, as if he had a sympathetic feeling for carvers who find themselves in front of a tough Duck or Goose, no matter how well they know where the joints ought to be found. "A Duck's legs are very short, and not only set far back on the body, but sunk into the skin quite up to the knees; so that the joints are very hard to find. This is planned to give the Duck more strength and ease in swimming, when the legs act like paddles. All Ducks' feet have three long toes in front and a short one behind, the front toes being loosely joined by two skin flaps which stretch between them when spread apart, making what we call web-feet."

"Something the way frogs' feet are?" asked Nat.

"Very much upon the same plan. Then Ducks have wide flat beaks of various shapes, with a sort of nail bent over like a hook at the end, and all along each side is a double row of little teeth, to help them take their food. Their stiff, pointed wings are quite strong enough to lift their heavy bodies off the ground or water into the air, and keep up an even flight, often more rapid than the swiftest express train."

"What do Wild Ducks eat?" asked Dodo, "seeds or bugs or fish?"

"They eat all those things and many others too, according to their various habits, which are as different as the expression of their faces or the color of their features. If you look at a case full of Wild Ducks in a museum, you will find that no two have the same-shaped head, or expression. Some look silly, some sly, while others seem either proud or inquisitive."

"How strange!" said Rap. "I never thought about Ducks' faces, except that they all looked foolish, with little pig-eyes and big beaks like shovels. And please, do they chew their food with the teeth you said they had?"

"Those are not true teeth, like ours, to chew with. You know a good many very different things are called teeth—those on a rake, for example, or a comb, or a cog-wheel. A Duck's teeth are horny like the skin that covers its whole beak, and act like strainers. When a Duck dabbles in the water, as you have all seen tame ones do, the water that gets into its mouth runs out at the sides between the teeth, but whatever food there is in the mouthful of water gets caught in the teeth, and can then be swallowed."

"Please tell us," continued Rap, "how many different kinds of Ducks there are in our country?"

"About forty," answered the Doctor; "but I shall not trouble you to learn more than a few of the common ones. They all belong to one family, which also contains the Geese and Swans. They are divided into three groups—Fishing Ducks, River or Fresh-water Ducks, and Sea Ducks.

"The Fishing Ducks are great swimmers and divers, living chiefly on the fish they catch by chasing them under water. Their beaks are narrow, hooked, and sharply toothed, which makes it easy for them to hold their slippery prey. But this oily food makes their flesh so rank that none of them is fit food for House People. They are all called Mergansers, and we have in this country four different species.

"The River Ducks are those that we see mostly in the spring and fall migrations; they have the handsomest plumage and the most delicate flesh. They feed along shallow rivers, ponds, and lakes, after the manner of barnyard Ducks—for the Mallard is one of them, and tame Ducks are domesticated Mallards, as I told you. In feeding, they bob head downward in the water with their tails straight up in the air, to find the roots, seeds, insects, small shell-fish, and other things they like to eat. They build very good nests, usually on the ground, and warmly lined with their own down, which the parent plucks from her breast to cover the eggs. The color of the eggs is always greenish, gray, drab, or buff, never with any spots. Most River Ducks nest in the far North, but there are some exceptions. The Wood Duck that Rap saw by the lake is one of these exceptions, and has the most beautiful plumage of all our Ducks. It does not build its nest on the ground, like most others of its family, but in a tree hole, like an Owl or a Woodpecker."

"How can the little Ducks get down to the ground—do their wings grow strong very soon?" asked Nat.

"You have seen that most birds come from the egg quite naked, and stay in the nest till their feathers grow, like Canaries and all other song birds, while others are hatched all covered with down, the same as Chickens are. The young of those living in open exposed places, such as sea and shore birds, are thickly clothed with down when hatched. Such downy plumage is not exactly like the feathers that sprout after a while, but it answers the same purpose; for the little things could not run about or swim if they were naked, you know."

"Yes, Ducklings are all downy; for I remember those that came out in June up at the Farm were, and their tiny little wings were as cunning and cute as could be," said Dodo.

"When little Wood Ducks are hatched and become quite dry, their mother takes them in her beak, by the wing, one by one, and flies down to the ground with them. As soon as her brood of ten or a dozen is thus collected, she leads them off to the nearest water, and the whole lot of Ducklings go in swimming, bobbing for food as if they were a year old instead of only a few hours. Then

Wood Duck.

mamma begins to drill them in danger-signalling, so that at the slightest hint from her they dive and swim out of harm's way.

"Sea Ducks do not always live on the ocean, as the name would lead you to expect, but prefer large open waters, either fresh like those of lakes, or salt, as in bays and sounds. They eat both animal and vegetable food, oftentimes diving deeply, and swimming far under water to find it. Of course they, in common with all other Ducks, must take a vast amount of mud and water into their mouths with their food; but instead of having to swallow this, it drains off through the little grooves on the inside edges of the bill, as a ship's deck is drained of water by means of the scuppers. But that I have explained to you already. Some Sea Ducks are more plentiful than their river brethren; and as they spend both their days and nights offshore, they run less danger of extermination. Most of them nest also in the far North, in much the same fashion as River Ducks do.

"Two celebrated members of this group are the Redhead and the Canvasback, who are always welcome guests at dinner, and are so much alike in the crisp brown company dress they wear on the table, with plenty of stuffing and gravy, that very few persons can tell them apart. But the most famous one of all is the Eider Duck—the one which yields such an abundance of exquisitely soft, warm down that we use it for making the best sort of bedquilts."

DUCKS AND DRAKES 273

"Can you always tell a Sea Duck from a River Duck by the feathers—or how?" asked Rap.

"You can always tell them by their feet," answered the Doctor; "for every Sea Duck has a little flap of skin hanging like an apron from the hind toe, while the hind toe of every River Duck is round and slim, like a Hen's."

"I should think there would always be plenty of Sea Ducks," said Rap; "for if they live so far out they ought to be able to take care of themselves and swim or fly away from everybody."

"You would think so, my boy, but when man with his many inventions sets out to kill, there is little chance of escape for bird or beast. Sea Ducks are hunted in their nesting homes, not only for their flesh and eggs, but for the downy feathers with which the nest is lined. In their migrations overland, every hand is set against them if they pause to rest or feed."

"But when they reach deep water, they must be safe; for they can fly faster than any boat can sail after them," said Rap.

"Sail—yes; but men go in gunning-punts, sneak-boats, and even steam-launches, to surround the flocks of Wild Ducks that are lying low, trusting perhaps to a covering of fog, and when it lifts these water pot-hunters commit slaughter which it would be slander to call sport."

"Oh, look!" cried Rap, "there are hundreds of Gulls over there, and Sea Swallows too. There is the island, for the breeze has come up and we have sailed ever so far without noticing it. There is a great flock of Gulls going off together—are they beginning their fall journey?"

"No, they are only going to some harbor to feed. They belong to a guild of water birds that I think we might call Sea Sweepers; for they clear from the surface of the water the refuse that the tide would otherwise throw upon the beaches. They also follow in the wake of ships for the same purpose. Neither Gulls nor Terns can dive far under water like Ducks, for their bodies are too light; but they all pounce down on wing and contrive to catch small fish swimming just below the surface.

"Look at the difference between the flight of the two! The Tern half folds his long pointed wings, and darts down like lightning; in a second he is up in the air again dashing off with capricious flight, holding his beak to his breast as the Woodcock does. But the Gull sails more slowly, settles deliberately, and often floats quietly on the surface; then when he rises on wing, with some ceremony, he flaps off with his beak held straight before him, like a Duck. Terns are the better flyers, but Gulls are decidedly the more expert swimmers."

"Are Gulls and Terns related?" asked Dodo.

"They both belong to one family of many members. These two that you have been watching are among the best known of all—the American Herring Gull, who lives on both lake and ocean; and the Common Tern, who mostly follows the sea-coast."

"Heads down!" called Olaf. The boom swung round, the sail dropped, and the boat ran into the shallow water of the beach at Great Gull Island. "You haven't given us any Duck tables, Uncle Roy," said Dodo.

"You cannot stop on this hot sand to write them out; but I will remember to give them to you as soon as we get back to the cabin."

"When shall we ever see these Ducks?" sighed Dodo, thinking of the long list there would be to write; "because I can remember better when I see things than if I only hear about them."

"Do you realize that when you go back to the Farm, it will be time for birds to begin their autumn journeys, and that they will be passing by until the snow is on the ground? Why may you not meet some of these Ducks by the river, or see them swimming on the pond? Or, if you are not so lucky, you must look for them in markets and museums. Some of them are sitting in my wonder room at this very minute."

(These are the Duck tables that Dodo afterward wrote in her book.)

THE WOOD DUCK

Length eighteen or twenty inches.

Male (the Drake, as the male of all Ducks is called): upper parts velvety black, shining
with bronzy, purplish, greenish, and violet tints.

Under parts rich purplish-chestnut on the breast, which is marked with chains
of white spots like polka-dots; belly white; a white band on each side of the
breast in front of the wing; the sides further back tan color with fine wavy
black lines, and still further back distinctly banded crosswise with black
and white.

Head beautifully crested and banded with white and the shining dark colors of the
back; bill prettily tinted with pink, lake-red, and black; eyes red; feet orange.

Female and young: much more plainly dressed than the male, but enough like him not
to be mistaken.

A Citizen of North America, who lives in the woods, unlike most other Ducks, and
nests in a hole in a tree, like a Woodpecker—but it has to be a much larger, natural
hollow. This beautiful Duck is not very plentiful now, and should not be shot for the
table, though its meat is excellent. It is by far the handsomest of its tribe, and is
sometimes kept in cages for its beauty.

THE BLACK DUCK

Length twenty or twenty-two inches.

Male and female (Drake and Duck) alike, which is the exception to the rule in this
family.

Plumage all over mottled and streaky with dusky shades and buff or tan colors, except
the beauty-spot or mirror on the wing, which is shining purple with a black border—
almost all Ducks have such a spot, which is called a mirror because it reflects many
glittering hues in different lights. There is no white
on the outside of the wings of this Duck,
and you can tell it from the female
Mallard by this character; but the
lining of the wings is mostly white.

A Citizen of eastern North
America, common along the
Atlantic coast from Florida
to Labrador. It nests on the ground,
like most Ducks, and is one of the
best for the table.

Black Duck.

THE MALLARD

Length twenty-two to twenty-four inches.

Male: head and part of neck shining dark green, with a white ring; back gray and
black; tail light gray, with two curly black feathers on top; mirror rich purple with a
black and white border.

Under parts rich chestnut on the breast, gray with wavy black lines on the belly, and
black under the tail.

Bill greenish; eyes brown; feet orange.

Female: like the Black Duck, but not so dark-colored, with more buff and tan markings, and the beauty-spot just the same as the Drake's.

Bill blotched with black and orange.

A Citizen of North America and many other parts of the world. This is the Wild Duck that has been domesticated and produced all kinds of tame ducks except the one called the Muscovy. Most of the domestic varieties you see in the barnyard look like the wild ones, but some are pure white. They can all sleep standing on one leg, with the head turned around so far that the bill points backward as it rests on the bird's back.

Mallard.

THE PINTAIL

Length up to thirty inches, though the body is not larger than a Mallard's; but the neck is longer, and the two middle feathers of the tail are from five to nine inches long; these are slender and sharp, whence the name Pintail.

Male: head and neck dark-colored, with a long white stripe lengthwise on each side. Back and sides finely waved with black and gray. Breast and belly pure white. Feathers under the tail jet-black. Long inner feathers of the wing striped lengthwise with velvet-black and silver-gray. Mirror on the wing glittering purple or violet, framed with black, white, and buff.

Female: not so handsome as the Drake, and the middle tail-feathers so much shorter that she is not over two feet long; but the neck is longer and slenderer than usual in this family in proportion to her size.

A Citizen of North America and many other countries, more common in the interior of the United States than on the Atlantic coast; nesting from the middle districts far northward, wintering in the Southern States and far beyond. A fine Duck for the table.

THE GREEN-WINGED TEAL

Length less than fifteen inches—all kinds of Teals are very small Ducks.

Pintail.

Male: head chestnut with black chin and a shining green patch on each side, and a little crest behind. Back and sides with fine wavy marks of black and gray. A curved white bar in front of the wing; mirror half purple and half green, bordered with black, white, and buff.

Under parts white, tinged with buff, with many round black spots; the feathers at the root of the tail black with a buff patch on each side.

Female: different from the male on the head and body, but the wings like his; besides, she is so small you cannot mistake her for any other kind of Duck.

Green-winged Teal.

A Citizen of North America, who nests from the Northern States northward and winters mostly in the Southern States or beyond. The flesh is delicious, and this Teal is so small it can be split and broiled like a spring Chicken.

THE BLUE-WINGED TEAL

Length fifteen or sixteen inches—a little more than the Green-winged Teal, but not much.

Male: head dark-colored with a very large white bar on each side in front of the eye. Body much variegated with black, brown, and gray. Most of the outside of the wing sky-blue, not bright, but as the sky looks on a dull day; the beauty-spot shining green, bordered with black, white, and buff.

Under parts gray spotted and mottled with black, and quite black under the tail, where there is a white spot on each side; the lining of the wings mostly white.

Female: differs from the male on the head and body, but the markings of the wings are much the same as his.

A Citizen of North America, chiefly its eastern half, with a very extensive breeding range, but mostly seen in the United States during the migrations and in winter. The flesh is excellent.

This Teal has a brother in the West, called the Cinnamon Teal from the color of his under parts.

Blue-winged Teal.

THE REDHEAD

Length twenty to twenty-three inches.

Male: head and upper part of neck rich chestnut with a bronze lustre. Rest of neck, fore back, and fore breast, black. Middle of back and sides of body finely waved with zigzag lines of black and white. Rump and tail-coverts black. No shining mirror on the wings, which are mostly ashy with white lining underneath.

Bill very broad and flat, dull blue with a black belt at the end. Feet grayish-blue, with dusky webs and claws. Eyes orange. Female: differs a good deal from the male, and it would make the table too long to tell all the difference; but she has the same markings on the wings, and the same shaped bill.

A Citizen of North America who goes far north to find his summer home, and is chiefly seen in the United States in winter or during the migrations. He is a twin brother of the Canvasback, and quite as good to eat. Very few persons can tell a Redhead from a Canvasback at the dinner table, though many think they can, because if the Redhead is in good order and well roasted, they say it is Canvasback, and if the Canvasback is tough and done too much, they say it is only a Redhead. Before the birds are plucked you can easily tell them apart; for the Canvasback has the head and beak differently shaped and much darker-colored; while the back is much whiter, because the black wavy lines are narrower than the white spaces between them, or even broken up in fine dots.

Redhead.

OLD SQUAW

Length from eighteen to twenty-three inches, the difference being due to the tail of the male, which in summer has the middle feathers eight or nine inches long.

This Duck differs more in summer and winter plumages than any other. In winter, the only season it is seen in the United States, the male varied with black, white, and silvery-gray, the bill orange and black. In summer he has much more black than white or silver, with some bright-reddish feathers on the wings. The bill is black and orange; the eyes are red.

A Citizen of North America and other parts of the northern hemisphere, never going very far south, and making his summer home in the Arctic regions. He is a noisy, lively, sociable Duck, who has in spring some pleasing notes, so mellow and musical that he may almost be said to sing; but he is not choice or dainty in his food, and the flesh is too rank for House People to eat. He has many absurd names besides "Old Squaw."[2]

Old Squaw.

THE HOODED MERGANSER

Length sixteen and a half to eighteen inches.

Male: a beautiful black and white crest rising up high in a rounded form, but very thin from side to side, like a hood ironed flat. Head, neck, and back black; belly and breast white; sides cinnamon-brown with fine black bars; a white mirror with black edges on the wing. Bill black, round like a lead-pencil, with a hook at the end, and strong saw-like teeth along the sides; eyes yellow.

Female: without any such crest as her mate has, and brown where he is black.

A Citizen of North America, very handsome and stylish when he is in full dress; but he is a Fishing Duck, and therefore not very good to eat, though not as rank as other Mergansers. Like the Wood Duck, but unlike nearly all other members of the Duck tribe, this Merganser builds his downy nest in a hollow tree or stump.

---

[2] The Old Squaw is now called the Long-tailed Duck. For more information on current efforts to rename racist names for birds, please see the introduction.

CHAPTER 31

Gulls and Terns at Home

Herring Gull.

Gull Island was only a great sand heap, anchored by rocks and covered with coarse grass; but the children had hardly taken a few steps along the beach when they began to exclaim at the number of strange birds. Some were flying, others walking about on the sand, where there were many tufts of grass and mats of seaweeds that looked as if they had been used for nests. Dodo nearly stepped upon a couple of greenish, dark-spotted eggs, that were nearly as large as a Hen's. "Are the Gulls still nesting, Uncle Roy? And what are those dark streaky birds over there?"

"These are left-over eggs that did not hatch, for nesting is over in July at latest, and the dark birds are young Gulls in their first plumage. They are brownish gray, streaked and spotted as you see, while the old birds are snow-white with pearl-gray backs, and black and white wing-markings in the summer, though their winter dress is not quite so pure, being streaked with gray on the neck."

"Then the very dark Gulls I have seen off our beach in winter are the young ones?" said Rap; "I never knew that before. I don't believe many people remember how birds change their colors, and a great many never heard about it at all, I guess."

"Gulls walk very nicely," said Nat. "Much better than Ducks; and how they bob up and down like little boats when they float!"

"Wake! wake! wake! wake!" screamed half a dozen, flying up as if to tell the Brotherhood of the coming of strangers.

"What can be the matter with all those Sea Swallows on the other side of the island?" asked Nat as they walked across, and a flock of a hundred or more Terns angled by, crying mournfully. "What a very sad noise they are making—do you think they are afraid of us?"

"They have reason enough to cry and be sad," answered Olaf, who was walking on, a little way ahead. "They have been driven from almost all these islands— shot for their pretty feathers, and had their nests robbed. There wouldn't be any here now, only that some people pay the light-keeper at the little island yonder to see that the law is kept and that no one hunts them here. See! He is coming over now to find out what we are doing here!"

"Who are the people that pay him, Uncle Roy?" asked Dodo; "the Wise Men?"

"Yes, the Wise Men, and some Wise Women too.[1] You can give a part of the money in your tin bank to help the poor birds if you wish."

"Oh yes—that is—I forgot," and Dodo whispered in her uncle's ear that she, as well as Nat, was saving money to buy Rap a *whole* bird book for Christmas.

"It seems to be a very open place for nests, out here on the sand," said Rap. "I suppose the little Gulls and Terns must be hatched with down-feathers on."

Common Tern.

---

[1] The light-keeper is playing the role of game warden, helping ensure that game laws are enforced. The warden is paid by the "Wise Men and Wise Women," a reference to women, like Mabel Osgood Wright, who were behind the reinvigoration of state-level Audubon Societies.

"Yes—though they are not able to take care of themselves as quickly as young Ducks. But as soon as they can leave the nest, they walk down to the water's edge and eat a sort of gluey stuff that floats in on the water. So you see that unless the law protected them they might be very easily stolen or destroyed before their wings were strong enough to fly."

"It must be very cold for them here in the winter."

"It would be if they were obliged to stay; but both Gulls and Terns scatter all over the country to winter, though the Terns travel much further south."

By this time the lighthouse keeper had made his way over to them. Finding who they were, he invited them to bring their luncheon and row over to Little Gull Island with him, to see the lighthouse.

There was a dancing breeze when they turned homeward that afternoon; the boat canted saucily, and little feathers of spray kept tickling Dodo's nose.

"Are there any more water birds that we are likely to see this fall?" asked Nat, as the Gull Islands disappeared behind them.

"There will be great flocks of Wild Geese coming down from the North, and they often rest on the mill pond; or a Loon may chance down the river, and a Grebe or two."

"Are Geese Ducks?" asked Dodo, and then laughed with the others at the question.

"Not precisely—no more than rats are mice," said the Doctor; "but both Ducks and Geese belong to the same family."

"And what are the others—the Loons and Grubs—are they wading or swimming birds?" "*Grebes*, not grubs," laughed the Doctor. "Loons and Grebes are swimming birds, like Ducks or Gulls, but both belong to quite a different order from any of the others and each of them belongs to a family of its own. They can barely move at all on land, and spend all their lives on the water, excepting in the nesting season, when they make curious floating nests of dead herbage in reedy marshes. Their legs are placed in such a backward position that they can sit upright in the water and swim as if they were walking, only keeping the tip of the bill above the surface."

"How can they get away if any one hunts them?" asked Rap.

"They can dive at the flash of a gun and swim long distances under water. Our familiar Pied-billed Grebe or Dabchick disappears so suddenly, that 'Water Witch' is one of its common names."

"What a lot of birds there are to watch for this fall!" said Nat very anxiously. "I only wish I knew how much more time we shall have before father and mother come for us."

"Why, there is one of the men from the Farm with a team," said Rap, as they tacked close to the beach half an hour later. "He is waving a letter or something, I think."

It did not take the party long to land, or the Doctor to read his letter, which said that Nat's and Dodo's parents were coming to the Farm in a couple of days.

Loon.

"So we must go home to-morrow," said the Doctor.

"I want to see mother awfully much," said Dodo, "and father too; but don't you think if you told them bird stories, Uncle Roy, you might be able to coax them to make you a long visit before they take us home?"

"*I* think father would rather go up to the logging camp, and see the coons that Rap says they catch there in the fall; there are red foxes, too, he says, and little fur beasts."

The Doctor did not give them a very satisfactory answer; but if they had looked they would have seen a merry twinkle in his eye. And Dodo, who had learned not to tease during her happy summer, nestled up to Olive and said, "I smell a secret somewhere, but I can wait; for I know that hereabouts secrets are always nice surprises."

When five more tables had been written—the last ones Uncle Roy gave the children this summer—they were like this:

THE CANADA GOOSE

Length three feet or more.

Body brown above, gray below, with black head, neck, tail, and long feathers of the wings, the tail white at the roots above and below, the head with a large white patch like a napkin folded under the chin.

Bill and feet black, the toes webbed like a Duck's or tame Goose's; but the wild Canada Goose is not the kind that our tame Geese came from.

A Citizen of North America, and a great traveller in spring and fall, when flocks fly high overhead in a wedge-shaped figure or in a long line, with one old Gander leading, and all crying "honk, honk, honk!"

The nest is placed on the ground, sometimes on a tree or cliff, in various parts of the United States and Canada. The flesh is excellent for the table if the roast Goose is a young tender one, but beware of an elderly Wild Goose!

THE AMERICAN HERRING GULL[2]

Length two feet.

Plumage pure white, with a pearly-blue mantle on the back and wings, the long feathers of the wings marked with black.

Bill yellow, with a red spot, stout and hooked at the end. Feet flesh-colored, the front toe webbed like a Duck's or Goose's, but the hind toe very short indeed.

In winter the head and neck streaked with gray. Young birds all patched with gray and black, the bill black.

Canada Goose.

A Citizen of North America, and a member of the guild of Sea Sweepers. He nests in summer in the Northern States, and in the fall travels south. He can sleep standing on one leg or floating on the water. His nest is usually built on the ground, but sometimes in a tree. He goes fishing and clamming for a living.

THE COMMON TERN OR SEA SWALLOW

Length thirteen to sixteen inches, according to the length of the tail, which is deeply forked with slender outside feathers, like a Barn Swallow's.

Plumage pure white, with a black cap on the head, a pearl-blue mantle, and silver-black shades on the long wing-feathers, which look as if they had hoar frost on them.

Bill coral-red with a black tip, slender and very sharp, without any hook at the end.

Feet coral-red, very small and weak, the front toes webbed like a Gull's.

Young ones are patched with various colors before they grow their pearly, snowy, and jet-black feathers.

[2] The American Herring Gull is now called the Herring Gull.

A Citizen of North America, chiefly its eastern portions, who travels far north in spring and far south in fall. He nests in large colonies on the sand or shingle of beaches, and cries very sadly when House People come to steal the eggs or kill the young ones. He belongs to the guild of Sea Sweepers, and eats little fishes.

THE LOON OR NORTHERN DIVER

Length two and a half to three feet, with a long neck like a Goose's, and a stout straight black bill, very sharp-pointed.

Plumage glossy black above, with a necklace of white streaks and many square white spots on the back; under parts white from the root of the neck backwards, but the sides of the breast streaky.

Young ones are speckled gray and white, without any glossy black, and the bill is not black.

A Citizen of North America, who nests in the far North and migrates into the United States for the winter.

A famous Sea Sweeper, who can catch fish by chasing them under water. He can dive like a flash and fly more than a hundred yards under water before coming up to breathe, but is very awkward and top-heavy on land because his legs are so far back that he has to stand up on end. His nest is on the ground and his flesh is not fit to eat, being too rank and fishy. You can hear his mournful cry a mile off.

THE PIED-BILLED GREBE, DABCHICK, OR WATER WITCH

Length thirteen inches.

Upper parts brownish-black. Breast and belly white, very smooth like satin. A black mark on the throat, and a black band on the bill, which is shaped like a Hen's. Feathers on top of the head bristly.

Feet very strange: they stick out far behind, because Grebes have no tail to be seen, and the toes are different from those of any other bird you have in your tables, being scalloped with flaps of skin instead of webbed like those of most Swimming Birds.

Pied-billed Grebe.

A Citizen of North America, whose nest is a wet bed of broken-down reeds, sometimes floating on the water of the marsh. He can dive and swim under water as well as a Loon. If you could catch one alive, he would make his flapper-like feet go so fast you could not see anything of them but a hazy film, as the Hummingbird does his wings when he poises in front of a flower.

CHAPTER 32

Chorus by the Birds

SWALLOWS WERE PERCHING on the same telegraph wires where they had met in May. Now it was September. There were Swallows of all kinds, both old and young, with whom a great many other birds stopped for a little chat.

"In a few weeks we must be off—how have you enjoyed the summer?" asked the Bank Swallow of his sharp-tailed brother from the barn.

"Excellently well! Times have changed for the better; not a single cat or rat has been seen in my hayloft all the season, and the window has been always open."

"So you have changed your mind about House People?" said the Bank Swallow slyly.

"Yes—that is, about *some* House People."

"I wish so many of the Bird Brotherhood did not leave in the winter; it makes me quite sad," murmured the Bluebird.

"Yes. Stay-at-homes, like yourself and Robins and Finches, must feel very lonely without us," said Barney kindly; "but I think likely these House People will scatter food about, so that at least you will not be hungry—that is, unless they migrate too, as the Catbird says they sometimes do."

"Dear, dear! *Think* of it, *think* of it!" warbled the Bluebird.

"Zeay! zeay!" screamed the Catbird, flying up. "N-e-w-s! N-e-w-s! The House People are to stay at our farm all winter! The man who owns this farm, the big girl, and the little girl and boy—and the mother and father bird they belong to—they are all down in the orchard, talking about it now—how they are going to something they call 'school,' over in the village, and how that boy who hops along on one leg with a stick under his wing is going with them."

"Did they say anything about the Bird Brotherhood?"

"No, but I heard them say that when the snow falls they are going up to those horrid dark Owl woods to see the foxes and little fur beasts—'Four-footed Americans' our House Man calls them."[1]

"He gave me a better name than that," said the Barn Swallow, "one day when he was telling the children about the Brotherhood, over in the old barn. He looked straight at me and said a whole tree full of nice things."

"What did he call you? What did he say about the Brotherhood?" asked all the others, crowding around Barney.

"He said that I swept the sky free of evil insects, that I was patriotic in coming back to my birthplace to nest, and that I worked to pay my rent and taxes, and—"

"And what?" cried the others in excitement.

"He called me 'Citizen Bird'! He said *all* well-behaved birds, who have their own nests, and belong to the guilds of the Brotherhood, are American Citizens and should be protected!"

"How badly the Cowbirds must feel!" said the chorus.

"Hip, hip, hurrah! for Citizen Bird and friendly House People!" drummed the Downy Woodpecker, beating away for dear life on a telegraph pole.

Then all the Swallows and Flycatchers began to dash about the air, whispering "Citizen Bird! Citizen Bird!" And the Bluebird flew down to the garden bushes to tell his winter companion, the Song Sparrow, all about it.

---

[1] In 1898, Macmillan published a sequel to *Citizen Bird*, devoted to American mammals: *Four-Footed Americans and Their Kin*. The book was written entirely by Wright, with Frank M. Chapman as the editor and Ernest Thompson Seton as the illustrator.

CHAPTER 33

The Procession of Bird Families

IN WHICH ALL THE BIRDS the children have learned in this little book are made to pass in orderly review, each bearing its scientific name, which the Wise Men write in Latin.[1]

I. ORDER OF PERCHING BIRDS   **Order Pas′seres**

Which have their feet best fitted for perching, with three toes in front and one behind, all on the same level.

Suborder of Singing Perching Birds   **Suborder Os′cines**

Which have music-boxes in their throats, though not all of them can sing.

   1. **FAMILY OF THRUSHES**   FAMILY TUR′DIDAE
       1. Bluebird   *Sia′lia sia′lis.*
       2. American Robin   *Mer′ula migrato′ria.*
       3. Wood Thrush   *Tur′dus musteli′nus.*
       4. Wilson's Thrush   *Tur′dus fusces′cens.*
       5. Hermit Thrush   *Tur′dus aonalasch′kae pal′lasi.*
       6. Olive-backed Thrush   *Tur′dus ustula′tus swain′soni.*

---

[1] The Latin names for the birds are written with an accent mark that indicates which syllable to stress. Additionally, some of these Latin names have changed since this 1897 publication. For example, the American Robin is called *Turdus migratorius*.

2. **FAMILY OF OLD-WORLD WARBLERS**
   7. Golden-crowned Kinglet

FAMILY SYLVI'IDAE

Reg'ulus sat'rapa.

3. **FAMILY OF NUTHATCHES**
   8. White-breasted Nuthatch

FAMILY SIT'TIDAE

Sit'ta carolinen'sis.

4. **FAMILY OF TITMICE**
   9. Chickadee

FAMILY PAR'IDAE

Par'us atricapil'lus.

5. **FAMILY OF CREEPERS**
   10. Brown Creeper

FAMILY CERTHI'IDAE

Cer'thia familia'ris america'na.

6. **FAMILY OF THRASHERS AND WRENS**
   11. Sage Thrasher
   12. Mockingbird
   13. Catbird
   14. Brown Thrasher
   15. Rock Wren
   16. House Wren
   17. Long-billed Marsh Wren

FAMILY TROGLODY'TIDAE

Oreoscop'tes monta'nus.
Mi'mus polyglot'tus.
Galeoscop'tes carolinen'sis.
Harporhyn'chus ru'fus.
Salpinc'tes obsole'tus.
Troglod'ytes ae'don.
Cistotho'rus palus'tris.

7. **FAMILY OF AMERICAN WARBLERS**
   18. Black-and-white Warbler
   19. Yellow Warbler
   20. Yellow-rumped Warbler
   21. Ovenbird
   22. Maryland Yellow-throat
   23. Yellow-breasted Chat
   24. American Redstart

FAMILY MNIOTIL'TIDAE

Mniotil'ta va'ria.
Dendroe'ca oesti'va.
Dendroe'ca corona'ta.
Siu'rus auricapil'lus.
Geoth'lypis tri'chas.
Icter'ia vi'rens.
Setoph'aga ruticil'la.

8. **FAMILY OF GREENLETS**
   25. Red-eyed Vireo

FAMILY VIREON'DAE

Vi'reo oliva'ceus.

9. **FAMILY OF SHRIKES**
   26. Great Northern Shrike

FAMILY LANI'IDAE

La'nius borea'lis.

THE PROCESSION OF BIRD FAMILIES 291

10. FAMILY OF WAXWINGS — FAMILY AMPE'LIDAE
   27. Cedar Waxwing — *Am'pelis cedro'rum.*

11. FAMILY OF SWALLOWS — FAMILY HIRUNDIN'IDAE
   28. Purple Martin — *Prog'ne su'bis.*
   29. Barn Swallow — *Cheli'don erythrogas'ter.*
   30. Tree Swallow — *Tachycine'ta bi'color.*
   31. Bank Swallow — *Clivi'cola ripa'ria.*

12. FAMILY OF TANAGERS — FAMILY TANAG'RIDAE
   32. Scarlet Tanager — *Piran'ga erytho'melas.*
   33. Louisiana Tanager — *Piran'ga ludovicia'na.*

13. FAMILY OF FINCHES, BUNTINGS, AND SPARROWS — FAMILY FRINGIL'LIDAE
   34. Pine Grosbeak — *Pinic'ola enu'cleator.*
   35. American Crossbill — *Lox'ia curviros'tra mi'nor.*
   36. American Goldfinch — *Spi'nus tris'tis.*
   37. Snowflake — *Plectrophe'nax niva'lis.*
   38. Vesper Sparrow — *Pooe'cetes gramin'eus.*
   39. White-throated Sparrow — *Zonotrich'ia albicol'lis.*
   40. Chipping Sparrow — *Spizel'la socia'lis.*
   41. Slate-colored Junco — *Jun'co hiema'lis.*
   42. Song Sparrow — *Melospi'za fascia'ta.*
   43. Towhee Bunting — *Pip'ilo erythrophthal'mus.*
   44. Cardinal — *Cardina'lis cardina'lis.*
   45. Rose-breasted Grosbeak — *Zamelo'dia ludovicia'na.*
   46. Indigo Bird — *Passeri'na cyan'ea.*

14. FAMILY OF BLACKBIRDS AND ORIOLES — FAMILY ICTER'IDEA
   47. Bobolink — *Dolicho'nyx oryziv'orus.*
   48. Cowbird — *Mol'othrus a'ter.*
   49. Orchard Oriole — *Ic'terus spu'rius.*
   50. Baltimore Oriole — *Ic'terus gal'bula.*
   51. Meadowlark — *Sturnel'la mag'na.*

292   CITIZEN BIRD

52. Red-winged Blackbird	*Ageloe'us phoeni'ceus.*
53. Purple Grackle	*Quis'calus quis'cula.*

15. FAMILY OF CROWS AND JAYS — FAMILY COR'VIDAE

54. American Crow	*Cor'vus america'nus.*
55. Blue Jay	*Cyanocit'ta crista'ta.*

Suborder of Songless Perching Birds — **Suborder Clamato'res**

Which have no music-boxes in their throats, and therefore cannot sing, though some of them can twitter.

16. FAMILY OF FLYCATCHERS — FAMILY TYRAN'NIDAE

56. Kingbird	*Tyran'nus tyran'nus.*
57. Phoebe	*Sayor'nis phoe'be.*
58. Wood Pewee	*Con'topus vi'rens.*

II. ORDER OF PICARIAN BIRDS — **ORDER PICA'RIAE**

Which have their feet fixed in various ways, but never quite like those of Perching Birds; though all of them can perch, none of them can sing.

Suborder of Hummingbirds — **Suborder Troch'ili**

Which make a humming sound with their wings when they fly.

17. FAMILY OF HUMMINGBIRDS — FAMILY TROCHIL'IDAE

59. Ruby-throated Hummingbird — *Troch'ilus col'ubris.*

Suborder of Long-handed Birds — **Suborder Cyp'seli**

Which can fly with great rapidity.

18. FAMILY OF SWIFTS — FAMILY MICROPO'DIDAE

60. Chimney Swift — *Choetu'ra pelag'ica.*

Suborder of Coracian Birds — **Suborder Cora'ciae**

Which are peculiar in many respects that cannot be understood by children.

THE PROCESSION OF BIRD FAMILIES 293

19. FAMILY OF GOATSUCKERS   FAMILY CAPRIMUL'GIDAE
     61. Nighthawk   *Chordei'les virginia'nus.*
     62. Whip-poor-will   *Antros'lomus vociferus.*

Suborder of Picine Birds   Suborder Pi'ci

Which have two toes in front and two behind, and most of which can climb.

20. FAMILY OF WOODPECKERS   FAMILY PIC'IDAE
     63. Downy Woodpecker   *Dryob'ates pubes'cens.*
     64. Red-headed Woodpecker   *Melaner'pes erythroceph'alus.*
     65. Yellow-bellied Sapsucker   *Sphyrap'icus va'rius.*
     66. Flicker   *Colap'tes aura'tus.*

Suborder of Halcyon Birds   Suborder Halcy'ones

Which have their front toes grown together so that they cannot walk on them.

21. FAMILY OF KINGFISHERS   FAMILY ALCEDIN'IDAE
     67. Belted Kingfisher   *Ceryle al'cyon.*

Suborder of Cuculine Birds   Suborder Cu'culi

Which have two toes in front and two behind, but which cannot climb like Woodpeckers.

22. FAMILY OF CUCKOOS   FAMILY CUCU'LIDAE
     68. Yellow-billed Cuckoo   *Coccy'zus america'nus.*

III. ORDER OF PARROTS   ORDER PSIT'TACI

Which have two toes in front and two behind, and beaks hooked like those of birds of prey. But this place is vacant in the procession, because cruel men have almost exterminated the only kind of Parrot that lives in North America—so he was afraid to fall in line with the rest.[2]

---

[2] This refers to the Carolina Parakeet, which was nearly extinct when *Citizen Bird* was written in 1897. The last known wild specimen was killed in Florida in 1904, and the last Carolina Parakeet in captivity died in the Cincinnati Zoo in 1918.

IV. ORDER OF BIRDS OF PREY   ORDER RAPTO'RES

Which have strong hooked beaks and claws, to catch and kill their living prey, and some of which are cannibal birds.

Suborder of Diurnal Birds of Prey   Suborder Accip'itres

Which can see well to take their prey by day.

23. FAMILY OF HAWKS AND EAGLES   FAMILY FALCON'IDAE

    69. Osprey   *Pandi'on haliae'tus carolinen'sis.*
    70. Bald Eagle   *Haliae'tus leucoceph'alus.*
    71. Golden Eagle   *Aq'uila chrysae'tus.*
    72. Red-shouldered Hawk   *Bu'teo linea'tus.*
    73. Marsh Hawk   *Cir'cus hudson'ius.*
    74. Sharp-shinned Hawk   *Accip'iter ve'lox.*
    75. Sparrow Hawk   *Fal'co sparve'rius.*

Suborder of Nocturnal Birds of Prey   Suborder Stri'ges

Which cannot see well in daylight, and mostly take their prey by night.

24. FAMILY OF OWLS   FAMILY STRIG'IDAE

    76. Screech Owl   *Meg'ascops a'sio.*
    77. Long-eared Owl   *A'sio wilsonia'nus.*
    78. Great Horned Owl   *Bubo virginia'nus.*
    79. Snowy Owl   *Nyc'tea nyc'tea.*

V. ORDER OF BIRDS THAT COO   ORDER COLUM'BAE

Which drink without raising the head at every sip, and feed the young in the nest on the contents of the crop.

25. FAMILY OF COLUMBINE BIRDS   FAMILY COLUM'BIDAE

    80. Passenger Pigeon   *Ectopis'tes migrato'rius.*
    81. Mourning Dove   *Zenaidu'ra macru'ra.*

THE PROCESSION OF BIRD FAMILIES   295

VI. ORDER OF BIRDS THAT SCRATCH   **ORDER GALLI'NAE**

Which when they drink raise the head at every sip, and whose young can run about and feed themselves almost as soon as they are hatched.

26. FAMILY OF PARTRIDGES   FAMILY PERDIC'IDAE
    82. Bob White   *Coli'nus virginia'nus.*

27. FAMILY OF GROUSE   FAMILY TETRAON'IDAE
    83. Ruffed Grouse   *Bona'sa umbel'lus.*

VII. ORDER OF SHORE BIRDS   **ORDER LIMIC'OLAE**

Which live in open places by the water's edge, for the most part, and whose young can run about and feed themselves almost as soon as they are hatched, like little Chickens.

28. FAMILY OF PLOVERS   FAMILY CHARADRI'IDAE
    84. Golden Plover   *Charad'rius dominicus.*

29. FAMILY OF TURNSTONES   FAMILY ARENARI'IDAE
    85. Turnstone   *Arena'ria inter'pres.*

30. FAMILY OF SNIPES   FAMILY SCOLOPAC'IDAE
    86. Woodcock   *Philo'hela mi'nor.*
    87. Wilson's Snipe   *Gallina'go delica'ta.*
    88. Spotted Sandpiper   *Acti'tis macula'ria.*
    89. Least Sandpiper   *Actodro'mas minutil'la.*

VIII. ORDER OF MARSH BIRDS   **ORDER PALUDIC'OLAE**

Which live for the most part in the thickest marshes, and whose young run about and feed themselves almost as soon as they are hatched, like young shore birds. Cranes belong to this order, but are left out of the procession because there are no Cranes where the children lived.

Suborder of Rails   **Suborder Ral'li**

Which are much smaller than Cranes, lay more eggs, and hide away better in the marshes.

31. FAMILY OF RAILS	FAMILY RAL'LIDAE
90. Virginia Rail	*Ral'lus virginia'nus.*

IX. ORDER OF SWAMP BIRDS — ORDER HERODIO'NES

Which live for the most part in swamps, and whose young have to be fed in the nest. All have very long legs and necks. Storks and Ibises belong to this order.

Suborder of Herons — Suborder Hero'dii

32. FAMILY OF HERONS	FAMILY ARDE'IDAE
91. American Bittern	*Botau'rus lentigino'sus.*
92. Snowy Egret	*Garzet'ta candidis'sima.*
93. Great Blue Heron	*Ar'dea hero'dias.*
94. Black-crowned Night Heron	*Nyctico'rax nyctico'rax noe'vius.*

X. ORDER OF SWIMMING BIRDS WITH TOOTHED BILLS — ORDER AN'SERES

Which are web-footed birds that can strain out their food from the water they take in their mouths.

33. FAMILY OF DUCKS, GEESE, AND SWANS	FAMILY ANAT'IDAE
95. Canada Goose	*Bran'ta canaden'sis.*
96. Wood Duck	*Aex spon'sa.*
97. Black Duck	*A'nas obscu'ra.*
98. Mallard	*A'nas bos'cas.*
99. Pintail	*Daf'ila acu'ta.*
100. Green-winged Teal	*Net'tion carolinen'sis.*
101. Blue-winged Teal	*Querqued'ula dis'cors.*
102. Red-head	*ÆEthy'ia america'na.*
103. Old Squaw	*Harel'da hiema'lis.*
104. Hooded Merganser	*Lophod'ytes cucul'a'tus.*

XI. ORDER OF SWIMMING BIRDS WITH LONG WINGS — ORDER GA'VIAE

Which are web-footed birds without any teeth along the edges of the bill.

THE PROCESSION OF BIRD FAMILIES   297

34. FAMILY OF GULLS AND TERNS

FAMILY LAR'IDAE

105. American Herring Gull
106. Common Tern

Larus argenta'tus smithsonia'nus.
Ster'na hirun'do.

XII. ORDER OF DIVING BIRDS

ORDER PYGOP'ODES

Which can dive like a flash and swim very far under water.

35. FAMILY OF WEB-FOOTED DIVERS

FAMILY URINATOR'IDAE

107. Loon

Urina'tor im'ber.

36. FAMILY OF LOBE-FOOTED DIVERS

FAMILY COLYM'BIDAE

108. Pied-billed Grebe

Podilym'bus pod'iceps.

Index of English Names

Latin names will be found in Procession of Bird Families.

Bee Martin, 130
Bittern, American, 253
Blackbird, Crow, 184
Blackbird, Red-winged, 183
Bluebird, 66
Bobolink, 174–175
Bob White, 243
Bunting, Bay-winged, 150
Bunting, Indigo, 169
Bunting, Snow, 148
Butcher Bird, 123
Cardinal, 165
Catbird, 95
Cedar Bird, 126
Chat, Yellow-breasted, 117
Chewink, 160
Chickadee, 86
Chippy, 154
Cowbird, 180–181
Creeper, Black-and-white, 107–108
Creeper, Brown, 87
Crossbill, American, 145
Crow, American, 190
Cuckoo, Yellow-billed, 221

Dove, Mourning, 238
Duck, Black or Dusky, 275
Duck, Blue-winged Teal, 277
Duck, Green-winged Teal, 276–277
Duck, Hooded Merganser, 279
Duck, Mallard, 275–276
Duck, Old Squaw, 278–279
Duck, Pintail, 276
Duck, Red-head, 278
Duck, Wood, 274
Ducks, 267–279
Eagle, Bald, 234
Eagle, Golden, 225
Eagle, White-headed Sea, 234
Egret, Snowy, 256–257
Finch, Grass, 150
Flicker, 218
Goldfinch, American, 147
Grackle, Purple, 184
Grebe, Pied-billed, 285–286
Grosbeak, Pine, 142
Grosbeak, Rose-breasted, 167
Grouse, Ruffed, 244
Gull, Herring, 284

INDEX OF ENGLISH NAMES

Gulls, 280–286

Hawk, American Sparrow, 233

Hawk, Marsh, 230–231

Hawk, Red-shouldered, 231–232

Hawk, Sharp-shinned, 231

Heron, Black-crowned Night, 253

Heron, Great Blue, 257

Heron, Snowy, 256–257

High-hole, 213

Hummingbird, 203

Indigo Bird, 169

Jay, Blue, 191

Junco, Slate-colored, 157

Kingbird, 196–197

Kingfisher, 220

Kinglet, Golden-crowned, 82

Kinglet, Ruby-crowned, 81

Loon, 285

Mallard, 275–276

Martin Bee, 130

Martin, Purple, 130

Martin, Sand, 131

Meadowlark, 186–187

Merganser, Hooded, 279

Mockingbird, 93

Nighthawk, 208

Nuthatch, White-breasted, 83–84

Old Squaw, 278–279

Old Wife, 278–279

Oriole, Baltimore, 179

Oriole, Orchard, 176–177

Osprey, American, 194

Ovenbird, 114–115

Owl, American Long-eared, 227–228

Owl, Great Horned, 229–230

Owl, Screech, 226

Owl, Snowy, 228–229

Pewee, Wood, 199

Phoebe, 198

Pigeon, Passenger, 237

Pigeon, Wild, 24

Pintail, 276

Plover, American Golden, 260

Quail, 240

Rail, Virginia, 266

Red-head, 278

Redstart, 119

Reedbird, 173

Ricebird, 173

Robin, American, 70

Robin, Ground, 160

Sandpiper, Least, 265–266

Sandpiper, Spotted, 265

Sapsucker, Yellow-bellied, 217–218

Shrike, Northern, 125–126

Snipe, Wilson's, 264–265

Snowbird, 156

Snowflake, 150

Sparrow, Chipping, 155

Sparrow, Song, 159

Sparrow, Vesper, 151

Sparrow, White-throated, 153

Stake-driver, 253

Swallow, 128–132

Swift, Chimney, 205

Tanager, Louisiana, 137

Tanager, Scarlet, 135

Teal, Blue-winged, 277

Teal, Green-winged, 276–277

Tern, Common, 284–285

Terns, 280–286

Thistlebird, 145

Thrasher, Brown, 98

Thrasher, Sage, 89–90

Thrush, Golden-crowned, 113

Thrush, Hermit, 76–77

Thrush, Song (Brown Thrasher), 98

Thrush, Wilson's, 75

INDEX OF ENGLISH NAMES 301

Thrush, Wood, 73

Titmouse, Black-capped, 85–86

Towhee, 161–162

Turnstone, 259–260

Veery, 75

Vireo, Red-eyed, 123

Warbler, Black-and-white, 107–108

Warbler, Myrtle, 112

Warbler, Yellow, 111

Warbler, Yellow-rumped, 112

Waxwing, Cedar, 127

Whip-poor-will, 210

Woodcock, 244

Woodpecker, Downy, 213–214

Woodpecker, Golden-winged, 212–213

Woodpecker, Red-headed, 215

Wren, House, 103

Wren, Long-billed Marsh, 104

Wren, Rock, 101

Wren, Winter, 101

Yellowbird, Summer, 111

Yellow-throat, Maryland, 116

APPENDIX 1

Supplementary Material
on *Citizen Bird*

INTRODUCTION AND APPENDIX TO THE 1923 EDITION OF *CITIZEN BIRD*

Greetings from Citizen Bird

To the Children Who Now Read These Stories

It was twenty-five years ago, when our friend the Doctor first went out with Olive, Nat, Rap, and Dodo to watch us, learn our names, see how we live, where we go, and what we eat.[1] He called us *Citizens* of the great out-door *Republic*, and said that we ought to go free everywhere, and never be caged or bought and sold. We, the birds that sing or at some time of the year eat the creeping things on flower, leaf, or branch that waste man's food.

When Mammy Bun told you how down in Louisiana where she came from the children stole little Mocking Birds from the nest and sold them three for a quarter, the Doctor said it must not be allowed, and he and the *Wise Men* thought and worked year in and year out until we have come truly to be Citizens and protected, so far as law may do it.[2]

But children, you who will be lawmakers in your turn, it is in your hands to see that these laws are kept in spirit and in letter. Many more of you go out into the fields and woods now than when Nat and Dodo were children. More people know about us and our ways than then.

---

[1] Mabel Osgood Wright, Introduction and Appendix, excerpt from *Citizen Bird* (New York: Macmillan and Co., 1923).

[2] For the Laws protecting migrating birds in the United States and Canada, see p. 435. [Here, Wright refers to the appendix to the 1923 edition of *Citizen Bird*, which explains the Federal Migratory Bird Law, and which is reprinted below in this appendix.]

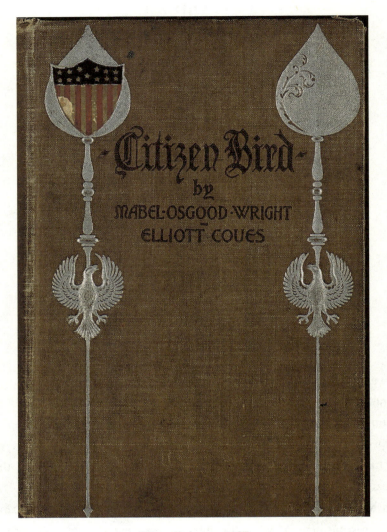

Citizen Bird cover, 1897.

The Boy and Girl Scouts and other Woodcraft Guilds go out and live in our Republic. But children, dear children, Citizen Bird begs this of you—Look at us, love us, protect us as far as may be without changing our world and habits. Then leave us to ourselves to live the life of freedom that has been won.

We wild things can be loved and studied to death, as well as stoned or shot to death! Remember! Hands off! Don't touch or peep into our nests even to make pictures!

BIRDCRAFT SANCTUARY, FAIRFIELD, CONN.,

JANUARY, 1923

Appendix

*The Old World Starling

(Often confused with our Red-winged Blackbird, Purple and Bronze Grackles, etc.)

About the length of a Catbird but more heavily built. Spring feathers purple and greenish with a metal lustre. Upper parts tipped with buff. *Bill yellow.*

Young birds and old in *fall* and *winter*. *Bill Brown.* Rusty tinge to feathers which are now heavily spotted with buff. Under parts spotted with white.

Young, just from the nest, dull grayish. Starlings *walk* like our grackles but never hop. First few notes of Spring song clear and musical. Flight rapid. *Wings long and pointed. Tail short and square.*

In early Spring when the marsh frogs begin to peep, a clear, whistled bird note will make you rush out of doors without stopping for coat or hat, calling "The Grackles have come back! Or maybe it is a Redwing; it doesn't sound quite right, but it must be one of the two!"

Then you look about for the bird who gave the whistle. There it is in the tree over the fence, and at that very moment it drops with widespread, motionless wings to the meadow below, followed by several others. Together they walk about prying into every hollow, pecking at the grubs they have uncovered with their powerful sharp bills.

Open your eyes wide, look and think at the same time, and you will see that though, at first, they look like their cousins the Blackbirds, not only are their markings different but they have *brown eyes*, while our Grackle's eyes are yellow. Also the gay shoulder feathers of the Red-wing are missing.

Listen! The birds fly again into the trees and soon you hear the sharp cries and fluttering that mark a bird fight.

One of the birds who has been exploring a large tree hole has met, face to face, a Flicker (the great pigeon-shaped Woodpecker) that has owned it for many years.

Round about they fly—squawk! Biff! We can now name the dark bird surely as the Starling. The Old World Starling that a bird lover, who did not think, introduced to this New World where it does not belong and is therefore a misfit, through no fault of its own.

"But," you ask, "why does its fighting the Flicker for its nest hole tell you its name?"

Because the Redwing nests in swamps and low meadows, setting its nest often on a bog tussock, and the Grackles choose trees, rarely nesting in holes of any kind. The Starlings for centuries have nested only in tree holes, the crevices between buildings, behind shutters, church towers, and belfries, or in the boxes set for other birds. For this reason, whatever its other qualities may prove, in this country the Starling is a nuisance, quarrelling with our song birds, prying them from their homes and stabbing their young most cruelly with their sharp bills.

Our beloved Bluebirds are among the chief sufferers, and I have seen fully grown Robins, who had dared to come to the same fruit tree, pecked to death.

Between the English Sparrow and Starling there is perpetual war. The Sparrow is becoming less numerous, perhaps also because there are fewer horses. For you know that the grain picked from horse-droppings was the Sparrow's chief food in winter weather.

Of the two birds the Starling is far the most unwelcome. From those few pairs set free in Central Park, New York City, in 1890–91, the flocks have spread for more than 100 miles in all directions, and this tide is still at its flood. Though the Starlings move about after the nesting season in great flocks, some are able to winter in all parts of the range. So you, who live anywhere that English Sparrows are found, may look out some morning and find that the Starling is with you; has dropped from the clouds overnight.

Starlings nest in early April, so that the flocks of mixed parents and young begin to gather in late May, all in good working order for cherry time! We may blame Robins, Catbirds, and Thrushes for berry stealing, but wait until you have seen a flock of Starlings swoop down upon my great "pie-cherry" tree, the fruit of which can be swallowed without even one bite!

Last year the crop, of several bushels, was safe in the morning; at noon all the outside cherries, at least two bushels, had been gobbled by Starlings!

In this same way the autumn and winter food of our own native birds is destroyed, bush-berries and tree fruits alike. In one day last autumn they stripped all the berries from two great Pepperidge trees in *Birdcraft Sanctuary* as quickly and more completely than they did my cherries in June.

**The Purple Finch

In size and build much like the English Sparrow. Male—body much streaked with brown and gray and washed with rose red. This colour is brightest on crown, breast and rump. Under parts whitish or light gray. Females and the young of the first season have no pink markings. They are much streaked with gray and brown and at the first glance might be taken for sparrows. The forked tail, heavy round bill and bristles over the nostrils will tell you the difference.

Though these handsome birds nest as far south as New Jersey, New York and Long Island, and are notable for their gushing, warbled song wherever they nest, they are most conspicuous when they come as winter visitors. Here at Birdcraft Sanctuary we are feeding a flock of between thirty and forty of them, about a third being the brilliantly coloured old males. They mingle with the Juncos, Tree Sparrows and all the smaller winter birds in complete accord, feeding on sunflower seeds.

Sometimes we must replenish the feeding trays two or three times a day, cold weather gives the birds such hearty appetites; besides, plenty of food is the fuel that keeps the birds warm and makes them able to stay with us.

The charming picture that they make against the snow banks and ice draped trees is pay enough for anything that humans can do for them, and then too, before they scatter to their summer homes, they always give us a joyous concert in early May.

The Federal Migratory Bird Law

State Laws for the protection of song and insect-eating birds and some other species, preventing them from being killed, possessed, or sold, have been safe-guarded and interlocked by the Federal (International) Game Laws. The result of the Convention called between the United States and Great Britain for the protection of Migratory Birds in the United States and Canada, was a Treaty signed at Washington on Aug. 16, 1916. Ratified by Great Britain, Oct. 20, 1916. Proclaimed, Dec. 8, 1916.

This treaty gives Federal protection to the birds specified, during flight over all lands and waters not covered by State protection. And such birds may nowhere be taken except by special Federal permit or for special purposes, even if unprotected by the laws of the State through which they pass.

Is not *Citizen Bird* being recognized everywhere as the property of the State and not the victim of the *Individual?*

M. O. W.

REVIEWS OF *CITIZEN BIRD*
Review in *The Auk* by Frank M. Chapman

'Citizen Bird' is a unique contribution to the literature of Ornithology.[3] It addresses an audience which ornithologists had previously neglected and does it in so attractive a manner that the reader's attention is held from cover to cover. With perhaps no desire for a knowledge of birds he is deluded into reading a story where the human element commands his interest, and if while reading he does not soon learn to care for birds for their own sake, it is because his nature is abnormally unsympathetic.

The plan of the book will explain how well adapted it is to achieve this end. 'Dr. Roy Hunter' with his daughter, nephew and niece, a country boy and two or three others, are passing the summer at 'Orchard Farm,' and the book is made up of a series of field and study talks in which the children are eager questioners and often keen observers, while the Doctor is ever present to explain in an always interesting manner the significance of the scenes from bird-life by which they are surrounded. The children themselves are so bright, the Doctor so responsive, that other children reading this record of a summer with the birds will not only become attached to its human characters, but to its feathered ones as well, and at the same time will unconsciously absorb an extensive and correct knowledge of ornithology.

The text is made more real by Mr. Fuertes's beautiful drawings, and their charm in turn is increased by the text, which makes us regard them as we would the portraits of the leading characters in a fascinating story. It is evident, therefore, that both authors and illustrator have made not only an important contribution to literature and art, but that they have rendered an invaluable service to science in so sharpening the entering wedge of bird-lore, that it may now find openings which before were closed to it.—F. M. C.

[3] Review from *The Auk* 14 (1895): 413–414.

SUPPLEMENTARY MATERIAL ON *CITIZEN BIRD* 309

Review in *Science* by Clinton Hart Merriam

Among the new books awaiting the reviewer on his recent return from the West is one which, from its authorship, attractive appearance and odd title, could not be put aside. 'Citizen Bird' is its name—a book for girls and boys.[4] It is admirably written and is illustrated by a remarkable series of original drawings.

In order to test the book, the reviewer called his children, two little girls, and read them the opening chapters. The younger (aged five years) was hardly able to follow the story, though interested in certain passages, but her elder sister (aged seven) was simply spell-bound from first to last; from which it may be inferred that the book will hold the attention of children of seven and upwards.

The subject-matter is very cleverly woven into a story of a family of bird lovers in their country home at 'Orchard Farm.' The owner of the farm, who is a doctor and something of an ornithologist, takes the children out into the woods and fields and tells them about the birds, their habits and their value to man; and afterward, in his 'wonder room,' gives them special talks on particular species, which are grouped by some easily remembered characteristic, as 'a silver-tongued family' (bluebirds, robins and thrushes), 'Peepers and Creepers' (creepers, kinglets, chickadees and nuthatches) and so on. The children at once become enthusiastic observers and ask innumerable questions, which, in the main, are admirably answered. The story is charmingly told, kindling an interest in bird-life which is kept up to the end. The child is taught a multitude of entertaining facts about nature, and at the same time filled with a healthy sentiment against the wanton destruction of birds and their eggs.

A few of the statements are a little lax from the standpoint of scientific precision, and one or two of the incidents narrated are liable to tax one's credulity, as when one of the boys tells of brushing newly-fallen snow from the back of a live woodcock on its nest; but the book as a whole may be commended as by far the best bird book for boys and girls yet produced in America.

The illustrations deserve more than passing notice. They are uncommonly good half-tone reproductions of wash drawings by young Fuertes, whose phenomenal talent in grasping bird attitudes was first brought to the attention of the public in Miss Florence A. Merriam's 'A' Birding on a Bronco'. The present series of more than a hundred drawings, published for the first time in 'Citizen

---

[4] Review from *Science* 6, no. 149 (1897): 706–707.

Bird,' fully sustains the artist's reputation. As would be expected in so large a series, a few are indifferent, but by far the greater number are remarkable for beauty, fidelity and power of expression. The pictures alone are worth the price of the book.

The typography and press work are of a high order of excellence, and the publishers are to be congratulated on the exceptional skill shown by their printer in handling difficult text figures. It is refreshing to find a book in the field of popular natural history which so distinctly raises the standard for its class and at the same time is offered for sale at so low a price.

C.H.M.

Review in *Nature* by W. Warde Fowler

This book consists of a series of pleasant dialogues between Dr. Roy Hunter and some children, at Orchard Farm in New England, in which the children learn the appearance and habits of a great number of the birds around them. It has been rather unfairly compared in a daily paper to "Sandford and Merton." It must be allowed that the didactic dialogue is apt to be tiresome, and in this case the children are of course a little unnatural in their acuteness and their ardent desire to learn. English boys would probably learn better from a sound and scholarly handbook: one in whose hands I to-day placed Sir Humphry Davy's "Salmonia," after a few days' trout-fishing, not unjustly complained that Halieutes and his pupils always caught exactly the fish they wanted—which was not the case when he was fishing. It may perhaps be doubted whether the experiment would answer on this side the water.

But the familiar names of Dr. Coues and Miss M. A. Wright are a more than sufficient guarantee of the excellence of the ornithological part of the book, and to English students of bird-life it will be of real value. Here we have the actual every-day life of the birds most familiar to the New Englander, which very few of us can hope ever to study in their own homes. Many of them, of course, closely resemble our own, and a very few are identical with ours. But the great majority are new to us, and of these we learn very pleasantly from this book something that we could not have picked up except by crossing the Atlantic our-selves. The photographic illustrations are excellent; and there is a useful index and a classification of North American birds. But perhaps the best thing in the book is the account given by Mammy Bun, the negress, of the mocking-bird as she knew it in the Southern States.

W. WARDE FOWLER.

MACMILLAN CIRCULAR IN *THE CRITIC* PROMOTING *CITIZEN BIRD*[5]

See page 312.

TRANSLATION OF MAMMY BUN SPEECH INTO STANDARD AMERICAN ENGLISH (EXCERPT FROM *CITIZEN BIRD*, CHAPTER 11)

The children followed Olive to the house and soon returned leading mammy, who was chuckling and out of breath, but evidently much pleased to be asked. She could not be persuaded to try the apple-tree perch, so they made her a sort of throne at the foot of the tree and sat respectfully in a row in front of her. Mammy wore a dark-blue print dress with some white figures on it, and she had a plaid handkerchief tied turban fashion around her head. As she talked she waved her hands a good deal, and her words had a soft comfortable sound like molasses pouring out of a big stone jug.

"Do I know the mockingbird? I reckon so—it's about the first thing I did know, except how to eat sugar-cane. Sugar-cane is good eating long into the early fall, but the Mocker ain't doing much singing by this time, at least not unless he's in a cage in a good sunshiny place. He's a kind of a pert gray bird, darker in some places, lighter in others, and clean as a parson. But come spring and time for planting the cotton seed, the Mocker he knows mighty well what's a-doin'. Along in March he comes into the bushes and orange scrub around the field making a fuss and telling folks to get along to work, or there won't be no cotton, and he keeps it straight up all the day long til' the cotton's out of bloom. All the day long kind of chatterin' and hurryin' the slaves up when they're dropping the seed in the line and scoldin' and hurryin' all the day long, where they're a-hoein' down the weeds. Then when it becomes night, the she-bird keep close on the

---

[5] Circular by Macmillan and Co. in *The Critic* 28, no. 808 (1897): n.p.

NEW BOOKS MACMILLAN COMPANY.

PUBLISHED BY THE

FOR THE YOUNG FOLKS. · FIFTH THOUSAND.

CITIZEN BIRD: A Story of Bird Life for Beginners.

By

MABEL OSGOOD WRIGHT,
Author of " Birdcraft," " Tommy Anne," etc.

Cloth, 12mo, $1.50.

and

Dr. ELLIOTT COUES.
Author of " Birds of North America," etc.

Illustrated with Drawings from Nature by LOUIS AGASSIZ FUERTES.

A charming story for the young people, which contains not only much Information about the life of birds in general, but also a guide to all the chief varieties of North American birds, their habits, economic value, etc.

" Teachers of natural science will find in Mrs. Wright's 'Citizen Bird' a delightful book for young people, written especially for those who are making a beginning in the study of bird life."— *From the New York Times*

" 'Citizen Bird ' is a delightful and at the same time a most instructive book. None of us know as much as we ought about birds, and whether old or young we can easily increase our knowledge by spending an hour or two in perusing 'Citizen Bird.' "— *From the New York Herald*

" There is no other book in existence so well fitted for arousing and directing the interest that all children of any sensibility feel towards the birds. — *From the Chicago Tribune.*

The Rural Science Series.

Edited by Professor L. H. BAILEY, Cornell University. Two new volumes.

The Principles of Fruit Growing.
Fundamentals Common to all kinds of Fruit Growing.

By Prof. L. H. BAILEY,
Professor of Horticulture, Cornell University
Cloth, 12mo, $1.25.

The Fertility of the Land:
A Discussion of the Relationship of Farm Practice to Saving and Augmenting the Productivity of the Soil.

By I. P. ROBERTS,
Director of the College of Agriculture Cornell University.
Fully Illustrated. $1.25.

Genesis of the Social Conscience.

The Relation between the Establishment of Christianity in Europe and the Social Question.

By HENRY S. NASH. *Professor in the Episcopal Theological School, Cambridge.*
Cloth, 12mo, $1.50.

" Professor Nash's volume fulfils the promise of its title. It does more, indeed, for the author is something more and better than a mere epitomizer of other men's thoughts Not only is his treatment of the great thesis which he has undertaken to discuss free and suggestive, but he shows himself to be a clear and original thinker."— From *The Tribune*, New York.

The Myths of Israel.

The Ancient Book of Genesis, with Analysis and Explanation of its Composition.

By AMOS K. FISKE,
Author of " The Jewish Scriptures," etc.
Cloth, 12mo, $1.50.

The author resolves the ancient Hebrew Book of Genesis into its component myths, explaining their significance and bearing in the literary and religious development of the Hebrew people.

The Social Teachings of Jesus:
An Essay in Christian Sociology.

By Professor SHAILER MATTHEWS, *Chicago University.*
Cloth, 12mo. *In Press*

It is based on the belief that Jesus as a strong thinker must have had some central truth of conception. Starting with this fundamental conception, the author endeavors to trace its application by Jesus himself to various aspects of social life.

NEW NOVELS FOR SUMMER HOLIDAY READING.

The Grey Lady.
By HENRY SETON MERRIMAN.
Cloth, crown 8vo, $1.50.

" Deeply interesting, original, and cleverly constructed."—*The Oakland Tribune.*

The Choir Invisible.
By JAMES LANE ALLEN,
Author of " A Kentucky Cardinal."
Cloth, cr. 8vo, $1.50.

In the Tideway.
By FLORA ANNIE STEEL,
Author of " On the Face of the Waters."
Cloth, 16mo, $1.25.

A Rose of Yesterday.

By F. MARION CRAWFORD. *Author of " Casa Braccio," etc* Cloth, Crown 8vo, $1.25.

Mr. Crawford is, as ANDREW LANG says, "the most versatile and various of modern novelists. . . . A master of the narrative style, he throws a subtle charm over all he touches." Mr Allen, also, so Bliss Carman writes, is "one of the best of our novelists to-day," with "a prose style of wonderful beauty," while Mrs. Steel's new book is described as ' a piece of evenly brilliant writing "

SHORT STORIES.

In the Land of the Snow Pearls.
Tales of Puget Sound.
By Mrs. ELLA HIGGINSON.
Cloth, cr 8vo, $1.50.

Old Times in Middle Georgia.
By the Author of " Dukesborough Tales."
By R. MALCOLM JOHNSTON.
Cloth, cr 8vo, $1.50.

Each of these volumes is a picture of life in one section of the country, very successful in preserving the local atmosphere. As the Detroit *Free Press* says of the tales of Puget Sound, "there is not a dull story in the book." To Mr. Johnston we owe the permanent possession of a view of life which now belongs to a vanished past.

JUST READY.

With the Turkish Army in Thessaly.

By CLIVE BIGHAM, *Author of " A Ride Through Western Asia "*
With Illustrations and Maps Cloth, 8vo Price, $2.50.

" This is the book which was reviewed at some length in the NATION last week with comments on the writer's "essential fairness," "studiously clear descriptions," " the powerful interest of his story," etc , and with the following paragraph in conclusion :

" The unity of effect achieved in this narrative is so happy that those who read it may almost regret as time misspent the attention given to piecemeal reports published in the daily press as the war proceeded A certain futility of perspective and lack of proportion is unavoidable so long as the events described are in progress, and renders the rearranging of a war correspondent's original material before it appears in permanent form obviously necessary. This has rarely been done to better purpose than in the present book."

ADDRESS

THE MACMILLAN COMPANY,   -   **66 Fifth Avenue, New York.**

---

nest, and the he-bird go in the scrub or the redwoods or the ginkgoes, near the clearin,' maybe right on the cabin roof, and he says to himself—"Now the slaves have done their work, I'll give them a tune to encourage them. Then he just lets himself begin his singin'. Sometimes he sings brave and bold, like he is saying big words like the missus and the folks that live in the big house. Then he whispers soft and low without any words, jest like a mammy was a-singin' to her baby. Then again he sings kind of soft and wheedlesome, like Sam when he comes a-courtin' me. Sure, now! Come to think of Sam, he never did like Mockers after one time he suspected a Mocker told tales on him. Master Branscome—he was a mighty fine man and your grand-dad, Miss Olive—he said he wouldn't have no person rob the nests of Mockers, not anywhere on his plantations. They did eat a pile o' fruit, but that was nothing. First place, he just loved to hear them sing and then he allowed that they were powerful fond of cotton worms, which were mighty bad some years.

"Now lots of slaves, they used to steal the young Mockers just before they left the nest and sell 'em to white trash that would tote 'em down the river and sell 'em again in New Orleans, to be fetched off in ships. And I used to hear tell that there ain't any such birds in other countries, and that the kings and queens just give their gold crowns off their heads to have a cage of Mockers.

"Those slaves never got no gold crowns, however. What they got was mostly a quarter for three he-birds. Now Sam was courtin' and wanted a banjo, and he didn't want no common truck, so he went to get one from New Orleans. So he agreed to pay for it in Mockers, and he thought he knew where he get them for sure. Mockers don't nest in the woods and wild places. They always keep round the plantations near where folks live.

"He knew he was doing wrong and he felt mighty uncomfortable; but he done took the young Mockers on our plantation right under the Master's nose. He was crafty and only took one out of each nest and at night when the old birds never miss them. When he got the banjo about paid for, that time he took a whole nestful of one of them and the birds that it belonged to saw what he was a-doin' and gave him a piece of their mind, and followed him around all day and sat on the roof of his quarters and talked all night, and told him to bring back those Mockers or they'd tell; and Sam was scared and wanted to put the birds back but he didn't. The next day, he supposed the he-Mocker went up to the big house, and told the Master about it, and he and Miss Jessamine—that was your ma—they came down to the quarters and told Sam he done took Mockers and asked what had he done with all of them. And he almost turned white, and he said, 'I sold them down the river'; and Master said, 'I have a great mind to sell you down the river too'—but he never sold nothing—gave us all our freedom. Now, no slave wants to be sold down the river, and Sam said, 'Oh, Miss Jessamine, here's three I didn't sell, and I'll give 'em back to that he-bird and ask his pardon.' Master he laughed and said, 'If that he-bird will excuse you, I will.' So Sam put 'em back and the he-bird acted as if he knew and talked a lot o' good advice to Sam, but I'm sure it was another slave that told on Sam.

"They used to have a song about the Mockers around the slave cabins, and a dance that went with it, because it was a very long song; but after that Sam done change it some when he used to sing it."

"A BIRD CLASS FOR CHILDREN," BY MABEL OSGOOD WRIGHT

One of the most frequent questions asked by those seeking to win children to an appreciation of birds is, "How, when we have awakened the interest, can we keep it alive?"[6]

The only way to accomplish this, to my thinking, is to take the children out-of-doors and introduce them to the 'bird in the bush,' to the bird as a citizen of a social world as real in all its duties and requirements as our own.

There is a group of people with ultra theoretical tendencies, who insist upon considering the bird merely as a feathered vertebrate that must not be in any way humanized, or taken from its perch in the evolutionary scheme, to be brought to the plane of our daily lives. In teaching children, I believe in striving to humanize the bird as far as is consistent with absolute truth, that the child may, through its own love of home, parents, and its various desires, be able to appreciate the corresponding traits in the bird. How can this best be done? By reading to children? That is one way; and good, accurate, and interesting bird books are happily plentiful. But when the outdoor season comes, little heads grow tired of books, and anything that seems like a lesson is repugnant.

Then comes the chance to form a bird class, or a bird party, if the word class seems too formidable. A dozen children are quite enough to be easily handled. The ages may range from six to twelve. Arrange to have them meet outdoors once a week, in the morning, during June and July. A pleasant garden or a vineclad piazza will do for a beginning; it is inadvisable to tire children by taking them far afield until they have learned to identify a few very common birds in their natural surroundings.

---

[6] Mabel Osgood Wright, "A Bird Class for Children," *Bird-Lore* 1, no. 3 (1899): 100–101.

SUPPLEMENTARY MATERIAL ON *CITIZEN BIRD* 315

Children who are familiar with even the very best pictures of birds must at first be puzzled by seeing the real bird at a distance, and perhaps partly screened by foliage. The value of the outdoor bird class is, that to be successful it must teach rapid and accurate personal observation.

"Very true," you say, "but the birds will not stay still while the children are learning to observe." Yes; yet this difficulty may be met in two ways. If you are so situated that you can borrow say twenty-five mounted birds from a museum or the collection of a friend, you will have a very practical outfit.

Choose four or five birds, not more for one day, take them outdoors, and place them in positions that shall resemble their natural haunts as much as possible. For example, place the Song Sparrow in a little bush, the Bluebird on a post, and the Chippy on a path. Let the children look at them near by and then at a distance, so that a sense of proportion and color value will be developed unconsciously.

After this, the written description of the habits of the birds, which you must read or tell the children, will have a different meaning. This method may be varied by looking up live specimens of the birds thus closely observed.

"True," you say again, "but I cannot beg or borrow any mounted birds."

Then take the alternative. Buy from the Massachusetts Audubon Society, 234 Berkeley St., Boston, for a dollar, one of its Audubon Bird Charts. This chart is printed in bright colors and is accompanied by a little pamphlet describing the twenty-six common birds that are figured. These are the (1) Downy Woodpecker, (2) Flicker, (3) Chimney Swift, (4) Ruby-throated Hummingbird, (5) Kingbird, (6) Bluejay, (7) Bobolink, (8) Red-winged Blackbird, (9) Baltimore Oriole, (10) Purple Finch, (11) American Goldfinch, (12) Chipping Sparrow, (13) Song Sparrow, (14) Scarlet Tanager, (15) Barn Swallow, (16) Cedar Bird, (17) Red-eyed Vireo, (18) Black and White Warbler, (19) Yellow Warbler, (20) Catbird, (21) House Wren, (22) Chickadee, (23) Golden-crowned Kinglet, (24) Wood Thrush, (25) American Robin, (26) Bluebird. Cut the birds carefully from the chart, back them with cardboard, and either mount them on little wooden blocks, like paper dolls, or arrange them with wires, so that they can be fastened to twigs or bushes.

You will be surprised to find how this scheme will interest the children, who may be allowed sometimes to place the birds themselves.

For those too old for the cut-out pictures, the teachers' edition of 'Bird-Life', with the colored plates in portfolios, will be found invaluable. The separate pictures may be taken outdoors and placed in turn on an easel behind a leaf-covered frame, with excellent effects—a few natural touches and the transition from indoors out often changing one's entire point of view.

One thing bearing on the question of bird study. If children ask you questions that you cannot answer, as they surely will, do not hesitate to say "I don't know."

Never fill their minds with fables guised as science, that they must unlearn.

Now a material point. When you have entertained your class for an hour, never more, lend the affair a picnic ending and give them a trifling lunch before they go; something very simple will do—cookies and milk, or even animal crackers! The young animal of the human species, as well as many others, is a complexity of stomach and brain, and it is well to administer food to each in just proportion.

M.O.W.

APPENDIX 2

Historical Materials on Nineteenth-Century Birding and Audubon

"THE SPRING SONG" BY MABEL OSGOOD WRIGHT AND ORIGINAL COVER

The Spring Song

What tidings hath the Swallow heard
That bids her leave the lands of summer
For woods and fields where April yields
Bleak welcome to the blithe newcomer?—Bourdillon.[1]

The trees are leafless, and there are snow patches in nooks and corners; the air is laden with chilly gusts, but at noon a little softness creeps into it; the days, though gray, hold twelve hours of light, and the vernal equinox is at hand.

Come to the window, my friend, you who are going to spend some days, weeks, or months upon the bird-quest. You say that you see nothing but the bare trees, not even "the sun making dust and the grass growing green," like sister Anne in the fairy tale. Open your window, or better still, go into the porch, for a procession is soon to pass, and you must hear the music. Listen! on the branch of the oak where the leaves still cling is the bugler, the Song Sparrow, calling through the silence, "They come! They come! They come! Prepare the way."

Then presently, instead of tramping feet, you will hear the rustling of the innumerable wings of the bird army. Happy for you if it is a long time in passing and if a large part of it camps for the season. Usually it sends forward a few scouts, and then a company or two, before the brigade, clad in its faultless

[1] Mabel Osgood Wright, "The Spring Song," excerpt from *Birdcraft* (New York: Macmillan and Co., 1895).

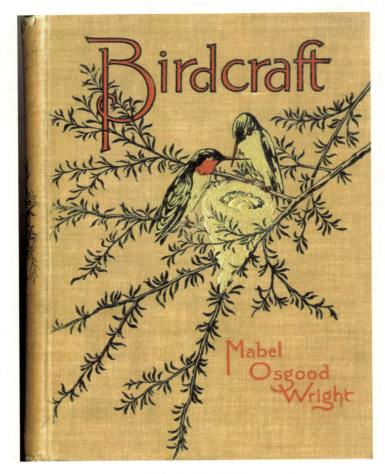

Birdcraft cover, 1895.

dress uniform, sweeps on, singing the greatest choral symphony of Nature,—the Spring Song.

There are many reasons, both of fact and of fancy, why it is best to begin the study of birds in the spring. The untrained eye becomes gradually accustomed to its new vocation before it is overtaxed. The matter of eyesight is of the first importance in the study of the living bird. Is your sight sufficiently good to allow you to exercise it in this way? The birds that you study will not be in the hand, but in the bush.

You may be accustomed to an out-door life, you may comprehend at a glance all the details of a landscape, or be able to detect a particular flower fields away; but in the quest of a bird which is oftentimes on the wing, your eyes will be obliged to distinguish certain details in a moving object backgrounded by a dazzling sky, and at the next moment refocus, to discover a bird, with perhaps very dull plumage, who is eluding you by circling in the black shadows of the pines. Thus you will be either peering into dim recesses or facing the strongest light twenty times to a single chance of seeing a bird in a clear light, with his plumage accentuated by a suitable background. If you squint and cannot face the sun, you must study birds in the museums, or learn to know them by their songs alone; a field-glass will lengthen the sight, but it will not give the ability to endure light.

Many people think that a bird wears the same plumage and sings the same songs all the year round, and expect to identify it by some easy and inflexible rule, which shall apply to all seasons and circumstances, but this is impossible.

When the birds come to us in spring they wear their perfect and typical plumage and are in the best voice, as befits those who are going courting. The male wears the most showy, or at least the most distinctly marked coat, and is generally slightly larger than the female, except in the case of Owls and a few others, where the female is the larger. In many families there is very little variation between the colouring of the male and female, and at a short distance you would probably notice none, except that the female is the paler of the two. But sometimes the difference is so marked that the novice invariably mistakes the female for a bird of another species; hence the importance of describing the plumage of both sexes.

The Scarlet Tanager has a green mate (there is great wisdom in this—a brilliant brooding bird would betray the location of the nest); the female Hummingbird lacks the ruby throat of her spouse; and the wife of the sleek black, white, and buff Bobolink wears sober brown. When the birds arrive in the spring, these colour distinctions are marked; but after the nesting time, which occurs mostly in May and June, a fresh complication arises. The young birds on leaving the nest, though fully grown perhaps and capable of strong flight, often wear hybrid feathers in which the characteristics of both parents are mingled. Soon after this time the summer moulting takes place, for the majority of birds moult twice a year. August is the time of this moulting. The jubilant love-song ceases, and the birds, dishevelled and moping, keep well in the shelter of the trees or retreat to the woods, as they are weakened and their power of flight is diminished. After the moulting comes another disturbing element, not only for the novice, but for those well versed in bird ways; with many birds the colours of the spring plumage are either wholly changed or greatly modified, and though the song may be in a measure renewed for a brief season, it is infrequent and not always true. The young birds are now associating with the old and adding their attempts at warbling, so that I think the snares that lie in the way of beginning the study of Song-birds after midsummer are quite evident.

The male Bobolink, after moulting, becomes brown like the female; the American Goldfinch, a late moulter, turns a dull olive; but the Bluebird's new feathers are rusty; many Warblers lose their identifying bands and streaks while the Baltimore Oriole keeps his flaming feathers.

After this moulting the bird's life as an individual ceases for a season; he is no longer swayed by sex, but by the flocking impulse of self-preservation, and in this case it is not always birds of a feather that flock together.

In the early spring, when the relaxing touch of the sun is felt, the second moulting occurs, and the feathers that have borne the wear and tear of winter give place to the fresh new coat, and the bird throat swells with the Spring Song.

From a residential standpoint, we have four distinct grades of birds to consider:—

I. The summer residents: Those birds which, coming to us in the spring, rear their young, and after shifting about somewhat in late summer, retreat more or less southward for the winter.

II. The residents: Comprising those species which are represented by individuals all the year round.

III. The winter residents: The birds who are inhabitants of boreal regions, breeding beyond the northern border of the United States, coming only to us in winter, and retiring northward at the time of the general upward migration.

IV. The migrants: Birds that are with us for a few weeks in spring, en route from the south to their more northern breeding haunts, and are also visible for a similar period during the return trip in autumn. We may class with these the casual visitors that appear for a brief visit either summer or winter.

The two movements of bird life in spring and fall are known as the great migrations, some birds being plentiful in spring and quite rare in the autumn, and vice versa, as the path chosen for the upward and downward trip may not be the same. The individuals belonging to these classes will be specified in turn, and they are mentioned here to show you that if you do not begin the bird-quest in spring, in time to meet the army of migrants, you may miss some of the most interesting species.

Conspicuous among the birds that lodge with us in April and May, letting us hear their song for a brief period, is the great Fox Sparrow, the White-throated and White-crowned Sparrows, the group of lovely Warblers, and, best of all, the Hermit Thrush, whose heavenly notes of invocation, if once heard, are never forgotten.

If you are ready for this quest when the sun crosses the equinox the 21. of March, you will be in good time, and your labours will be lightened by studying the birds as they come one by one, hearing each voice in a solo, before all have gathered in late May and individual notes blend in the chorus. In this locality there is very little general upward movement before the vernal equinox, for the weather is too capricious. A few Song Sparrows and Bluebirds begin to sing, but the Yellowbirds that have wintered with us are still wearing their old coats, and have not broken into song. Last spring (1894) I noted in my diary the return of the Song Sparrows March 5, but the flocks of Bluebirds and Robins did not come until the 13. when a flock of a hundred or more Fox Sparrows also arrived, and the White-throated Sparrows followed them.

The birds oftentimes arrive singly or by twos or threes, and then again suddenly in great flocks. One afternoon there may not be a White-throat in sight, the next morning they will be feeding upon the ground like a drift of brown leaves. Almost all birds migrate at night, and every dawn will show you some new arrival, pluming and drying his feathers in the first rays of the sun. Birds who depend upon insect diet, like the Phoebe, the commonest of the fly-catchers, may arrive too soon, before insect life has quickened, and suffer much through their miscalculation. Often the appearance of individuals of a species does not indicate the beginning of the general return, as they may be birds that have not gone far away, but have merely been roving about all winter.

From the last of March until the first of June the spring migration is in full swing, some of the earlier birds to arrive will have passed on, before the Tanagers and Black-polls, and other late Warblers, appear. The last week of May the Spring Song is at its height; let us look at the order in which the singers begin and end their daily music.

You must be up in the long twilight that precedes dawn, if you wish to hear the little precentor—the Chipping Sparrow—give the signal on his shrill pitch pipe. Then the Song Sparrow sounds his reveille of three notes and a roulade—"Maids, maids, maids, put your kettle-ettle on." The Robin answers with his clarion notes, and the Bluebird, mildly plaintive, seems to regret that the quiet night is past, and sighs—"Dear, dear, think of it, think of it." Then the various Swallows begin their twitterings, and the Chimney Swift redoubles his winged pursuit of insects, and the Purple Martins, rising in pairs, coquette in mid-air, and their cheerful warble seems to drop from the clouds. As it becomes light, the Phoebe joins his "Pewit, phoebe-a," with the Wood Pewee's—"Pewee, pewee peer," and the Field Sparrow whistles and trills somewhat in the key of the Chipping Sparrow. Then up from the meadow wells the song of the Bobolink, our only bird that rivals the English Lark in singing and soaring, pouring out its delicious melody with virile fervour, while in the same field the Meadowlark rings his bell-like—"Spring o' the year, spring o' the year!" and the Indigo Bunting lisps from the briars.

One by one, the Oriole, the Song and Wood Thrushes, the Mourning Dove, Catbird, Towhee, Wrens, Warblers, Chat, and the obstreperous Vireos chime in. These are the birds that you may hear in your garden and the near-by meadows. Down in the lowlands the Red-winged Blackbird "flutes his okalee," the Crows keep up an incessant cawing, and in the woods between these lands and the marshes, the Herons cry; while from the marshes themselves the Snipe call. The flocking Sandpipers "peep" from the beach edge, and the migrating Ducks call as they settle in the flags.

Above the inland woods the Nighthawk, the Whip-poor-will's kinsman, skirling, circles a few times before hiding from day. There are Hawk cries, as Cooper's Hawk (the dreaded chicken-killer) bears a tender morsel to her nestlings already well fledged, who are in the top of the tall hickory, and the Quail whistles "Bob-white! Poor Bob-white!" the Ruffed Grouse clucks henlike, and the Woodcock calls like his brother Snipe.

It is in these woods, within sound of running water, that you may hear the Veery, though he is not so much the bird of dawn as of twilight, and in this same spot some day the Hermit Thrush may give a rehearsal for your private ear, of the music with which he will soon thrill the northern woods.

This is the Matin Song. When it ceases, you must watch for the individual birds as they go to and fro, feeding or building, or perching on some favourite twig to sing, either to their mates or from pure exultation. From nine o'clock in the morning until five in the afternoon, the principal singers are the Bobolink, Meadowlark, Vireos; the Redstart, who declares that every morsel he swallows is "Sweet, sweet, sweeter!" the Black-throated Green Warbler, who flashes his yellow feathers calling, "Will you co-ome, will you co-ome, will you?" the sprightly Maryland Yellow-throat, who almost beckons as he dashes about laughing,

"Follow me, follow me"; the Baltimore Oriole, who alternately blows his mellow horn or complains querulously; and the Song Sparrow, who sings equally at all times.

Towards five o'clock the Evensong begins, and the Purple Finch, perching in the elm top, warbles in continuous bursts—"List to me, list to me, hear me, and I'll tell you, you, you," each peal being more vigorous than the last. The Wood Thrushes take up their harp-like "Uoli Uoli-, aeo-lee-lee," the Vesper Sparrow tunes, the birds of morning follow, one by one; but there are new voices that we did not hear in the matinal that continue after the chorus is hushed—the Rose-breasted Grosbeak, the Veery, and the Whip-poor-will.

The Veery rings his echo notes in the morning also, but his evensong is the best; and, as the dusk deepens, his notes have a more solemn quality. The Grosbeak has a sweet, rounded, warbling song that it is difficult to render in syllables intelligently, but when you hear it in the twilight you will know it, because it is unlike anything else. The Mockingbird is not heard freely as a night singer in this latitude, but further south he gives his best song only to the night wind; not his mocking, jeering ditty of squeaks and cat-calls, but his natural heart-song; and when you hear it, you may listen for the martial note of the Cardinal, who seems to tell the hours, adding to each—"All's well." Then the Whip-poor-will calls, and the Owls answer, hooting, laughing, purring, according to the specific note.

When you go through garden, lane, and wood, on your happy quest, circling the marshes that will not yield you foothold, remember that if you wish to hear the Spring Song and identify the singers, you must yourself be in tune, and you must be alert in keeping the record, lest the troop slip by through the open doorway of the trees, leaving you to regret your carelessness all the year.

As you listen to the song and look at the birds, many will disappear, and you will know that these are the migrants who have gone to their various breeding haunts; and that those who are busy choosing their building sites, and are carrying straw, clay and twigs, are the summer residents. Then you must glide quietly among the trees to watch the next scene of the bird year—the building of the nest—which is the motive of the Spring Song, and you will feel that in truth—

"Hard is the heart that loveth nought
In May."

"COLLECTING BIRDS' EGGS."

If it be true that the child, in his individual life from the cradle up, is a fair representative of the various stages in the advance of the race, then at some particular period every boy must be a young savage.[2] One peculiarity of the savage is his recklessness of life, and it is therefore important that the boy should be educated out of that stage as fast as possible. It is sometimes hard to do this, and at the same time develop a taste for natural history. But the two can go hand in hand, if there be wise instructors. Is it wise, however, as has been suggested, to advise the robbing of birds' nests as one step in this development in street boys? Even those who should know better destroy many rare birds by taking the eggs. The rarer the birds, indeed, the more diligently does the professional collector seek for their eggs.

Mr. Eldridge E. Fish, the author of that charming book The Blessed Birds, says with reference to this: "The Agassiz Association, itself a worthy organization, with laudable aims, soon had thousands in its ranks who degenerated into mere specimen-gatherers. The egg-collecting craze infected boys alike in cities, villages, and rural districts. The country was scoured far and near for nests and eggs. Lawns, hedges, orchards, fields, and highways were mercilessly ransacked, and every nest, common or rare, despoiled; even cemeteries, always favorite resorts for the birds, were not exempt from the destroyer. Within the last few years millions of eggs have thus been destroyed, and little scientific knowledge gained by this manner of study.... I have had thousands brought to me by boys for identification.... The boys had little or no knowledge of the subject, often not knowing what species they had robbed. These eggs were to them as so many marbles, or other toys,—trophies, valuable only as objects of barter; but the effects on the bird population were none the less injurious. Our birds have all been identified and described, and a further persecution of them in that direction is selfishly barbarous, and ought not longer to be tolerated."

[2] "Collecting Birds' Eggs," unsigned article from *Atlantic Monthly*, February 1895, p. 288.

HISTORICAL MATERIALS   325

By all means let the boys learn to know the birds. Mr. H. E. Parkhurst, in The Birds' Calendar, tells how that can be done without killing a bird or robbing a nest. And if boys wish to know more about the eggs of the different species, any city lad can have the privilege of studying eggs at the various natural history museums, and can exercise his skill in other directions by making wax imitations of them. A complete description of the way to do this is given in The Extermination of Birds, by Edith Carrington.

An egg seems a trifle, but if it is the cradle from which might have sprung a wood thrush or a bobolink, it is a serious loss to crush it.

One of the surest ways of acquiring an influence over rough boys is to instill into their hearts a love of nature, or rather to develop that love which is dormant in most of us. But is it not better, along with such an education, to give also lessons in self control; to teach them to find nests, study them, and even examine the eggs, without touching them; to gather for botanical purposes only as many flowers as are really necessary, leaving some to beautify the earth and to multiply their kind; to study trees without girdling the trunks; and to hunt for frog spawn without stoning the frogs? A genuine love of nature means such sympathy with all nature's children, animal and vegetable, that the lover learns to exercise a jealous care lest they suffer at his hands. With this proviso, let the street boys go into the fields and woods; the more of them, the better.

"PUNCH'S PLEA FOR THE WHITE-PLUMED HERONS."

"BUTCHERED to make a Roman holiday,"[3]
That roused hard anger in indignant metre
Butchered to make a lady's bonnet gray!—
    Sounds that much sweeter?
Little white heron, with the shoulder plume
Which stirs the milliner's remorseless passion,
You guess not how your finery seals your doom
    At beck of Fashion.
The little egret's nuptial plumes are sought

---

[3] "Punch's Plea for the White-Plumed Herons (An Appeal to all English Ladies with Pitiful Hearts)," *Punch*, February 29, 1896.

Above all other feathers by Eve's daughter,
And hence the heronry with woe is fraught,
  A scene of slaughter.
Poor, pretty, bridal-plumed, nest-loyal birds,
At breeding-time alone you grow gregarious.
The hunter comes, and scenes too sad for words
  Grieve e'en the hilarious.
The mothers hovering near their helpless brood,
Are shot in hundreds; 'tis such easy killing!
The plumelets are plucked out, since they are good
  For many a shilling.
The young birds starve, whilst, festering in white heaps,
Their displumed parents lie in scores about them.
When men say at the thought their chill blood creeps,
  Will ladies doubt them?
Male thralls of Mammon do the murderous deed,
But if the slaves of Mode could feel compassion,
Young herons need not starve, nor old ones bleed.
  To—follow Fashion!
The heronries are fast destroyed, 'tis said,
The pretty egrets fast exterminated.
It seems a pity! Betwixt Mode and Trade
  Are the birds fated?
Nay, lovely woman, prithee just say "Nay"
In mere humanity and love of beauty!
Punch loves the sex, and to his pets would pray,
  "Dears—do your duty!"

"DESTRUCTION OF BIRDS."

Twenty to thirty years ago it was not an unusual sight to see even the scarlet tanager, a bright red bird with black wings and tail, flitting from tree to tree in the heart of our cities like a fiery meteor in the sunlight, and to find their nests, built very lightly of straws and similar material, on the horizontal limbs of our shade trees.[4]

---

[4] "Destruction of Birds," *Locomotive Engineer's Monthly Journal*, March 1887.

HISTORICAL MATERIALS 327

But they were killed off and driven back to the woods long before the advent of bird millinery as a fashion. They were, indeed, a "shining mark," and everybody wanted a specimen, or thought they did, until at the present time the scarlet tanager is really a very rare bird throughout the New England States.

The Baltimore oriole, so named because the colors of the bird, black and yellow, resembled those of Lord Baltimore, has almost met the same fate, as it has done duty in ornamenting thousands of ladies' bonnets within the past five years. Four years ago this bird was quite plenty on the elms of Boston and suburbs. The hanging nests, made of hemp, old twine, etc., were quite common. But the past season showed a great change. These birds have been shot so ruthlessly, both while here and at the South, and during the migration, that hardly a pair could be found during the breeding season of 1886. The ragged nests are occasionally seen, belonging to years gone by, as it sometimes takes the storms of many winters to beat them to the ground. If the different societies organized to protect our native birds do their whole duty, these beautifully plumaged insectivorous birds will soon become common once more.

YOUNG WOMAN MODELING FEATHERED HAT[5]

See page 328.

"ON THE PRESENT STATUS OF PASSER DOMESTICUS IN AMERICA, WITH SPECIAL REFERENCE TO THE WESTERN STATES AND TERRITORIES," BY ELLIOTT COUES

Now that the enormous increase and rapid dispersion of the European House Sparrow in America have resulted in the appearance of this objectionable bird in various portions of the Western States and Territories, it is time to consider what means may be taken to check for its westward extension; for the agriculturists of that portion of our country have already enough to do to content with the grasshopper scourge without having to guard their crops against a plague only

---

[5] *Young Woman Modeling: Back view, head and shoulders, wearing feathered hat,* photograph by Fitz W. Guerin, n.d.

less formidable and imminent.[6] Should the noxious birds become as numerous and as widely diffused in the West as they are already in the thickly-settled portions of the United States, they would there prove even more destructive to the crops than they are known to be in the East. For here they still live for the most part in cities, towns, and villages, where they derive their subsistence chiefly from street-garbage, especially horse-manure; but in the West, where such supplies are limited, these granivorous birds would at once and continually prey upon the crops. I am not informed to what extent they may have multiplied already in some of the places, as at Salt Lake City, to which they have been transported, and where they have obtained a foothold; but it may not be too late, if vigorous measures are taken at once, to stamp out the plague. The strongholds of the birds are few, comparatively speaking, and isolated to such a degree that the eradication of the birds from that part of the United States may not be now absolutely impracticable, as unfortunately seems to be the case in the East. The Great Plains offer a natural barrier to the westward progress of the birds from the Mississippi; and if pains be taken to destroy the advance guard as fast as they move westward, the evils now suffered in the East may be long delayed or even avoided. In most parts of the West where the Sparrows have appeared, it is believed that they have been imported, not that they reached these spots by spontaneous migration or natural dispersion. If this be the case, indeed, it may not be a matter of the greatest difficulty to destroy them, root and branch, in the comparatively few places in which they have already become naturalized. Should this be done, and laws be passed prohibiting the introduction of the birds into the Western States and Territories, immunity from invasion might be secured for a practically unlimited period. To bring this

---

[6] Elliott Coues, "On the Present Status of Passer Domesticus in America, with Special Reference to the Western States and Territories," United States Geological and Geographical Survey, 1879.

matter to the attention of the people in the West, and to urge that such measures be taken without further dangerous delay, is the object of the present paper.

This may seem like an extreme course, to the few who still look favorably upon the presence of the Sparrow in America; but such may be assured that it is no more than the exigencies of the case demand. Unless the Sparrows can be made to devour grasshoppers, there is absolutely no occasion for their naturalization in the West, not even the flimsy excuse for them that we sometimes hear made in the East. That they will not subsist upon grasshoppers to any extent or upon potato beetles, may be regarded as a foregone conclusion; and in the absence of other sources of food supply, they will infallibly fall upon the crops.

Though it must appear to all well-informed persons a work of supererogation to point out what mischief the Sparrows have done, what worse evils are in prospect, and what thoroughly undesirable birds these are from every standpoint, yet the people of the West may not be fully apprised as yet of the actual state of the case. Their attention is therefore called to the present status of the Sparrow in America, as fully exhibited in the following review of the situation.

For it occurs to me that the facts in the case can in no way be more forcibly presented or more clearly illustrated than by the simple and lucid method of setting forth, in sufficient detail, the controversy which the introduction of the Sparrow into America has occasioned, and analyzing the massive evidence we have accumulated. To such a record, moreover, attaches a degree of historical interest. Instead of expressing my own views, or of preparing statements which might be open to an even unfounded charge of prejudice, I have therefore thrown what I have to say in the form of a commentary on the record itself, leaving each one to form his own opinion on the subject.

The following record forms a portion of a more elaborate article which I have in preparation upon the general subject. Though very incomplete,—in fact, representing but a fragment of the literature which the Sparrow Question has occasioned,—it is sufficient for present purposes. It is compiled from all available sources, without partiality or prejudice, and the commentary is written without fear, favor, or affection. It includes every article which I have seen, and a few others, the titles of which I have taken from Mr. T. G. Gentry's book. For some, I am indebted to the kindness of Prof. C. V. Riley. Articles in favor of, as well as those unfavorable to, the Sparrow, have been collated with equal care; but those of the former character are so few and weak in comparison with those of the latter category, that if the contributions to the subject made by the eminent ornithologist, Dr. Thomas M. Brewer, be expected, little remains on that side of the question. Additional titles of articles bearing upon the off side of the controversy are therefore the special desiderata of this piece of bibliography; but any additions to the list or corrections of errors which may be detected will be very acceptable to the compiler.

"THE DESTRUCTION OF BIRDS BY TELEGRAPH WIRE," BY ELLIOTT COUES

This is a subject which has already attracted deserved attention in Europe, and I believe that much has been said about it, particularly by German writers.[7] But in this country the facts in the case seem to have been to a great degree overlooked, or at any rate insufficiently set forth in the random notices which, like the accounts of the mortality caused by lighthouses, have occasionally appeared. Yet the matter is one of much interest, as I shall here take opportunity to note. Few persons, probably, even among ornithologists, realize what an enormous number of birds are killed by flying against these wires, which now form a murderous network over the greater part of the country. And so recently, I had myself no adequate idea of the destruction that is so quietly, insidiously, and uninterruptedly accomplished. My observations do not enable me to form even an approximate estimate of the annual mortality, and I suppose we shall never possess accurate data; but I am satisfied that *many hundred thousand birds* are yearly killed by the telegraph. The evidence I shall present may be considered sufficient to bear out a seemingly extravagant statement.

I recently had occasion to travel on horseback from Denver, Colorado, to Cheyenne, Wyoming, a distance of one hundred and ten miles, by the road which, for a considerable part of the way, coincided with the line of the telegraph. It was over rolling Prairie, crossed by a few affluents of the South Platte, along the eastern base of the Rocky Mountains. The most abundant birds of the stretch of country, at the time (October), were horned larks (*Eremophila*), flocks of which were almost continually in sight; and the next most characteristic species was Maccown's bunting (*Plectrophanes Maccownii*). Almost immediately upon riding by the telegraph wire, I noticed a dead lark; and as I passed several more

---

[7] Elliott Coues, "The Destruction of Birds by Telegraph Wire," *The American Naturalist* 10, no. 12 (1876): 734–736.

in quick succession, my attention was aroused. The position of the dead birds enabled me to trace cause and effect, before I actually witnessed a case of the killing. The bodies lay in every instance nearly or directly beneath the wire. A crippled bird was occasionally seen fluttering along the road. Becoming interested in the matter, I began to count, and desisted only after actually counting *a hundred* in the course of one hour's leisurely riding—representing perhaps a distance of three miles. Nor was it long before I saw birds strike the wire, and fall stunned to the ground; three such cases were witnessed during the hour. One bird had its wing broken; another was picked up dying and convulsions from the force of the blow. The eyeballs of several dead ones I examined were started from their sockets, and the feathers of the forehead were torn off, indicating a violent blow upon the head; but in most cases there was left no outward mark of the fatal internal injury. Along some particular stretches of wire where, for whatever reason, some birds had congregated, the dead ones averaged at least one to every interval between the pole; sometimes two or three lay together, showing where a flock had passed by, and been decimated. The great majority of the birds destroyed consisted of lark; I noticed perhaps half a dozen buntings, one meadow starling (*Sturnella magna neglecta*), and one green winged teal (*Querquedula Carolinensis*). The proportion of larks was probably due in the main simply to their greater abundance; but I presume that their singularly wayward, impulsive flight may have increased the risk of striking the wires. They were the only birds I saw knocked down; and I noticed, or fancied I noticed, some hesitation and confusion in their flight when the flocks crossed the line of wire.

From these facts, which I simply narrate, one may attempt to estimate, if he wishes, the extent of the destruction which, as I have already said, goes on incessantly. Given, one hundred dead birds to three miles of wire, all killed, perhaps, within a week; or, given three birds seen to strike and fall in one hour; how many are annually killed by the telegraph wires of the United States? I should be sorry to suppose, however, that the rate of destruction I witnessed is not at or near the maximum; For I have seldom seen more birds to the acre than during the day to which I particularly refer, and never under circumstances more likely to result in the disaster of which I speak.

Usually, a remedy has been or may be provided for any unnecessary or undesirable destruction of bird; but there seems to be none in this instance. Since we cannot conveniently abolish the telegraph, we must be content with fewer birds. The only moral I can discern is that larks must not fly against telegraph wires.

SECOND REPORT OF THE AUDUBON OF THE SOCIETY OF CONNECTICUT FOR THE PROTECTION OF BIRDS (EXCERPTS).

President,
Mrs. James Osborne Wright.
(Mabel Osgood Wright), Fairfield.[8]

Report of the Secretary.

This report of your Secretary is the first one to cover an entire year. It deals with the work done from June 1898 to June 1899.

The first Annual Meeting of the Audubon Society of Connecticut, was held in the Town Hall of Fairfield, on June 4th, 1898. Members of the Association from all parts the State were present to the number of 250.

After a delightful day and the mutual felicitations on the outlook for the work of the Society so auspiciously begun, the meeting adjourned.

Your Executive Committee, immediately after the Annual Meeting, on the motion of your President, turned to the practical side of the task our Society aims to perform. It was recognized that something more must be done besides saying, "Don't wear feathers, and don't shoot birds." So it was moved and voted that the Executive Committee appropriate the sum of $130.00 to procure two sets of lantern slides to be used by local Secretaries of the Society. Literary material to accompany the lectures was promised from the President, as set forth on the last page of the Annual Report, these lantern slides were accurately colored under the supervision of Mr. F. M. Chapman. These slides portraying the chief species of New England song, game and waterbirds and accompanied by typewritten explanatory lectures, and the whole intended as a circulating lecture bureau for the use of the Societies, local Secretaries and such teachers as may desire to promote bird study in their schools, but lack funds necessary to higher lecturers, were duly prepared and the history of their successful missionary tours through Connecticut will be separately reported to you here to-day.

In order to give as wide publicity as possible to the aims and works of the Society, the most accurate report of the Annual Meeting was sent to every paper

[8] Excerpts from the *Second Report of the Audubon of the Society of Connecticut for the Protection of Birds*, 1899.

in the State. 500 copies of the Annual Report were also printed and one sent to each member.

Although your Executive Committee has deemed it wise to abstain from attempting to pass restrictive legislation in this State lest it should stir up various conflicting interests, it has nevertheless taken what it deems a great forward step in procuring instructive legislation. It was proposed by your committee and carried, that the state authorities be petitioned to "amend an act relating to Arbor Day," as follows: "Resolved by this Assembly that Section 1756 of the Revised Statues of 1888 be amended so that the same shall read as follows:

Section 1756. The Governor shall annually in the spring, designate by official proclamation an Arbor and Bird Day to be observed in the schools and in any other way as shall be indicated in such official proclamation."

The President of your Society with three members of the Executive Committee went to Hartford under the guidance of Mr. H. H. Knapp as legal counsel, and were accorded a hearing by the committee on "Fisheries and Game." No opposition developed against the proposed legislation. It was deemed, however, a valuable opportunity to place the objects of your Society before the Legislature, and an effort having been made in a certain part of the State to allow the killing of yellow-hammers, the President of your Society was enabled to make a statement as to these birds and their habitats, which demolished the argument for their destruction. At the same time she clearly indicated to the Committee the value of birds to farmers, and in other ways cleared up various misapprehensions apparently at work among the persons present at the hearing. Our effort as a Society was entirely successful and an act passed substantially as asked for, whereby the Governor did issue an Arbor and Bird Day proclamation to be observed in the schools of the State.

The thanks of the Society are due to Mr. Frank Sherwood, representative for Fairfield, for presenting our petition to the Legislature and for his aid in seeing it through the House and Senate. And especially do we owe our thanks to Mr. H. H. Knapp for unwearied interest and legal acumen in steering our bark in the untried seas of bird legislation.

Mr. C. D. Hine of the State Board of Education, has loyally aided us in every way to get Bird Day before the schools. In order to re-inforce the Governor's proclamation and help to carry into effect its recommendations, the Executive Committee had printed 5000 copies of the Bird Law of Connecticut, as to the killing, etc., of birds, and one copy sent to every school teacher, public and private, and a carefully drawn up programme of exercises for the schools on Bird Day was sent at the same time. So that we feel that every assemblage of children in our State had laid before them on that day urgent reasons for learning to love and protect our beautiful feathered world.

The by-laws of this Society, as printed in the First Report, were necessarily somewhat tentative. And so during the past winter they have been revised and amended in various ways, which we hope will commend themselves to your attention and approval.

As to membership, the Society has gained steadily. It has one honorary member, Mr. Frank M. Chapman, 7 Patrons, 35 Sustaining members, 771 regular members, making in all a total membership of 814, an increase of 514 over last year's list.

In order to remove misapprehensions as to fees, we reiterate the statement that sustaining members are the only class of members from whom annual dues are required. That fact should be understood, and attention is called to the printed statement to that effect in the Report.

We have distributed during the last year about 2,000 circulars on the "Protection of Birds," 500 leaflets on the Aigrette, purchased from the New York Audubon Society, 200 leaflets with a list of books on bird study and nature, 100 small books called "Helps to Bird Study," obtained from Massachusetts Audubon Society. The Society has had a pin of blue enamel and silver gilt made, which members may obtain from the Secretary for $1.10.

Most encouraging reports have come in from the local secretaries. In many places lectures have been given, literature distributed, and a special effort made to arouse an interest among the school children.

The Treasurer's Report will show you how the finances stand. The year closes with a balance in the treasury, and as some expenses of the past year will not come up again, the outlook is very favorable.

Reports of Local Secretaries.

Bridgeport (by its Local Secretary) reports: "Since May 15, 1898, seventeen members have been brought in: five adult members, one sustaining member, three teachers, eight children. Over one hundred circulars have been distributed, and all the literature has been put out. The lantern slides have been shown in Bridgeport twice, and are advertised for one more exhibition during this month for the special benefit of children. A successful bird lecture was given in November by Mrs. Tryon. From this lecture a surplus of $12.00 remains which Bridgeport will be very glad to give to the Audubon Society. At least fifty tickets can be used for the Annual Meeting.

Torrington: "Seven times since March 1st in as many communities, I have talked upon the subject of "Birds," trying to simulate in my hearers a love for bird study and observations, and in every address, since becoming a member of the organization, have referred to the influence and the work of the Connecticut Audubon Society. Two weeks ago I invited a number of children who would care to become members of a Junior Audubon Society to meet with me and talk the matter over. And already fifty-three small bird lovers have asked to have their names enrolled. Each child has a note-book, and records his observations for the week, and each Wednesday afternoon the members of the Society meet for reports. Already the children's bright eyes have made many discoveries, and they are eager to learn the unfamiliar birds. Though quite young, these boys and girls are proving genuine little bird enthusiasts who will always, I believe, befriend right loyally their "little brothers of the air.""

West Redding: "Documents received have been distributed. I think most of the people in town have at least heard of the Audubon Society, and that an interest is growing, is demonstrated by the fact that many have asked me about it, and have expressed pleasure at receiving circulars, which were not merely formal remarks but savored of genuine interest. As for my school and myself, bird life has for us a new and ever increasing interest, and it is very pleasurable to note the quick ear and eye of the children as they begin to understand and appreciate the birds. We observed Arbor and Bird Day by planting a few trees and flowers and inviting the parents and friends in to help us with the little program which I enclose:

Arbor and Bird Day was observed at the Diamond Hill School on Friday. The following program was rendered: Reading of proclamation, followed by a sketch of the life of John James Audubon; concert recitation by school, entitled "Brothers of the Air;" reading, "Birds of Killingworth," by Miss Boughton; song, "Chick-a-dee-dee," by school; reading "The Pebble and the Acorn," by Miss Field; reading, Teacher's Leaflet, "The Birds and I;" concert recitation, "Woodman Spare that Tree;" song, "America."

Wethersfield: Reports forty-two members, a gain of twenty-nine since last June. It is difficult to secure adult members here, although the parents are in sympathy with the aims of the Society. The children are very interested and are anxious for information about birds. A meeting of the junior members was held at a private residence, May 20th, at which each boy and a girl contributed a reading, recitation or paper on some particular bird, and we devoted the afternoon to the subject of birds. The principal of the high school included this subject in the program for the exercises on Arbor Day, and the teachers in the primary schools gave some instruction in regard to the birds. I find the leaflets published by the "Humane Societies" of Boston and Providence very helpful in this work."

Salisbury: Reports "very general interest in the subject, and great enthusiasm in the lecture, "The Birds We Know," given last March, and a desire to have in the autumn, the one which follows. Last Saturday, May 13, a meeting was called of the school children to interest them in the love of birds and to form a branch of the Society. About forty was present and ten joined about that time, with a promise of others at the next meeting. Miss Leverich, who conducted it, is a warm lover of nature, and had out-of-door lore made vivid by William Hamilton Gibson, four successive summers being his pupil, so that she is admirably adapted to inspire enthusiasm in others."

Ridgefield: Reports "in the Ridgefield school of West Lane, the teacher, Miss Mary Kelley, herself a bird lover, has helped me to awaken the children, and I found unexpected response in the homes I was able to visit—often, fathers and mothers gladly telling of the individual birds that had nested in their door-yards, and showing the spirit, which, if more common, would remove the need of our Society. I have to record the enrollment on our membership list of seven adult and forty-two junior members since June 1, 1898."

New Milford: Reports "the result of the year's work in the number of subscribers secured for our Society is much smaller than it should be on account of the Secretary's long absence. There is a certain amount of apathy to be overcome, and enthusiasm to be aroused among parents for their children, which requires time. The seed is sowed and will become a tree so that the birds of the air will come and lodge on the branches thereof." A beginning has been made which will, I trust, show good results in the coming year. One teacher in the public school is thoroughly interested and zealously working with the children in her department. Arbor and Bird Day were celebrated together, instruction being given from leaflets. The outlook is encouraging. The leaven hidden will surely leaven the whole lump."

Stamford: Reports "that introductory and educational work has been done. I cannot state the exact number of members gained, as under the rule those wishing to become members sign and forward their applications direct. A large amount of literature has been distributed, principally through the medium of the schools, and we were fortunate in securing the co-operation of the Superintendent of Schools, and of the head master of the high school, and through their courtesy also, were enabled to utilize the services of Mr. Frank M. Chapman in giving, at the building, a public lecture, which was highly appreciated. The illustrated lecture of the Society on 'The Birds about Home' we have three times, about one hundred and seventy-five persons hearing it. The daily press has kindly published, by request, various items of interest concerning birds, as well as the laws of the State for their protection. Bird Day was observed by appropriate and interesting exercises at the high school.

We trust that much interest has been aroused in the protection of birds, and although the results in membership seem small, we confidently hope to see an increase during the coming year."

Respectfully submitted,

HARRIET D. C. GLOVER,

Secretary.

Fairfield, Conn., June 1st, 1899.

APPENDIX 3

Other Works of Nineteenth-Century Nature Writing and Children's Literature

"FEATHERED PHILOSOPHERS," BY MABEL OSGOOD WRIGHT

You cannot with a scalpel find
The poet's soul, or yet the wild bird's song.
A Wood Song.

Man's kingdom is a bit of ground and his birthright a resting-place on the earth's bosom.[1] Out of the ground grow the trees that hang their leaves in the wood to shelter him, the flowers that unfold in the sun, the ferns that deepen the silence in the shadowy byways where the lichens traced their cryptograms on the rocks. Above this bit of ground is a scrap of sky holding its rotary star treasure, showing the seasons various signs, and on the ground, in the trees, and in the sky, are the birds; through the heat, and in the cold, sociable or remote, one for each thought, one for each mood, one for every passion. A bird for every day, from the ghostly white owl skimming the January meadows, to the hummingbird that darts roseward in the midsummer twilight.

The sun in its journey from equinox to equinox marks out the seasons, but they are brought nearer to the eye and the heart by the shifting calendar of feathers that measures the seasons by its songs, changes of colour, and comings and goings. The birds are more time-true than the flowers, who may be hidden by the late snows, or cut off by early frosts. To claim the confidence of one

---

[1] Mabel Osgood Wright, "Feathered Philosophers," excerpt from *The Friendship of Nature: A New England Chronicle of Birds and Flowers* (New York: Macmillan and Co., 1894).

feathered brother, to compass his ways and learn his secrets, to fathom his traits and philosophy, to gain recognition from him, is a labour worthy of trial.

The character study of the bird is beyond the mazes of classification, beyond the counting of bones, out of the reach of the scalpel and the literature of the microscope. We comprehend its air-filled bones, and its physical evolution, uses, and limitations. We know that it is frailly mortal,—but still a bird will seem like a voice from some unknown region. The beasts of the earth are bound to its face, and manned also, for science, as yet, can guide but very poorly even the most limited aerial navigation; but the bird appears, and away, to surmount the attraction of gravitation, and, as its eulogist Michelet says, "feels itself strong beyond the limits of its action."

Instinct may serve to designate such acts as the sex impulse or that bear the stamp of heredity, but a wider scope must be allowed to the brain of the bird, which with keen sense and a trite philosophy often outshines in manners and morals some of the human animals.

Have birds a language? Surely they have between themselves a spoken understanding, which the least discerning man may translate, and distinguish between their cries of joy and of fear; may separate their love songs and their scolding from their subtle ventriloquism that lures the searcher from a nest. The chronicler of the Val Sainte Veronique says that a superstition still lingers there,—the belief that every bird repeats some phrase of its own, and that in every village there is some one who understands and could interpret it, but that he is in honour bound to guard the knowledge until when on his death-bed; then he may reveal it to his nearest of kin; at such a time, however, his thoughts being upon other things, the secret is lost.

It is more likely that in the sleep which precedes birth, the forces of nature stamp impressions upon the white brain mass and string the latent senses to keen susceptibility, which later, in their full development, vibrate at Nature's lightest touch. So from prenatal circumstances some beings are more closely drawn toward the creatures of air and earth and comprehend their voices:—

> "We are what sons and winds and waters make us;
> The mountains are our sponsors and the rills
> Fashion and win their nursling with their
> smiles."—LANDOR.

People who care little for birds because of their lovable qualities, or for their ministry to eye and ear, still associate them with signs, warnings, and supernatural power. In an old legend, Death is pictured going through the land with a bird perched upon his shoulder and choosing his victims by its aid. The bird tapped at a window, and if, through heedlessness or fear, the casement remained closed and shelter was refused it, Death knocked the same night. If the bird was admitted, Death passed on.

> "'Knock at this window,' said Death.
> In flew the bird, scant of breath:
> They fed him, succoured him, let him fly.
>   Death passed by."

And even now people shiver when a wind-driven bird dashes against the pane, and half-smiling, fear, as they do when a mirror quivers and breaks. The negress also, a victim of voodoo, with rolling eyes and bated breath tells stories of the magic Zombi bird, which if it is killed and eaten continues to sing inside its murderer, revealing the sin of which he has been guilty.

What is more human in its expression than the despair shown by a caged wild bird? Its first mad impotent struggles, the head turned back as it searches in vain for a loophole of escape, and then the silent drooping attitude of heartbroken anguish. Such things always move me to a pitying vengeance. "I can't get out, no, I can't get out," wailed the starling, when Sterne tore up vainly at the wires of its cage, and he wrote: "I never had my affections more tenderly awakened."

By accident, I once had two wild birds that showed a human likeness in the different ways with which they bore imprisonment. One bitterly cold Christmas eve, I bought them from a street pedlar, my only wish being to take them in from the numbing cold, and in spring to let them fly away. One was an English goldfinch and the other a siskin. Each had a cage with water and food, placed in a subdued light, to calm its struggling more easily. The siskin was of a Byronic mood, fought against comfort, twisted the cage wires, would neither eat nor drink, and in the morning I found him hanging dead with his head between the bars. The goldfinch, when I brought him home, let me hold his draggled body in my hands, until their warmth had unbent his stiffened claws, so they might grasp the perch; then he shook himself, took a sip of water and a seed or two, and fell to smoothing out his wings and coat, pluming slowly. If a feather hung besmeared and broken he bravely pulled it out, and, his self-respect restored, he settled comfortably for the night, head under wing.

Never afterward did he show any signs of fear, but when I whistled to him he would always come close to the cage bars and make a soft kissing sound and part his beak. When springtime came, I found that to let him fly meant solitude and perhaps starvation. One mild day, I hung his cage in a low tree, when suddenly a tremor shook him, and throwing back his head he looked up through the leaves where the insects buzzed, as if the remembrance of some forgotten time had come back to him, and beating his wings, he fell from the perch with his eyes closed; but when taken indoors he rallied quickly, and lived, singing and cheerful, for many years.

* * *

The sky was gray, unrevealing, dumb; the earth was covered with ice crystals; snow dropped its obliterating veil between the two, and there was no sun to mark this season by its position. Was it midwinter? No one could tell by mere sense of vision. Colin lifted his head, and extending his moist, vibrating nostrils, sniffed suspiciously. The black-capped tit-mice, the brown and white buntings, and the slate-coloured juncos fearlessly picked up the crumbs near his kennel, and the nuthatch, less trustful, seizing a morsel, took it to a more quiet place. Colin, raising himself, crept softly toward the copse of spruces, lifting his feet from the new snow with cat-like deliberation. Did he hear the crossbill snapping the scales from the pine cones? Hardly that, for the flock, seeing him, had changed their position, and he halted before the spruces with his paw raised and tail rigid. Was it midwinter? Ah! The dog had found augurs to answer that question. Perched in the spruces were a score of sturdy male robins, not the gaunt resident birds who had fasted and battled with the rigours of winter, but the plump scouts of the coming spring, with the alert, well-fed air of migrants. The gray sky and white earth may cling to the winter curtain, but the bird heart beating warm leads us to March in the calendar; and when the snow-cloud divided, I could see that the sun was hurrying toward the vernal equinox, and I knew that the snow buntings would soon hasten northward after the white owls.

Again the sky was gray and the woods were choked and matted with brown leaves, the storm-stirred brook was brown, and the grass also. Was it dead autumn or unawakened spring? There stole into the sky a rift of blue, and on the ground lay the azure feather of a bluebird's wing, his spring sign this, for his autumn coat is rusty. The dun sky swallowed up the blue again, and near the bluebird's feather lay a hawk's barred quill. Comedy and tragedy side by side. Which overcame? The hawk by force, or the bluebird by escape,—who knows? But in a neighbouring farm-yard above a hen-coop swung a dead hawk, compelled by the wind to flap his wings in warning.

In early April two robins came to the leafless vine on the western piazza and began a nest. In the morning snow fell, and in the evening lightning blazed. The birds were discouraged, but after a few days returned and completed their dwelling, and another pair chose a trellis over the foot-path, and still another an evergreen branch by the roadside. All three nests were in plain sight, and I watched their comings and goings at intervals from morning until evening. The father and mother alternately covered the eggs and supplied the wants of the nestlings; but at night if I looked at the nest by the aid of a lantern, the mother alone was sitting, and no peering or shaking of the branches revealed the perch of the father. This seemed a little unusual, as in the case of others of the same family, the wood thrush and the catbird, I had seen the male perch on the edge of the nest, on a twig nearby, or huddling close to the female.

One bright moon-lit June night, chancing to go near the pines in the loneliest part of the garden, a hubbub arose as some night bird flapped in among the branches, and there sounded the rapid "quick! quick!" of alarm from a score or two of robins. But daylight did not reveal the trace of a nest in these pines, and after much watching and debating, I discovered that the birds which congregated there nightly were males, who gathered from sundown until an hour or so after, and roosted while their mates guarded the nests.

Bradford Torrey has noted this trait at length, with many interesting details, telling of roosts where the robins troop in nightly by hundreds, from a widely extended region; but this roost was in a garden where there were many passers, and seemed like a most exclusive coterie, or a very select bit of clubdom. They continued roosting in this way until early July, when, joined by their young, they disappeared for a time.

Have you ever noticed the oriole's fleetness of wing, foot, and eye? He is the fiery hang-bird who, wearing Lord Baltimore's colours, flits about among the sweeping elm branches in May, searching for a wand both strong and supple, where he may safely anchor his sky cradle. There is much thought required in the choosing of a location, with a dense leafy spray above it like an umbrella, and no twigs underneath to chafe when the wind rocks.

Near here is a garden, arched by elms and beeches, where all the season the most gorgeous flowers blaze upon the even turf, from the gold of the first crocus until the last chrysanthemum yields to the frost, and even then glass-shielded orchids and a mist of ferns and regal roses bridge the winter. The keeper of this garden lives with the flowers, watching the signs of sky and bird, and at night follows the moths with his net and lantern, and he told me this story of an oriole's power of thought.

Late in May, three pairs of orioles were locating their nests in the garden elms and there had been much skirmishing, fighting, and singing. Suddenly there arose a wonderful noise and commotion. Robins were giving the alarm to the bluebirds, thrushes, and sparrows, for high in the fork of a branch, a female oriole, who had slipped or was caught in flying, hung by the neck. Near by sat the three males, more quiet than agitated, while the other birds dashed about in the wildest excitement. The females cried, hovering about their unfortunate sister, pulling and jerking her tail, yet only succeeding in wedging her still more firmly. At last a gorgeous male darted up, and with wings spread dropped quickly on the forking prison, and with feet braced seized the choking bird by the neck with his beak, with one jerk releasing her, unhurt save for the loss of some feathers.

How the bird colours ebb and flow from spring until autumn! The grays of March and April are glinted by flying colour, though the earliest birds are more soberly clad than those that arrive when the leafage has grown. Wise Mother Nature, to drape your scouts in browns and russets with a dash of sky-blue or bark-green! How would the tanager, oriole, redstart, the chat and Maryland yellow-throat, or the bouquet of warblers escape the birds of prey, if when they came they found only bare branches? And the great, gold, swallow-tailed butterflies also, with the blue, the brick-red, and the variegated Apollo, reign in the torrid months, when their bird enemies have mostly gone northward, and they share the garden with the humming-bird.

The humming-bird hides his nest, or rather conceals it, by a trick of construction, which blends the nest with the branch, binding the soft bed of fern-wool and lichens to it so closely that the eye passes it over, and I seldom have found more than one nest in a season, though the flocks of parents and young give indications of at least a dozen. In a nest that I saw this year, saddled aslant on a drooping beech bough, were two little hummers, a day or so from the egg, who bore hardly a bird-like feature, looking like tiny black beans pricked over with stiff dark bristles, but in two weeks they were wearing their iridescent coats of mail.

What becomes of the father birds, with their wonderfully ruby gorgets, after the young are reared? All through July and August the birds have lived in the garden and swarmed in flocks about the sweet peas, carnations, and Japanese lilies, but I have never seen a ruby throat among them since the nesting time. In middle July, when I was training a vine to the arbour, a flock of humming-birds flew so close that I could have touched them with my hand. Contrary to their restless habits, they frequently perched on the trellis, and with a swift circular motion of the tongue licked the aphids from the curled edges of the leaves. They were newly fledged young wearing the female colours, as many birds do in their babyhood, but differing from their mothers in their lack of endurance, in a soft and infantile roundness, and in a total absence of fear. The old birds seldom alight, and I have seen one return from a dizzy flight and cover her nest without even grazing the margin. Sometimes the flock would number thirty or forty, and all the summer from dawn until sunset they fed in the garden, uttering harsh little cries, whirling and fighting, and only yielding their haunt to the hawk-moths at dusk. When there came with September some few days of dark, stormy weather, they circled high in excitement, and the next morning, as a flock, they had passed to the south, though a few stragglers remained all through October.

On the top of the trellis where the humming-birds and butterflies gathered, in a blaze of July sunshine, was a young cowbird. It did not perch, it sat, its only comprehension seeming to be the possession of a stomach, and the only sound it made was a sort of wheezing. At its side, a little beneath, was the nest of a chipping sparrow, the alien egg in its nest being one of the commonest tales of bird-land sociology. The little sparrow, however, seemed proud of the rank, ungainly offspring, and lavished special care upon it, stretching on tiptoe to give the food that its size demanded, while her own nestlings, hungry and meager, clamoured feebly. The cowbird typifies matter and craft, a dangerous conjunction, and the sparrow a case where scant sense is entirely subservient to the maternal instinct; tragedies that are not alone of the nest arise from such combinations.

* * *

The swallows distrusted the new barn; perhaps the paint startled them, or the slope of the eaves was inconvenient, and the glazed hay-loft windows repelled them. In a few years the paint grew dim and weather-stained, chrysalids hung in the groovings, and the glazed sash was left down to air the hay so that its sweets, floating out, reassure them. In June a belated pair were looking for lodgings, and the outside not satisfying them, they ventured in at the window and busied themselves with a minute examination of every beam and rafter, prying here and there and peering about with the gait of woodpeckers. Then they attempted a nest, and all one day brought clay, with which, together with hay-straws, they moulded a bracket; but the second day it fell all in a lump, the smooth wood having in some way upset their plan of adhesion. They began another tour of inspection, and they found a support that was made of mellow old timber, sound and firm, but with a rough cuticle which absorbed more quickly and to which the clay stuck firmly. Here they again essayed, and in two days they had really completed their building.

The brood was ready to fly one warm day in the early part of August, or the parents at least thought so, but the nestlings were perfectly content where they were; the table was good and the view unexceptional. Coaxing did not avail, so next day the parents relentlessly pushed them out on the hay, and there they stayed for two days more. But they either could not or would not fly, and seemed to have cramps in their claws and weak ankles (tarsi is the more accurate term). The third day the parents refused to come further in than the window-sill, where they uttered a lisping chirp, fluttered their wings, and held out insects temptingly. In this way the young were lured up, and finally spent the night on the sill, cuddled together.

Next morning the wind blew sharply and the perch was disagreeable and draughty, so with encouraging cries the youngsters were coaxed to the limbs of the hemlock, the nearest tree to the window, but one which offered only a perilous footing. Two of the four found rest in the most steady branches, but two grasped bending twigs and swung over head downward, having no strength of grip with which to regain an upright position. Under one bird were tiers of soft green branches, under the other a stone wall, rough and jagged. The old birds gave a few sibilant twitters and darted invisibly high; in a minute or two the sky was alive with swallows, fluttering about the bird who was suspended over the wall; so many swallows had not been seen this season in all the village. To and fro they wheeled, keeping always above the little one, as if to attract its attention. The parents stayed nearer, and the mother held a moth in her beak and seemed to urge an effort to secure it. In a few minutes the bird who hung over the branches, relaxing his hold, turned, and spreading his wings slightly dropped to the branch beneath, where he settled himself comfortably.

Still above the wall the other hung motionless, except that its head was slowly drooping backward, and the circling birds grew more vociferous. Suddenly the parent who held the butterfly lit on the branch at the spot where the bird was clinging, and its mate darted swiftly close beneath. Whether the darting bird really pushed the little one up, or only made the rush to startle it to sudden action, I could not discover, but in a flash the deed was accomplished and the bird righted and led into a bushy cover. The visiting swallows wheeled and lisped for a minute, and then were engulfed by the sky as mist in the air blends with the sunlight.

Tell me, positive science, where these manœuvres merely instinctive? Or, if you cannot, then confess bravely that there are things that you may not fathom.

TOMMY-ANNE AND THE THREE HEARTS, BY MABEL OSGOOD WRIGHT

... "Say, say! What's the row? I'm awake, so are you," jeered Miou, the gray Catbird, tipping his black-capped head on one side and flicking his tail.[2]

"Winter's over, winter's over! Hear me laughing, laughing,—see!" sang the black and white Bobolink, soaring high above the meadow grass.

Tommy-Anne started, rubbing her eyes, saw that the sun had risen some time ago, heard the bird music, and then scolded Waddles, who had found his way, as usual, to the foot of her bed, and was walking very slowly, yawning and making a bow of his back.

"Oh, Waddles, Waddles! I told you to remind me,—'to-morrow early,'—and it's late now, and there's bath and breakfast before we can go out. I could take my breakfast in my pocket, but not my bath. I wonder if the anniversary has begun." And she hung out of the window, looking anxiously toward the meadow, which could not be seen because of the trees.

A tiny brown Wren, wild with good spirits, chattered at her from the honey-suckle. "Perhaps he will tell me something about it," she said.

"Tell you something about what?" he answered pertly, never stopping his nervous hopping from twig to twig. "What do you want to know—who I am? I'm Johnny Wren; I live here in this little box; soon there will be spotted brown eggs in it—perhaps five—perhaps ten—who knows—do you? If we like it here—and no cats come—we'll stay—make another nest in the next box later on. New nest

---

[2] Mabel Osgood Wright, *Tommy-Anne and the Three Hearts*, excerpt (New York: The Macmillan Co., 1896).

Let's shake hands.

for every brood—best way—more neat—some birds don't, though—we are neat—are you? Here comes my wife—hear her scold—good-bye!"

"Now I know what a chatterbox is," said Tommy-Anne, drawing a long breath. "He asked us if we are neat, Waddles. Perhaps he was hinting about that bath. I think I had better set about it, because it's a *must be*, that only stops for two things,—a bad cold and frozen water pipes."

Tommy-Anne and her father had their breakfast together on a little table in the piazza, and Tommy-Anne poured out his coffee and carried it to him as steadily as if she was not eager to be down in the meadow. They often breakfasted together on this way, for her mother was not very strong and slept late, and Aunt Prue simply would *not* take a meal outdoors. "Dining rooms are to eat in," she said; "if one is to eat with bugs and ants crawling over the butter, and flies in the milk, one might as well be a pedlar and live in a cart."

A Robin flew past, calling, "Quick! Quick!" It was only his fussy way, but Tommy-Anne thought that he was telling her to hurry; and her father, seeing her earnestness, let her go, first asking if she had on her thick boots.

Yes, she had; for thick boots were her dear friends, and a *why* that she thoroughly understood, after a summer spent in the company of ankles bruised with stones and striped with briar scratches, to say nothing of colds.

"We are too late, Waddles; I'm sure we are too late," she sighed, as they crossed the bridge, and standing under a great apple tree, the beginning of the old orchard, looked over the meadow toward the woods. "The Bobolinks are here, but they always are; they make flat pie nests in the grass. I stepped in one last summer; but lucky for them it was empty. They are too giddy to tell us anything. As soon as they see any one coming, they sail straight up in the air and sing so fast that they forget the words and have to come down again to think."

"Mistress," said Waddles, who had been sniffing where the grass was trampled down in a long trail, "the Miller's bull, Taw, is out for a walk *without* the Miller. Now the last time Taw went walking alone a great many accidents happened. My particular friend, the Doctor's dog, Flo, sprained her back, our pasture fence fell over, and the Egg Woman, who was going across lots to the store, spilled four dozen fresh eggs and had to climb up this very tree that we are standing under, in an awful hurry.

"When the Miller came to find the bull, Taw roared at him terribly from over the river, and shook his brass nose-ring, saying 'I'm out for the day,'—and so he was. For the Miller knows that there is no use in contradicting a bull in an open field, when there is no rope tied to his nose-ring. I think, mistress, that you had better climb this apple tree *now*, for there is a queer noise over in the wood." So saying, Waddles made himself into a very small package behind the gnarled trunk, where he could see and not be seen.

There certainly was a commotion in the wood. Birds were chattering at a great rate, not singing, but giving their call notes and alarm cries.

"The anniversary must be beginning," said Tommy-Anne, from her perch; "don't you want to come where you can see better, Waddles? I can pull you up, and there is a nice wide branch for you to sit on, if you keep quite still."

"No thank you; it's against the custom of our family to climb trees. I might be disgraced by being mistaken for a cat. Look quick, mistress!"

The clamour was coming nearer. Swallows darted above the river, whispering excitedly. Robins flew from tree to bush, calling hurriedly. A flame-colored Oriole shot over, and perching in the old apple tree above Tommy-Anne's head, gave some notes like a bugle call. Down from the woods came a strange procession of birds: hundreds and hundreds of them; some walking, some flying close above the ground,—but all keeping in groups of a colour or a family, like the companies of a regiment, led by a large Owl walking between a Thrush and a Crow.

So many birds moving at once made Tommy-Anne almost dizzy, and she looked up to ask the Oriole what it all meant, when she saw that he had left the tree, and a dark gray bird, who was bowing and trying to attract her attention, was in his place. "Say, say!" it called—"Prut, prut—say say! hi, hi! victory!" It was Miou, the Catbird.

"Good-morning," cried Tommy-Anne, in delight. "You are the very person I wanted to see, because you are always so sociable, and seem to really enjoy telling what you know."

"Good-morning," he piped gaily, for he felt very much complimented by being called a person. "Good-day, good-day! excuse me for not taking off my cap, but I can't, you see, because *it grows on.*" And he laughed at his own little joke.

"Now, Miou," said Tommy-Anne, "please tell me about the anniversary, and where all those birds came from." And she pointed at the procession that was fast breaking up into little parties that explored the meadow and neighboring orchard.

"Don't you really know about them? They are coming from Cock Robin's funeral."

"Cock Robin's funeral!" she cried, in amazement. "I thought that he was an English Robin, and that he died years ago. I heard about it when I was *very* young, I am sure."

"So he was, so he did," chattered Miou, delighted to have a listener. "It is not the real funeral, but the anniversary of it, that we celebrate. We are his kinsmen, you know; and we do it to make us remember that we have declared war against the English Sparrow who killed him.

> "'Who killed Cock Robin?'
> 'I' said the Sparrow;
> 'With my bow and arrow
> I killed Cock Robin.'"

sang Miou, softly.

"I never thought of that before," said Tommy-Anne, "and I've often wondered why the Sparrows were always fighting with other birds. I suppose that is why people celebrate anniversaries of battles and things, so that they can remember to feel angry; and birthdays for fear they shall forget how old they are. Only, Miou, have you noticed that some people don't seem to have any birthdays? That must be because they want to forget."

The bird began to look bored, as talkative people are apt to when some one else is speaking, and seemed anxious to go on with his story.

"Pray excuse me," said Tommy-Anne; "but at the real funeral the bull tolled the bell. How do you manage that?"

"That is quite a long story," said Miou, contently settling himself on his twig. "For years and years we *imagined* the bull,—left a place for him in the procession and played that he was there, you know. This year, Dahinda, the greatest Bull-frog in the pond, told Wawa, the Wild Goose, who was swimming near him, that our anniversary was getting to be very dull, and that he had heard the birds say, when they were bathing, that they would stop coming to it if there was not more variety.

"Wawa asked him what he could suggest, and Dahinda said, 'Have a real bull in the procession, and kept on saying, 'B-u-ll! B-u-ll!' all day, until the Council of Birdland agreed with him.

"That was the beginning of the trouble. We all knew Taw, the Miller's bull, very well, and Ko-ko-ko-ho, the Horned Owl, who sleeps near the barn, promised to invite him. Taw said he would be happy to come, but did not know how he could get out alone, unless the Council could make a plan. So they appointed the Owl, the Jay, the Wood Dove, and the Wren a committee of arrangement to do the work. They chose the Owl because he looked wise; the Jay, because he was not troubled with too many scruples; the Dove, because he agreed with almost everyone; and the Wren, because he was energetic. Tchin, the Jay, who promised to get Taw out, asked his friend, the Red Fox, to run swiftly through the barnyard early in the morning, when the Miller's boy was leaving Taw to the water-trough. So far all went well. The boy dropped the rope that was fastened in Taw's nose-ring, to chase the fox, and Taw pushed open the gate and came to us."

"Where did you get the bell for him to toll, and where is he now?" said Tommy-Anne, unable to resist asking questions; "he did not come back with the procession."

"You go too fast; give me time," said Miou. "We had to *imagine* the bell because we hadn't any, and if we had one, the noise would have told the Miller exactly were Taw was and spoiled everything."

"Of course!" ejaculated Tommy-Anne. "Half the *whys* would answer themselves if they took time to think. But where is Taw now?"

"Ah!" said Miou; "that is the trouble. After the celebration, when he should have come back with us to this tree to hear the stories and songs—"

"Stories? what stories?" cried she.

"After the anniversary we always have a feast, and sing, and tell stories about where we have spent the winter; for it is the first time that we have all met since last year. It is very interesting."

"Shall I hear these stories?" said Tommy-Anne, her eyes dancing with pleasure.

"I don't think, by the way you interrupt *me*, that you *wish* to hear stories," said Miou, severely.

"Please forgive me," she begged; "but Heart of Nature said that I might ask questions of all the things *themselves*, so that I could learn a great many *whys*."

"That is different," said Miou, and then added suspiciously, "Do you know the pass-word?"

"Yes; it is Brotherhood!" she replied promptly.

"Very good. Now to go back to Taw. After we had imagined that we had buried Cock Robin, and were starting to return through the wood, one of those bad Cowbirds, who have nothing to do but meddle and gossip, perched on Taw's back and whispered in his ear, 'There's fine fall grain over the other way; fresh green eating. Come see,' and went walking off to show the way, Taw following. We were all well frightened, and the Council ordered the Committee of Management to bring Taw back.

"Ko-ko-ko-ho would do nothing about it, because he is a night owl, and he says the light hurts his eyes; Tchin, the Jay, said he had only agreed to bring Taw *out, not* get him *back.* The Dove tiptoed and said nothing, and the Wren tried to argue with Taw, who only laughed at her, and she flew away threatening to call the Miller.

"Meanwhile, Taw is eating all the beautiful young wheat, and we are sorry, because it belongs to the Blacksmith, and he is very good to us and keeps the boys from robbing our nests hereabouts, and feeds those of us who stay all winter."

BIRDS OF VILLAGE AND FIELD: A BIRD BOOK FOR BEGINNERS, BY FLORENCE MERRIAM BAILEY

HOW TO FIND A BIRD'S NAME.—As this book is intended for beginners, scientific classification has been disregarded, and the birds which readers are most likely to know and see are placed first, the rarer ones left until later.[3] For the benefit of those who have a definite bird to name, a color key based on markings visible in the field has been made to all the birds taken up (see pp. xxix–xlix); this, when run down, will lead by page reference to the description and picture of the bird in the body of the book. If the family to which the bird belongs is known, the species will be found more quickly by turning to the key of the family, referred to in the index.

If no definite bird is to be looked up, and one goes to the field unembarrassed by knowledge, with the whole bird world freshly opening for conquest, the matter of naming the birds and learning their ways is not a difficult one. Four things only are necessary—a scrupulous conscience, unlimited patience, a notebook, and an opera-glass. The notebook enables one to put down the points which the opera-glass has brought within sight, and by means of which the bird may be found in the key; patience leads to trained ears and eyes, and conscience prevents hasty conclusions and doubtful records. Two notebooks should be kept, one for permanent records and a pocket one for field use, as elaborations from memory are of little value to one's self, and still less to posterity. One of the best forms of permanent notebook is a pad, punched and fastened in an adjustable cover. The notes on each bird should be written on separate pages, and as they

---

[3] Florence Merriam Bailey, *Birds of Village and Field: A Bird Book for Beginners,* excerpt, American Museum of Natural History Library (Boston: Houghton, Mifflin and Co., 1898).

accumulate, the pages slipped out of the cover and arranged alphabetically for easy reference....

WHERE TO FIND BIRDS.—Shrubby village door-yards, the trees of village streets and orchards, roadside fences, overgrown pastures, and the borders of brooks and rivers are among the best places to look for birds. Such places afford food and protection, for there are more insects and fewer enemies in villages and about country houses than in forests; while brooks and river banks, though without the protection afforded by man, give water and abundant insect life. Very few birds care for deep woods. The heart of the dark, coniferous Adirondack forest is silent—hardly a bird is to be found there. It is along the edges of sunny, open woodland that most of the wood-loving species go to nest.

HOW TO WATCH BIRDS.—In looking for birds be careful not to frighten them away. As shyer kinds are almost sure to fly before you in any case, the best way is to go quietly to a good spot and sit down and wait for them to return and proceed with their business unconscious of spectators. Do not look toward the sun, as colors will not show against the light.

In nesting time, birds may be found at home at any hour, as the nestling's meal-time comes without regard for callers; but during migration, birds are moving, and best seen from 4.30 to 8.30 A.M. and 4 to 8 P.M.

If you begin watching birds in the spring, when they are coming back from a winter in the south, you will be kept busy looking up the names of the new arrivals; but even when intent on the distinguishing marks of the birds, you may make a great many interesting discoveries as to their ways of life. It is one of the pleasures of the season to keep a dated list of the migrants as they come north. The first year this will be exciting from the daily surprises of new arrivals; and as the years go by it will be of increasing interest from anticipations based on old dates, and the changes that occur with variations of season....

HOW TO KEEP BIRDS ABOUT OUR HOUSES.—Protection from enemies, food to live on, and suitable nesting sites are the three considerations that determine a bird's place of residence. As insects are most numerous on cultivated land, about houses, gardens, and fields where crops are grown, most birds, if not molested, prefer to live where man does. Their worst enemies are gunners and cats. Gunners may be kept away by posting one's woods with signs forbidding shooting, and one's yard may be kept free from cats by fencing. Mr. William Brewster, president of the American Ornithologists' Union, has found after. many experiments that the best fence for the purpose is tarred fish net or seine, six feet high, attached at the top to flexible poles; at the bottom threaded by rods pinned to the ground by tent pegs. When a cat jumps against this fence, the poles bend toward her so that she falls backwards unable to recover herself or spring over.

When we have protected our birds from their enemies, the next thing is to provide them with suitable nesting places. They are particularly fond of tangles of shrubbery; and by planting a corner of the yard with sunflowers and wild berry-bearing bushes we can at once supply them with food and with good shelter for their nests. Pans of water add greatly to the comfort of birds and attract them to drink and bathe. Birds like Martins, Bluebirds, Wrens, and Chickadees will usually occupy artificial nesting places provided for them—such as cans, gourds, and bird houses.

In the summer it is a very simple matter to keep the birds about us by supplying the necessary conditions; but people who live in the country can get more pleasure from the companionship of birds in winter than summer, and the question is how to draw the winter ones from the woods. It can be done very easily by taking a little pains to feed them.

Bones and a few pieces of suet or the fat of fresh pork nailed to a tree are enough to attract Chickadees, Nuthatches, Woodpeckers, and Blue Jays; and a rind of salt pork will draw the salt-eating Crossbills when they are in the neighborhood. For food that can be blown away or snowed under—such as grain, or crumbs from the table—it is well to nail up boxes with open fronts, placing them with the back to the prevailing wind.

As some birds prefer to feed on the ground, it is a good thing to keep a space clear of snow under a window, from which food can be thrown without disturbing them: shy birds like Grouse will come more freely to corn or buckwheat scattered on a barrel under the cover of an evergreen. A window shelf protected by awning is also an admirable thing.

Most of these devices have been employed with great success by Mrs. Davenport, in Brattleboro', Vermont. She has fed the birds hemp seed, sunflower seed, nuts, fine-cracked corn, and bread. As wheat bread freezes quickly, in very cold weather she uses bread made from one third wheat and two thirds Indian meal.

Her flock, during the winter of 1895–96, included, as daily visitors, seven to ten Blue Jays, more than twenty Chickadees, three Downy Woodpeckers, one Hairy Woodpecker, three Nuthatches, more than forty Tree Sparrows, and one Junco. After the first of February new recruits joined her band—more Juncos, Song Sparrows, Fox Sparrows, a Redpoll Linnet, and two Red-breasted Nuthatches; and in March a Swamp Sparrow came. A flock of Siskins were so tame that when the seed she threw to them rattled on their backs, they merely shook themselves. In March a flock of Tree Sparrows sang so cheerfully their chorus 'made the March morning like June.' Before the snow had gone, Purple Finches came, and they remained all summer. On June 15, 1896, the birds that came were Purple Finches, Downy Woodpeckers, Nuthatches, Robins, Orioles, Blue Jays, Chipping Sparrows, and sometimes a Scarlet Tanager or a Thrush. Then followed the interest of the nesting season, when the old birds brought their broods to the house to drink and bathe. Altogether the response to the hospitality offered the birds was so eager that throughout the year the family almost never had a meal by daylight without the presence of birds on the window shelf.

The pleasure Mrs. Davenport gets from her flock is particularly worthy of record, because it is open to such a large number of bird-lovers at the cost of a little trouble, and, as she herself tells us, "however much one may do for the birds, that which comes in the doing is a revelation of sources of happiness not before suspected."

Bluebird: *Sialia sialis*.

Adult male, upper parts deep blue; throat and breast reddish brown; belly white. *Adult female*, upper parts grayish blue; under parts duller. *Young*, in nestling plumage, spotted with whitish.

Length, about 7 inches.

GEOGRAPHIC DISTRIBUTION.—Eastern United States; breeds from the Gulf states to Manitoba and Nova Scotia; winters from southern Illinois and southern New York southward.

Although the Bluebird did not come over in the Mayflower, it is said that when the Pilgrim Fathers came to New England this bird was one of the first whose gentle warblings attracted their notice, and, from its resemblance to the beloved Robin Redbreast of their native land, they called it the Blue Robin. From that time on, this beautiful bird has shown itself so responsive to friendly treatment that it has won a deep place in the affections of the people. The bird houses that were put up for it insured its presence in villages and city parks until the introduction of the House Sparrow, but since that time the old familiar friend has had to give way before the quarrelsome stranger. Mr. Nehrling, however, gives us the grateful information that by a simple device the Bluebird boxes may be protected from the Sparrow. It seems that the Sparrow, being no aeronaut,—not to say of earthly mind,—finds difficulty in entering a hole unless there is a perch beside it where, as it were, he can have his feet on the ground. The Bluebird, on the contrary, aside from his mental cast, is so used to building in old Woodpecker holes, none of which are blessed with piazzas or front-door steps, that he has no trouble in flying directly into a nest hole. So, by making the Bluebird houses without perches, the Sparrows may be kept away. Mr. Nehrling urges that cigar boxes should never be used for bird houses, which is surely wise, for we would neither offend the nostrils of feathered parents nor contaminate the feathered youth. In the south, he tells us, the cypress knees furnish excellent materials for them. He suggests, moreover, that sections of hollow branches and hollow tree trunks can be used in addition to the usual board houses. When this is done, the section of the branch should be sawed in two, bored out for the nest cavity, and then nailed or glued together and capped at each end to keep out the rain. It should then be fastened securely to a branch or tree trunk with strong wire. Bird houses of some sort are especially necessary on the prairie and in other regions where few natural nesting sites are to be found.

One of the most effective ways to attract the bluebird, however, is by planting wild berry- bearing bushes, particularly in the west, where such bushes do not grow naturally. For while three quarters of the Bluebird's food consists of grasshoppers, crickets, caterpillars, and similar insects, and it is "exceedingly useful to the horticulturist and farmer, destroying myriads of larvae and insects which would otherwise increase and multiply to the great injury of vegetation," the Bluebird is not a bird of one idea, but extends his dietary to wild fruits, and by means of them may be brought about our houses. A variety of bushes can be planted, for he has been found to eat bird cherry, chokeberry, dogwood, bush cranberry, huckleberry, greenbrier, Virginia creeper, strawberry-bush, juniperberry, bittersweet, pokeberry, false spikenard, partridgeberry, holly, rose haws, sumac, and wild sarsaparilla.

Wilson, in speaking of the Bluebird engaged in courting his mate, says in his delightful way: "If a rival makes his appearance,... he quits her in a moment, attacks and pursues the intruder as he shifts from place to place, in tones that bespeak the jealousy of his affection, conducts him, with many reproofs, beyond the extremities of his territory, and returns to warble out his transports of triumph beside his beloved mate."

As we watch the Bluebird, one of the most noticeable things about him, in spite of his familiar friendliness, is a certain untamable spirit of the woods and fields. As he sits on a branch lifting his wings, there is an elusive charm about his sad quavering *tru-al-ly, tru-al-ly*. Ignoring our presence, he seems preoccupied with unfathomable thoughts of field and sky.

"A BIRD'S FOREFATHERS," BY JAMES NEWTON BASKETT.

The birds form one of the five great groups of the vertebrates, and of course their ancestry began when the backbone was a gristly cord on the lower border of the fishes.[4] Perhaps we might begin later, when the backbone of the higher fish-forms had become bony and jointed and a brain case had expanded upon its forward end; for birds are certainly brainy creatures. Later still, we might set our beginning when the numerous rays of the fins of fishes gave way to the few fingers and toes of the four-footed, land-tending amphibians, and where the fringed gill of the water breather yielded to the simple lung sack of the air breather; for our bird has certainly four limbs only, with few fingers and toes on each, and it is the best adapted to air breathing of all earth's creatures. Or possibly our story might begin at that point where the young ceased to have a tadpole or larval state, but began at once to resemble its parents as soon as it was hatched or born; for we shall see later that a baby bird at once begins to look like his mother.

Perhaps we might set out at that parting of the ways between the reptiles and the mammals and between the reptiles and the amphibians, where the large egg

---

[4] James Newton Baskett, "A Bird's Forefathers," excerpt from *The Story of the Birds* (New York: D. Appleton and Co., 1896).

comes in and the young are capable of being nourished for a long time independent of the parent or of position in the water; for the yoke of the bird's egg feeds the young bird till hatched, and in some cases a short while after, and the hatching is independent of water.

Then there is the region of better or more cellular lungs at which we might begin, or that of a better or more extensively chambered heart with warm blood pulsing through it; but that would be getting up within the realm of the bird itself almost—at least upon the borderland. Yet the duckbill (with its kin) has all these traits and lays an egg and incubates it, but it is not a bird or in the line of the bird's ancestry.

Surely we may say that birdward tendencies were set up when Nature began by skin appendages to carry the lizards through the air; but the development of this might have missed the bird completely, for these lizards are certainly not the ancestors of the bird any more than bats are its fellows or descendants. They were only evolved out of the same conditions.

Here, indeed, however, is the true region, for the dawning of bird life closely follows the dawning of vertebrate flight. Had there been no tendency to fly, the true bird could never have been deployed. The ancestral outlook of the birds, therefore, lies in the aspirations of the lizards.

But real bird life begins higher up the line still, where flight became very special—not by skin, but by scales with some changes wrought in them. So far as our knowledge goes, no creature except a bird ever *flew by feathers*. It may be possible that there were some soft modifications of the scales among the active terrestrial reptiles, but, so far as we now know, nothing but a bird has ever worn feathers—except a woman and a savage. Better to say that nothing but a bird *grows* feathers.

Birds show that their forefathers were among the reptiles by the following characters common to both, and by many others too technical for our discussion:

The large egg noted, found nowhere else except in that three-way connecting link between birds, reptiles, and mammals—the duckbill group; by the lack of complete diaphragm below the heart and lungs; by having only a *single* ball-and-socket joint where the head turns on the neck, whereas the mammals and amphibians have two; by many peculiarities of structure about the head, especially by having the lower jaw connected to the skull by an intervening (quadrate) bone not found in the mammals. So also there are peculiar arrangements of the circulatory system and of the bones of the feet, etc., that are found only in these two groups. Finally, as distinctive of the groups, they neither pass through a tadpole or incomplete state after birth, as the amphibians, or have special glands (*mammæ*) to nourish their young as the mammals.

While they differ from each other in the bird having hot blood and feathers (instead of cold blood and scales), great naturalists are inclined to make one class of the two groups. The oldest bird which we know of yet is the fossil *Archæopteryx*, and had not the print of the feathers on its wings, tail, and legs been left in the rocks along with its bones, it is probably that it would have been classed simply as a flying lizard.

Thinking back over what has been noted, we may say of the bird that it is—

A back-boned, four-limbed, lung-breathing, egg-laying, hot-blooded, feather-covered, upright-walking creature, having its fore legs adapted to flight; for, however flightless a bird may be now, there is sufficient evidence that it has come out of an ancestry whose wings were once really complete and useful.

Whether all birds have had the same forefather is a much discussed question out of place in this connection, but it is further slightly referred to in Chapter III.

"THE FATE OF MR. JACK SPARROW," BY JOEL CHANDLER HARRIS.

"You'll tromple on dat bark twel hit won't be fitten fer ter fling 'way, let 'lone make hoss-collars out'n," said Uncle Remus, as the little boy came running into his cabin out of the rain.[5] All over the floor long strips of "wahoo" bark were spread, and these the old man was weaving into horse-collars.

"I'll sit down, Uncle Remus," said the little boy.

"Well, den, you better, honey," responded the old man, "kaze I 'spizes fer ter have my wahoo trompled on. Ef 'twuz shucks, now, hit mout be diffunt, but I'm a gittin' too ole fer ter be projickin' longer shuck collars."

For a few minutes the old man went on with his work, but with a solemn air altogether unusual. Once or twice he sighed deeply, and the sighs ended in a prolonged groan, that seemed to the little boy to be the result of the most unspeakable mental agony. He knew by experience that he had done something which failed to meet the approval of Uncle Remus, and he tried to remember what it

---

[5] Joel Chandler Harris, "The Fate of Mr. Jack Sparrow," excerpt from *Uncle Remus, His Songs and His Sayings: The Folk-Lore of the Old Plantation* (New York: D. Appleton and Co., 1886).

was, so as to frame an excuse; but his memory failed him. He could think of nothing he had done calculated to stir Uncle Remus's grief. He was not exactly seized with remorse, but he was very uneasy. Presently Uncle Remus looked at him in a sad and hopeless way, and asked:

"W'at dat long rigmarole you bin tellin' Miss Sally 'bout yo' little brer dis mawnin?"

"Which, Uncle Remus?" asked the little boy, blushing guiltily.

"Dat des w'at I'm a axin' un you now. I hear Miss Sally say she's a gwineter stripe his jacket, en den I knowed you bin tellin' on 'im."

"Well, Uncle Remus, he was pulling up your onions, and then he went and flung a rock at me," said the child, plaintively.

"Lemme tell you dis," said the old man, laying down the section of horse-collar he had been plaiting, and looking hard at the little boy—"lemme tell you dis—der ain't no way fer ter make tattlers en tail-b'arers turn out good. No, dey ain't. I bin mixin' up wid fokes now gwine on eighty year, en I ain't seed no tattler come ter no good een'. Dat I ain't. En ef ole man M'thoozlum wuz livin' clean twel yit, he'd up'n tell you de same. Sho ez youer settin' dar. You 'member w'at 'come er de bird w'at went tattlin' 'roun' 'bout Brer Rabbit?"

The little boy didn't remember, but he was very anxious to know, and he also wanted to know what kind of bird it was that so disgraced itself.

"Hit wuz wunner deze yer uppity little Jack Sparrers, I speck," said the old man; "dey wuz allers bodder'n' longer udder fokes's bizness, en dey keeps at it down ter dis day—peckin' yer, and pickin' dar, en scratchin' out yander. One day, atter he bin fool by ole Brer Tarrypin, Brer Rabbit wuz settin' down in de woods studdyin' how he wuz gwineter git even. He feel mighty lonesome, en he feel mighty mad, Brer Rabbit did. Tain't put down in de tale, but I speck he cusst en r'ar'd 'roun' considerbul. Leas'ways, he wuz settin' out dar by hisse'f, en dar he sot, en study en study, twel bimeby he jump up en holler out:

"'Well, doggone my cats ef I can't gallop 'roun' ole Brer Fox, en I'm gwineter do it. I'll show Miss Meadows en de gals dat I'm de boss er Brer Fox,' sezee.

"Jack Sparrer up in de tree, he hear Brer Rabbit, he did, en he sing out:

"'I'm gwine tell Brer Fox! I'm gwine tell Brer Fox! Chick-a-biddy-win'-a-blowin'-acuns-fallin'! I'm gwine tell Brer Fox!'"

Uncle Remus accompanied the speech of the bird with a peculiar whistling sound in his throat, that was a marvelous imitation of a sparrow's chirp, and the little boy clapped his hands with delight, and insisted on a repetition.

"Dis kinder tarrify Brer Rabbit, en he skasely know w'at he gwine do; but bimeby he study ter hisse'f dat de man w'at see Brer Fox fus wuz boun'ter have de inturn, en den he go hoppin' off to'rds home. He didn't got fur w'en who should he meet but Brer Fox, en den Brer Rabbit, he open up:

"'W'at dis twix' you en me, Brer Fox?' sez Brer Rabbit, sezee. 'I hear tell you gwine ter sen' me ter 'struck-shun, en nab my fambly, en 'stroy my shanty,' sezee.

"'Den Brer Fox he git mighty mad.

"'Who bin tellin' you all dis?' sezee.

"Brer Rabbit make like he didn't want ter tell, but Brer Fox he 'sist en 'sist, twel at las' Brer Rabbit he up en tell Brer Fox dat he hear Jack Sparrer say all dis.

"'Co'se,' sez Brer Rabbit, sezee, 'w'en Brer Jack Sparrer tell me dat I flew up, I did, en I use some langwidge w'ich I'm mighty glad dey wern't no ladies 'round' nowhars so dey could hear me go on,' sezee.

"Brer Fox he sorter gap, he did, en say he speck he better be sa'nter'n on. But, bless yo' soul, honey, Brer Fox ain't sa'nter fur, 'fo' Jack Sparrer flipp down on a 'simmon-bush by de side er de road, en holler out:

"'Brer Fox! Oh, Brer Fox!—Brer Fox!'

"Brer Fox he des sorter canter 'long, he did, en make like he don't hear 'im. Den Jack Sparrer up'n sing out agin:

'Brer Fox! Oh, Brer Fox! Hole on, Brer Fox! I got some news fer you. Wait Brer Fox! Hit'll 'stonish you.'

"Brer Fox he make like he don't see Jack Sparrer, ner needer do he hear 'im, but bimeby he lay down by de road, en sorter stretch hisse'f like he fixin' fer ter nap. De tattlin' Jack Sparrer he flew'd 'long, en keep on callin' Brer Fox, but Brer Fox, he ain't sayin' nuthin'. Den little Jack Sparrer, he hop down on de groun' en flutter 'roun' 'mongst de trash. Dis sorter 'track Brer Fox 'tenshun, en he look at de tattlin' bird, en de bird he keep on callin':

"'I got sump'n fer ter tell you, Brer Fox.'

"'Git on my tail, little Jack Sparrer,' sez Brer Fox, sezee, 'kaze I'm de'f in one year, en I can't hear out'n de udder. Git on my tail,' sezee.

"Den de little bird he up'n hop on Brer Fox's tail.

"'Git on my back, little Jack Sparrer, kaze I'm de'f in one year en I can't hear out'n de udder.'

"Den de little bird hop on his back.

"'Hop on my head, little Jack Sparrer, kaze I'm de'f in bofe years.'

"Up hop de little bird.

362   APPENDIX 3

"'Hop on my toof, little Jack Sparrer, kaze I'm de'f in one year en I can't hear out'n de udder.'

"De tattlin' little bird hop on Brer Fox's toof, en den—"

Here Uncle Remus paused, opened wide his mouth and closed it again in a way that told the whole story.[6]

"Did the Fox eat the bird all—all—up?" asked the little boy.

"Jedge B'ar come long nex' day," replied Uncle Remus, "en he fine some fedders, en fum dat word went roun' dat ole man Squinch Owl done kotch nudder watzizname."

---

[6] An Atlanta friend heard this story in Florida, but an alligator was substituted for the fox, and a little boy for the rabbit. There is another version in which the impertinent gosling goes to tell the fox something her mother has said, and is caught; and there may be other versions. I have adhered to the middle Georgia version, which is characteristic enough. It may be well to state that there are different versions of all the stories—the shrewd narrators of the mythology of the old plantation adapting themselves with ready tact to the years, tastes, and expectations of their juvenile audiences.

APPENDIX 4

Further Reading

Anderson, Lorraine, and Thomas S. Edwards, eds. *At Home on This Earth: Two Centuries of U.S. Women's Nature Writing.* Hanover, NH: University Press of New England, 2002.

Arluke, Arnold, and Clinton R. Sanders. *Regarding Animals.* Philadelphia: Temple University Press, 1996.

Barrow, Mark V., Jr. *A Passion for Birds: American Ornithology after Audubon.* Princeton, NJ: Princeton University Press, 1998.

Brodhead, Michael J. "Elliott Coues and the Sparrow War." *New England Quarterly* 44, no. 3 (1971): 420–432.

Burroughs, John. *Birds and Poets.* New York: Hurd and Houghton, 1877.

Burroughs, John. *Wake-Robin.* New York: Hurd and Houghton, 1871.

Capek, Stella M. "Of Time, Space, and Birds: Cattle Egrets and the Place of the Wild." In *Mad about Wildlife: Looking at Social Conflict over Wildlife*, edited by Ann Herda-Rapp and Theresa Goedeke, 195–222. Leiden: Brill, 2005.

Cherry, Elizabeth. *For the Birds: Protecting Wildlife through the Naturalist Gaze.* New Brunswick, NJ: Rutgers University Press, 2019.

Cutright, Paul Russell, and Michael J. Brodhead. *Elliott Coues: Naturalist and Frontier Historian.* Urbana: University of Illinois Press, 1981.

Doughty, Robin W. *Feather Fashions and Bird Preservation: A Study in Nature Protection.* Berkeley: University of California Press, 1975.

Dunlap, Thomas R. *In the Field, among the Feathered: A History of Birders and Their Guides.* New York: Oxford University Press, 2011.

Fine, Gary Alan, and Lazaros Christoforides. "Dirty Birds, Filthy Immigrants, and the English Sparrow War: Metaphorical Linkage in Constructing Social Problems." *Symbolic Interaction* 14, no. 4 (1991): 375–393.

Gibbons, Felton, and Deborah Strom. *Neighbors to the Birds: A History of Birdwatching in America.* New York: W. W. Norton, 1988.

Graham, Frank, and Carl W. Buchheister. *The Audubon Ark: A History of the National Audubon Society.* New York: Knopf, 1990.

Greven, Philip J. *The Protestant Temperament: Patterns of Child-Rearing, Religious Experience, and the Self in Early America.* Chicago: University of Chicago Press, 1988.

Greven, Philip J. *Spare the Child: The Religious Roots of Punishment and the Psychological Impact of Physical Abuse.* New York: Knopf, 1991.

Hays, Samuel P. *Conservation and the Gospel of Efficiency: The Progressive Conservation Movement, 1890–1920.* Pittsburgh: University of Pittsburgh Press, 1999.

Johnson, Benjamin Heber. *Escaping the Dark, Gray City: Fear and Hope in Progressive-Era Conservation.* New Haven, CT: Yale University Press, 2017.

Kohlstedt, Sally Gregory. *Teaching Children Science: Hands-on Nature Study in North America, 1890–1930.* Chicago: University of Chicago Press, 2010.

Lewis, Daniel. *The Feathery Tribe: Robert Ridgway and the Modern Study of Birds.* New Haven, CT: Yale University Press, 2012.

Lutts, Ralph H. *The Nature Fakers: Wildlife, Science, and Sentiment.* Charlottesville: University Press of Virginia, 1990.

Norwood, Vera. *Made from This Earth: American Women and Nature.* Chapel Hill: University of North Carolina Press, 1993.

Peck, Robert McCracken. *A Celebration of Birds: The Life and Art of Louis Agassiz Fuertes.* New York: Walker and Company, 1982.

Philippon, Daniel J. *Conserving Words: How American Nature Writers Shaped the Environmental Movement.* Athens: University of Georgia Press, 2004.

Stradling, David, ed. *Conservation in the Progressive Era: Classic Texts.* Seattle: University of Washington Press, 2015.

Strom, Deborah, ed. *Birdwatching with American Women: A Selection of Nature Writings.* New York: W. W. Norton, 1989.

Taylor, Dorceta E. *The Rise of the American Conservation Movement: Power, Privilege, and Environmental Protection.* Durham, NC: Duke University Press, 2016.

Weidensaul, Scott. *Of a Feather: A Brief History of American Birding.* Orlando, FL: Harcourt, 2007.

Acknowledgments

FIRST AND FOREMOST we would like to thank Peter Mickulas, without whom this teaching edition of *Citizen Bird* would not exist. Thank you for bringing this project to us, for your patience during the pandemic and pandemic-related interruptions, and for your good humor, keen eye, and steadfast support throughout the entire process. We hope that you have found us an easier pair to work with than George P. Brett likely found Mabel Osgood Wright and Elliott Coues.

We would also like to thank everyone else at Rutgers University Press who worked on this project, including the peer reviewers; and to the production team, we promise not to request changing the size of the paper on which this book is printed at the last moment, like a certain author may or may not have done with *Citizen Bird*'s first printing.

This work would not have been possible without access to the authors' and illustrator's letters to one another (and the gossipy letters about one another to their publisher). We had far too much fun perusing their letters in the Macmillan Company records in the New York Public Library's Manuscripts and Archives Division (Astor, Lenox, and Tilden Foundations), as well as the Louis Agassiz Fuertes Papers in the Rare and Manuscript Collections of the Cornell University Library. Special thanks to Edward Surato and Diane Lee of the Fairfield Museum and History Center for our access to the archives and for permission to use the image of Mabel Osgood Wright and her bird study class.

Our work benefited greatly from the constructive comments of colleagues from a variety of disciplines at many different conferences throughout the past several years. In particular, we would like to thank Dolly Jorgensen and the folks from the Green House at Stavanger University for the invitation to the Enviro-Citizen Conference in Brussels, Belgium. We also benefited from colleagues' feedback on our presentations at the meetings of the Northeast Modern Language Association in Baltimore, Maryland; the American Society for Environmental History in Boston, Massachusetts; and the Animal History Group in Lincoln, United Kingdom.

We would like to thank the students in our environmental sociology and children's literature classes for being our first audiences for this project and for convincing us of its viability as a teaching text. Your enthusiasm for and your thoughtful observations about "The Citizen" informed this project in numerous ways.

Finally, Liz would like to thank Meghan for her Victorian detective eye and her ability to find the most interesting nuggets of information in a seemingly innocuous line of text. Liz also thanks her husband, Anthony, for his unwavering support for all of her professional and personal endeavors, including looking up citations and letting her incorporate birding into all of their trips. Special thanks to her canine companion Cooper, who knows when it is 5:00 P.M., and it is time to quit working and play.

And Meghan would like to thank Liz for inviting her on the journey that has been *Citizen Bird* and for teaching her everything she currently knows about birds (including the much- maligned English Sparrow), birding, and animal studies. While she will never be enough of a morning person to be a true birder, she now has a favorite bird and can distinguish a Starling from a Grackle. Meghan also would like to thank her husband, Jeff, for all of the ways he has supported her and this project through all of the major life changes that have marked these past few years. For the many hours he spent discussing *Citizen Bird* with her, she dedicates her part in this book to him.

About the Contributors

AUTHORS AND ILLUSTRATOR

MABEL OSGOOD WRIGHT (1859–1934) founded the Connecticut Audubon Society and the Birdcraft Museum and Sanctuary in Connecticut, published several books on birds and birding, and helped revive and reestablish the National Audubon Society through her work as editor and writer for *Bird-Lore*, the precursor to *Audubon Magazine*. Her book *Birdcraft: A Field Book of Two Hundred Song, Game, and Water Birds* (1895) is widely regarded as the first true field guide for birds, and her book *Citizen Bird: Scenes from Bird-Life in Plain English for Beginners* (1897) is cited by the Library of Congress as a milestone in the conservation movement.

ELLIOTT COUES (1842–1899) was one of the founders, and later the president, of the American Ornithologists' Union (now the American Ornithological Society), published numerous books and scientific papers on ornithological topics, and edited the AOU's publication *The Auk*. His *Key to North American Birds* (1872), a highly regarded scientific bird identification manual, was revised and reprinted in six editions. One of the American Ornithological Society's most prestigious annual awards is named after Elliott Coues.

LOUIS AGASSIZ FUERTES (1874–1927) was a highly sought-after American bird illustrator, second in prominence today only to John James Audubon. He produced thousands of illustrations for many important works, including Merriam Bailey's *Handbook of Birds of the Western United States* (1902), Keyser's *Birds of the Rockies* (1902), Coues's *Key to North American Birds* (1903), Eaton's *Birds of New York* (1910–1914), and Forbush's *Birds of Massachusetts* (1925–1929). The Wilson Ornithological Society has named its most prestigious award after Louis Agassiz Fuertes.

EDITORS

ELIZABETH CHERRY is a professor of sociology at Manhattanville University, where she teaches courses on human-animal studies, environmental sociology, culture, and social movements. Her primary areas of research include birding, environmental activism, the animal rights movement, veganism, and animals in art. She is the author of *For the Birds: Protecting Wildlife through the Naturalist Gaze* (Rutgers University Press).

MEGHAN FREEMAN is the fellowship and internship librarian at the Beinecke Rare Book and Manuscript Library at Yale University. Her primary area of research is nineteenth-century British and American literature and culture, with specializations in women's writing, children's literature, and material culture. Among other topics, she has written on museum-going and tourism in Victorian literature, environmentalism and utopian thinking in the Arts and Crafts movement, and women's arts education in the nineteenth century.

Index

Abbott, Jacob, xlv, xlviii
Academy, The, xxviii
Allen, J. A., xii, xxxv, lviii, lxi
American Museum of Natural History, ix, xiv, xxxv
American Naturalist, lvii
American Ornithological Society, lxxiv
American Ornithologists' Union (AOU), x, xi, xlii, lviii, lxxiv; founding of, xii, xxxv–xxxvi, lxii
anthropocentrism, lii–liii
anthropomorphism, xl, lix–lxi
AOU. *See* American Ornithologists' Union
AOU Code of Nomenclature and Check-List of North American Birds, The, xii
Arbor Day, xxxi
ASPCA, xli
Atlantic Monthly, xlv
Audubon, John James, xxii, xxxviii, lxxiv
Audubon Magazine x, xxxix, xlii
Audubon Society, x, lviii–liv, lxxiv; and Bird Day, xxx–xxxi, lv; founding of, xxx, xli, xlii–xliii

Audubon Society of Connecticut, x, xxx, xxxi, xlii
Auk, The, xii, xxvii, xxix, xxxv

Babcock, C. A., xxxi
Bailey, Florence Merriam, xiv, xxxiii, xxxvi, xxxvii, xxxix, xli, lxxvi
Baird, Spencer Fullerton, xi, xii, xxxvii
Baskett, James Newton, xxv, lxxvi
binoculars, xxxviii–xxxix
Birdcraft (Wright), ix, x, xxvi, xxxvii, xliv; as a field guide, xxxiv, xxxix, xl; illustrations for, xviii, xxi, xxiii; reviews of, xii, xv
Birdcraft Sanctuary, x
Bird Day, x, xxx–xxxiii, lv, lxxiv, lxxv
bird illustration, xxv, xxvi, xxxiv, xxxv, xxxvii–xli; Louis Agassiz Fuertes, xv, xx–xxi, xxii, xxix–xxx. *See also* Audubon, John James
birding. *See* birdwatching
Bird-Lore, x, xxxii, lxxv
birds: conservation, xxvi–xxvii, xxx, xli–xliii, lxxii–lxxiv; feathers in hats,

birds (cont.)
xlii–xliii, lviii, lxxvi; migration, lvi–lvii;
skins, xxix, xxxvi, xxxvii, xxxviii
Birds of America, The (Audubon), xxxviii
*Birds of Village and Field: A Bird Book for
Beginners* (Bailey), lxxvi
Birds through an Opera-Glass (Bailey),
xxxvii, xxxix
birdwatching, viii, xxx, xxxiv,
xxxv–xxxvii; field guides, vii, xxxiv,
xxxvii–xli, xliii, liii, lxxv–lxxvi
Brett, George P., Sr., ix, xv–xxiv
Brewer, T. M., xxxvii, lxi
Brewster, William, xii, xxxv

Chapman, Frank M., x, xiv, xxvii, xxix, xl,
xlii, lv
Chicago Tribune, xxvi
children, vii; education, xxx–xxxiii, lxxiii;
literature, vii, viii, xxvi–xxvii, xliii–lvi,
liii–liv; readers, xxvii–xxix
Civil War, xliv–xlvi
citizenship, lii–liii, lix–lxii, lxiv–lxvi,
lxxv
class. *See* social class
Coues, Elliott, vii, x, xvii–xx, xxii, xxix,
xli–xlii, xliv, lvii; American Ornithologists' Union, xxxv–xxxvi; biography
of, xi–xiii; mentor to Louis Agassiz
Fuertes, xiv, xv–xvii, xx, xxi, xxiii,
xxxviii; ornithological manuals,
xxxiv, xxxvii, xl; Sparrow Wars,
lxi–lxii, lxxvi
cowbirds, xl–xli, liii, lxii–xiii
Critic, The, xxiv
crows, lxii–lxiii

Dogtown (Wright), lv
Dream Fox Story Book, The (Wright), lv

Edgeworth, Maria, xlv, xlviii
education, xxxii–xxxiii; of British
children, xxviii; public schools, xxxi,
xlviii. *See also* Bird Day; Wright,
Samuel Osgood
egg collecting, xxvii, xl, li, lxii, lxxiii,
lxxvi
egrets, xliii
English sparrows, lx–lxiii, lxxiii. *See also*
Sparrow Wars
environment: conservation, viii, xxvi–xxvii,
xxxiv, xli–xliii, lviii, lxxii–lxxiv; preservation, xxvii–xxviii, lviii
environmental movement, lviii–lix
ethnicity, lxii–lxvi, lxxv
extinction, xxvii, liv

Fairfield, Connecticut, viii, x, xi, xxxii
Field Guide to the Birds, A (Peterson), xl–xli
Flowers and Ferns in Their Haunts (Wright),
x, lv
Forest and Stream, xxiii, xlii
Four-Footed Americans and Their Kin
(Wright), x, lv
Fowler, W. Warde, xxviii
*Friendship of Nature: A New England Chroni-
cle of Birds and Flowers, The* (Wright), ix,
xxxviii, xliv, lxxvi
Fuertes, Louis Agassiz, vii, x, xii, xv–xxv,
xxix–xxx, xxxiv, xxxviii; biography,
xiii–xiv; *Birdcraft,* xxvi

Garden of the Commuter's Wife, The (Wright), x
gender, xvii, xxxvi, xli–xliii; in literature,
xlviii–xlix; women's fashion, xlii–xliii
Grinnell, George Bird, xlii

Harris, Joel Chandler, lxvii, lxviii, lxix, lxxvi
heart of nature, xlii, xliv, lxxi

INDEX 371

History of North American Birds (Ridgway), xxxvii

house sparrows. *See* English sparrows

immigration, lii, lix–lxvi, lxxv

industrialization, xli, xlvi, lvi–lix, lxii–lxiv

Jim Crow period, lxiii, lxix

Journal of Education, xxxii

Key to North American Birds (Coues), xii, xiv, lxi

Lacey Act, lviii

lighthouses, lvi–lviii, lxxvi

Macmillan Company, ix, xii, xv–xxvi, xliv

Mammy Bun (character), lxiv–lxv, lxvi–lxxi, lxxv

migration: of birds, liii, lvi, lvii; of people, lxiii–lxiv

Migratory Bird Treaty Act, lix, lxxii

Miller, Olive Thorne, xxxiii

mockingbirds, lxviii–lxx

Mosswood, viii, xlvii, liv

My New York (Wright), xlviii, lxvii

Nation, The, xv

National Association of Audubon Societies. *See* Audubon Society

nation-building, lix–lxii

Nature, xxviii

nature writing, viii, x, xxxiii, xxxvii–xxxviii

nest parasitism, xl–xli

New York Herald, xxvi

New York Times, xxvi, xxvii, xxix, xxxiii

Nuttall Ornithological Club, xii, xxxv, lviii, lxii

opera glasses. *See* binoculars

ornithology, vii, viii, xiv, xxii, xxvii, xxxiv–xxxvii, xxxvii, lxv, lxxii–lxxiv; and bird conservation, lvii–lviii; Elliott Coues, xi, xii, xviii; field guides and manuals, xxxvii–xxxviii, xl; gender, xlii; illustrations, xxx; Mabel Osgood Wright, ix; Sparrow Wars, lxi–lxii. *See also* American Ornithologists' Union; Nuttall Ornithological Club

Osgood, Rev. Samuel, viii, xliv–xlvii

Outlook, xxvi–xxvii

Pater, Walter, l

Peterson, Roger Tory, xl–xli

photography, xi, xxxix

poaching, lviii

Progressive Era, vii, x, xxxiii, lvi, lix, lx, lxiii–lxiv, lxxi

race, xliii, xlix, lxii–lxv, lxvi–lxxi, lxxiii–lxv, lxxv; eye dialect, lxviii, lxxv; mammy figure, lxvii; slavery, lxvii–lxx; stereotypes, lxiv, lxvii

Reconstruction, xliv–xlvi, lxiii, lxvii

Ridgway, Robert, xv, xxxvii, xl

Roosevelt, Theodore, xli

Science, xxviii

Seton, Ernest Thompson, xv, xx, xxi, lv

Sierra Club, xli

Smithsonian Institution, xi, xv

social class, xxix, xxx, xliii, xlviii–xlix, lii–liii, lxiv

Sparrow Wars, lxi–lxii

Story of the Birds, The (Baskett), xxv, lxxvi

Stowe, Harriet Beecher, lxvii, lxviii

taxidermy, xxxv, xxxvi. *See also* birds: skins

telegraph lines, lvi–lvii, lxxvi

Tommy Anne and the Three Hearts (Wright), x, xliv, lv, lxxvi

Tubman, Harriet, lxxiii–lxxiv

Uncle Remus: His Songs and Sayings (Harris), lxvii, lxxvi

Uncle Tom's Cabin (Stowe), lxvii

urbanization, lvi–lix, lxii, lxiii–lxiv

Wabeno the Magician (Wright), lv

Wilson, Lucy Landon, xxxiii

Wright, James Osborne, ix

Wright, Mabel Osgood, vii, xxiii–xxv, xxviii, xxxiv, liii–liv, lix, lxxv–lxxvi; in the American Ornithologists' Union, xxxvi; biography, viii–xi; *Birdcraft*, xxxix–xli; Bird Day, xxx–xxxiii; childhood, xlvi–xlix, lxvii; children's literature, xliv, lv; Connecticut Audubon Society, xlii–xliii; Heart of Nature book series, xlii, lv; nature writing, xxxvii–xxxviii; working with Elliott Coues, xii, xv–xxii; working with Louis Agassiz Fuertes, xxix–xxx

Zoologist, The, xxviii